BMA's
TALENT & OLYMPIAD
EXAMS RESOURCE BOOK

CLASS IX

BRAIN MAPPING
A C A D E M Y
Mapping Your Future

www.bmatalent.com

Published by:

Brain Mapping Academy

#16-11-16/1/B, First Floor, Farhath Hospital Road,
Saleem Nagar, Malakpet, Hyderabad–500 036.
© 040–66135169, 65165169.
E-mail: info@bmatalent.com
Website: www.bmatalent.com

ISBN: 978-81-906877-6-8

Disclaimer

Every care has been taken by the compilers and
publishers to give correct, complete and updated information.
In case there is any omission, printing mistake or any
other error which might have crept in inadvertently,
neither the compiler / publisher nor any of the
distributors take any legal responsibility.

*In case of any dispute, all matters are subjected to the exclusive
jurisdiction of the courts in Hyderabad only.*

First Edition   : 2003

Second Edition : 2006

Revised Edition as per the latest syllabus

Printed at:
Sri Vinayaka Art Printers, Hyderabad.

Publisher's Note

Sometimes the understanding of fundamental concepts alone does not help the students to crack the competitive exams as most of them are objective in structure. Students need rigorous training to familiarize themselves to the style of the exams they are attempting. The board exams which are of qualifying, but not competitive, nature do not completely address the needs of students in testing them in objective type format.

To bridge this gap and to enable the students to face the reality of competitive exams, Brain Mapping Academy, decided to bring out an all-objective questions reference book at the secondary level education.

A crisp summary of the topics and useful equations were provided at the beginning of each chapter so that the students can memorize the important points.

Care has been taken to design thought-provoking questions. These should help students to attain a deeper understanding of principles. The questions have been reviewed to fill the gaps in problem coverage and to build the confidence in the students. They have also been expanded to impart reasoning/logical/analytical skills. Hints have been provided for the difficult questions that stimulate the mental muscles.

This book will cater all the requirements of the students who are approaching national/state level talent search examinations and all Olympiad exams. This book also complements the additional preparation needs of the students for the regular board exams.

We took utmost care to make this the best resource book available for the talent exams aspirants. We welcome criticism from the students, teacher community and educators, especially concerning any errors and deficiencies which may have remained in this edition and the suggestions for improvement for the next edition.

NATIONAL LEVEL SCIENCE TALENT SEARCH EXAMINATION

Aim of this examination

The focus on fundamentals at the secondary level is so important that without a firm understanding of them, a child cannot be expected to face the reality of the competitive world once he/she finishes the formal education. Even while opting for higher studies the student has to go through a complete scan of what he/she knows. Exams like IIT-JEE, AIEEE, AIIMS, AFMC, CAT, SAT, GRE, GMAT, etc. are so designed to test the fundamental strength of a student. Hence the need of the hour is building the fundamental base as strong as possible.

A successful life emerges out from healthy and sound competition. Competition is the only way for the students to shake lethargy. It's the only way to get introduced for manly worthiness. Firm standards in education and competition are the tonic for a promising and talented future.

This exactly is the philosophy behind the Unified Council's NSTSE.

Organisation

National Science Talent Search Examination is conducted by Unified Council. Unified Council is India's first ISO 9001 certified organisation in the educational testing and assessment sector. It is a professionally managed progressive organisation in the field of education established in the year 1994 by eminent personalities and academicians from diverse domains of education. Since its inception, Unified Council has put together the best brains in an endeavour to make the younger generation fundamentally stronger and nourish their brains for a bright and enterprising future.

Eligibility : Students of classes 2, 3, 4,5,6,7,8,9,10,11&12 are eligible to participate in this examination.

Medium & Syllabus: This exam is conducted in only English medium and is suitable for all the students following CBSE/ICSE/State Board Syllabi.

Examination Pattern

There will be a separate question paper for each class. All questions are objective-type multiple choice with no negative marking for wrong answers.

No. of Questions: 50   **Marks:** 50 (for 2nd class)

No. of Questions: 75   **Marks:** 75 (for 3rd class)

No. of Questions: 100   **Marks:** 100 (for classes 4th to 12th)

Duration: 90 minutes

Date : Conducted every year on the last Sunday of January.

Test Centres : Spread across the country.

DIVISION OF MARKS

FOR CLASS II

Mathematics	:	25 marks
General Science	:	25 Marks

FOR CLASS III

Mathematics	:	40 marks
General Science	:	35 Marks

FOR CLASSES IV & V

Mathematics	:	45 marks
General Science	:	45 Marks
General Questions	:	10 marks

FOR CLASSES VI TO X

Mathematics	:	25 marks
Physics	:	25 marks
Chemistry	:	20 marks
Biology	:	20 marks
General Questions	:	10 marks

FOR CLASS XI & XII(PCM)

Mathematics	:	40 marks
Physics	:	25 marks
Chemistry	:	25 marks
General Questions	:	10 marks

FOR CLASS XI & XII(PCB)

Biology	:	40 marks
Physics	:	25 marks
Chemistry	:	25 marks
General Questions	:	10 marks

Infrastructure

The Council makes use of ultra-modern equipment such as **Optical Mark Recognition (OMR)** *equipment to evaluate the answer papers to proficiently assess students' performance. The examination procedure is* **completely computerised.**

Unique Service from Unified Council:

Unique analysis reports like Student's Performance Report for students, General School Report & Individual School Report for schools will be provided. These reports will be very much helpful for students & schools to analyse their strengths and weaknesses.

General School Report (GSR) analyses the performance of students participating in the exam (subject-wise and class-wise). The report, in graphical format will have Ogive and Histogram Graphs, which are useful to schools that wish to improve their students' performance by benchmarking the areas of weaknesses and building upon them. This report is provided free of cost.

Individual School Report (ISR) analyses the performance of your school when compared to the rest of the students participating in this examination (subject-wise, class-wise and question-wise). This report acts as a tool for the schools to improve their students' performance in the future by benchmarking the areas of weaknesses and building upon them. ISR is also provided free of cost.

Awards & Scholarships:

Top 100 members in each class will be awarded with Scholarships, Cash Awards & Rewards etc.

Presentation Ceremony:

The awards for the toppers and Institutional Awardees will be presented by eminent personalities at a grand celebration in Hyderabad before an impressive gathering of thousands of students, parents& teachers.

For further details write to **Unified Council**

#16-11-16/1/B, Farhath Hospital Road, Saleem Nagar, Malakpet, Hyderabad-500 036
Phones : 040-24557708, 24545862, 66139917
E-mail: exam @ unifiedcouncil.com, Website: www.unifiedcouncil.com

CONTENTS

Mathematics

1. Number Systems   1
2. Polynomials   33
3. Co-ordinate Geometry   53
4. Linear Equations in two Variables   55
5. Lines & Angles   58
6. Triangles   77
7. Quadrilaterals   85
8. Areas of Parellograms & Triangles   104
9. Circles   106
10. Constructions   125
11. Heron's Formula   131
12. Surface Areas & Volumes   137
13. Statistics   155
14. Probability   168

Model Test Paper   **174**

Physics

1. Motion   180
2. Force & Laws of Motion   200
3. Gravitation & Pressure   215
4. Work, Energy & Power   234
5. Sound   250

Model Test Paper   **268**

Chemistry

1. Matter   275
2. The Nature of Matter   283
3. Atoms & Molecules   289
4. Structure of the Atom   309

Model Test Paper   **329**

Biology

1. Fundamental Unit of Life   334
2. Tissues   347
3. Diversity in Living Organisms   359
4. Health & Diseases   376
5. Natural Resources   383
6. Improvement in Food Resources   391

Model Test Paper   **400**

MATHEMATICS

Chapter 1

Number Systems

Number systems :

1. **Natural numbers (N) :**

   1, 2, 3 ,4 ... etc., are called Natural numbers.

2. **Whole numbers (W) :**

   0,1, 2, 3,..... etc., are called Whole numbers.

3. **Integers (Z) :**

   ......, -3, -2, -1, 0, 1, 2, 3, ... etc., are called Integers.

   1, 2, 3, 4,... etc., are called positive integers and denoted by Z^+

   -1, -2, -3, -4, ... etc., are called Negative integers and denoted by Z^-

   Note :- "0" is neither positive nor negative.

4. **Fractions :**

   The numbers of the form $\dfrac{x}{y}$, where x and y are natural numbers, are known as fractions.

   E.g. :- $\dfrac{3}{5}, \dfrac{2}{1}, \dfrac{1}{125}, \ldots\ldots$etc.

5. **Rational numbers (Q) :**

   A number of the form $\dfrac{p}{q}$ (q ≠ 0), where p and q are integers, is called a rational number .

   E.g. :- $\dfrac{-3}{17}, \dfrac{5}{-19}, \dfrac{10}{1}, \dfrac{-11}{-23}, \ldots\ldots$ etc.

   Note :- "0" is a rational number, since $0 = \dfrac{0}{1}$

6. A rational number $\dfrac{p}{q}$ is positive if p and q are either both positive or both negative.

   E.g. :- $\dfrac{3}{5}, \dfrac{-2}{-7}$

7. A rational number $\dfrac{p}{q}$ is negative if one of p and q is positive and the other one is negative. E.g. :- $\dfrac{-5}{9}, \dfrac{7}{-23}$

8. *Properties of rational numbers :*

   1. If $\dfrac{p}{q}$ is a rational number and 'm' is a nonzero integer, then $\dfrac{p}{q} = \dfrac{p \times m}{q \times m}$

      E.g. : Let us take $\dfrac{3}{4}$, a rational number and m = 2, 3, 4, ... which are nonzero integers.

      Then $\dfrac{3}{4} = \dfrac{3 \times 2}{4 \times 2} = \dfrac{3 \times 3}{4 \times 3} = \dfrac{3 \times 4}{4 \times 4} = \ldots$

2. If $\dfrac{p}{q}$ is a rational number and 'm' is a common divisor of p and q, then $\dfrac{p}{q} = \dfrac{p \div m}{q \div m}$

E.g. :- Let us take $\dfrac{-36}{48}$, a rational number, and m=12, 6, 3, ... which are common divisors.

Then $\dfrac{-36}{48} = \dfrac{-36 \div 12}{48 \div 12} = \dfrac{-36 \div 6}{48 \div 6}$

$= \dfrac{-36 \div 3}{48 \div 3} = \cdots \cdots$

3. Two rational numbers are equivalent only when the product of numerator of the first and the denominator of the second is equal to the product of the denominator of the first and the numerator of the second.

Thus $\dfrac{p}{q} = \dfrac{r}{s}$ only when $p \times s = q \times r$

E.g. :- $\dfrac{-15}{18} = \dfrac{5}{-6}$

$(-15) \times (-6) = (5)(18)$

$90 = 90.$

So they are equivalent.

Note : $\dfrac{-p}{q} = \dfrac{p}{-q} = -\dfrac{p}{q}$

9. *Standard form of a rational number :*

A rational number $\dfrac{p}{q}$ is said to be in standard form if q is positive and the integers p and q have no common divisors other than 1.

E.g. :- Express $\dfrac{22}{-77}$ in standard form.

$\dfrac{22}{-77} = \dfrac{22 \times (-1)}{-77 \times (-1)} = \dfrac{-22}{77}$

(denominator is positive)

Now find LCM of 22 and 77. It is 11. So, divide both numerator and denominator by 11.

i.e., $\dfrac{-22}{77} = \dfrac{-22 \div 11}{77 \div 11} = \dfrac{-2}{7}$

$\therefore \dfrac{-2}{7}$ is the standard from of $\dfrac{22}{-77}$.

10. *Comparison of two rational numbers :*

Step 1 : Express each one of the two given rational numbers with positive denominator.

Step 2 : Take the LCM of these positive denominators.

Step 3 : Express each rational number with this LCM as common denominator.

Step 4 : The number having greater numerator is greater.

E.g. :- Which of the two rational numbers $\dfrac{2}{-3}$ and $\dfrac{-4}{5}$ is greater?

Step 1 : $\dfrac{2}{-3} = \dfrac{2 \times (-1)}{-3 \times (-1)} = \dfrac{-2}{3}$

$\dfrac{-4}{5}$ already in the standard form.

Step 2 : LCM of 3 and 5 = 15

Step 3 : $\dfrac{-2}{3} = \dfrac{-2}{3} \times \dfrac{5}{5} = \dfrac{-10}{15}$

$\dfrac{-4}{5} = \dfrac{-4}{5} \times \dfrac{3}{3} = \dfrac{-12}{15}$

Step 4 : Since -10 > -12, $\dfrac{-2}{3} > \dfrac{-4}{5}$

Shortcut method :

$\dfrac{-2}{3}, \dfrac{-4}{5}$

$-2 \times 5, \quad -4 \times 3$

$-10, \quad -12$

Since, $-10 > -12$, we have $\dfrac{-2}{3} > \dfrac{-4}{5}$.

11. Three important properties of rational numbers are

    1. For each rational number x, exactly one of the following is true.

       (a) x > 0   (b) x = 0   (c) x < 0

    2. For any two rational numbers x and y, exactly one of the following is true.

       (a) x > y   (b) x = y   (c) x < y

    3. If x, y, z be rational numbers such that x > y and y > z then x > z.

12. *Addition of Rational Numbers :*

    1. To add two rational numbers with the same denominator, we simply add their numerators and divide by the common denominator.

       E.g. $\dfrac{-5}{7} + \dfrac{1}{7} = \dfrac{-5+1}{7} = \dfrac{-4}{7}$

    2. When denominators of given numbers are unequal we take the LCM of their denominators and express each one of the given rational numbers with this LCM as the common denominator. Now add as shown above.

E.g.. $\dfrac{-3}{8} + \dfrac{5}{4}$

LCM of 8 and 4 is 8.

$\dfrac{-3}{8} = \dfrac{-3}{8} \times \dfrac{1}{1} = \dfrac{-3}{8}$

$\dfrac{5}{4} = \dfrac{5}{4} \times \dfrac{2}{2} = \dfrac{10}{8}$

$\dfrac{-3}{8} + \dfrac{5}{4} = \dfrac{-3}{8} + \dfrac{10}{8} = \dfrac{-3+10}{8} = \dfrac{7}{8}$

Alter : $\dfrac{-3}{8} + \dfrac{5}{4}$

$\dfrac{-3 \times 4 + 5 \times 8}{8 \times 4} = \dfrac{-12+40}{32} = \dfrac{28}{32} = \dfrac{7}{8}$

Properties :

Closure Property :

The sum of two rational numbers is always a rational number.

Thus if a and b are any two rational numbers then (a+b) is also a rational number.

Commutative Property :

Two rational numbers can be added in any order.

Thus if a and b are any two rational numbers then a + b = b + a.

Associative Property :

While adding three (or) more rational numbers they can be grouped in any order.

Thus if a,b and c are any three rational numbers then

$$a + (b + c) = (a + b) + c$$

Identity Property :

The sum of any rational number and zero is the rational number itself.

Thus if a is a rational number then

$$a + 0 = 0 + a = a$$

Note : 0 is called the identity element for addition of rational numbers.

Inverse Property :

If a and b be two rational numbers such that a + b = b + a = 0 then a and b are called additive inverse of each other.

Here 0 is the additive identity.

13. **Subtraction of Rational Numbers:**

If a and b are any two rational numbers then we define a - b = a + (-b)

Thus subtracting a rational number means adding its additive inverse.

Note : Except closure property, the other properties mentioned above do not hold good for the subtraction of rational numbers.

14. **Multiplication of Rational Numbers :**

Product of two rational numbers

$$= \frac{\text{product of numerators}}{\text{product of denominators}}$$

Properties :

Closure Property :

The product of two rational numbers is always a rational number.

Thus if a, b are two rational numbers, then ab is also a rational number.

Commutative Property :

Two rational numbers can be multiplied in any order.

Thus if a and b are two rational numbers, then ab = ba.

Associative Property :

While multiplying three (or) more rational numbers, they can be grouped in any order.

Thus if a, b and c be any three rational numbers, then a (bc) = (ab) c

Identity Property :

The product of any rational number with 1 is the rational number itself.

Thus if a is any rational number, then
$$a \times 1 = 1 \times a = a$$

Note : 1 is called the multiplicative identity for rational numbers.

Distributive Property :

If a, b and c are any three rational numbers then

$$a \times (b + c) = (a \times b) + (a \times c)$$

This is called distributive property of multiplication over addition.

Note :

1. A rational number a is called the reciprocal or multiplicative inverse of a rational number b if

   $$a \times b = b \times a = 1$$

   i.e., $b = \dfrac{1}{a}$ (or) $a = \dfrac{1}{b}$

2. Zero has no reciprocal.

3. 1 and -1 are the only rational numbers having their own reciprocals.

4. The reciprocal or the multiplicative inverse of a nonzero rational

number $\dfrac{a}{b}$ is written as $\left(\dfrac{a}{b}\right)^{-1}$

15. Division of Rational Numbers :

If a and b are integers such that $b \neq 0$, then

$$a \div b = a \times (\text{reciprocal of b}) = a \times \dfrac{1}{b}.$$

Here a is called the dividend, b is called the divisor and the result is known as quotient.

Note : Division by zero is not defined.

Properties :

Closure Property :

If a and b are two rational numbers such that $b \neq 0$, then $a \div b$ is always a rational number.

1. For any rational number $\dfrac{a}{b}$

we have (i) $\dfrac{a}{b} \div 1 = \dfrac{a}{b}$

and (ii) $\dfrac{a}{b} \div (-1) = -\dfrac{a}{b}$

2. For every nonzero rational number $\dfrac{a}{b}$, we have

(i) $\dfrac{a}{b} \div \dfrac{a}{b} = 1$

(ii) $\dfrac{a}{b} \div \left(\dfrac{-a}{b}\right) = -1$

(iii) $\left(\dfrac{-a}{b}\right) \div \left(\dfrac{a}{b}\right) = -1$

16. Absolute value of a rational number :

1. The absolute value of a rational number is the number without any regard to its sign.

Thus, for any rational number x,

The absolute value of x =

$$|x| = \begin{cases} x, \text{if } x > 0 \\ 0, \text{if } x = 0 \\ -x, \text{if } x < 0 \end{cases}$$

2. $|x + y| \leq |x| + |y|$, where x and y are rational numbers.

3. $|x \times y| = |x| \times |y|$, where x and y are rational numbers.

4. If x and y are any two rational numbers such that $x < y$ then $\dfrac{1}{2}(x+y)$ is a rational number lying between x and y.

17. Some results on irrational numbers :

(a) The –ve of an irrational number is an irrational number.

(b) The sum of a rational and an irrational number is an irrational number.

(c) The product of a non–zero rational number with an irrational number is always an irrational number.

18. Real numbers :

The totality of all rational and all irrational numbers forms the set R of all real numbers.

19. Properties of all real numbers :

(a) *Closure property of addition :* The sum of two real numbers is always a real number.

(b) *Commutative law for addition :*
$a + b = b + a$, $\forall$ real numbers 'a' and 'b'.

(c) *Associative law for addition :*
$(a + b) + c = a + (b + c)$, $\forall$ real numbers a, b and c.

(d) *Existence of additive identity :*
Zero is the additive identity.
$a + 0 = 0 + a = a$, $\forall$ real numbers a.

(e) *Existence of additive inverse :*
For each real number 'a', there exists a real number '–a' such that $a + (-a) = (-a) + a = 0$.

(f) *Closure property for multiplication :*
The product of two real numbers is a real number.

(g) *Commutative law of multiplication :*
$ab = ba$, $\forall$ real numbers a and b.

(h) *Associative law of multiplication :*
$(ab)c = a(bc)$, $\forall$ real numbers a, b and c.

(i) *Existence of multiplicative identity :*
1 is called the multiplicative identity.

$1.a = a.1 = a$, $\forall$ real numbers a.

(j) *Existence of multiplicative inverse :*
Every non–zero real number 'a' has its multiplicative inverse $\dfrac{1}{a}$.

(k) *Distributive law of multiplication over addition :*
$a(b + c) = ab + ac$, $\forall$ real numbers a, b and c.

20. Zero is a real number which has no multiplicative inverse.

21. *Real numbers are of two types :*
   (i) Rational numbers
   (ii) Irrational numbers

Modulus of a real number is given by $|x|$.

If $|x| = a \Rightarrow x = \pm a$

$|x| < a \Rightarrow -a < x < a$

$|x| > a \Rightarrow x > a$ or $x < -a$

$|x - a| < l \Rightarrow a - l < x < a + l$

$|x - a| > l \Rightarrow x > a + l$ or $x < a - l$

If "a" is rational number and "n" is a positive integer such that $a^{\frac{1}{n}}$ is irrational, then $a^{\frac{1}{n}}$ is called the surd of order 'n'.

$a^{\frac{1}{n}} = \sqrt[n]{a}$ is a surd. It is also called radical. Rational number 'a' is called radicand.

22. *Laws of surds :*

1. $\left(\sqrt[n]{a}\right)^n = a$

2. $\left(a^{\frac{1}{n}} \cdot b^{\frac{1}{n}}\right)^n = ab$

3. $a^{\frac{1}{n}} \cdot b^{\frac{1}{n}} = (ab)^{\frac{1}{n}}$

4. $\left(\dfrac{a^{\frac{1}{n}}}{b^{\frac{1}{n}}}\right)^n = \dfrac{a}{b}$; $b \neq 0$

5. $\left(a^m\right)^{\frac{1}{n}} = \left(a^{\frac{1}{n}}\right)^m = a^{\frac{m}{n}}$

6. $a^{\frac{1}{m}} \times a^{\frac{1}{n}} = a^{\frac{1}{m} + \frac{1}{n}}$

7. $a^{\frac{1}{mn}} = \left(a^{\frac{1}{m}}\right)^{\frac{1}{n}} = \left(a^{\frac{1}{n}}\right)^{\frac{1}{m}}$

A surd whose rational factor is unity is called pure surd.

Eg : $\sqrt{3},\ \sqrt{2},\ \sqrt[3]{4}$ etc.

A surd whose rational factor is any number other than unity is called mixed surd.

Eg : $2\sqrt{3},\ 2\sqrt[3]{5}$ etc.

Surds having same irrational factors are called similar or like surds.

Eg : $\sqrt{2},\ 5\sqrt{2},\ \frac{1}{2}\sqrt{2}$ etc.

23. *Rational Factor (RF) :*

If the product of two surds is a rational number then each is called the rationalising factor (RF) of the other.

RF of monomial surd $a^{\frac{1}{n}}$ is $a^{1-\frac{1}{n}}$

RF of binomial surd $\sqrt{a} + \sqrt{b}$ is $\sqrt{a} - \sqrt{b}$

Multiple Choice Questions

1. Which of the following is not a rational number?

   (A) $\sqrt{2}$ (B) $\sqrt{4}$ (C) $\sqrt{9}$ (D) $\sqrt{16}$

2. Set of natural numbers is a subset of

   (A) set of even numbers

   (B) set of odd numbers

   (C) set of composite numbers

   (D) set of real numbers

3. The two irrational numbers between $\sqrt{2}$ and $\sqrt{3}$ are

   (A) $2^{\frac{1}{2}},\ 6^{\frac{1}{4}}$ (B) $3^{\frac{1}{4}},\ 3^{\frac{1}{6}}$

   (C) $6^{\frac{1}{8}},\ 3^{\frac{1}{4}}$ (D) none

4. Which of the following is a rational number?

   (A) $\sqrt{5}$ (B) $\sqrt{6}$

   (C) $\sqrt{8}$ (D) $\sqrt{9}$

5. Representation of $3.\bar{6}$ in rational number form is

   (A) $\dfrac{11}{3}$ (B) $\dfrac{3}{11}$

   (C) $\dfrac{36}{10}$ (D) $\dfrac{33}{10}$

6. The number $\left(6 + \sqrt{2}\right)\left(6 - \sqrt{2}\right)$ is

   (A) rational   (B) irrational

   (C) can't say   (D) none

7. Which of the following numbers has the terminal decimal represen - tation?

   (A) $\dfrac{1}{7}$ (B) $\dfrac{1}{3}$

   (C) $\dfrac{3}{5}$ (D) $\dfrac{17}{3}$

8. The distance between -3 and $|-3|$ is

   (A) 6   (B) 0

   (C) can't say   (D) none

9. The values of x are such that $1 < x < 2$. Then which of the following interval is true?

(A) $(1, 2)$ (B) $[1, 2)$

(C) $(1, 2]$ (D) $[1, 2]$

10. The value of x in $|x - 2| = 12$ is

(A) 14, 10   (B) 14, − 10

(C) −14, − 10   (D) −14, 10

11. Solution of $|2x - 1| \geq 5$ is

(A) $x \geq -2, x \geq 3$ (B) $x \leq -2, x \leq 3$

(C) $x \leq -2, x \geq 3$ (D) $x \leq -2, x \leq 3$

12. The number $\left(\sqrt{2} + \sqrt{3}\right)^2$ is

(A) rational number

(B) irrational number

(C) can't say

(D) none

13. The number $\left(\sqrt{x} + \sqrt{y}\right)\left(\sqrt{x} - \sqrt{y}\right)$ where x, y > 0 is

(A) rational   (B) irrational

(C) both   (D) none

14. The sum of rational and irrational number is always

(A) rational   (B) irrational

(C) both   (D) can't say

15. The product of rational and irrational number is always

(A) rational   (B) irrational

(C) both   (D) can't say

16. The domain of the function

$f(x) = |x| + |x - 1| + |x - 2|$ is

(A) $R - \{2\}$

(B) $R - \{1, 2\}$

(C) $R - \{1, 2, 3\}$

(D) R

17. The domain of the function

$f(x) = \left(\sqrt{x - 1}\right)\left(\sqrt{4 - x}\right)$

(A) $1 \leq x \leq 4$ (B) $1 < x < 4$

(C) R (D) $R - \{1, 4\}$

18. The domain of the function

$f(x) = \dfrac{2x}{x^2 + 1}$

(A) R (B) $A = \{-1, 1\}$

(C) $R - \{1\}$ (D) $R - \{-1\}$

19. Rational number between $\sqrt{2}$ and $\sqrt{3}$ is

(A) $\dfrac{\sqrt{2} + \sqrt{3}}{2}$ (B) $\dfrac{\sqrt{2} \times \sqrt{3}}{2}$

(C) 1.5   (D) 1.8

20. The irrational number between 2 and 3 is

(A) $\sqrt{2}$ (B) $\sqrt{3}$

(C) $\sqrt{5}$ (D) $\sqrt{11}$

21. The value of a if $f(x) = \dfrac{1}{x} + ax$ and

$f\left(\dfrac{1}{5}\right) = \dfrac{28}{5}$

(A) 3   (B) 2

(C) 1   (D) 0

22. The number $\dfrac{3 - \sqrt{3}}{3 + \sqrt{3}}$ is

(A) rational   (B) irrational

(C) both   (D) can't say

23. The rational number between $\frac{1}{2}$ and $\frac{1}{3}$ is

(A) $\frac{2}{5}$　　　　(B) $\frac{1}{5}$

(C) $\frac{3}{5}$　　　　(D) $\frac{4}{5}$

24. The domain of the function

$f(x) = \sqrt{x-4} + \sqrt{x-5} + |x| + x^2$

(A) $R - \{4\}$　　　(B) $R - \{4, 5\}$

(C) R^+　　　　(D) R

25. The equivalent rational form of

$17.\overline{6}$ is

(A) $\frac{53}{3}$　　　　(B) $\frac{88}{5}$

(C) $\frac{44}{25}$　　　(D) none

26. The value of x if $|3x + 2| = 8$

(A) 2　　　　　(B) –2

(C) $\frac{10}{3}$, –2　　　(D) $-\frac{10}{3}$, 2

27. The value of b if $f(x) = x^2 + 4\sqrt{x} + b$ and $f(16) = 275$ is

(A) 3　　　　(B) 2

(C) 1　　　　(D) 0

28. The value of a and b if $f(x) = ax + b$ and $f(2) = 8$, $f(3) = 11$ is

(A) a = 3, b = –2　(B) a = –3, b = 2

(C) a = –3, b = –2　(D) a = 3, b = 2

29. The domain of the function

$f(x) = \frac{\sqrt{x}}{|x|}$ is

(A) x > 0, x ∈ R　(B) x < 0, x ∈ R

(C) can't say　　(D) none

30. The domain of the function

$\frac{1}{x^2 - 5x + 6}$

(A) $R - \{2\}$　　(B) $R - \{2, 3\}$

(C) $\{R - 3\}$　　(D) $R - \{-2, -3\}$

31. The solution set of $|3 - 5x| > 2$

(A) $x < \frac{1}{5}$ or $x > 1$

(B) $x < 1$ or $x > \frac{1}{5}$

(C) $x < 1$ or $x > -\frac{1}{5}$

(D) $x < -\frac{1}{5}$ or $x > 1$

32. The value of x from $1 < |x| < 2$

(A) $1 < x < 2$

(B) $\{-2 < x < -1\} \cup \{1 < x < 2\}$

(C) $-2 < x < -1$

(D) none of these

33. The ascending order of the following surds $\sqrt[3]{2}, \sqrt[6]{3}, \sqrt[9]{4}$ is

(A) $\sqrt[9]{4}, \sqrt[6]{3}, \sqrt[3]{2}$　(B) $\sqrt[9]{4}, \sqrt[3]{2}, \sqrt[6]{3}$

(C) $\sqrt[3]{2}, \sqrt[6]{3}, \sqrt[9]{4}$　(D) $\sqrt[6]{3}, \sqrt[9]{4}, \sqrt[3]{2}$

34. Which of the following is a pure surd?

    (A) $4\sqrt{3}$ (B) $3\sqrt[3]{5}$

    (C) $\sqrt{12}$ (D) $\frac{3}{4}\sqrt{8}$

35. The greatest among $\sqrt[3]{4}$, $\sqrt[4]{5}$, $\sqrt[4]{3}$ is

    (A) $\sqrt[3]{4}$ (B) $\sqrt[4]{5}$

    (C) $\sqrt[4]{3}$ (D) none of these

36. The greater among $\sqrt{17}-\sqrt{12}$ and $\sqrt{11}-\sqrt{6}$ is

    (A) $\sqrt{17}-\sqrt{12}$ (B) $\sqrt{11}-\sqrt{6}$

    (C) both are equal   (D) can't say

37. $\sqrt{a} > \sqrt{b} > \sqrt{c} > \sqrt{d}$ where d, c, b, a are consecutive natural numbers. Then which of the following is true?

    (A) $\sqrt{a}-\sqrt{b} > \sqrt{c}-\sqrt{d}$

    (B) $\sqrt{c}-\sqrt{d} > \sqrt{a}-\sqrt{b}$

    (C) $\sqrt{a}-\sqrt{c} > \sqrt{b}-\sqrt{d}$

    (D) None of these

38. The smaller among the following surds is

    $\sqrt{\frac{1}{2}}$, $\sqrt[3]{\frac{2}{3}}$, $\sqrt{\frac{1}{3}}$, $\sqrt{\frac{1}{4}}$

    (A) $\sqrt{\frac{1}{2}}$ (B) $\sqrt[3]{\frac{2}{3}}$

    (C) $\sqrt{\frac{1}{3}}$ (D) $\sqrt{\frac{1}{4}}$

39. The product of $\sqrt[3]{2}$, $\sqrt[4]{3}$ is

    (A) $(234)^{\frac{1}{12}}$ (B) $(324)^{\frac{1}{12}}$

    (C) $(432)^{\frac{1}{12}}$ (D) $(433)^{\frac{1}{12}}$

40. Divide $\sqrt[6]{12}$ by $\sqrt{3}\,\sqrt[3]{2}$.

    (A) $\frac{1}{\sqrt[2]{3}}$ (B) $\frac{1}{\sqrt[3]{3}}$

    (C) $\frac{1}{\sqrt[4]{3}}$ (D) $\frac{1}{\sqrt[5]{3}}$

41. The rationalising factor of $2\sqrt[3]{5}$ is

    (A) $\sqrt[3]{5}$

    (B) $\sqrt[3]{5^2}$

    (C) 5^2

    (D) 5^3

42. The rationalising factor of $\sqrt[5]{a^2b^3c^4}$ is

    (A) $\sqrt[5]{a^3b^2c}$ (B) $\sqrt[4]{a^3b^2c}$

    (C) $\sqrt[3]{a^3b^2c}$ (D) $\sqrt{a^3b^2c}$

43. The rationalising factor of $\sqrt{108}$ is

    (A) $\sqrt{3}$ (B) $\sqrt[3]{3}$

    (C) $\sqrt[3]{27}$ (D) $\sqrt[3]{15}$

44. The rational denominator of the surd $\frac{3\sqrt[3]{5}}{\sqrt[3]{9}}$ is

    (A) 1   (B) 2

    (C) 3   (D) 4

45. Given that $\sqrt{2} = 1.414$, $\sqrt{3} = 1.732$, $\sqrt{5} = 2.236$. Then the value of $\dfrac{1}{\sqrt{10}}$ up to three decimal places is

(A) 2.414

(B) 0.316

(C) 1.079

(D) 3.162

46. If both 'a' and 'b' are rational numbers then 'a' and 'b' from the following

$\dfrac{3-\sqrt{5}}{3+2\sqrt{5}} = a\sqrt{5} - b$ are

(A) $a = \dfrac{9}{11}$, $b = \dfrac{19}{11}$

(B) $a = \dfrac{19}{11}$, $b = \dfrac{9}{11}$

(C) $a = \dfrac{2}{11}$, $b = -\dfrac{8}{11}$

(D) $a = \dfrac{10}{11}$, $b = \dfrac{21}{11}$

47. The value of $\dfrac{\sqrt{5}-2}{\sqrt{5}+2} - \dfrac{\sqrt{5}+2}{\sqrt{5}-2}$ is

(A) $-\sqrt{5}$ (B) $-2\sqrt{5}$

(C) $-4\sqrt{5}$ (D) $-8\sqrt{5}$

48. If $x = 2 - \sqrt{3}$ then the value of $x^2 + \dfrac{1}{x^2}$ and $x^2 - \dfrac{1}{x^2}$ is

(A) $14, 8\sqrt{3}$ (B) $-14, -8\sqrt{3}$

(C) $14, -8\sqrt{3}$ (D) $-14, 8\sqrt{3}$

49. The value of

$\dfrac{1}{1+\sqrt{2}} + \dfrac{1}{\sqrt{2}+\sqrt{3}} + \dfrac{1}{\sqrt{3}+\sqrt{4}} + \dfrac{1}{\sqrt{4}+\sqrt{5}}$

$+ \dfrac{1}{\sqrt{5}+\sqrt{6}} + \dfrac{1}{\sqrt{6}+\sqrt{7}} + \dfrac{1}{\sqrt{7}+\sqrt{8}} + \dfrac{1}{\sqrt{8}+\sqrt{9}}$

(A) 0 (B) 1

(C) 2 (D) 4

50. If $x = 3 + \sqrt{8}$ then $x^3 + \dfrac{1}{x^3} = $

(A) 216 (B) 198

(C) 192 (D) 261

51. If $x = \dfrac{\sqrt{3}+1}{2}$ then the value of

$4x^3 + 2x^2 - 8x + 7$ is

(A) 10 (B) 8

(C0 6 (D) 4

52. If $x = \dfrac{\sqrt{a}+\sqrt{b}}{\sqrt{a}-\sqrt{b}}$, $y = \dfrac{\sqrt{a}-\sqrt{b}}{\sqrt{a}+\sqrt{b}}$ then the value of $x^2 + xy + y^2$ is

(A) $\dfrac{4(a-b)}{(a+b)}$ (B) $\dfrac{4(a+b)}{(a-b)}$

(C) $\dfrac{2(a+b)}{a-b}$ (D) $\dfrac{2(a-b)}{a+b}$

53. The smallest positive number from the numbers below is

(A) $10 - 3\sqrt{11}$

(B) $3\sqrt{11} - 10$

(C) $18 - 5\sqrt{13}$

(D) $51 - 10\sqrt{26}$

54. $\dfrac{2\sqrt{6}}{\sqrt{2}+\sqrt{3}+\sqrt{5}}$ equals

(A) $\sqrt{2}+\sqrt{3}-\sqrt{5}$

(B) $4-\sqrt{2}-\sqrt{3}$

(C) $\sqrt{2}+\sqrt{3}+\sqrt{6}-5$

(D) $\dfrac{1}{2}\left(\sqrt{2}+\sqrt{5}-\sqrt{3}\right)$

55. The value of $\left(\sqrt[6]{27}-\sqrt{6\dfrac{3}{4}}\right)^{2}$

(A) $\dfrac{\sqrt{3}}{2}$ (B) $\dfrac{3}{2}$

(C) $\dfrac{\sqrt{3}}{4}$ (D) $\dfrac{3}{4}$

56. Which of the following is closest to $\sqrt{65}-\sqrt{63}$?

(A) 0.12   (B) 0.25

(C) 0.14   (D) 0.15

57. The value of $\sqrt{8}+\sqrt{18}$ is

(A) $\sqrt{26}$ (B) $2\left(\sqrt{2}+\sqrt{3}\right)$

(C) 7   (D) $5\sqrt{2}$

58. The fraction $\dfrac{2\left(\sqrt{2}+\sqrt{6}\right)}{3\left(\sqrt{2+\sqrt{3}}\right)}$ is equal to

(A) $\dfrac{2\sqrt{2}}{3}$ (B) 1

(C) $\dfrac{2\sqrt{3}}{3}$ (D) $\dfrac{4}{3}$

59. If $N=\dfrac{\sqrt{\sqrt{5}+2}+\sqrt{\sqrt{5}-2}}{\sqrt{\sqrt{5}+1}}-\sqrt{3-2\sqrt{2}}$

then N equals to

(A) 1   (B) $2\sqrt{2}-1$

(C) $\dfrac{\sqrt{5}}{2}$ (D) none of these

60. If $t=\dfrac{1}{1-\sqrt[4]{2}}$ then t equals to

(A) $\left(1-\sqrt[4]{2}\right)\left(2-\sqrt{2}\right)$

(B) $\left(1-\sqrt[4]{2}\right)\left(1+\sqrt{2}\right)$

(C) $-\left(1+\sqrt[4]{2}\right)\left(1+\sqrt{2}\right)$

(D) $\left(1+\sqrt[4]{2}\right)\left(1+\sqrt{2}\right)$

61. If $x=\sqrt{3}+\sqrt{2}$ then $x^{2}+\dfrac{1}{x^{2}}$ is

(A) $2\sqrt{3}$ (B) 10   (C) 12   (D) 14

62. The biggest surd among $\sqrt[3]{2}$, $\sqrt{3}$, $\sqrt[3]{5}$ is

(A) $\sqrt[3]{2}$ (B) $\sqrt{3}$

(C) $\sqrt[3]{5}$ (D) none

63. The value of the surd $4\sqrt{3}-3\sqrt{12}+2\sqrt{75}$ is

(A) $2\sqrt{3}$ (B) $4\sqrt{3}$

(C) $6\sqrt{3}$ (D) $8\sqrt{3}$

64. The product of $\sqrt[3]{4}$ and $\sqrt[3]{22}$ is

(A) $2\sqrt[3]{11}$ (B) $3\sqrt{11}$

(C) $4\sqrt{11}$ (D) none

65. The value of

$$\frac{a+\sqrt{a^2-b^2}}{\sqrt{a^2+b^2}+b}+\frac{\sqrt{a^2+b^2}-b}{a-\sqrt{a^2-b^2}}$$

(A) $\dfrac{a^2}{b^2}$ (B) $\dfrac{b^2}{a^2}$

(C) $\dfrac{a}{b}$ (D) none

66. If p : Every fraction is a rational number and

     q : Every rational number is a fraction, then which of the following is correct?

(A) p is True and q is False

(B) p is False and q is True

(C) Both p and q are True

(D) Both p and q are False

67. Which of the following is a rational number(s)?

(A) $\dfrac{-2}{9}$ (B) $\dfrac{4}{-7}$

(C) $\dfrac{-3}{-17}$ (D) All the three

68. If p : All integers are rational numbers and

     q : Every rational number is an integer, then which of the following statement is correct?

(A) p is False and q is True

(B) p is True and q is False

(C) Both p and q are True

(D) Both p and q are False

69. $\dfrac{-3}{0}$ is a _____.

(A) positive rational number

(B) negative rational number

(C) either positive or negative rational number

(D) neither positive nor negative rational number

70. A rational number equivalent to $\dfrac{-5}{-3}$ is

(A) $\dfrac{-25}{15}$ (B) $\dfrac{25}{-15}$

(C) $\dfrac{25}{15}$ (D) none of these

71. $\dfrac{-2}{-19}$ is a

(A) positive rational number.

(B) negative rational number.

(C) either positive or negative rational number

(D) neither positive nor negative rational number

72. The rational number $\dfrac{0}{7}$

(A) has a positive numerator

(B) has a negative numerator

(C) has either a positive numerator or a negative numerator

(D) has neither a positive numerator nor a negative numerator

73. Which of the following rational numbers is in the standard form?

    (A) $\dfrac{8}{-36}$ (B) $\dfrac{-7}{56}$

    (C) $\dfrac{3}{-4}$ (D) None

74. Which of the following statement is true?

    (A) $\dfrac{3}{-8} > \dfrac{-12}{32}$ (B) $\dfrac{3}{-8} = \dfrac{-12}{32}$

    (C) $\dfrac{3}{-8} < \dfrac{-12}{32}$ (D) $\dfrac{3}{5} > \dfrac{4}{3}$

75. If $\dfrac{-3}{5} = \dfrac{-24}{x}$, then x = _____

    (A) 40 (B) -40

    (C) ± 40 (D) none

76. If $\dfrac{-3}{x} = \dfrac{x}{27}$ then x is _____.

    (A) a rational number
    (B) not a rational number
    (C) an integer
    (D) a natural number

77. A rational number $\dfrac{-2}{3}$

    (A) lies to the left side of 0 on the number line

    (B) lies to the right side of 0 on the number line

    (C) it is not possible to represent on the number line

    (D) cannot be determined on which side the number lies

78. Which of the following statements is true?

    (A) $\dfrac{-5}{8}$ lies to the left of 0 on the number line

    (B) $\dfrac{3}{7}$ lies to the right of 0 on the number line

    (C) The rational numbers $\dfrac{1}{3}$ and $\dfrac{-7}{3}$ are on opposite sides of 0 on the number line
    (D) All the above

79. Out of the rational numbers $\dfrac{-5}{11}, \dfrac{5}{-12}, \dfrac{-5}{17}$, which is greater?

    (A) $\dfrac{-5}{11}$ (B) $\dfrac{5}{-12}$

    (C) $\dfrac{-5}{17}$ (D) None

80. Out of the rational numbers $\dfrac{7}{-13}, \dfrac{-5}{13}, \dfrac{-11}{13}$ which is smaller?

    (A) $\dfrac{7}{-13}$ (B) $\dfrac{-5}{13}$

    (C) $\dfrac{-11}{13}$ (D) None

81. Which of the following statements is true?

    (A) $\dfrac{-2}{3} < \dfrac{4}{-9} < \dfrac{-5}{12} < \dfrac{7}{-18}$

    (B) $\dfrac{7}{-18} < \dfrac{-5}{12} < \dfrac{4}{-9} < \dfrac{-2}{3}$

    (C) $\dfrac{4}{-9} < \dfrac{7}{-18} < \dfrac{-5}{12} < \dfrac{-2}{3}$

    (D) $\dfrac{-5}{12} < \dfrac{-2}{3} < \dfrac{4}{-9} < \dfrac{7}{-18}$

82. Arrange the following numbers in descending order. $-2, \dfrac{4}{-5}, \dfrac{-11}{20}, \dfrac{3}{4}$

(A) $\dfrac{3}{4} > -2 > \dfrac{-11}{20} > \dfrac{4}{-5}$

(B) $\dfrac{3}{4} > \dfrac{-11}{20} > \dfrac{-4}{5} > -2$

(C) $\dfrac{3}{4} > \dfrac{4}{-5} > -2 > \dfrac{-11}{20}$

(D) $\dfrac{3}{4} > \dfrac{4}{-5} > \dfrac{-11}{20} > -2$

83. The given rational numbers are $\dfrac{1}{2}, \dfrac{4}{-5}, \dfrac{-7}{8}$. If these numbers are arranged in the ascending order or descending order, then the middle number is

(A) $\dfrac{1}{2}$ (B) $\dfrac{-7}{8}$

(C) $\dfrac{4}{-5}$ (D) None

84. The average of the middle two rational numbers if $\dfrac{4}{7}, \dfrac{1}{3}, \dfrac{2}{5}, \dfrac{5}{9}$ are arranged in ascending order is

(A) $\dfrac{86}{90}$ (B) $\dfrac{86}{45}$ (C) $\dfrac{43}{45}$ (D) $\dfrac{43}{90}$

85. What is the percentage of least number in the greatest number if $\dfrac{3}{5}, \dfrac{9}{5}, \dfrac{1}{5}, \dfrac{7}{5}$ are arranged in ascending or descending order?

(A) $11\dfrac{1}{9}\%$ (B) 10%

(C) 20%   (D) 25%

86. The difference between the greatest and least numbers of $\dfrac{5}{9}, \dfrac{1}{9}, \dfrac{11}{9}$ is

(A) $\dfrac{2}{9}$ (B) $\dfrac{4}{9}$ (C) $\dfrac{10}{9}$ (D) $\dfrac{2}{3}$

87. If x, y, z be rational numbers such that x > y and z < y then _____

(A) z > x   (B) z < x

(C) y < z   (D) y > x

88. For any two rational numbers x and y, which of the following properties are correct?

(i) x < y   (ii) x = y   (iii) x > y

(A) Only (i) and (ii) are correct

(B) Only (ii) and (iii) are correct

(C) Only (ii) is correct

(D) All (i), (ii) and (iii) are correct

89. If A : The quotient of two integers is always a rational number and

R : $\dfrac{1}{0}$ is not rational,

then which of the following statements is true?

(A) A is True and R is the correct explanation of A

(B) A is False and R is the correct explanation of A

(C) A is True and R is False

(D) Both A and R are False

90. If A: Every whole number is a natural number and

R : 0 is not a natural number,

Then which of the following statement is true?

(A) A is False and R is the correct explanation of A

(B) A is True and R is the correct explanation of A

(C) A is True and R is False

(D) Both A and R are True

91. $2 - \dfrac{11}{39} + \dfrac{5}{26} = $ ....

(A) $\dfrac{149}{39}$ (B) $1 + \dfrac{71}{78}$

(C) $\dfrac{149}{76}$ (D) $\dfrac{149}{98}$

92. $\dfrac{-143}{21} = $ ....

(A) $-6 + \dfrac{17}{21}$ (B) $6 + \left(\dfrac{-17}{21}\right)$

(C) $(-6) + \left(\dfrac{-17}{21}\right)$ (D) none

93. Addition of rational numbers does not satisfy which of the following property?

(A) Commutative   (B) Associative
(C) Closure   (D) None

94. $\dfrac{-7}{5} + \left(\dfrac{2}{-11} + \dfrac{-13}{25}\right) = \left(\dfrac{-7}{5} + \dfrac{2}{-11}\right) + \dfrac{-13}{25}$

This property is

(A) closure

(B) commutative

(C) associative

(D) identity

95. Which of the following statements is correct?

(A) 0 is called the additive identity for rational numbers.

(B) 1 is called the multiplicative identity for rational numbers.

(C) The additive inverse of 0 is zero itself.

(D) All the above

96. The sum of two rational numbers is -3. If one of the numbers is $\dfrac{-7}{5}$, then the other number is

(A) $\dfrac{-8}{5}$ (B) $\dfrac{8}{5}$

(C) $\dfrac{-6}{5}$ (D) $\dfrac{6}{5}$

97. What number should be added to $\dfrac{-5}{6}$ so as to get $\dfrac{3}{2}$?

(A) $\dfrac{-7}{3}$ (B) $2\dfrac{1}{3}$

(C) $\dfrac{8}{3}$ (D) $\dfrac{-8}{3}$

98. Which of the following alternatives is wrong? Given that

(i) difference of two rational numbers is a rational number

(ii) subtraction is commutative on rational numbers

(iii) addition is not commutative on rational numbers.

(A) (ii) and (iii)   (B) (i) only
(C) (i) and (iii)   (D) All the above

99. Which of the following statements is true?

(A) The reciprocals 1 and -1 are themselves

(B) Zero has no reciprocal

(C) The product of two rational numbers is a rational number

D) All the above

100. Name the property of multiplication illustratedby

$$\frac{-4}{3} \times \left(\frac{-6}{5} + \frac{8}{7}\right) = \left(\frac{-4}{3} \times \frac{-6}{5}\right) + \left(\frac{-4}{3} \times \frac{8}{7}\right).$$

(A) Associative property
(B) Commutative property
(C) Distributive property
(D) None of these

101. The product of a rational number and its reciprocal is

(A) 0   (B) 1   (C) -1   (D) none

102. The product of two rational numbers is $\frac{-9}{16}$. If one of the numbers is $\frac{-4}{3}$, then the other number is

(A) $\frac{36}{48}$ (B) $\frac{25}{64}$

(C) $\frac{27}{49}$ (D) $\frac{27}{64}$

103. By what rational number should $\frac{-8}{39}$ be multiplied to obtain 26?

(A) $\frac{507}{4}$ (B) $\frac{-507}{4}$

(C) $\frac{407}{4}$ (D) None

104. How many pieces of equal size can be cut from a rope of 30 metres long, each measuring $3\frac{3}{4}$ meters?

(A) 8   (B) 10
(C) 6   (D) 12

105. If A : Rational numbers are always closed under division and

R : Division by Zero is not defined, then which of the following statement is correct?

(A) A is True and R is the correct explanation of A

(B) A is False and R is the correct explanation of A

(C) A is True and R is False

(D) None of these

106. π is

(A) rational   (B) irrational
(C) imaginary   (D) an integer

107. The set of all irrational numbers is closed for

(A) addition

(B) multiplication

(C) division

(D) none of thse

108. The additive inverse of $\frac{-a}{b}$ is

(A) $\frac{a}{b}$ (B) $\frac{b}{a}$

(C) $\frac{-b}{a}$ (D) $\frac{-a}{b}$

109. Multiplicative inverse of '0' is

(A) $\dfrac{1}{0}$

(B) 0

(C) does not exist

(D) none of these

110. Which of the following statement is false?

(A) Every fraction is a rational number

(B) Every rational number is a fraction

(C) Every integer is a rational number

(D) All the above

111. A rational number can be expressed as a terminating decimal if the denominator has factors

(A) 2 or 5

(B) 2 ,3 or 5

(C) 3 or 5

(D) none of these

112. Express 0.75 as rational number.

(A) $\dfrac{75}{99}$

(B) $\dfrac{75}{90}$

(C) $\dfrac{3}{4}$

(D) None

113. Express $0.\overline{75}$ as rational number.

(A) $\dfrac{75}{90}$

(B) $\dfrac{25}{33}$

(C) $\dfrac{3}{4}$

(D) None

114. Express $0.3\overline{58}$ as rational number.

(A) $\dfrac{358}{1000}$

(B) $\dfrac{358}{999}$

(C) $\dfrac{355}{990}$

(D) All

115. Which of the following statements is true?

(A) $\dfrac{5}{7} < \dfrac{7}{9} < \dfrac{9}{11} < \dfrac{11}{13}$

(B) $\dfrac{11}{13} < \dfrac{9}{11} < \dfrac{7}{9} < \dfrac{5}{7}$

(C) $\dfrac{5}{7} < \dfrac{11}{13} < \dfrac{7}{9} < \dfrac{9}{11}$

(D) $\dfrac{5}{7} < \dfrac{9}{11} < \dfrac{11}{13} < \dfrac{7}{9}$

116. A rational number between $\dfrac{1}{4}$ and $\dfrac{1}{3}$ is

(A) $\dfrac{7}{24}$

(B) 0.29

(C) $\dfrac{13}{48}$

(D) all the above

117. An irrational number is

(A) a terminating and nonrepeating decimal

(B) a nonterminating and non-repeating decimal

(C) a terminating and repeating decimal

(D) a nonterminating and repeating decimal

118. Which of the following statements is true?

    (A) Every point on the number line represents a rational number

    (B) Irrational numbers cannot be represented by points on the number line

    (C) $\frac{22}{7}$ is a rational number

    (D) None of these

119. The set of real numbers does not satisfy the property of

    (A) multiplicative inverse

    (B) additive inverse

    (C) multiplicative identity

    (D) none of these

120. Which step in the following problem is wrong?

    a = b = 1

    a = b

    step–1 = a² = ab

    step–2 = a² – b² = ab – b²

    step–3 = (a + b) (a – b) = b(a – b)

    step 4 : $a + b = \dfrac{b(a-b)}{a-b}$

    a + b = b

    1 + 1 = 1

    2 = 1

    (A) Step–4

    (B) Step–3

    (C) Step–2

    (D) Step–1

121. If 'm' is an irrational number then '2m' is _____ .

    (A) a rational number

    (B) an irrational number

    (C) a whole number

    (D) a natural number

122. The value of $\sqrt{3}$ is

    (A) 1.414   (B) 2.256

    (C) 1.732   (D) none

123. The sum of a rational and an irrational number is _____ .

    (A) an irrational number

    (B) a rational number

    (C) an integer

    (D) a whole number

124. The product of two irrationals is

    (A) a rational number

    (B) an irrational number

    (C) either A or B

    (D) neither A nor B

125. The value of $1.\overline{34} + 4.1\overline{2}$ is

    (A) $\dfrac{133}{99}$ (B) $\dfrac{371}{90}$

    (C) $\dfrac{5169}{990}$ (D) $\dfrac{5411}{990}$

126. The value of $4 - \dfrac{5}{1 + \dfrac{1}{3 + \dfrac{1}{2 + \dfrac{1}{4}}}}$ is

    (A) $\dfrac{40}{31}$ (B) $\dfrac{4}{9}$

    (C) $\dfrac{1}{8}$ (D) $\dfrac{31}{40}$

127. The sum of the additive inverse and multiplicative inverse of 2 is

(A) $\dfrac{3}{2}$ (B) $\dfrac{-3}{2}$

(C) $\dfrac{1}{2}$ (D) $\dfrac{-1}{2}$

128. If $\sqrt{6}$ = 2.449 then the value of $\dfrac{3\sqrt{2}}{2\sqrt{3}}$ is close to

(A) 1.225   (B) 0.816

(C) 0.613   (D) 2.449

129. The value of $\sqrt{5\sqrt{5\sqrt{5\sqrt{5.....}}}}$ is

(A) 0

(B) 5

(C) can't be determined

(D) none

130. The greatest among the following is

I. $\sqrt[3]{1.728}$ II. $\dfrac{\sqrt{3}-1}{\sqrt{3}+1}$

III. $\left(\dfrac{1}{2}\right)^{-2}$ IV. $\dfrac{17}{8}$

(A) I   (B) IV

(C) II   (D) III

131. A fraction $\dfrac{a}{b}$ can be expressed as a terminating decimal, if b has no prime factors other than

(A) 2, 3   (B) 3, 5

(C) 2, 5   (D) 2, 3, 5

132. $\dfrac{217}{143}$ can be expressed in the decimal form as

(A) $1.5\overline{17}$ (B) $1.\overline{517}$

(C) $1.5\overline{17}$ (D) 1.517...

133. $\dfrac{961}{625}$ is a

(A) terminating decimal
(B) nonterminating decimal
(C) cannot be determined
(D) none of these

134. 2.003 can be expressed in the rational form as

(A) $\dfrac{2003}{100}$ (B) $\dfrac{2003}{1000}$

(C) $\dfrac{2003}{10000}$ (D) $\dfrac{2003}{10}$

135. $0.\overline{018}$ can be expressed in the rational form as

(A) $\dfrac{18}{1000}$ (B) $\dfrac{18}{990}$

(C) $\dfrac{18}{9900}$ (D) $\dfrac{18}{999}$

136. $2.53\overline{6}$ can be expressed in the rational form as

(A) $\dfrac{716}{300}$ (B) $\dfrac{761}{3000}$

(C) $\dfrac{761}{300}$ (D) $\dfrac{716}{3000}$

137. $0.\overline{23} + 0.\overline{22} =$

(A) $0.\overline{45}$ (B) $0.\overline{43}$

(C) $0.4\overline{5}$ (D) 0.45

138. Which of the following statement(s) is true?

(A) $|x \times y| = |x| \cdot |y|$, where x and y are rational numbers

(B) Infinite number of rational numbers lie between any two rational numbers

(C) $|x| = -x$ if $x < 0$ where x is a rational number

(D) All the above

139. If A : If the denominator of a rational number has 2 as a prime factor, then that rational number can be expressed as a terminating decimal and R : $\dfrac{83}{64}$ is a terminating decimal, then which of the following statements is correct?

(A) A is False and R is True

(B) A is True and R is False

(C) A is True and R is an example of A

(D) A is False and R is an example supporting A

140. If x and y are two rational numbers, then which of the following statements is wrong?

(A) $|x + y| \le |x| + |y|$

(B) $|x \times y| = |x| \times |y|$

(C) $|x - y| \le |x| - |y|$

(D) None of these

Answers

1. A	2. D	3. C	4. D	5. A	6. A	7. C	8. A	9. A	10. B
11. C	12. B	13. A	14. B	15. B	16. D	17. A	18. A	19. C	20. C
21. A	22. B	23. C	24. B	25. A	26. D	27. A	28. D	29. A	30. B
31. A	32. B	33. A	34. C	35. A	36. B	37. B	38. B	39. C	40. B
41. B	42. A	43. A	44. C	45. B	46. A	47. D	48. C	49. C	50. B
51. A	52. B	53. D	54. A	55. D	56. B	57. D	58. D	59. A	60. C
61. B	62. B	63. D	64. A	65. D	66. A	67. D	68. B	69. D	70. C
71. A	72. C	73. D	74. B	75. A	76. B	77. A	78. D	79. C	80. C
81. A	82. B	83. C	84. D	85. A	86. C	87. B	88. D	89. B	90. A
91. B	92. C	93. D	94. C	95. D	96. A	97. B	98. A	99. D	100. C
101. B	102. D	103. B	104. A	105. B	106. B	107. D	108. A	109 C	110. B
111. A	112. C	113. B	114. C	115. A	116. D	117. B	118. D	119 D	120. A
121. B	122. C	123. A	124. C	125. D	126. C	127. B	128. A	129 B	130. D
131. C	132. D	133. A	134. B	135. D	136. C	137. A	138. D	139 C	140. C

1. **(A)** $\sqrt{2}$ is not a rational number. It can't be expressed in the fractional form.

5. **(A)** Let $x = 3.\overline{6}$; $10x = 36.6$

   $\Rightarrow 9x = 33$

   $x = \dfrac{33}{9} = \dfrac{11}{3}$

6. **(A)** $\left(6+\sqrt{2}\right)\left(6-\sqrt{2}\right) = 6 - 4 = 2$

7. **(C)** $\dfrac{3}{5} = 0.6$ where as other numbers have non-terminating decimals.

8. **(A)** $3 - (-3) = 3 + 3 = 6$

10. **(B)** $|x - 2| = 12 \Rightarrow x - 2 = 12$

    $x = 14,$
    or
    $-(x - 2) = 12$
    $x - 2 = -12$
    $x = -10$

11. **(C)** $|2x - 1| >, 5$

    $\Rightarrow -5 \geq 2x - 1 \geq 5$

    $\Rightarrow x \leq -2, x \geq 3$

12. **(B)** $\left(\sqrt{2} + \sqrt{3}\right)^2 = 5 + 2\sqrt{6}$

    is an irrational number.

17. **(A)** $f(x)$ is a real valued function

    $x - 1 \geq 0, \quad 4 - x \geq 0$
    $x \geq 1 \qquad \quad -x > -4$
    $\qquad \qquad \qquad x \leq 4$

18. **(A)** Since $f(x)$ is real valued function,

    $x^2 + 1 \neq 0$
    $x^2 \neq -1$
    $x \neq \pm\sqrt{-1}$.
    There is no real value of x such that $x^2 + 1 = 0$.

19. **(C)** A and B are irrational. Number D is does not lie between $\sqrt{2}$ and $\sqrt{3}$

21. **(A)** $f\left(\dfrac{1}{5}\right) = \dfrac{28}{5} \Rightarrow 5 + \dfrac{a}{5} = \dfrac{28}{5}$

    $\therefore a = 3$

22. **(B)** $3 - \sqrt{3}$ is an irrational number.

    $3 + \sqrt{3}$ is also an irrational number.

    $\dfrac{3 - \sqrt{3}}{3 + \sqrt{3}}$ is an irrational number.

24. **(B)** $\sqrt{x-4}$ and $\sqrt{x-5}$ will be positive only if $x > 4, x > 5$.

25. **(A)** Let $x = 17.\overline{6}$; $10x = 176.\overline{6}$

    $9x = 159$

    $x = \dfrac{159}{9}$

    $17.\overline{6} = \dfrac{53}{3}$

26. **(D)** $3x + 2 = \pm 8 \Rightarrow x = -\dfrac{10}{3}, 2$.

27. **(A)** $f(16) = 275 \Rightarrow 16^2 + 16 + b = 275$

    $\therefore b = 3$.

28. **(D)** $f(2) = 8 \Rightarrow 2a + b = 8 \dots\dots (1)$
    $f(3) = 11 \Rightarrow 3a + b = 11$
    Solving (1) & (2) we get
    $a = 3, b = 2$.

30. **(B)** The factors of $x^2 - 5x + 6$ are $(x - 2)(x - 3)$.

    $f(x) = \dfrac{1}{x^2 - 5x + 6}$ takes all the values except 2 and 3.

31. (A)
$|3 - 5x| > 2$

$-2 > 3 - 5x > 2,$

$-2 > 3 - 5x \Rightarrow x > 1$

$3 - 5x > 2 \Rightarrow x < \dfrac{1}{5}.$

32. (B)
$1 < -x < 2 \Rightarrow -2 < x < -1$

$1 < x < 2 \Rightarrow 1 < x < 2$

$\therefore \{-2 < x < -1\} \cup \{1 < x < 2\}$

33. (A)
$2^{\frac{1}{3}}, \ 3^{\frac{1}{3}}, \ 4^{\frac{1}{9}}$

LCM of 3, 6, 9 is 18.

$2^{\frac{1}{3}} = 2^{\frac{6}{18}}, \ 3^{\frac{1}{6}} = 3^{\frac{3}{18}}, \ 4^{\frac{1}{9}} = 4^{\frac{2}{18}}$

$(64)^{\frac{1}{18}}, \ (27)^{\frac{1}{18}}, \ (16)^{\frac{1}{18}}$

$(16)^{\frac{1}{18}}, \ (27)^{\frac{1}{18}}, \ (64)^{\frac{1}{18}}$

$\sqrt[9]{4}, \ \sqrt[6]{3}, \ \sqrt[3]{2}$

35. (A)
$4^{\frac{1}{3}}, \ 5^{\frac{1}{4}}, \ 3^{\frac{1}{4}}$

LCM of 3, 4, 4 is 12

$4^{\frac{4}{12}}, \ 5^{\frac{3}{12}}, \ 3^{\frac{3}{12}}$

$\Rightarrow \left(4^4\right)^{\frac{1}{12}}, \ \left(5^3\right)^{\frac{1}{12}}, \left(3^3\right)^{\frac{1}{12}}$

$\sqrt[12]{256}, \ \sqrt[12]{125}, \ \sqrt[12]{27}$

36. (B)
$\sqrt{11} - \sqrt{6}$ is the difference of smaller surds.

$\sqrt{17} - \sqrt{12}$ is the difference of bigger surds.

$\therefore \ \sqrt{11} - \sqrt{6} > \sqrt{17} - \sqrt{12}$

38. (B)
$\left(\dfrac{1}{2}\right)^{\frac{1}{2}}, \left(\dfrac{2}{3}\right)^{\frac{1}{3}}, \left(\dfrac{1}{3}\right)^{\frac{1}{2}}, \left(\dfrac{1}{4}\right)^{\frac{1}{2}}$

$\left(\dfrac{1}{2}\right)^{\frac{3}{6}}, \left(\dfrac{2}{3}\right)^{\frac{2}{6}}, \left(\dfrac{1}{3}\right)^{\frac{3}{6}}, \left(\dfrac{1}{4}\right)^{\frac{3}{6}}$

$\left(\dfrac{1}{8}\right)^{\frac{1}{6}}, \left(\dfrac{4}{9}\right)^{\frac{1}{6}}, \left(\dfrac{1}{27}\right)^{\frac{1}{6}}, \left(\dfrac{1}{64}\right)^{\frac{1}{6}}$

The biggest surd is $\left(\dfrac{4}{9}\right)^{\frac{1}{6}}$

39. (C)
$\sqrt[3]{2} \times \sqrt[4]{3} = 2^{\frac{1}{3}} \times 3^{\frac{1}{4}}$

$= 2^{\frac{4}{12}} \times 3^{\frac{3}{12}}; \ \left(2^4\right)^{\frac{1}{12}} \times \left(3^3\right)^{\frac{1}{12}}$

$= (16 \times 27)^{\frac{1}{12}}$

$= (432)^{\frac{1}{12}}$

40. (B)
$\dfrac{\sqrt[6]{12}}{\sqrt{3}\sqrt[3]{2}} = \dfrac{(12)^{\frac{1}{6}}}{3^{\frac{1}{2}} \times 2^{\frac{1}{3}}} = \dfrac{(12)^{\frac{1}{6}}}{3^{\frac{3}{6}} \times 2^{\frac{2}{6}}}$

$= \dfrac{(12)^{\frac{1}{6}}}{(27)^{\frac{1}{6}} \times (4)^{\frac{1}{6}}}$

$= \left(\dfrac{12}{27 \times 4}\right)^{\frac{1}{6}} = \left(\dfrac{1}{9}\right)^{\frac{1}{6}}$

$\left(3^{-2}\right)^{\frac{1}{6}} = 3^{-\frac{1}{3}} = \dfrac{1}{\sqrt[3]{3}}$

41. (B) Rationalising factor of

$5^{\frac{1}{3}} = 5^{1 - \frac{1}{3}} = 5^{\frac{2}{3}}$

$\therefore \ 5^{\frac{2}{3}} = \sqrt[3]{5^2}$

42. (A)
$\sqrt[5]{a^2 b^3 c^4} = \left(a^2 b^3 c^4\right)^{\frac{1}{5}}$

$= a^{\frac{2}{5}} \ b^{\frac{3}{5}} \ c^{\frac{4}{5}}$

RF of $a^{\frac{2}{5}} \ b^{\frac{3}{5}} \ c^{\frac{4}{5}} = a^{\frac{3}{5}} \ b^{\frac{2}{5}} \ c^{\frac{1}{5}}$

$$= \sqrt[5]{a^3 b^2 c}$$

43. (A) $\sqrt{108} = \sqrt{36 \times 3}$

$= 6 \times \sqrt{3} = 6\sqrt{3}$

RF of $6\sqrt{3} = \sqrt{3}$.

44. (C) RF of $\sqrt[3]{9} = 3^{\frac{2}{3}}$ is $3^{\frac{1}{3}}$

$\therefore \ 3^{\frac{2}{3}} \times 3^{\frac{1}{3}} = 3^1$

45. (B) $\dfrac{1}{\sqrt{10}} = \dfrac{1}{\sqrt{2} \times \sqrt{5}} = \dfrac{1}{1.414 \times 1.732}$

$= 0.316$

46. (A) $\dfrac{\left(3 - \sqrt{5}\right)}{\left(3 + 2\sqrt{5}\right)} \dfrac{\left(3 - 2\sqrt{5}\right)}{\left(3 - 2\sqrt{5}\right)} = \dot{a}\sqrt{5} - b$

$\left[\dfrac{9 - 9\sqrt{5} + 10}{-11} = a\sqrt{5} - b \right.$

$-\dfrac{19}{11} + \dfrac{9}{11}\sqrt{5} = a\sqrt{5} - b$

$\left. \Rightarrow a = \dfrac{9}{11}, \ b = \dfrac{19}{11} \right]$

47. (D) $\dfrac{\sqrt{5} - 2}{\sqrt{5} + 2} - \dfrac{\sqrt{5} + 2}{\sqrt{5} - 2}$

$= \dfrac{\left(\sqrt{5} - 2\right)^2 - \left(\sqrt{5} + 2\right)^2}{\left(\sqrt{5} + 2\right)\left(\sqrt{5} - 2\right)}$

$= \dfrac{-8\sqrt{5}}{1}$

48. (C) $x^2 + \dfrac{1}{x^2} = \left(x + \dfrac{1}{x}\right)^2 - 2$;

$x^2 - \dfrac{1}{x^2} = \left(x + \dfrac{1}{x}\right)\left(x - \dfrac{1}{x}\right)$

$x = 2 - \sqrt{3}$

$\dfrac{1}{x} = \dfrac{1}{2 - \sqrt{3}} = \dfrac{2 + \sqrt{3}}{1}$

$x^2 + \dfrac{1}{x^2} = 16 - 2 = 14$

$x^2 - \dfrac{1}{x^2} = 4\left(-2\sqrt{3}\right) = -8\sqrt{3}$

49. (C) Rationalising   each denominator, we get

$\sqrt{2} - \sqrt{1} + \sqrt{3} - \sqrt{2} + \sqrt{4} - \sqrt{5}$

$+ \sqrt{5} - \sqrt{4} + \sqrt{6} - \sqrt{5} + \sqrt{7} - \sqrt{6}$

$+ \sqrt{8} - \sqrt{7} + \sqrt{9} - \sqrt{8}$

$= -\sqrt{1} + \sqrt{9} = 2.$

50. (B) $x = 3 + \sqrt{8}, \ \dfrac{1}{x} = 3 - \sqrt{8}$;

$x + \dfrac{1}{x} = 6$

$x^3 + \dfrac{1}{x^3} = \left(6\right)^3 - 3\left(6\right)$

$= 216 - 18$

$= 198.$

51. (A) $4\left(\dfrac{\sqrt{3} + 1}{2}\right)^3 + 2\left(\dfrac{\sqrt{3} + 1}{2}\right)^2$

$-8\left(\dfrac{\sqrt{3} + 1}{\cdot 2}\right) + 7 = 10$

52. (B) $x^2 + xy + y^2$
$= (x + y)^2 - xy$

$= \dfrac{4\left(a + b\right)}{\left(a - b\right)}$

$$x^2 + xy + y^2 = \frac{4(a+b)}{(a-b)}$$

53. (D) $10 - 3\sqrt{11} = \sqrt{100} - \sqrt{99}$

$3\sqrt{11} - 10 = \sqrt{99} - \sqrt{100}$

$18 - 5\sqrt{13} = \sqrt{324} - \sqrt{325}$

$51 - 10\sqrt{26} = \sqrt{2601} - \sqrt{2600}$

Obviously smallest one is

$\sqrt{2601} - \sqrt{2600}$. Difference of the larger surds is smaller.

54. (A) $m = \sqrt{2}$, $n = \sqrt{3}$

$$\frac{2\sqrt{6}}{\sqrt{2} + \sqrt{3} + \sqrt{5}} = \sqrt{2} + \sqrt{3} - \sqrt{5}$$

55. (D) $\left(\sqrt[6]{27} - \sqrt{6\dfrac{3}{4}} \right)^2$

$$\left((27)^{\frac{1}{6}} - \left(\frac{27}{4}\right)^{\frac{1}{2}} \right)^2$$

$$= \frac{1}{4}\left[2.(3)^{\frac{1}{2}} - 3^{\frac{3}{2}} \right]^2$$

$$= \frac{\left(3^{\frac{1}{2}} \right)^2}{4}[2 - 3]^2 = \frac{3}{4}.$$

56. (B) $\sqrt{64+1} - \sqrt{64-1} < 2/\sqrt{64}$

$< 2/8$

$< 1/4 = 0.25.$

57. (D) $\sqrt{8} + \sqrt{18}$

$\sqrt{4 \times 2} + \sqrt{9 \times 2} = 2\sqrt{2} + 3\sqrt{2}$

$= 5\sqrt{2}.$

58. (D) $\left\{ \dfrac{2\left(\sqrt{2} + \sqrt{6}\right)}{3\left(\sqrt{2} + \sqrt{3}\right)} \right\}^2$

$$= \frac{4\left(2 + 6 + 2\sqrt{12}\right)}{9\left(2 + \sqrt{3}\right)}$$

$$= \frac{4\left(8 + 4\sqrt{3}\right)}{9\left(2 + \sqrt{3}\right)}$$

$$= \frac{4 \times 4\left(2 + \sqrt{3}\right)}{9\left(2 + \sqrt{3}\right)}$$

$$= \frac{16}{9}$$

$\therefore$ Required answer $= \sqrt{\dfrac{16}{9}} = \dfrac{4}{3}.$

59. (A) $\left\{ \dfrac{\sqrt{\sqrt{5}+2} + \sqrt{\sqrt{5}-2}}{\sqrt{\sqrt{5}+1}} \right\}^2 = 2$

$\sqrt{3 - 2\sqrt{2}} = \sqrt{2 - 2\sqrt{2} + 1}$

$= \sqrt{\left(\sqrt{2} - 1\right)^2}$

$= \sqrt{2} - 1$

$\therefore \dfrac{\sqrt{\sqrt{5}+2} + \sqrt{\sqrt{5}-2}}{\sqrt{\sqrt{5}+1}} = \sqrt{2} - \left(\sqrt{2} - 1\right)$

$= \sqrt{2} - \sqrt{2} + 1$

$= 1.$

60. (C) $t = \dfrac{1}{1-2^{\frac{1}{4}}} \cdot \dfrac{1+2^{\frac{1}{4}}}{1+2^{\frac{1}{4}}} = \dfrac{1+2^{\frac{1}{4}}}{1-2^{\frac{1}{2}}}$

$$= \dfrac{\left(1+2^{\frac{1}{4}}\right)\left(1+2^{\frac{1}{2}}\right)}{\left(1-2^{\frac{1}{2}}\right)\left(1+2^{\frac{1}{2}}\right)}$$

$$= \dfrac{\left(1+\sqrt[4]{2}\right)\left(1+\sqrt[2]{2}\right)}{-1}$$

61. (B) $x = \sqrt{3}+\sqrt{2} \Rightarrow \dfrac{1}{x} = \sqrt{3}-\sqrt{2}$

$$x^2 + \dfrac{1}{x^2} = \left(x+\dfrac{1}{x}\right)^2 - 2$$

$$\Rightarrow \left(2\sqrt{3}\right)^2 - 2 = 10.$$

62. (B) $2^{\frac{1}{3}}, 3^{\frac{1}{2}}, 5^{\frac{1}{3}} \Rightarrow 2^{\frac{2}{6}}, 3^{\frac{3}{6}}, 5^{\frac{2}{6}}$

$$(4)^{\frac{1}{6}}, (27)^{\frac{1}{6}}, (25)^{\frac{1}{6}}$$

63. (D) $4\sqrt{3} - 6\sqrt{3} + 10\sqrt{3} = 8\sqrt{3}$

64. (A) $4^{\frac{1}{3}} \times 22^{\frac{1}{3}} = (88)^{\frac{1}{3}}$

$$= (8 \times 11)^{\frac{1}{3}}$$

$$= 2\sqrt[3]{11}$$

66. (A) Let us suppose fraction $= \dfrac{3}{5}$

and rational number $= \dfrac{-4}{7}$.

By definition, $\dfrac{3}{5}$ is a rational number.

So, P is True. By definition, $\dfrac{-4}{7}$ is not a fraction.

Since, -4 is not a natural number.

So, q is False.

67. (D) Since in all fractions both numerator and denominator are integers.

68. (B) Since every integer is having the denominator 1 can be expressed in $\dfrac{p}{q}$ form, p is True.

Since a rational number with denominator other than 1 is not an integer (e.g. $\dfrac{3}{5}$), q is False.

69. (D) Since denominator is 0, it is not a rational number.

70. (C) $\because \dfrac{-5}{-3} = \dfrac{-5}{-3} \times \dfrac{-5}{-5} = \dfrac{25}{15}$

71. (A) Since both numerator and denominator are negative (i.e., same sign)

72. (C) Since 0 is having either a positive sign or a negative sign.

73. (D) Since in A and C, the denominator is negative. In B we have to divide both numerator and denominator by 7 (i.e., LCM).

74. (B) Since $\dfrac{3}{-8} = \dfrac{3}{-8} \times \dfrac{-4}{-4} = \dfrac{-12}{32}$

75. (A) $\dfrac{-3}{5} = \dfrac{-24}{x}$

$-3 \times x = -24 \times 5$

$x = \dfrac{-24 \times 5}{-3} = 40.$

76. (B) $\dfrac{-3}{x} = \dfrac{x}{27}$

$x \times x = -3 \times 27$

$x^2 = -81$

$x = \sqrt{-81}$

x is not a rational number.

77. (A) Since $\dfrac{-2}{3} < 0$, it lies on left side of 0 on the number line.

78. (D) All the above given statements are true.

79. (C) $\dfrac{-5}{11}, \dfrac{-5}{12}, \dfrac{-5}{17}$

∵ All have same numerator. So the rational number having the least denominator is the greatest. But here all have negative sign. So the number having greatest denominator is greater.

Hence $\dfrac{-5}{17}$ is greater.

Alter : Take any two given numbers,

$\dfrac{-5}{11}, \dfrac{-5}{12}$

-5 x 12,   -5 x 11

-60,   -55

∵ -55 > -60

So $\dfrac{-5}{12}$ is greater.

Now compare this with $\dfrac{-5}{17}$.

$\dfrac{-5}{12}, \dfrac{-5}{17}$

-5 x 17,   -5 x 12

-85,   -60

∵ -60 > -85

So $\dfrac{-5}{17}$ is greater.

80. (C) Take any two given rational numbers.

$\dfrac{-7}{13}, \dfrac{-5}{13}$

-7 x 13,   -5 x 13

-91,   -65

∵ -65 > -91

So $\dfrac{-7}{13}$ is smaller.

Now compare this with $\dfrac{-11}{13}$.

$\dfrac{-7}{13}, \dfrac{-11}{13}$

-7 x 13,   -11 x 13

-91,   -143

∵ -91 > -143

So $\dfrac{-11}{13}$ is smaller.

81. (A) This question is very easy if we solve it by verification process.

Take (A) i.e.,

$\dfrac{-2}{3} < \dfrac{4}{-9} < \dfrac{-5}{12} < \dfrac{7}{-18}.$

First take $\dfrac{-2}{3}, \dfrac{-4}{9}.$

-2 x 9, -4 x 3

-18, -12

$\because -12 > -18$

So $\dfrac{-4}{9} > \dfrac{-2}{3}$ i.e., $\dfrac{-2}{3} < \dfrac{-4}{9}$.

Now, take $\dfrac{-4}{9}, \dfrac{-5}{12}$.

-4 x 12, -5 x 9

-48, -45

$\because -45 > -48$

So $\dfrac{-5}{12} > \dfrac{-4}{9}$, i.e., $\dfrac{-4}{9} < \dfrac{-5}{12}$.

Finally $\dfrac{-5}{12}, \dfrac{-7}{18}$

-5 x 18, -7 x 12

-90, -84

$\because -84 > -90$

So $\dfrac{-7}{18} > \dfrac{-5}{12}$, i.e., $\dfrac{-5}{12} < \dfrac{-7}{18}$.

$\therefore \dfrac{-2}{3} < \dfrac{-4}{9} < \dfrac{-5}{12} < \dfrac{-7}{18}$

You can identify the answer by observing the question by practicing this method.

82. **(B)** By verification process,

A $\rightarrow \dfrac{3}{4}, \dfrac{-2}{1}, \dfrac{-11}{20}, \dfrac{-4}{5}$

3×1, -2×4,

3, -8

Correct.

-2×20, -11×1,

-40, -11

Wrong.

B $\rightarrow \dfrac{3}{4}, \dfrac{-11}{20}, \dfrac{-4}{5}, \dfrac{-2}{1}$

3×20, -11×4

60, -44

$\dfrac{3}{4} > \dfrac{-11}{20}$

-11×5, -4×20,

-55, -80

$\therefore \dfrac{-11}{20} > \dfrac{-4}{5}$

-4×1, -2×5,

-4, -10

$\therefore \dfrac{-4}{5} > -2$

So B is the correct answer.

83. **(C)** Let given numbers arranged in the descending order.

$\dfrac{1}{2}, \dfrac{-4}{5}, \dfrac{-7}{8}$

-4×8, 5×-7

-32, -35

$\dfrac{-4}{5} > \dfrac{-7}{8}$

The descending order is

$\dfrac{1}{2} > \dfrac{-4}{5} > \dfrac{-7}{8}$

So middle number is $\dfrac{-4}{5}$.

84. **(D)** $\dfrac{4}{7}, \dfrac{1}{3}, \dfrac{2}{5}, \dfrac{5}{9}$

The above numbers in ascending order are

$\dfrac{1}{3} < \dfrac{2}{5} < \dfrac{5}{9} < \dfrac{4}{7}$

Middle two numbers are $\dfrac{2}{5}$ & $\dfrac{5}{9}$.

$$\therefore \text{ Average} = \frac{\frac{2}{5}+\frac{5}{9}}{2} = \frac{43}{90}.$$

85. (A) The given numbers can be arranged in the ascending order as

$$\frac{1}{5} < \frac{3}{5} < \frac{7}{5} < \frac{9}{5}$$

Greatest number $= \frac{9}{5}$;

Least number $= \frac{1}{5}$.

We have, $\frac{9}{5} \times \frac{x}{100} = \frac{1}{5}$

$$x = \frac{100}{9} = 11\frac{1}{9}\%$$

86. (C) The ascending order of given numbers is $\frac{1}{9}, \frac{5}{9}, \frac{11}{9}$

$\therefore$ Required difference

$$= \frac{11}{9} - \frac{1}{9} = \frac{10}{9}$$

87. (B) $x > y$, $z < y$

$x > y$, $y > z$

then we have $x > z$ or $z < x$.

88. (D) By the properties of rational numbers, all (i), (ii), (iii) are correct.

89. (B) Since $\frac{1}{0}$ is not rational, the quotient of two integers is not rational.

90. (A) Zero (0) is a whole number but not a natural number.

91. (B) $\frac{2}{1} - \frac{11}{39} + \frac{5}{26}$

$$= \frac{156 - 22 + 15}{78} = \frac{149}{78} = 1\frac{71}{78} = 1 + \frac{71}{78}$$

92. (C) $\frac{-143}{21} = (-6) + \left(\frac{-17}{21}\right)$

93. (D) Addition of rational numbers satisfy commutative, associative and closure properties.

94. (C) Since $a + (b + c) = (a + b) + c$ is associative property.

95. (D) All the given statements are correct.

96. (A) Let x be the required number.

So $x + \left(\frac{-7}{5}\right) = -3$

$$x = -3 + \frac{7}{5} = \frac{-15 + 7}{5} = \frac{-8}{5}$$

97. (B) $x + \left(\frac{-5}{6}\right) = \frac{3}{2}$

$$x = \frac{3}{2} + \frac{5}{6} = \frac{9 + 5}{6} = \frac{14}{6} = \frac{7}{3} = 2\frac{1}{3}$$

98. (A) Since the statements (ii) and (iii) are wrong.

99. (D) All the given statements are true.

100. (C) Since $a \times (b + c) = (a \times b) + (a \times c)$ is distributive.

101. (B) Since $a \times \frac{1}{a} = 1$.

102. (D) $x \times \frac{-4}{3} = \frac{-9}{16}$

$$x = \frac{-9/16}{-4/3} = \frac{-9}{16} \times \frac{-3}{4} = \frac{27}{64}$$

103. (B) $\quad x \times \dfrac{-8}{39} = 26$

$$x = \frac{26}{-8/39} = 26 \times \frac{39}{-8} = \frac{-507}{4}$$

104. (A) $\quad \dfrac{30}{3\frac{3}{4}} = \dfrac{30}{15/4} = 30 \times \dfrac{4}{15} = 8$

105. (B) Let us take two rational

numbers $\dfrac{3}{5}$ and $\dfrac{0}{3}$.

Then the division $3/5 \div 0/3$ is not a rational number.

So division is not closure because division by zero is not defined.

106. (B) $\quad \pi$ is irrational. (See synopsis)

107. (D) The set of irrational numbers does not satisfy the closure property.

108. (A) $\quad \because P + (-P) = (-P) + P = 0'$ is the additive inverse property.

So additive inverse of $\dfrac{-a}{b}$ is $\dfrac{a}{b}$.

109. (C) Does not exist since division by zero is not defined.

110. (B) Every rational number is not a fraction. Therefore, in rational numbers, we use integers and in fractions, we use only natural numbers.

111. (A) When the denominator has factors 2 (or) 5, then only a rational number is expressible as a terminating decimal.

112. (C) $\quad 0.75 = \dfrac{75}{100} = \dfrac{3}{4}$

113. (B) $\quad 0.\overline{75} = \dfrac{75}{99} = \dfrac{25}{33}$

114. (C) $\quad 0.3\overline{58} = \dfrac{358 - 3}{990} = \dfrac{355}{990}$

115. (A) $\quad \dfrac{5}{7} = 0.71 \qquad \dfrac{7}{9} = 0.77$

$$\dfrac{9}{11} = 0.81 \qquad \dfrac{11}{13} = 0.84$$

So $\dfrac{5}{7} < \dfrac{7}{9} < \dfrac{9}{11} < \dfrac{11}{13}$.

116. (D) $\quad \dfrac{1}{4} = 0.25, \ \dfrac{1}{3} = 0.33$

$$\dfrac{7}{24} = 0.29, \ \dfrac{13}{48} = 0.27$$

So $\dfrac{7}{24}, \ \dfrac{13}{48}$ and 0.29 are lying

between $\dfrac{1}{4}$ & $\dfrac{1}{3}$.

117. (B) An irrational number is a non-terminating and nonrepeating decimal. (See synopsis)

118. (D) All the given statements are false.

119. (D) All the properties are satsified by real numbers.

120. (A) $\quad \because a = b = 1 \Rightarrow a - b = 0$

Division by zero is not defined.

So we cannot divide by $(a - b)$.

121. (B) An irrational number.

122. (C) $\quad \sqrt{3} = 1.732$

123. (A)   An irrational number.

124. (C)   Either a rational number or an irrational number.

125. (D) $1.\overline{34} = \dfrac{133}{99}$

$4.1\overline{2} = \dfrac{371}{90}$

$1.\overline{34} + 4.1\overline{2} = \dfrac{133}{99} + \dfrac{371}{90}$

$= \dfrac{4081 + 1330}{990}$

$= \dfrac{5411}{990}$

127. (B) $-2 + \dfrac{1}{2} = \dfrac{-3}{2}$

128. (A) $\dfrac{3\sqrt{2}}{2\sqrt{3}} \times \dfrac{\sqrt{3}}{\sqrt{3}} = \dfrac{3\sqrt{6}}{2 \times 3}$

$= \dfrac{\sqrt{6}}{2} = \dfrac{2.449}{2} = 1.2245$

129. (B)   Let x = $\sqrt{5\sqrt{5\sqrt{5....}}}$

$x = \sqrt{5x}$

$x^2 - 5x = 0$

$x(x-5) = 0$

$x = 0$ (or) $x = 5$

$x = 0$ is impossible.

$\therefore$ x can only be 5.

130. (D) $\sqrt[3]{1.728} = 1.2$

$\dfrac{\sqrt{3}-1}{\sqrt{3}+1} \times \dfrac{\sqrt{3}-1}{\sqrt{3}-1} = \dfrac{4-2\sqrt{3}}{3-1}$

$= 2 - \sqrt{3} = 2 - 1.732 = 0.268$

$\left(\dfrac{1}{2}\right)^{-2} = (2)^2 = 4$

$\dfrac{17}{8} = 2.125$

$\therefore \left(\dfrac{1}{2}\right)^{-2}$ is greatest.

132. (D)
```
143) 2 1 7 (1.517....
     1 4 3
     ----------
       7 4 0
       7 1 5
     ----------
         2 5 0
         1 4 3
       -------------
         1 0 7 0
         1 0 0 1
       -------------
             6 9 0
       -------------
```

133. (A)   Since $625 = 5 \times 5 \times 5 \times 5$, 5 is the only prime factor of 625.

So $\dfrac{961}{625}$ is a terminating decimal.

134. (B) $2.003 = \dfrac{2003}{1000}$

135. (D) $0.\overline{018}$ is a pure recurring decimal.

So $0.\overline{018} = \dfrac{18}{999}$.

136. (C)   Since $2.53\overline{6}$ is a mixed recurring decimal.

So $2.5\overline{36} = \dfrac{2536 - 253}{900}$

$= \dfrac{2283}{900} = \dfrac{761}{300}$

137. (A) $0.\overline{23} = 0.232323......$

$0.\overline{22} = 0.222222......$

$= 0.454545........$

$= 0.\overline{45}$

138. (D) All the given statements are true.

139. (C) Since $64 = 2 \times 2 \times 2 \times 2 \times 2 \times 2$, the only prime factor = 2.

$\therefore \dfrac{83}{64}$ is a terminating decimal.

140. (C) Since $|x - y| \geq |x| - |y|$.

◆ ◆ ◆

Chapter 2

Polynomials

2

---

1. A combination of constants and variables connected by $+, -, \times$ and $\div$ is known as an algebraic exp-ression.

   Eg : $2 - 3x + 5x^{-2}y^{-1} + \dfrac{1}{3}\dfrac{x}{y^3}$

2. An algebraic expression in which the variables involved have only nonnegative integral powers is called a polynomial.

   Eg : $2 - 3x + 5x^2y - \dfrac{1}{3}xy^3$

3. In the case of a polynomial in one variable, the highest power of the variable is called the degree of the polynomial.

   Eg : $5x^3 - 7x + \dfrac{3}{2}$ is a polynomial in x of degree 3.

4. In the case of polynomials in more than one variable, the sum of the powers of the variables in each term is taken up and the highest sum so obtained is called the degree of the polynomial.

   Eg : $5x^3 - 2x^2y^2 - 3x^2y + 9y$ is a polynomial of degree 4 in x and y.

5. A polynomial of degree 1 is called a linear polynomial.

6. A polynomial of degree 2 is called a quadratic polynomial.

7. A polynomial of degree 3 is called a cubic poynomial.

8. A polynomial of degree 4 is called a biquadratic polynomial.

9. A polynomial containing 1 term is called a monomial.

10. A polynomial containing 2 terms is called a bionomial.

11. A polynomial containing 3 terms is called a trinomial.

12. A polynomial containing one term consisting of a constant is called a constant polynomial.

13. The degree of a constant polynomial is zero.

14. The terms of a polynomial are said to be in ascending (or) descending order if they increase (or) decrease in degrees respectively.

    Eg : (1) $3 - 7x + 5x^2 - 2x^3$ is in ascending order

    (2) $-2x^3 + 5x^2 - 7x + 3$ is in descending order.

15. Terms with same variables and which have the same exponents are called like or similar terms, otherwise they are called unlike (or) dissimilar terms.

    Eg : (1) $3x^3, \dfrac{1}{2}x^3, -9x^3, \dots$ etc, are like terms

    (2) $x^2y, 3xy^2, -4x^3, \dots$ etc, are unlike terms.

16. Dividend =

    $(\text{divisor} \times \text{quotient}) + \text{reminder}$

17. P(x) is a polynomial of degree ≥ 1. 'a' is any real number. If P(x) is divided by $(x - a)$ then the remainder is P(a).

---

18. P(–a) is remainder on dividing P(x) by (x + a).

19. $P\left(\dfrac{b}{a}\right)$ is remainder on dividing P(x) by (ax - b)

20. $P\left(-\dfrac{b}{a}\right)$ is remainder on dividing P(x) by (ax + b).

21. **Factor Theorem :**

P(x) is a polynomial of degree ≥ 1 and "a" is a real number then

(i) p(a) = 0 $\Rightarrow$ (x - a) is a factor of p(x)

(ii) (x-a) is a factor of p(x) then p(a)=0

(iii) ax - b is a factor of p(x) then

$$p\left(\dfrac{b}{a}\right) = 0$$

(iv) ax + b is a factor of p(x) then

$$p\left(\dfrac{-b}{a}\right) = 0$$

(v) (x - a) is a factor of $x^n - a^n$ where "n" is any integer

(vi) (x + a) is a factor of $x^n + a^n$ where "n" is an odd positive integer.

(vii) (x + a) is a factor of $x^n - a^n$ where "n" is positive even integer

(viii) $(x^n + a^n)$ is not divisible by x + a when "n" is even

(ix) $x^n + a^n$ is not divisible by x - a for any "n"

(x) If x - 1 is a factor of polynomial of degree 'n' then the condition is sum of the coeffecients is zero.

(xi) If (x+1) is a factor of polynomial of degree 'n' then the condition is sum of the coefficients of even terms is equal to the coefficients of odd terms.

22. The process of writing an algebraic expression as the product of two or more algebraic expressions is called factorization.

23. *Some important identities :*

1. $(a + b)^2 = a^2 + 2ab + b^2$

2. $(a - b)^2 = a^2 - 2ab + b^2$

3. $(a + b)(a - b) = a^2 - b^2$

4. $(a + b + c)^2 = a^2 + b^2 + c^2 + 2ab + 2bc + 2ca$

5. $(a + b)^3 = a^3 + b^3 + 3ab(a + b)$
   $= a^3 + b^3 + 3a^2b + 3ab^2$

6. $(a - b)^3 = a^3 - b^3 - 3ab(a - b)$
   $= a^3 - b^3 - 3a^2b + 3ab^2$

7. $a^3 + b^3 = (a + b)(a^2 - ab + b^2)$

8. $a^3 - b^3 = (a - b)(a^2 + ab + b^2)$

9. $a^3 + b^3 + c^3 - 3abc = $
   $(a + b + c)$
   $(a^2 + b^2 + c^2 - ab - bc - ca)$

10. If a+b+c = 0 then $a^3+b^3+c^3 = 3abc$

Multiple Choice Questions

1. Which of the following expressions is a polynomial?

   (A) $3x^{\frac{1}{2}} - 4x + 3$

   (B) $4x^2 - 3\sqrt{x} + 5$

   (C) $3x^2y - 2xy + 5x^4$

   (D) $2x^4 + \dfrac{3}{x^2} - 1$

2. The degree of the polynomial $5x^3 - 6x^3y + 4y^2 - 8$ is

   (A) 3

   (B) 4

   (C) 2

   (D) can't be determined

3. What must be added to $x^3 + 3x - 8$ to get $3x^3 + x^2 + 6$?

   (A) $2x^3 + x^2 - 3x + 14$

   (B) $2x^2 + x^2 + 14$

   (C) $2x^3 + x^2 - 6x - 14$

   (D) None of these

4. What must be subtracted from $x^3 - 3x^2 + 5x - 1$ to get $2x^3 + x^2 - 4x + 2$?

   (A) $-x^3 + 4x^2 - 9x + 3$

   (B) $x^3 + 4x^2 - 9x + 3$

   (C) $x^3 - 4x^2 + 9x - 3$

   (D) $-x^3 - 4x^2 + 9x - 3$

5. Divide $(-56mnp^2)$ by $(7mnp)$.

   (A) $-8p$ (B) $8mnp$

   (C) $8p$ (D) None

6. A factor of $x^3 - 1$ is

   (A) $x - 1$ (B) $x^2 + x + 1$

   (C) either A or B   (D) none of these

7. The product of $\dfrac{2}{3}xy$ by $\dfrac{3}{2}xz$ is

   (A) $\dfrac{1}{6}xyz$ (B) x^2yz

   (C) $6x^2yz$ (D) none of these

8. Divide $8x^2y^2 - 6xy^2 + 10x^2y^3$ by $2xy$.

   (A) $4xy - 3y + 5xy^2$

   (B) $4xy + 3y - 5xy^2$

   (C) $8xy + 3y - 5xy^2$

   (D) $4xy - 3y - 5xy^2$

9. The product of $(x^2 + 3x + 5)$ and $(x^2 - 1)$ is

   (A) $x^4 + 3x^3 - 4x^2 - 3x - 5$

   (B) $x^4 + 3x^3 + 4x^2 - 3x - 5$

   (C) $x^4 + 3x^3 + 4x^2 + 3x - 5$

   (D) none of these

10. If quotient $= 3x^2 - 2x + 1$, remainder $= 2x - 5$ and divisor $= x + 2$ then the dividend is

    (A) $3x^3 - 4x^2 + x - 3$

    (B) $3x^3 - 4x^2 - x + 3$

    (C) $3x^3 + 4x^2 - x + 3$

    (D) $3x^3 + 4x^2 - x - 3$

11. If $(x - 2)$ is one factor of $x^2 + ax - 6 = 0$ and $x^2 - 9x + b = 0$ then $a + b =$ _____ .

    (A) 15   (B) 13

    (C) 11   (D) 10

12. The remainder obtained when $t^6 + 3t^2 + 10$ is divided by $t^3 + 1$ is

    (A) $t^2 - 11$ (B) $t^3 - 1$

    (C) $3t^2 + 11$ (D) none

13. The value of the product $(3x^2 - 5x + 6)$ and $(-8x^3)$ when $x = 0$ is

    (A) $\dfrac{1}{2}$ (B) 2

    (C) 1   (D) 0

14. The difference of the degrees of the polynomials $3x^2y^3 + 5xy^7 - x^6$ and $3x^5 - 4x^3 + 2$ is

    (A) 2   (B) 3

    (C) 1   (D) none

15. What must be added to $x^2 + 5x - 6$ to get $x^3 - x^2 + 3x - 2$?

    (A) $x^3 - 2x^2 - 2x - 4$

    (B) $x^3 + 2x^2 - 2x + 4$

    (C) $x^3 - 2x^2 - 2x + 4$

    (D) None

16. What must be subtracted from $x^4 + 2x^2 - 3x + 7$ to get $x^3 + x^2 + x - 1$?

    (A) $x^4 - x^3 + x^2 - 4x + 8$

    (B) $x^3 + x^2 - 4x + 8$

    (C) $x^4 - x^3 + x^2 + 4x - 8$

    (D) $x^4 - x^3 - x^2 + 4x - 8$

17. The product of x^2y and $\dfrac{x}{y}$ is equal to the quotient obtained when x^2 is divided by _____ .

(A) 0   (B) 1

(C) x   (D) $\dfrac{1}{x}$

18. If $(3x - 4)(5x + 7) = 15x^2 - ax - 28$ then a = _____ .

(A) 1   (B) –1

(C) –2   (D) none

19. The product of two factors with unlike signs is_____

(A) positive

(B) negative

(C) cannot be determined

(D) none of these

20. Subtract $x^3 - xy^2 + 5x^2y - y^3$ from $-y^3 - 6x^2y - xy^2 + x^3$.

(A) $2y^3 - 8x^2y + 3xy^2 - 2x^3$

(B) $2x^3 - 2xy^2 - x^2y - 2y^3$

(C) $- 11x^2y$

(D) None of these

21. The real factors of $x^2 + 4$ are

(A) $(x^2 + 2) (x^2 - 2)$

(B) $(x + 2) (x - 2)$

(C) does not exist

(D) none of these

22. One of the factors of $x^4 + 4$ is

(A) $x^2 + 2$ (B) $x^2 - 2x + 2$

(C) $x^2 - 2$ (D) none of these

23. The factors of $x^4 + 2x^2 + 9$ is

(A) $(x^2 - 2x + 3) (x^2 + 2x + 3)$

(B) $(x^2 + 3) (x^2 - 3)$

(C) factorization is not possible

(D) none of these

24. For $x^2 + 2x + 5$ to be a factor of $x^4 + px^2 + q$, the values of p and q must be

(A) –2, 5   (B) 5, 25

(C) 10, 20   (D) 6, 25

25. The factors of $x^2 + xy - 2xz - 2yz$ are

(A) $(x - y) (x + 2z)$

(B) $(x + y) (x - 2z)$

(C) $(x - y) (x - 2z)$

(D) $(x + y) (x + 2z)$

26. $x^9 - x$ is having

(A) 5 factors

(B) 4 factors

(C) 2 factors

(D) cannot be determined

27. The factors of $\dfrac{x^2}{4} - \dfrac{y^2}{9}$ are

(A) $\left(\dfrac{x}{4} + \dfrac{y}{9}\right)\left(\dfrac{x}{4} - \dfrac{y}{9}\right)$

(B) $\left(\dfrac{x}{2} + \dfrac{y}{9}\right)\left(\dfrac{x}{2} - \dfrac{y}{9}\right)$

(C) $\left(\dfrac{x}{2} + \dfrac{y}{3}\right)\left(\dfrac{x}{2} - \dfrac{y}{3}\right)$

(D) none of these

28. The factors of $1 - p^3$ are

(A) $(1 - p) (1 + p + p^2)$

(B) $(1 + p) (1 - p - p^2)$

(C) $(1 + p) (1 + p^2)$

(D) $(1 + p) (1 - p^2)$

29. The factors of $x^4 + y^4 + x^2y^2$ are

(A) $(x^2 + y^2) (x^2 + y^2 - xy)$

(B) $(x^2 + y^2) (x^2 - y^2)$

(C) $(x^2 + y^2 + xy) (x^2 + y^2 - xy)$

(D) factorization is not possible

30. The factors of $15x^2 - 26x + 8$ are

(A) $(3x - 4)(5x + 2)$

(B) $(3x - 4)(5x - 2)$

(C) $(3x + 4)(5x - 2)$

(D) $(3x + 4)(5x + 2)$

31. One of the factors of
$a^3(b - c)^3 + b^3(c - a)^3 + c^3(a - b)^3$ is

(A) $a - b$

(B) $b - c$

(C) $c - a$

(D) all the above

32. One of the factor of
$a^3 + 8b^3 - 64c^3 + 24abc$ is

(A) $a + 2b - 4c$

(B) $a - 2b + 4c$

(C) $a + 2b + 4c$

(D) $a - 2b - 4c$

33. The value of

$$\frac{0.76 \times 0.76 \times 0.76 + 0.24 \times 0.24 \times 0.24}{0.76 \times 0.76 - 0.76 \times 0.24 + 0.24 \times 0.24} \text{ is}$$

(A) 0.52   (B) 1

(C) 0.01   (D) 0.1

34. The factors of $a^2 + b - ab - a$ are

(A) $(a - 1)(a - b)$

(B) $(a + b)(a - 1)$

(C) $(a + 1)(a - b)$

(D) none

35. One of the factors of

$$x^2 + \frac{1}{x^2} + 2 - 2x - \frac{2}{x} \text{ is}$$

(A) $x - \dfrac{1}{x}$ (B) $x + \dfrac{1}{x} - 1$

(C) $x + \dfrac{1}{x}$ (D) $x^2 + \dfrac{1}{x^2}$

36. If the factors of $a^2 + b^2 + 2(ab + bc + ca)$ are $(a + b + m)$ and $(a + b + nc)$, then the value of $m + n$ is

(A) 0   (B) 2

(C) 4   (D) 6

37. If $(x^2 + 3x + 5)(x^2 - 3x + 5) = m^2 - n^2$, then m = _____

(A) $x^2 - 3x$ (B) $3x$

(C) $x^2 + 5$ (D) none

38. One of the factors of
$(a^2 - b^2)(c^2 - d^2) - 4abcd$ is

(A) $(ac - bd + bc + ad)$

(B) $ac - bd + bc - ad$

(C) cannot be determined

(D) none of these

39. The factors of

$\sqrt{3}x^2 + 11x + 6\sqrt{3}$ are

(A) $\left(x - 3\sqrt{3}\right)\left(\sqrt{3}x + 2\right)$

(B) $\left(x - 3\sqrt{3}\right)\left(\sqrt{3}x - 2\right)$

(C) $\left(x + 3\sqrt{3}\right)\left(\sqrt{3}x - 2\right)$

(D) $\left(x + 3\sqrt{3}\right)\left(\sqrt{3}x + 2\right)$

40. One of the factors of $x^7 + xy^6$ is

(A) $x^2 + y^2$

(B) x

(C) either A or B

(D) neither A nor B

41. Factors of $x^3 + x^2 + x + 1$

(A) $(x + 1)(x^2 - 1)$

(B) $(x - 1)(x^2 + 1)$

(C) $(x - 1)(x^2 - 1)$

(D) $(x + 1)(x^2 + 1)$

42. Factors of $x^2 + (a + b + c)x + ab + bc$

(A) $(x + a) (x + b + c)$

(B) $(x + a) (x + a + c)$

(C) $(x + b) (x + a + c)$

(D) $(x + b) (x + b + c)$

43. Factors of $x^3 - 3x^2 + 3x + 7$

(A) $(x + 1) (x^2 - 4x + 7)$

(B) $(x - 1) (x^2 + 4x + 7)$

(C) $(x + 1) (x^2 + 4x + 7)$

(D) $(x - 1) (x^2 - 4x + 7)$

44. The value of

$(a + b)^3 + (a - b)^3 + 6a(a^2 - b^2)$

(A) $6a^3$ (B) $8a^3$

(C) $10a^3$ (D) $12a^3$

45. Factorise $x^2 + 3\sqrt{2}x + 4$

(A) $(x + 2\sqrt{2}) (x + \sqrt{2})$

(B) $(x + 2\sqrt{2}) (x - \sqrt{2})$

(C) $(x - 2\sqrt{2}) (x + \sqrt{2})$

(D) $(x + 2\sqrt{2}) (x - \sqrt{2})$

46. Factorise $x^{12} - y^{12}$

(A) $(x - y) (x^2 + xy + y^2) (x + y)$
$(x^2 - xy + y^2) (x^2 + y^2)$
$(x^4 - x^2y^2 + y^4)$

(B) $(x + y) (x^2 - xy + y^2) (x + y)$
$(x^2 - xy + y^2) (x^2 + y^2)$
$(x^4 - x^2y^2 + y^4)$

(C) $(x + y) (x^2 + xy - y^2) (x + y)$
$(x^2 - xy + y^2) (x^2 + y^2)$
$(x^4 - x^2y^2 + y^4)$

(D) $(x - y) (x^2 - xy + y^2) (x + y)$
$(x^2 - xy + y^2) (x^2 + y^2)$
$(x^4 - x^2y^2 + y^4)$

47. If $x + y + z = 0$ then $x^3 + y^3 + z^3$ is

(A) xyz (B) $2xyz$

(C) $3xyz$ (D) zero

48. If $a + b + c = 0$, evaluate

$$\frac{a^2}{bc} + \frac{b^2}{ca} + \frac{c^2}{ab}$$

(A) 1   (B) 2

(C) 3   (D) 4

49. Factors of $ab + bc + ax + cx$

(A) $(a + c) (x + b)$

(B) $(a - c) (x - b)$

(C) $(a + b) (x + c)$

(D) $(x + a) (a + b)$

50. Factors of $20a^2 - 45$

(A) $5(3 - 2a) (3 + 2a)$

(B) $5(2a + 3) (2a - 3)$

(C) $3(5 + 2a) (5 - 2a)$

(D) $3(2a + 5) (2a - 5)$

51. Resolve into factors.

$6x^3 - 24xy^2 - 3x^2y + 12y^3$

(A) $3(2x - y) (x + 2y) (x - 2y)$

(B) $3(2x - y) (x + y) (x + 2y)$

(C) $3(2x - y) (x - 2y) (x + y)$

(D) $3(2x + y) (x - y) (x + 2y)$

52. Factors of $\frac{1}{2}x^2 - 3x + 4$

(A) $\left(\frac{1}{4}x - 1\right)(x - 2)$

(B) $(x - 4)\left(\frac{1}{2}x - 1\right)$

(C) $(x - 4) (x - 2)$

(D) $(x - 4) (x - 1)$

53. Factorise $(3 - 4y - 7y^2)^2 - (4y + 1)^2$

(A) $(4 - 7y^2)(2 - 8y - 7y^2)$

(B) $(7y^2 - 4)(2 - 8y - 7y^2)$

(C) $(4 - 7y^2)(7y^2 + 8y - 2)$

(D) $(7y^2 - 4)(7y^2 - 8y - 2)$

54. Factorise $3\sqrt{3}x^3 + y^3$

(A) $\left(\sqrt{3}x + y\right)\left(3x^2 - \sqrt{3}xy + y^2\right)$

(B) $\left(\sqrt{3}x - y\right)\left(\sqrt{3}x^2 + \sqrt{3}xy + y^2\right)$

(C) $\left(\sqrt{3}x + y\right)\left(3x^2 + \sqrt{3}xy + y^2\right)$

(D) $\left(\sqrt{3}x - y\right)\left(3x^2 - \sqrt{3}xy - y^2\right)$

55. Factorise $1 - x + x^2 - x^3$

(A) $(1 + x)(1 - x^2)$

(B) $(1 - x)(1 + x^2)$

(C) $(1 - x)(1 - x^2)$

(D) $(1 + x)(1 + x^2)$

56. Factorise $49y^2 - 14y + 1 - 25x^2$

(A) $(7y - 1 + 5x)(7y - 1 - 5x)$

(B) $(5x - 1 + 7y)(5x - 1 - 7y)$

(C) $(7y - 1 + 5x)(7y - 1 + 5x)$

(D) $(5x + 7y - 1)(5x + 7y + 1)$

57. Factorise $x^2 - 1 - 2a - a^2$

(A) $(x - a - 1)(x + a - 1)$

(B) $(x + a + 1)(x - a - 1)$

(C) $(x + a + 1)(x - a + 1)$

(D) $(x - a + 1)(x + a - 1)$

58. Factors of $x^4 - x^2 - 12$

(A) $(x + 2)(x - 2)(x^2 + 3)$

(B) $(x + 3)(x - 3)(x^2 + 2)$

(C) $(x + 2)(x - 2)(x^2 - 3)$

(D) $(x^2 + 2)(x^2 - 6)$

59. Factors of $a^3 + b^3 + a + b$

(A) $(a + b)(a^2 + b^2 - ab + 1)$

(B) $(a - b)(a^2 + b^2 - ab + 1)$

(C) $(a + b)(a^2 - b^2 + ab - 1)$

(D) $(a + b)(a^2 - ab - b^2 - 1)$

60. If $x + \dfrac{1}{x} = a + b$ and $x - \dfrac{1}{x} = a - b$ then

(A) $ab = 1$ (B) $a = b$

(C) $ab = 2$ (D) $a + b = 0$

61. If $\left(a + \dfrac{1}{a}\right)^2 = b$ then $a^3 + \dfrac{1}{a^3}$ is equal to

(A) b^3 (B) $b^{\frac{3}{2}}$

(C) $b^{\frac{3}{2}} - 3b^{\frac{1}{2}}$ (D) $b^{\frac{3}{2}} + 3b^{\frac{1}{2}}$

62. The value of $2^{\frac{1}{4}} . 4^{\frac{1}{8}} . 16^{\frac{1}{16}} . (256)^{\frac{1}{32}}$ is equal to

(A) 1   (B) 2

(C) 4   (D) 8

63. Factors of $x - 8xy^3$

(A) $x(1 - 2y)(1 + 2y + 4y^2)$

(B) $x(1 + 2y)(1 + 2y + 4y^2)$

(C) $x(1 - 2y)(1 - 2y + 4y^2)$

(D) $x(1 + 2y)(1 - 2y + 4y^2)$

64. Factors of $(m - n)^6 - 8m^3$

(A) $\left\{(m - n)^3 + 4m\right\}\left\{(m - n)^3 - 2m^2\right\}$

(B) $\left\{(m - n)^3 - (2m)^3\right\}\left\{(m - a)^3 + (m^3)\right\}$

(C) $\left\{(m - n)^2 - 2m\right\}\left\{(m - n)^4 + (m - n^2)2m + 4m^2\right\}$

(D) none of those

65. If $a^{\frac{1}{2}} + b^{\frac{1}{2}} - c^{\frac{1}{2}} = 0$ then the value of $(a + b - c)^2$ is

(A) 2ab   (B) 2bc

(C) 4ab   (D) 4ac

66. Factorise $a^{2x} - b^{2x}$

(A) $(a^x + b^x)(a^x - b^x)$

(B) $(a^x - b^x)^2$

(C) $(a^x + b^x)(a^2 - b^2)$

(D) $(a^x - b^x)(a^2 + b^2)$

67. If $x = \dfrac{a-b}{a+b}$, $y = \dfrac{b-c}{b+c}$, $z = \dfrac{c-a}{c+a}$ then the value of $\dfrac{(1+x)(1+y)(1+z)}{(1-x)(1-y)(1-z)}$ is

(A) abc   (B) $a^2b^2c^2$

(C) 1   (D) -1

68. Factorise $8a^3 - 2a^2 - 15ab^2$

(A) $(4a + 5b)(2a^2 - 3ab)$

(B) $(4a - 5b)(2a^2 - 3ab)$

(C) $(4a - 5b)(2a^2 + 3ab)$

(D) $(4a + 5b)(2a^2 + 3ab)$

69. If $p = (2 - a)$ then $a^3 + 6ap + p^3 - 8$ is

(A) 0   (B) 1

(C) 2   (D) 3

70. The value of $(x - a)^3 + (x - b)^3 + (x - c)^3 - 3(x - a)(x - b)(x - c)$ when $a + b + c = 3x$

(A) 3   (B) 2

(C) 1   (D) 0

71. Factorise $a^2 + b^2 + 2(ab + bc + ca)$

(A) $(a + b)(a + b + 2c)$

(B) $(b + c)(c + a + 2b)$

(C) $(c + a)(a + b + 2c)$

(D) $(b + a)(b + c + 2a)$

72. Factorise $px^2 + (4p^2 - 3q)x - 12pq$

(A) $(x - 4p)(px - 3q)$

(B) $(x + 4p)(px - 3q)$

(C) $(x + 4p)(px + 3q)$

(D) $(x - 4p)(px + 3q)$

73. Factorise $y^3 - 2y^2 - y + 2$

(A) $(y - 2)(y - 1)(y + 1)$

(B) $(y + 2)(y - 1)(y + 1)$

(C) $(y - 2)(y + 1)^2$

(D) $(y + 1)(y - 1)^2$

74. If $x^{\frac{1}{3}} + y^{\frac{1}{3}} + z^{\frac{1}{3}} = 0$ then

(A) $x^3 + y^3 + z^3 = 0$

(B) $x + y + z = 27xyz$

(C) $(x + y + z)^3 = 27xyz$

(D) $x^3 + y^3 + z^3 = 27xyz$

75. The remainder when $P(x) = 4x^4 - 3x^3 - 2x^2 + x - 7$ is divided by $x - 1$ is

(A) -7   (B) -6

(C) 7   (D) 6

76. If the polynomials $2x^3 + ax^2 + 3x - 5$ and $x^3 + x^2 - 4x + a$ leave the same remainder when divided by $x - 2$ then the value of a is

(Hint : Substitute $x = 2$ in both polynomials and equate.)

(A) $\dfrac{3}{13}$ (B) $\dfrac{3}{14}$

(C) $-\dfrac{13}{3}$ (D) $-\dfrac{3}{13}$

77. If R_1 and R_2 are remainders when $x^3 + 2x^2 - 5ax - 7$ and $x^3 + ax^2 - 12x + 6$ are divided by $x + 1$ and $x - 2$ and if $2R_1 + R_2 = 6$ then the value of a is

(A) 1   (B) 2

(C) 3   (D) 4

78. If $x^2 - 1$ is a factor of $ax^4 + bx^3 + cx^2 + dx + e$ then the condition is

(A) $a + c + e = b + d$ (B) $a - c - e = b - d$

(C) $a + c - e = b - d$ (D) $a + c + e = d - b$

79. Factors of $x^3 + 7x^2 + 14x + 8$

(A) $(x - 1) (x - 2) (x - 4)$

(B) $(x + 1) (x + 2) (x - 4)$

(C) $(x + 1) (x - 2) (x - 4)$

(D) $(x + 1) (x + 2) (x + 4)$

80. $f(x) = ax^7 + bx^3 + cx - 5$ where a, b, c are constants. If $f(-7) = 7$ then $f(7)$ equals to

[**Hint :** find $f(-x)$, and find the sum of $f(-x)$ and $f(x)$]

(A) -17   (B) -7

(C) 14   (D) 21

81. Find the value of a if the polynomials $2x^3 + ax^2 + 3x - 5$ and $x^3 + x^2 - 4x - a$ leave the same remainder when divided by x - 1.

[**Hint :** Apply remainder theorem]

(A) a = -1   (B) a = 1

(C) a = 2   (D) a = -2

82. The value of P if (x - 3) is a factor of $p^2x^3 - px^2 + 3px - p$ is

(A) 27   (B) -27

(C) $\dfrac{1}{27}$ (D) $-\dfrac{1}{27}$

83. The value of a if (x - a) factor of $x^6 - ax^5 + x^4 - ax^3 + 3x - a + 2 = 0$ is

(A) a = 1   (B) a = -1

(C) a = 2   (D) a = -2

84. For what value of K is the polynomial $2x^4 + 3x^3 + 2kx^2 + 3x + 6$ is exactly divisible by (x + 2)?

(A) k = 1   (B) k = -1

(C) k = 2   (D) k = -2

85. Is (x - 1) a factor of $x^3 - 6x^2 + 11x - 6$?

(A) Yes

(B) No

(C) Can't say

(D) None

86. The remainder when

$p(x) = x^4 + 2x^3 - 3x^2 + x - 1$ is

divided by x - 2 is

(A) 21   (B) -21

(C) 47   (D) -47

87. The remainder when

$f(x) = 2x^4 - 6x^3 + 2x^3 - x + 2$ is

divided by $g(x) = x + 2$ is

(A) 29   (B) -29

(C) 92   (D) -92

88. What should be added to $8x^3 - 4x^2 + 2x + 7$ so as to make the sum $10x^3 - 2x^2 + 7x + 20$?

(A) $- 2x^3 + 2x^2 + 5x + 3$

(B) $2x^3 + 2x^2 + 5x + 3$

(C) $- 2x^3 - 2x^2 - 5x + 13$

(D) $2x^3 + 2x^2 + 5x - 13$

89. If $p(x) = 4x^3 - 3x^2 + 2x + 1$, $q(x) = x^3 - x^2 + x + 1$, $r(x) = x^2 - 2x + 1$ then the value of $3p(x) + 7q(x) + r(x)$ is

(A) $19x^3 - 15x^2 + 11x + 11$

(B) $-19x^3 - 15x^2 + 11x - 11$

(C) $19x^3 - 15x^2 - 11x + 11$

(D) $19x^3 - 15x^2 - 11x - 11$

90. The value of m if

$2y^3 + my^2 + 11y + m + 3$ is

exactly divisible by 2y - 1 is

(A) 7   (B) -7

(C) 6   (D) -6

91. If $y - 2$ and $y - \dfrac{1}{2}$ are the factors of $py^2 + 5y + r$ then
    (A) $p > r$ (B) $p = r$
    (C) $p < r$ (D) none

92. What must be substracted from $4x^4 - 2x^3 - 6x^2 + x - 5$ so that the result is exactly divisible by $2x^2 + x - 2$?
    (A) $-3x - 5$ (B) $3x - 5$
    (C) $-3x + 5$ (D) $3x - 5$

93. If $(x + 1)$ and $(x - 1)$ are the factors of $px^3 + x^2 - 2x + q$ then the values of p and q are
    (A) $p = -1, q = 2$ (B) $p = 2, q = -1$
    (C) $p = 2, q = 1$ (D) $p = -2, q = -2$

94. The value of m if $(x - 2)$ is a factor of $2x^3 - 5x^2 + 5x + m$
    (A) -1 (B) 0
    (C) 2 (D) -2

95. If $p(x, y) = a^2 - y^2 - xy$

    and $q(x, y) = -x^2 + y^2 + 3xy$ then the value of $4p(x, y) - 5q(x, y)$ is

    (A) $9x^2 - 9y^2 - 19xy$

    (B) $9x^2 + 9y^2 - 19xy$

    (C) $-9x^2 + 9y^2 + 19xy$

    (D) $9x^2 - 9y^2 + 19xy$

96. The value of a if $(x - a)$ is a factor of $x^6 - ax^5 + x^4 - ax^3 + 3x - a + 2$
    (A) $a = -1$ (B) $a = 2$
    (C) $a = -2$ (D) $a = 1$

97. Using factor therem, factorise the cubic polynomial $x^3 - 6x^2 + 11x - 6$.
    (A) $(x + 1)(x - 3)(x - 2)$
    (B) $(x - 1)(x - 3)(x - 2)$
    (C) $(x + 1)(x + 3)(x - 2)$
    (D) $(x + 1)(x - 3)(x + 2)$

98. Factorise $x^3 - 2x^2 - x + 2$.
    (A) $(x - 1)(x - 2)(x + 1)$
    (B) $(x + 1)(x + 2)(x - 1)$
    (C) $(x - 2)(x - 1)^2$
    (D) $(x + 2)(x - 1)(x - 2)$

99. When f(x) is divided by $2x + 3$ then the remainder is?
    (A) $f(2)$ (B) $f(3)$
    (C) $f(3/2)$ (D) $f(-3/2)$

100. When $x^{11} + 1$ is divided by $x + 1$ then the remainder is
    (A) 0 (B) 2
    (C) 1 (D) -1

101. Using factor theorem the factors of $y^3 - 2y^2 - y + 2$ is
    (A) $(y - 2)(y + 1)(y - 1)$
    (B) $(y + 2)(y + 1)(y - 1)$
    (C) $(y - 2)(y + 2)(y - 1)$
    (D) $(y - 2)(y + 2)(y + 1)$

102. When $x^9 - a^9$ is divided by $x - a$ then the remainder is
    (A) 0 (B) 1
    (C) -1 (D) 2

103. If $11^7 + 4^7$ is divided by 15 then the remainder is

(A) 0   (B) 1

(C) 2   (D) -2

104. If $5^{2n} - 2^{3n}$ is divisible by 17 then the remainder is

(A) 0   (B) 1

(C) -1   (D) 2

105. The value of $25x^2 + 16y^2 + 40xy$ at x = 1 and y = −1 is

(A) 81   (B) −49

(C) 1   (D) none

106. Find the missing term in the following problem.

$$\left(\frac{3x}{4} - \frac{4y}{3}\right)^2 = \frac{9x^2}{16} + \underline{\quad} + \frac{16y^2}{9}$$

(A) 2xy   (B) −2xy

(C) 12xy   (D) −12xy

107. The value of

$$\frac{7.83 \times 7.83 - 1.17 \times 1.17}{6.66} \text{ is}$$

(A) 9   (B) 6.66

(C) 1.176   (D) none

108. If $x - \dfrac{1}{x} = \sqrt{6}$ then $x^2 + \dfrac{1}{x^2} = \underline{\quad}$

(A) 2   (B) 4

(C) 6   (D) 8

109. If $x^2 + \dfrac{1}{x^2} = 79$ then $x + \dfrac{1}{x} = \underline{\quad}$

(A) $\sqrt{75}$ (B) 9

(C) $\sqrt{79}$ (D) none

110. If $3x - 7y = 10$ and $xy = -1$ then the value of $9x^2 + 49y^2$ is

(A) 58   (B) 142

(C) 104   (D) −104

111. If $a + b + c = 10$ and $a^2 + b^2 + c^2 = 36$ then $ab + bc + ca = \underline{\quad}$

(A) 136   (B) 64

(C) 32   (D) 68

112. If $x - y = 4$ and $xy = 21$ then $x^3 - y^3 =$

(A) 361   (B) 316

(C) −188   (D) none

113. $(a + b)^3 - (a - b)^3 = \underline{\quad}$

(A) $b^3 + 3a^2b$

(B) $2(b^3 + 3a^2b)$

(C) $2(a^3 + 3ab^2)$

(D) 0

114. The product of $(4x - 3y)$ and $(16x^2 + 12xy + 9y^2)$ is

(A) $(4x - 3y)^3$

(B) $(16x^2 + 12xy + 9y^2)^2$

(C) $64x^3 - 27y^3$

(D) none

115. $(3x - 5y)^3 - (5x - 2y)^3 + (2x + 3y)^3$

(A) $(3x - 5y)(5x - 2y)(2x + 3y)$

(B) $3(3x - 5y)(5x - 2y)(2x + 3y)$

(C) $(3x - 5y)(2y - 5x)(2x + 3y)$

(D) $-3(3x - 5y)(5x - 2y)(2x + 3y)$

116. If $a + b + c = 9$ and $ab + bc + ca = 26$, then the value of $a^3 + b^3 + c^3 - 3abc$ is

(A) 27   (B) 29

(C) 495   (D) 729

117. If $x^3 + y^3 + z^3 = 3xyz$ then the relation between x, y and z is

(A) $x + y + z = 0$

(B) $x = y = z$

(C) either $x + y + z = 0$ (or) $x = y = z$

(D) neither $x + y + z = 0$ nor $x = y = z$

118. The equality $b^2 + 5 > 9b + 12$ is satisfied if

(A) $b > 9$ (or) $b < 1$

(B) $b > 9$ (or) $b < 0$

(C) $b = 10$ (or) $b = -1$

(D) $b > 8$ (or) $b < 0$

119. If $0 < a < 1$, then the value of

$$a + \frac{1}{a} \text{ is}$$

(A) greater than 2

(B) less than 2

(C) greater than 4

(D) less than 4

120. What is the zero of the binomial $ax + b$?

(A) 0   (B) $\dfrac{b}{a}$

(C) $\dfrac{-a}{b}$ (D) $\dfrac{-b}{a}$

Answers

1. C	2. B	3. A	4. D	5. A	6. C	7. B	8. A	9. B	10. D
11. A	12. C	13. D	14. B	15. C	16. A	17. D	18. B	19. B	20. C
21. C	22. B	23. A	24. D	25. B	26. A	27. C	28. A	29. C	30. B
31. D	32. A	33. B	34. A	35. C	36. B	37. C	38. A	39. D	40. C
41. D	42. C	43. A	44. B	45. A	46. A	47. C	48. C	49. A	50. B
51. A	52. B	53. A	54. A	55. B	56. A	57. B	58. A	59. A	60. A
61. C	62. B	63. A	64. C	65. C	66. A	67. C	68. A	69. A	70. D
71. A	72. B	73. A	74. C	75. A	76. C	77. B	78. A	79. D	80. A
81. A	82. C	83. B	84. B	85. A	86. A	87. C	88. B	89. A	90. B
91. C	92. A	93. B	94. D	95. A	96. A	97. B	98. A	99. D	100. A
101. A	102. A	103. A	104. A	105. C	106. B	107. A	108. D	109. B	110. A
111. C	112. B	113. B	114. C	115. D	116. A	117. C	118. B	119. A	120. D

2. *Polynomials*   *Class IX–Maths*

1. (C) For polynomials power should be non-negative integer.

2. (B) $\because$ highest power is $3 + 1 = 4$.

3. (A)

$$\begin{array}{l} 3x^3 + x^2 \qquad\ \ + 6 \\ (+)\, x^3 \qquad (+)3x\ -8 \\ \underline{\quad -\qquad\ \ -\qquad +\quad} \\ \\ \underline{2x^3 + x^2 - 3x + 14} \end{array}$$

4. (D)

$$\begin{array}{l} x^3 - 3x^2 + 5x\ - 1 \\ +2x^3 + x^2 - 4x\ + 2 \\ \underline{\ -\quad -\quad +\quad\ -\ } \\ \\ \underline{-x^3 - 4x^2 + 9x - 3} \end{array}$$

5. (A) $\dfrac{-56\ mnp^2}{7\ mnp} = -8p$

6. (C) $x^3 - 1 = x^3 - 1^3 = (x - 1)(x^2 + x + 1)$

7. (B) $\dfrac{2}{3}xy \times \dfrac{3}{2}xz = x^2yz$

8. (A) $\dfrac{8x^2y^2 - 6xy^2 + 10x^2y^3}{2xy}$

$$= \dfrac{8x^2y^2}{2xy} - \dfrac{6xy^2}{2xy} + \dfrac{10x^2y^3}{2xy}$$

$$= 4xy - 3y + 5xy^2$$

9. (B) $(x^2 + 3x + 5) \times (x^2 - 1)$

$= x^2 \times x^2 + 3x \times x^2 + 5 \times x^2 +$

$\qquad x^2 \times -1 + 3x \times -1 + 5 \times -1$

$= x^4 + 3x^3 + 5x^2 - x^2 - 3x - 5$

$= x^4 + 3x^3 + 4x^2 - 3x - 5$

10. (D) Dividend

$=$ divisor $\times$ quotient $+$ remainder

$= (3x^2 - 2x + 1) \times (x + 2) + (2x - 5)$

$= 3x^3 + 4x^2 - x - 3$

11. (A)

$x^2 + ax - 6 = 0$	$x^2 - 9x + b = 0$
$2^2 + a(2) - 6 = 0$	$2^2 - 9(2) + b = 0$
$2a = 2$	$b = 14$
$a = 1$	

$\therefore\ a + b = 1 + 14 = 15.$

12. (C)

$$t^3 + 1\ )\ t^6 + 3t^2 + 10\ (\ t^3 - 1$$
$$\begin{array}{l} \underline{t^3 + t^6} \\ -t^3 + 3t^2 + 10 \\ \underline{-t^3 \qquad\quad -1} \\ 3t^2 + 11 \end{array}$$

13. (D) $(3x^2 - 5x + 6) \times -8x^3$

$= -24x^5 + 40x^4 - 48x^3$

Put $x = 0$

$-24(0)^5 + 40(0)^4 - 48(0)^3 = 0.$

14. (B) $8 - 5 = 3$

15. (C)

$$\begin{array}{l} x^3 - x^2 + 3x - 2 \\ (-)\ \underline{\quad x^2 + 5x - 6} \\ \underline{x^3 - 2x^2 - 2x + 4} \end{array}$$

16. (A)

$$\begin{array}{l} x^4 + 0 + 2x^2 - 3x + 7 \\ (-)\ \underline{\quad x^3 +\ x^2 +\ x - 1} \\ \underline{x^4 - x^3 + x^2 - 4x + 8} \end{array}$$

17. (D) $x^2y \times \dfrac{x}{y} = x^3$

$$x^2 \div \frac{1}{x} = x^3.$$

18. (B) $(3x - 4)(5x + 7) = 15x^2 - ax - 28$

$15x^2 + x - 28 = 15x^2 - ax - 28$

Comparing we get a = -1.

19. (B) Negative

20. (C) $x^3 - 6x^2y - xy^2 - y^3$

$(-) \quad x^3 + 5x^2y - xy^2 - y^3$

$\overline{\qquad\qquad -11x^2y \qquad\qquad}$

21. (C) Real factors do not exist for $x^2 + 4$.

22. (B) $x^4 + 4 = (x^4 + 4x^2 + 4) - 4x^2$

$= (x^2 + 2)^2 - (2x)^2$

$= (x^2 + 2x + 2)(x^2 - 2x + 2)$

23. (A) $x^4 + 2x^2 + 9 =$

$(x^4 + 6x^2 + 9) - 4x^2$

$= (x^2 + 3)^2 - (2x)^2$

$= (x^2 + 2x + 3)(x^2 - 2x + 3)$

24. (D) Let the other factor be $x^2 + ax + b$.

We have

$(x^2 + 2x + 5)(x^2 + ax + b)$

$\qquad\qquad = x^4 + px^2 + q$

$x^4 + (2 + a)x^3 + (2a + b + 5)x^2 +$

$\qquad (5a + 2b)x + 5b = x^4 + px^2 + q$

Comparing the coefficients

$2a + b + 5 = p$ —— (1)

$\qquad 5b = q$ —— (2)

$2 + a = 0 \Rightarrow a = -2$.

$5a + 2b = 0 \Rightarrow b = 5$.

$\therefore p = 2a + b + 5 = 2(-2) + 5 + 5 = 6$.

$q = 5b = 5(5) = 25$.

25. (B) $x^2 + xy - 2xz - 2yz$

$= x(x + y) - 2z(x + y)$

$= (x + y)(x - 2z)$

26. (A) $x^9 - x = x(x^8 - 1)$

$x\left[\left(x^4\right)^2 - (1)^2\right] = x\left(x^4 + 1\right)\left(x^4 - 1\right)$

$= x(x^4 + 1)(x^2 + 1)(x + 1)(x - 1)$

27. (C) $\dfrac{x^2}{4} - \dfrac{y^2}{9} = \left(\dfrac{x}{2}\right)^2 - \left(\dfrac{y}{3}\right)^2$

$= \left(\dfrac{x}{2} + \dfrac{y}{3}\right)\left(\dfrac{x}{2} - \dfrac{y}{3}\right)$

28. (A) $1 - p^3 = 1^3 - p^3$

$= (1 - p)(1 + p + p^2)$

29. (C) $x^4 + y^4 + x^2y^2$

$= (x^4 + y^4 + 2x^2y^2) - x^2y^2$

$= (x^2 + y^2)^2 - (xy)^2$

$= (x^2 + y^2 + xy)(x^2 + y^2 - xy)$

30. (B) $15x^2 - 26x + 8 = 15x^2 - 20x - 6x + 8$

$= 5x(3x - 4) - 2(3x - 4)$

$= (3x - 4)(5x - 2)$

31. (D) $\left[a(b - c)^3\right] + \left[b(c - a)\right]^3 + \left[c(a - b)\right]^3$

$= 3a(b - c)\,b(c - a)\,c(a - b)$

$= 3abc(a - b)(b - c)(c - a)$

32. (A) $a^3 + 8b^3 - 64c^3 + 24abc$

$= (a)^3 + (2b)^3 + (-4c)^3 - 3(a)(2b)(-4c)$

$= (a + 2b - 4c)(a^2 + 4b^2 + 16c^2 -$

$\qquad\qquad\qquad 2ab + 8bc - 4ac)$

33. (B) $\dfrac{0.76 \times 0.76 \times 0.76 + 0.24 \times 0.24 \times 0.24}{0.76 \times 0.76 - 0.76 \times 0.24 + 0.24 \times 0.24}$

$= \dfrac{(0.76)^3 + (0.24)^3}{(0.76)^2 - 0.76 \times 0.24 + (0.24)^2}$

$= 0.76 + 0.24 = 1$.

34. (A) $a^2 + b - ab - a$

$= a^2 - ab + b - a$

$= a(a - b) - 1(a - b)$

$= (a - 1)(a - b)$

35. (C) $x^2 + \dfrac{1}{x^2} + 2 - 2x - \dfrac{2}{x}$

$= \left(x^2 + \dfrac{1}{x^2} + 2\right) - 2\left(x + \dfrac{1}{x}\right)$

$= \left(x + \dfrac{1}{x}\right)^2 - 2\left(x + \dfrac{1}{x}\right)$

$= \left(x + \dfrac{1}{x}\right)\left(x + \dfrac{1}{x} - 2\right)$

36. (B) $a^2 + b^2 + 2ab + 2bc + 2ca + c^2 - c^2$

$= (a + b + c)^2 - c^2$

$= (a + b)(a + b + 2c)$

On comparision we get

$m = 0, n = 2$

$m + n = 0 + 2 = 2$

37. (C) $(x^2 + 3x + 5)(x^2 - 3x + 5)$

$= (x^2 + 5 + 3x)(x^2 + 5 - 3x)$

$= (x^2 + 5)^2 - (3x)^2$

$\therefore m = x^2 + 5.$

38. (A) $(a^2 - b^2)(c^2 - d^2) - 4abcd$

$= (ac - bd)^2 - (bc + ad)^2$

$= (ac - bd + bc + ad)(ac - bd - bc - ad)$

39. (D) $\sqrt{3}x^2 + 11x + 6\sqrt{3}$

$= \sqrt{3}x^2 + 9x + 2x + 6\sqrt{3}$

$= \sqrt{3}x\left(x + 3\sqrt{3}\right) + 2\left(x + 3\sqrt{3}\right)$

$= \left(x + 3\sqrt{3}\right)\left(\sqrt{3}x + 2\right)$

40. (C) $x^7 + xy^6 = x(x^6 + y^6)$

$= x\left[\left(x^2\right)^3 + \left(y^2\right)^3\right]$

$= x\left(x^2 + y^2\right)\left(x^4 - x^2y^2 + y^4\right)$

41. (D) $x^3 + x^2 + x + 1$

$x^2(x + 1) + (x + 1)$

$(x + 1)(x^2 + 1)$

42. (C) $x^2 + ax + bx + cx + ab + bc$

$(x^2 + bx) + (ax + ab) + (cx + bc)$

$x(x + b) + a(x + b) + c(x + b)$

$(x + b)(x + a + c)$

43. (A) $x^3 - 3x^2 + 3x - 1 + 8$

$(x - 1)^3 + 2^3$

$\Rightarrow (x + 1)(x^2 - 2x + 1 - 2x + 2 + 4)$

$\Rightarrow (x + 1)(x^2 - 4x + 7)$

44. (B) Let $a + b = A, a - b = B$

$\therefore A + B = 2a$

$(a + b)^3 + (a - b)^3 + 6a(a^2 - b^2)$

$A^3 + B^3 + 3(A + B)AB = (A + B)^3$

$\qquad\qquad = (2a)^3 = 8a^3$

45. (A) $x^2 + 3\sqrt{2}\,x + 4$

$= x^2 + 2\sqrt{2}\,x + \sqrt{2}\,x + 4$

$= (x + 2\sqrt{2})(x + \sqrt{2})$

46. (A) $x^{12} - y^{12}$

$\left(x^6 + y^6\right)\left(x^6 - y^6\right)$

$(x^4 - x^2y^2 + y^4)(X^2 + Y^2)$

$(x - y)(x^2 + xy + y^2)(x + y)(x^2 - xy + y^2)$

47. (C) $x + y = -z$

$(x + y)^3 = (-z)^3$

$x^3 + y^3 + 3xy(x + y) = -z^3$

$x^3 + y^3 + z^3 = 3xyz$

48. (C) $\dfrac{a^2}{bc} + \dfrac{b^2}{ca} + \dfrac{c^2}{ab} = \dfrac{a^3 + b^3 + c^3}{abc}$

$= \dfrac{3abc}{abc} = 3$

49. (A) $ab + bc + ax + cx$

$b(a + c) + x(a + c) \Rightarrow (b + x)(a + c)$

50. (B) $20a^2 - 45$

$5(4a^2 - 9) \Rightarrow 5(2a + 3)(2a - 3)$

51. (A) $6x^3 - 24xy^2 - 3x^2y + 12y^3$

$6x^3 - 3x^2y - 24xy^2 + 12y^3$

$3x^2(2x - y) - 12y^2(2x - y)$

$(2x - y)(3x^2 - 12y^2)$

$\Rightarrow 3(2x - y)(x + 2y)(x - 2y)$

52. (B) $\dfrac{1}{2}x^2 - 3x + 4 = \dfrac{1}{2}x^2 - 2x - x + 4$

$= \dfrac{1}{2}x(x - 4) - 1(x - 4)$

$= \left(\dfrac{1}{2}x - 1\right)(x - 4)$

53. (A) $(3 - 4y - 7y^2)^2 - (4y + 1)^2$

$(4 - 7y^2)(2 - 8y - 7y^2)$

54. (A) $3\sqrt{3}x^3 + y^3 =$

$\left(\sqrt{3}x + y\right)(3x^2 - \sqrt{3}xy + y^2)$

55. (B) $1 - x + x^2 - x^3$

$(1 - x) + x^2(1 - x) \Rightarrow (1 + x^2)(1 - x)$

56. (A) $49y^2 - 14y + 1 - 25x^2$

$= (7y - 1)^2 - (5x)^2$

$= (7y - 1 + 5x)(7y - 1 - 5x)$

57. (B) $x^2 - 1 - 2a - a^2 = x^2 - (a^2 + 2a + 1)$

$= x^2 - (a + 1)^2$

$= (x + a + 1)(x - a - 1)$

58. (A) $x^4 - x^2 - 12 = x^4 - 4x^2 + 3x^2 - 12$

$= x^2(x^2 - 4) + 3(x^2 - 4)$

$= (x^2 + 3)(x^2 - 4)$

$= (x^2 + 3)(x + 2)(x - 2)$

60. (A) $\Rightarrow 2x = 2a \therefore x = a$

Similarly $\dfrac{2}{x} = 2b; \dfrac{1}{x} = b$

$x \times \dfrac{1}{x} = a \times b \Rightarrow ab = 1$

61. (C) $\left(a + \dfrac{1}{a}\right)^2 = b \Rightarrow a + \dfrac{1}{a} = \sqrt{b}$

$a^3 + \dfrac{1}{a^3} = b^{\frac{3}{2}} - 3b^{\frac{1}{2}}$

62. (B) $2^{\frac{1}{4}} . 4^{\frac{1}{8}} . 16^{\frac{1}{16}} . (256)^{\frac{1}{32}}$

$2^{\frac{1}{4}} . 2^{\frac{1}{4}} . 2^{\frac{1}{4}} . 2^{\frac{1}{4}} . = 2^{\frac{1}{4} + \frac{1}{4} + \frac{1}{4} + \frac{1}{4}}$

$= 2^1$

63. (A) $x - 8xy^3 = x(1 - 8y^3)$

$= x[1^3 - (2y)^3]$

$= x(1 - 2y)(1 + 2y + 4y^2)$

64. (C) $(m - n)^6 - 8m^3$

$\left\{(m - n)^2\right\}^3 - (2m)^3$

$\left\{(m - n)^2 - 2m\right\}\left\{(m - n)^4 - (m - n)^2 2m + 4m^2\right\}$

65. (C) $a^{\frac{1}{2}} + b^{\frac{1}{2}} - c^{\frac{1}{2}} = 0 \Rightarrow a^{\frac{1}{2}} + b^{\frac{1}{2}} = c^{\frac{1}{2}}$

$\left(a^{\frac{1}{2}} + b^{\frac{1}{2}}\right)^2 = \left(c^{\frac{1}{2}}\right)^2$

$a + b + 2\sqrt{ab} = c$

$a + b - c = -2\sqrt{ab}$

$(a + b - c)^2 = 4ab$

66. (A) $\left(a^x\right)^2 - \left(b^x\right)^2$

$= \left(a^x + b^x\right)\left(a^x - b^x\right)$

67. (C) $\dfrac{x}{1} = \dfrac{a - b}{a + b}$

Applying compedendo and dividendo process, we get

$$\frac{x+1}{x-1} = \frac{a-b+a+b}{a-b-(a+b)} \Rightarrow \frac{x+1}{x-1} = \frac{a}{-b}$$

$$\frac{1+x}{1-x} = +\frac{a}{b}$$

Similarly $\dfrac{1+y}{1-y} = \dfrac{b}{c}, \dfrac{1+z}{1-z} = \dfrac{c}{a}$

$$\frac{1+x}{1-x} \times \frac{1+y}{1-y} \times \frac{1+z}{1-z} = \frac{a}{b} \times \frac{b}{c} \times \frac{c}{a}$$

$$= 1$$

68. (A) Factorise $8a^3 - 2a^2b - 15ab^2$

$8a^3 + 10a^2b - 12a^2b - 15ab^2$

$(4a + 5b)(2a^2 - 3ab)$

69. (A) $a + p + (-2) = 0$

$\Rightarrow a^3 + p^3 + (-2)^3 = 3(a)(p)(-2)$

$a^3 + p^3 - 8 + 6ap = 0$

70. (D) $a + b + c - 3x = 0$ or

$3x - a - b - c = 0$

$\Rightarrow (x - a) + (x - b) + (x - c) = 0$

$\Rightarrow (x - a)^3 + (x - b)^3 + (x - c)^3$
$\quad - 3(x - a)(x - b)(x - c) = 0$

71. (A) $a^2 + b^2 + 2ab + 2bc + 2ca$

$(a + b)^2 + 2c(a + b)$

$\Rightarrow (a + b)(a + b + 2c)$

72. (B) $px^2 + 4p^2x - 3qx - 12pq$

$px(x + 4p) - 3q(x + 4p)$

$(x + 4p)(px - 3q)$

73. (A) $y^2(y - 2) - 1(y - 2)$

$(y^2 - 1)(y - 2) = (y + 1)(y - 1)(y - 2)$

74. (C) $x^{\frac{1}{3}} + y^{\frac{1}{3}} + z^{\frac{1}{3}} = 0$

$\Rightarrow x + y + z = 3x^{\frac{1}{3}}y^{\frac{1}{3}}z^{\frac{1}{3}}$

$\Rightarrow (x + y + z)^3 = 27xyz$

75. (A) Remainder $= p(1) = -7$

76. (C)

$2(2)^3 + a(2)^2 + 3(2) - 5 = (2)^3 + (2)^2 - 4(2) + a$

$$3a = -13 \Rightarrow a = -\frac{13}{3}$$

77. (B)

$(-1)^3 + 2(-1)^2 - 5a(-1) - 7 = R_1 \therefore R_1 = -6 + 5a$

$(2)^3 + a(2)^2 - 12(2) + 6 = R_2 \therefore R_2 = -10 + 4a$

$2R_1 + R_2 = 6 \Rightarrow -12 + 10a - 10 + 4a = 6 \therefore a = 2$

78. (A) $x^2 - 1 = (x + 1)(x - 1)$

Since $(x + 1)$, $(x - 1)$ are factors of the given polynomial, consider $(x + 1)$ is a factor $a + c + e = b + d$.

79. (D) The sum of the coefficients of even terms is equal to the sum of the coefficients of odd terms.

$\therefore (x + 1)$ is a factor.

$\therefore x^3 + 7x^2 + 14x + 8 = (x + 1)(x^2 + 6x + 8)$

$\qquad\qquad = (x+1)(x+2)(x+4)$

80. (A) $f(-x) = -ax^7 - bx^3 - cx - 5$

$f(x) + f(-x) = -10$

$f(7) + f(-7) = -10 \Rightarrow f(7) + 7 = -17$

81. (A)

$2(1)^3 + a(1)^2 + 3(1) - 5 = (1)^3 + (1)^2 - 4(1) - a$

$2 + a + 3 - 5 = 1 + 1 - 4 - a$

$2a = -2 \therefore a = -1$

82. (C) $(x - 3)$ is a factor of $p^2x^3 - px^2 + 3px - p$ then

$p^2(3)^3 - p(3)^2 + 3p(3) - p = 0$

$\therefore p = \dfrac{1}{27}$

84. (B) $2(-2)^4 + 3(-2)^2 + 2K(-2)^2 + 3(-2) + 6 = 0$
$\Rightarrow K = -1$

85. (A) If **x - 1** is a factor then
$(1)^3 - 6(1)^2 + 11(1) - 6 = 0$

86. (A) $\therefore$ p(2) $= (2)^4 + 2(2)^3 - 3(2)^2 + 2 - 1$
$= 21$

87. (C) $f(-2) = 2(-2)^4 - 6(-2)^3 + 2(-2)^2 - (-2) + 2$
$= 92$

88. (B)
$8x^3 - 4x^2 + 2x + 7 + A = 10x^3 - 2x^2 + 7x + 10$
$A = 2x^3 + 2x^2 + 5x + 3$

89. (A)
$3p(x) + 7q(x) + r(x) = 12x^3 - 9x^2 + 6x + 3 + 7x^3 + 7x^2$
$+ 7x + 7 + x^2 - 2x + 1$
$= 19x^3 - 15x^2 + 11x + 11$

90. (B)
$2\left(\dfrac{1}{2}\right)^3 + m\left(\dfrac{1}{2}\right)^2 + 11\left(\dfrac{1}{2}\right) + m + 3 = 0$
$\Rightarrow m = -7$

91. (C) $y - 2$ is a factor of $py^2 + 5y + r$
then $p(2)^2 + 5(2) + r = 0$
$4p + r + 10 = 0 \ldots\ldots(1)$

$y - \dfrac{1}{2}$ is a factor of $py^2 + 5y + r$

then $p\left(\dfrac{1}{2}\right)^2 + 5\left(\dfrac{1}{2}\right) + r = 0$

$\dfrac{p}{4} + \dfrac{5}{2} + r = 0 \ldots\ldots\ldots(2)$

By solving (1) & (2) we get p$= \dfrac{-2}{3}$

$r = \dfrac{22}{3}$

92. (A)
$2x^2 + x - 2 \,)\, 4x^4 - 2x^3 - 6x^2 + x - 5 \,(\, 2x^2 - 2x$
$\underline{ 4x^4 \pm 2x^3 \underset{+}{-} 4x^2}$

$\underline{ - 4x^3 - 2x^2 + x - 5}$
$\underset{+}{-}\, 4x^3 \underset{+}{-} 2x^2 \pm 4x$

$\underline{ - 3x - 5}$

$-3x - 5$ to be subtracted from $4x^4 - 2x^3 - 6x^2 + x - 5$ so that it is divisible by $2x^2 + x - 2$.

93. (B) Since $(x + 1)$ and $(x - 1)$ are factors of $px^3 + x^2 - 2x + q$.
Then $p(-1)^3 + (-1)^2 - 2(1) + q = 0$
$-p + q = -3 \ldots\ldots(1)$
$p(1)^3 + (1)^2 - 2(1) + q = 0$
$p + q = 1 \ldots\ldots(2)$
By solving we get p = 2, q = -1.

94. (D) Since $(x - 2)$ is a factor of
$2x^3 - 6x^2 + 5x + m$
$2(2)^3 - 6(2)^2 + 5(2) + m = 0$
$\Rightarrow m = -2$

95. (A) $4p(x, y) - 5q(x,y)$
$9x^2 - 9y^2 - 19xy$

96. (A) $a^6 - a(a)^5 + (a)^4 - a(a)^3 + 3a - a + 2 = 0$
$a^6 - a^6 + a^4 - a^4 + 3a - a + 2 = 0$
$\Rightarrow a = -1$

97. (B) The sum of the coefficients in the polynomial is zero. Then $(x - 1)$ is a factor.

$\dfrac{x^3 - 6x^2 + 11x - 6}{x - 1} = (x^2 - 5x + 6)$

$\therefore x^3 - 6x^2 + 11x - 6$
$= (x - 1)(x - 2)(x - 3)$

98. (A) Sum of the coefficients of $x^3 - 2x^2 - x + 2$ is zero. Then $x - 1$ is a factor.

$$\frac{x^3 - 2x^2 - x + 2}{x - 1} = (x + 1)(x - 2)$$

$x^3 - 2x^2 - x + 2 = (x - 1)(x + 1)(x - 2)$

99. (D) When f(x) is divided by $2x + 3$ reminder will be $f\left(\dfrac{-3}{2}\right)$.

100. (A) Since x is odd,

$\therefore \dfrac{x^{11} + 1}{x + 1}$ is exactly divisible.

$\therefore$ remainder is zero.

101. (A) $(y^3 - 2y^2 - y + 2) \div (y - 1)$ Quotient will be $y^2 - y - 2$.

$\therefore$ The factors will be

$(y - 1)(y + 1)(y - 2)$

102. (A) $x^n - a^n$ is always divisible by $(x - a)$ for any 'n'.

$\therefore$ the remainder is zero.

103. (A) $x^n + a^n$ is divisible by $x + a$ when 'n' is odd. $11^7 + 4^7$ is exactly divisible by 15.

104. (A) $5^{2n} - 2^{3n} = \left(5^2\right)^n - \left(2^3\right)^n = (25)^n - (8)^n$

$(25)^n - (8)^n$ is divisible by $(25 - 8)$ for any integer 'n'.

105. (C) $25x^2 + 16y^2 + 40xy$
at x = 1 and y = –1
$25(1)^2 + 16(-1)^2 + 40(1)(-1)$
= 25 + 16 – 40
= 1.

106. (B) $\left(\dfrac{3x}{4} - \dfrac{4y}{3}\right)^2 =$

$\left(\dfrac{3x}{4}\right)^2 - 2\left(\dfrac{3x}{4}\right)\left(\dfrac{4y}{3}\right) + \left(\dfrac{4y}{3}\right)^2$

$$= \frac{9x^2}{16} - 2xy + \frac{16y^2}{9}$$

$$= \frac{9x^2}{16} + (-2xy) + \frac{16y^2}{9}.$$

107. (A) $\dfrac{7.83 \times 7.83 - 1.17 \times 1.17}{6.66}$

$$= \frac{(7.83 + 1.17)(7.83 - 1.17)}{6.66}$$

$$= \frac{9 \times 6.66}{6.66} = 9.$$

108. (D) $x - \dfrac{1}{x} = \sqrt{6}$

Squaring on both sides

$$\left(x - \frac{1}{x}\right)^2 = \left(\sqrt{6}\right)^2$$

$$x^2 + \frac{1}{x^2} - 2.x.\frac{1}{x} = 6$$

$$x^2 + \frac{1}{x^2} = 6 + 2 = 8.$$

109. (B) $\left(x + \dfrac{1}{x}\right)^2 = x^2 + \dfrac{1}{x^2} + 2$

= 79 + 2 = 81

$\therefore x + \dfrac{1}{x} = \sqrt{81} = 9.$

110. (A) $3x - 7y = 10$
Squaring on both sides
$(3x - 7y)^2 = 10^2$
$9x^2 + 49y^2 - 42xy = 100$
$9x^2 + 49y^2 = 100 - 42 = 58.$

111. (C) $a + b + c = 10$
Squaring on both sides
$a^2 + b^2 + c^2 + 2ab + 2bc + 2ca = 100$

36 + 2 (ab + bc + ca) = 100

2 (ab + bc + ca) = 100 − 36 = 64

$ab + bc + ca = \dfrac{64}{2} = 32$.

112. (B)　$x − y = 4$

Cubing on both sides

$(x − y)^3 = (4)^3$

$x^3 − y^3 − 3xy(x − y) = 64$

$x^3 − y^3 − 3(21)(4) = 64$

$x^3 − y^3 = 316$.

113. (B)　$(a + b)^3 − (a − b)^3$

$= (a^3 + b^3 + 3a^2b + 3ab^2)−$

　　$(a^3 − b^3 − 3a^2b + 3ab^2)$

$= 2(b^3 + 3a^2b)$.

114. (C)　$(4x − 3y) (16x^2 + 12xy + 9y^2)$

$= (4x − 3y) [(4x)^2 + (4x)(3y) + (3y)^2]$

$= (4x)^3 − (3y)^3$

$\left[(a − b)(a^2 + ab + b^2) = a^3 − b^3 \right]$

$= 64x^3 − 27y^3$.

115. (D)　let a = 3x − 5y

　　　b = 2y − 5x

　　　c = 2x + 3y

　　a + b + c = 0.

We have

If a + b + c = 0 then

$a^3 + b^3 + c^3 = 3abc$.

So, $(3x − 5y)^3 − (5x − 2y)^3 + (2x + 3y)^3$

$= 3(3x − 5y) (2y − 5x) (2x + 3y)$

$= − 3(3x −5y) (5x − 2y) (2x + 3y)$.

116. (A)　a + b + c = 9

Squaring on both sides

$(a + b + c)^2 = 81$

$a^2 + b^2 + c^2 + 2ab + 2bc + 2ca = 81$

$a^2 + b^2 + c^2 + 2(ab + bc + ca) = 81$

$a^2 + b^2 + c^2 + 2(26) = 81$

$a^2 + b^2 + c^2 = 81 − 52 = 29$

$a^3 + b^3 + c^3 − 3abc$

$= (a + b + c) (a^2 + b^2 + c^2$

　　　　　$− ab − bc − ca)$

$= (a + b + c) [(a^2 + b^2 + c^2)$

　　　　　$−(ab + bc + ca)]$

$= (9) (29 − 26)$

$= 9 × 3 = 27$.

117. (C)　We have

$x^3 + y^3 + z^3 − 3xyz$

$= (x + y + z) (x^2 + y^2 + z^2 − xy − yz − zx)$

$0 = (x + y + z) (x^2 + y^2 + z^2$

　　　　　$− xy − yz − zx)$

So either x + y + z = 0 (or)

$x^2 + y^2 + z^2 − xy − yz − zx = 0$

$x^2 + y^2 + z^2 − xy − yz − zx = 0$

$2x^2 + 2y^2 + 2z^2 − 2xy − 2yz − 2zx = 0$

$(x^2 − 2xy + y^2) + (y^2 − 2yz + z^2) +$

　　　　　$(z^2 − 2zx + x^2) = 0$

$(x − y)^2 + (y − z)^2 + (z − x)^2 = 0$

$\Rightarrow x = y = z$

∴ either x + y + z = 0 or x = y = z

118. (B)　b > 9 (or) b < 0.

119. (A)　Let a = 0.5

∴ $a + \dfrac{1}{a} = 0.5 + \dfrac{1}{0.5} = 2.5 > 2$

120. (D)　ax + b = 0

　　　ax = -b

　　　x = -b/a

Chapter 3

Coordinate Geometry

3

1.   *Co-ordinate geometry* : The branch of mathematics in which geometric problems are solved through algebra by using the coordinate system is known as coordinate geometry.

2.   In coordinate geometry, every point is represented by an ordered pair, called coordinates of that point.

3.   A pair of numbers 'a' and 'b' listed in a specific order with 'a' at the first place and 'b' at the second place is called an ordered pair (a, b).

   $$(a, b) \neq (b, a)$$

   If (a, b) = (c, d)

   then a = c and b = d.

4.   The position of a point in a plane is determined with reference to two fixed mutually perpendicular lines called the coordinate axes.

5.   The horizontal line is called X-axis and vertical line is called Y-axis.

6.   The point of intersection of these axes is called origin (0, 0).

7.   In a point P(a, b), 'a' is called X coordinate or first coordinate or abscissa and 'b' is called Y-coordinate or second coordinate or ordinate.

8.   The axes divide the plane into four quadrants.

9.   XOY- I Quadrant (Q_1), x>0, Y>0, (+, +)

   X^1OY- II Quadrant (Q_2), x<0, Y>0, (-, +)

   X^1OY^1- III Quadrant (Q_3), x<0, Y<0, (-, -)

XOY^1-IV Quadrant (Q_4), x>0, Y<0, (+, -)

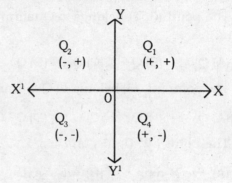

The coordinates of any point on X-axis is of the form (a, 0) [Y-coordinate zero].

10.   The coordinates of any point on Y-axis is of the form (0, b) [X-coordinate zero].

Multiple Choice Questions

1.   The point of intersection of X and Y axes is called

   (A) origin
   (B) null point
   (C) common point
   (D) none

2.   The point (2, 3) is at a distance of _____ units from X-axis.

   (A) 2 units   (B) 5 units
   (C) 3 units   (D) None

3.   The point (3, 2) is at a distance of _____ units from Y-axis.

   (A) 2 units   (B) 3 units
   (C) 5 units   (D) none

4. The point (-3, 2) belongs to Quadrant _____

(A) Q_1 (B) Q_2 (C) Q_3 (D) Q_4

5. The point (2, -3) belongs to Quadrant _____

(A) Q_1 (B) Q_2 (C) Q_3 (D) Q_4

6. The point (3, 2) belongs to Quadrant _____

(A) Q_1 (B) Q_2 (C) Q_3 (D) Q_4

7. The point (-2, -3) belongs to Quadrant

(A) Q_1 (B) Q_2 (C) Q_3 (D) Q_4

8. The point (-2, 0) lies on

(A) +ve X-axis   (B) +ve Y-axis
(C) -ve X-axis   (D) -ve Y-axis

9. The point (0, -2) lies on

(A) +ve X-axis   (B) +ve Y-axis
(C) -ve X-axis   (D) -ve Y-axis

10. The point (3, 0) lies on

(A) +ve X-axis   (B) +ve Y-axis
(C) -ve X-axis   (D) -ve Y-axis

11. The point (0, 3) lies on

(A) +ve X-axis   (B) +ve Y-axis
(C) -ve X-axis   (D) -ve Y-axis

Match the following

12. $x>0, y>0$ [   ]   (A) Q_2

13. $x<0, y>0$ [   ]   (B) Q_1

14. $x<0, y<0$ [   ]   (C) -ve X-axis

15. $x>0, y<0$ [   ]   (D) Q_3

16. $x>0, y=0$ [   ]   (E) +ve X-axis

17. $x<0, y=0$ [   ]   (F) +ve Y-axis

18. $x=0, y<0$ [   ]   (G) Q_4

19. $x=0, y>0$ [   ]   (H) -ve Y-axis

20. The distance of the point (2, 0) from the origin is _____

(A) 1 unit

(B) 2 units

(C) 4 units

(D) None of these

Answers

1. A	2. C	3. B	4. B	5. D	6. A	7. C	8. C	9. D	10. A
11. B	12. B	13. A	14. D	15. G	16. E	17. C	18. H	19. F	20. B

✦ ✦ ✦

Chapter 4

Linear Equations in two variables

4

Synopsis

1. An equation of the form $ax + by + c = 0$, where a, b and c are real numbers, such that 'a' and 'b' are not both zero, is called a linear equation in two variables.

2. A linear equation in two variables has infinitely many solutions.

3. The graph of every linear equation in two variables is a straight line.

4. $x = 0$ is the equation of y-axis.

5. $y = 0$ is the equation of x-axis.

6. The graph of $x = a$ is a straight line parallel to the y-axis.

7. The graph of $y = a$ is a straight line parallel to the x-axis.

8. An equation of the type $y = mx$ represents a line passing through the origin.

9. Every point on the graph of a linear equation in two variables is a solution of the linear equation. Moreover, every solution of the linear equation is a point on the graph of the linear equation.

Multiple Choice Questions

1. $y = 4x - 3$ has _____

    (A) a unique solution

    (B) only two solutions

    (C) infinitely many solutions

    (D) cannot be determined

2. The solution of the equation $x - 3y = 2$ is _____

    (A) (2, 3)　　　　(B) (−3, 2)

    (C) (2, −3)　　　 (D) (5, 1)

3. If $x = -2$ and $y = 3$ is the solution of the equation $3x - 5y = k$, then the value of 'k' is _____

    (A) −21　　　　 (B) −9

    (C) −18　　　　 (D) 19

4. An equation of the form $ax + by + c = 0$, where a, b are non-zero numbers represents _____

    (A) a straight line

    (B) a circle

    (C) a triangle

    (D) a quadrilateral

5. The equation of the line parallel to y-axis is _____

    (A) $y = -2$　　　(B) $y = 0$

    (C) $y = 5$　　　 (D) $x = -4$

6. The equation of x-axis is _____

(A) x = 0

(B) x = –2

(C) y = 0

(D) none of these

7. The line x + 1 = 0 is _____

(A) parallel to y-axis

(B) parallel to x-axis

(C) passing through the origin

(D) none of these

8. The equation of the line passing through the origin is _____

(A) y = 2   (B) x = 4

(C) y = 5x   (D) none of these

9. The line y –2=0 is _____

(A) parallel to x-axis

(B) parallel to y-axis

(C) passing through the origin

(D) none of these

10. Which of the following graph represents x + y = 7 ?

(B)
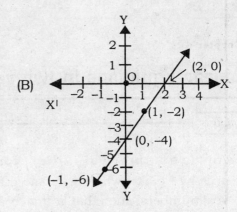

(C)
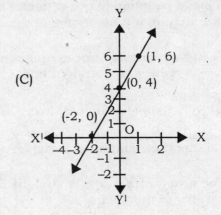

(A)
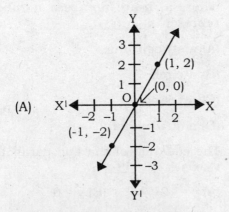

(D)
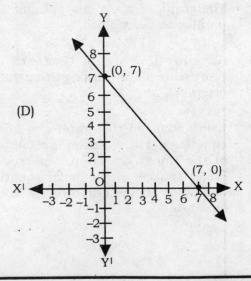

Answers

1. C	2. D	3. A	4. A	5. D	6. C	7. A	8. C	9. A	10. D

Explanatory Answers

1. (C) A linear equation in two variables has infinitely many solutions.

2. (D) $x - 3y = 2$

putting $x = 5$ and $y = 1$

$5 - 3(1) = 2$

$\Rightarrow 2 = 2$

Hence $(5, 1)$ is the solution of $x - 3y = 2$

3. (A) Given that,

$x = -2$ and $y = 3$ is the solution of $3x - 5y = k$

So,

$k = 3(-2) - 5(3)$

$= -6 - 15$

$= -21$

4. (A) $ax + by + c = 0$ represents a straight line

5. (D) The equation of the line parallel to y–axis is $x = a$.

Hence $x = -4$ is the required equation.

6. (C) The equation of x–axis is $y = 0$

7. (A) $x + 1 = 0$

$\Rightarrow x = -1$

It represents a line parallel to y-axis.

8. (C) The equation of the line passing through the origin is $y = mx$.

Hence $y = 5x$ is the required equation.

9. (A) $y - 2 = 0$

$\Rightarrow y = 2$

It represents a line parallel to x-axis.

10. (D) The graph given in option (D) represents $x + y = 7$.

✦ ✦ ✦

Chapter 5

Lines and Angles

5

Synopsis

Angle is a figure formed by two rays with the same end point. The common end point is called vertex and the two rays are called arms of the angle.

Measure of right angle is 90°

Straight angle is 180°

Acute angle > 0° and < 90°

Obtuse angle > 90° and < 180°

Reflex angle > 180° and < 360°

When two lines or line segments meet each other by forming a right angle then they are said to be perpendicular to each other.

Symbol '⊥' is used to denote the perpendicularity of two lines and is read as 'perpendicular to'.

Pair of angles :

Adjacent angles : Two angles with a common vertex and a common arm are called adjacent angles.

Linear Pair : Adjacent angles whose sum is 180° is called a linear pair.

Two angles whose sum is 90° are called complementary angles

Two angles whose sum is 180° are called supplementary angles.

Complementary angles need not be adjacent.

All linear pairs are supplementary angles where as all supplementary angles are not linear pairs.

Two angles opposite to each other are called vertically opposite angles.

Vertically opposite angles are equal.

Two lines or line segments which do not intersect and whose perpendicular distance remains constant are called parallel lines.

Symbol for parallel is '||' and is read as 'parallel to'.

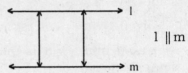

$$l \parallel m$$

Transversal is a line or line segment which intersects two or more straight lines or line segments at different points.

Angles made by a transversal :

Eight angles are made by a transversal when it intersects a pair of lines.

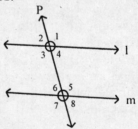

P is the transversal.

Of these 8 angles made

∠1 and ∠5

∠2 and ∠6

∠3 and ∠7

∠4 and ∠8 are called corresponding angles.

$\angle 1$ and $\angle 3$ $\angle 6$ and $\angle 8$
$\angle 2$ and $\angle 4$ $\angle 5$ and $\angle 7$ are
called vertically opposite angles.

$\angle 2$ and $\angle 8$ $\angle 3$ and $\angle 5$
$\angle 1$ and $\angle 7$ $\angle 4$ and $\angle 6$ are
called alternate angles.

All corresponding, vertically opposite and alternate angles are equal.
$\angle 4 + \angle 5 = 180°$
$\angle 3 + \angle 6 = 180°$
$\angle 3$ and $\angle 6$ & $\angle 4$ and $\angle 5$ are interior angles which lie on the same side of transversal.
Corresponding angles lie on the same side of the transversal.
Alternate angles lie on the opposite side of the transversal.
A plane figure bounded by three line segments which are formed by joining three noncollinear points is called triangle.
Three sides, three angles and three vertices are called elements of a triangle.
Points which lie inside the triangle are said to be in interior region.
Points which lie on the boundary of a triangle are said to be on region.
The interior and boundary of a triangle is called triangular region.

Classification of triangles :

A triangle with all three acute angles is called an acute angled triangle.
A triangle with one right and two acute angles is called a right angled triangle.
A triangle with one obtuse angle and two acute angles is called an obtuse angled triangle.
A triangle with three equal sides is called an equilateral triangle.
A triangle with two equal sides is called an isosceles triangle.

A triangle with three unequal sides is called scalene triangle.

Properties of a triangle :

Angle sum Property : Sum of all the three interior angles of a triangle is 180°.

Inequality Property : Sum of any two sides of a triangle is always greater than the third side.

When any side of a triangle is extended beyond the vertex it forms an exterior angle with the other side at the same vertex.

An exterior angle is equal to the sum of two interior opposite angles.

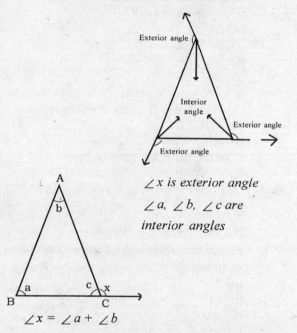

$\angle x$ is exterior angle
$\angle a$, $\angle b$, $\angle c$ are interior angles

$\angle x = \angle a + \angle b$

Exterior angle = sum of two interior opposite angles
Every triangle has six exterior angles and three interior angles.
To get exterior angles the sides of the triangle are to be produced in one direction only either in clockwise or in anticlockwise.

Multiple Choice Questions

1. If B lies between A and C, AC = 15 cm and BC = 9 cm then AB^2 is
   (A) 306   (B) 144
   (C) 36   (D) 24

2. The difference of two complimentary angles is 40^0. Then the angles are
   (A) $65^0, 25^0$ (B) $70^0, 20^0$
   (C) $70^0, 30^0$ (D) $60^0, 30^0$

3. The measure of an angle is four times the measure of its supplementary angle. Then the angles are
   (A) $36^0, 144^0$ (B) $40^0, 160^0$
   (C) $18^0, 72^0$ (D) $50^0, 200^0$

4. Which of the following pair is a complementary?
   (A) $37^0, 43^0$
   (B) $28^0, 52^0$
   (C) $55^0, 35^0$
   (D) $34^0, 66^0$

5. If two supplementary angles are in the ratio 4 : 5 then the angles are
   (A) $80^0, 100^0$
   (B) $85^0, 95^0$
   (C) $40^0, 50^0$
   (D) $60^0, 120^0$

6. Complement of 25^0 is
   (A) 75^0 (B) 65^0
   (C) 85^0 (D) 55

7. From the adjoining figure the value of x^0 is
   (A) 15^0
   (B) 60^0
   (C) 30^0
   (D) none of these

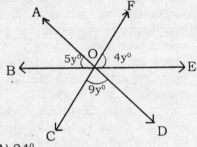

8. From the adjoining figure x = 30^0. The value of y^0 is
   (A) 25^0
   (B) 24^0
   (C) 36^0
   (D) 45^0

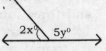

9. From the adjoining figure ∠POR, ∠QOR from a linear pair and a – b = 40^0. Then a, b are
   (A) $110, 70^0$
   (B) $70, 100^0$
   (C) $80, 120^0$
   (D) $120, 80^0$

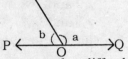

10. Two supplementary angles differ by 34^0. Then the angles are
    (A) $73^0, 107^0$ (B) $107^0, 73^0$
    (C) $120^0, 60^0$ (D) $72^0, 108^0$

11. The supplement of an angle is one third of itself. Then the angle of its supplement are
    (A) $135^0, 45^0$ (B) $60^0, 180^0$
    (C) $120^0, 360^0$ (D) $60^0, 120^0$

12. From the adjoining figure the value of y is

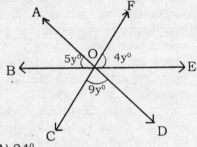

(A) 24^0
(B) 22^0
(C) 20^0
(D) 10^0

13. The difference of two complementary angles is 40^0. Then the angles are
    (A) $50^0, 40^0$ (B) $65^0, 25^0$
    (C) $70^0, 30^0$ (D) $40^0, 50^0$

14. From the adjoining figure the value of x is
    (A) 95^0
    (B) 90^0
    (C) 85^0
    (D) 80^0

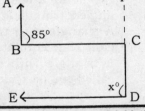

15. The sum of the two angles in a triangle is 95^0 and their difference is 25^0. Then the angles of a triangle is

(A) $75^0, 50^0, 55^0$

(B) $85^0, 65^0, 30^0$

(C) $50^0, 45^0, 85^0$

(D) $60^0, 35^0, 85^0$

16. The sides BC, CA and AB of $\triangle ABC$ are produced in order to form exterior angles $\angle ACD, \angle BAE$ and $\angle CBF$ then $\angle ACD + \angle BAE + \angle CBF$ is

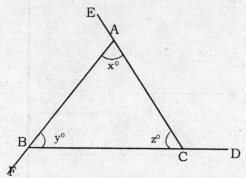

(A) 180^0

(B) 270^0

(C) 360^0

(D) 540^0

17. From the adjoining figure the value of x is

(A) 60^0

(B) 75^0

(C) 90^0

(D) 120^0

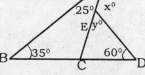

18. In the given figure the value of x^0 is

(A) 60^0

(B) 80^0

(C) 80^0

(D) 90^0

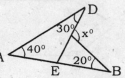

19. In the figure, the bisectors of B and C meet at 0. Then $\angle BOC$ is

(A) $90 + \dfrac{1}{2} \angle A$

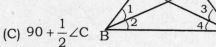

(B) $90 + \dfrac{1}{2} \angle B$

(C) $90 + \dfrac{1}{2} \angle C$

(D) none of these

20. In the adjoining figure BO, CO are angle bisectors of external angles of $\triangle ABC$. Then $\angle BOC$ is

(A) $90^0 - \dfrac{1}{2} \angle A$

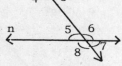

(B) $90^0 + \dfrac{1}{2} \angle A$

(C) $180^0 - \dfrac{1}{2} \angle A$

(D) $180^0 + \dfrac{1}{2} \angle A$

21. From the adjoining figure, if $\angle 2 = 55^0$ and $\angle 5 = 60^0$ then the lines m and n are

(A) parallel

(B) not parallel

(C) cannot say

(D) none of these

22. In the adjoining figure, the value of $\angle A + \angle B + \angle C + \angle D + \angle E + \angle F$ is

(A) 360^0

(B) 270^0

(C) 540^0

(D) 180^0

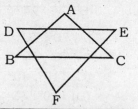

23. In a $\triangle PQR$ the angle bisectors of the $\angle PQR$, $\angle PRQ$ meet at O^0. If $\angle QPR = 80^0$ then $\angle QOR$ is

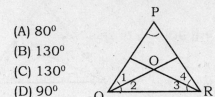

(A) 80^0
(B) 130^0
(C) 130^0
(D) 90^0

24. In the adjoining figure $AM \perp BC$ and AN is the bisector of $\angle BAC$. If $\angle B = 70^0$ and $\angle C = 35^0$ then $\angle MAN$ is

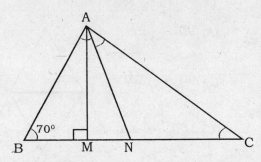

(A) 17.5^0
(B) 27.5^0
(C) 37.5^0
(D) 47.5^0

25. An exterior angle of a triangle is 110^0 and one of the interior of opposite angles is 40^0. Then the other two angles of a triangle are

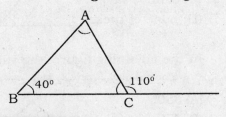

(A) $70^0, 70^0$
(B) $70^0, 40^0$
(C) $110^0, 40^0$
(D) $110^0, 75^0$

26. From the adjoining figure $AB \parallel DE$ Then the value of x^0 is

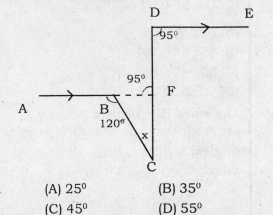

(A) 25^0 (B) 35^0
(C) 45^0 (D) 55^0

27. In the figure find x if $AB \parallel CD$.

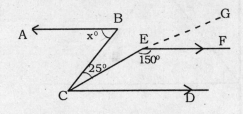

(A) 45^0 (B) 55^0
(C) 60^0 (D) 70^0

28. The value of internal and the external bisectors of an angle is

(A) 90^0
(B) 180^0
(C) 270^0
(D) none

29. In the adjoining figure the value of x is

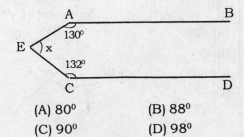

(A) 80^0 (B) 88^0
(C) 90^0 (D) 98^0

30. In the given figure BO and CO are the bisectors of the exterior angles of B and C. Then $\angle BOC$ is

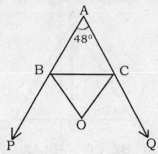

(A) 46^0 (B) 56^0

(C) 66^0 (D) 76^0

31. In the figure AB = AC, CH = CB and HK ∥ BC. If the exterior angle CAX is 140^0 then the angle HCK is

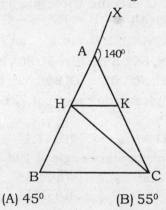

(A) 45^0 (B) 55^0

(C) 50^0 (D) 40^0

32. In a $\triangle$ ABC if $\angle A = 90^0$ and AB = AC, then $\angle B$ and $\angle C$ are

(A) 30^0, 60^0

(B) 45^0, 45^0

(C) 60^0, 30^0

(D) 75^0, 15^0

33. The angles ABC and BDC are right angles. If AD = 9 cm and DC = 16 cm and AB = 15 cm then the length of BD is

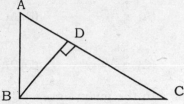

(A) 12 cm   (B) 16 cm

(C) 15 cm   (D) 25 cm

34. In a right angled triangle, the square of the hypotenuse is equal to twice the product of the other two sides. One of the acute angles of the triangle is

(A) 60^0 (B) 45^0

(C) 30^0 (D) 75^0

35. In the given figure PQ∥RS

$\angle PAB = 70^0$, $\angle ACS = 110^0$ then

$\angle BAC$ is

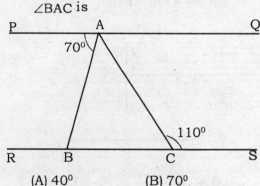

(A) 40^0 (B) 70^0

(C) 110^0 (D) 30^0

36. In the adjoining figure AB∥CD, $\angle 1 : \angle 2 = 3 : 2$. Then $\angle 6$ is

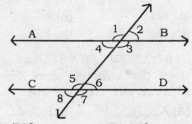

(A) 72^0 (B) 36^0

(C) 108^0 (D) 144^0

37. If D is a mid point of the hypotenuse AC of a right triangle ABC then BD is equal to

(A) $\frac{1}{2}$AC   (B) AC

(C) $\frac{3}{2}$AC   (D) 2AC

38. In the given figure PQ > PR and QS, RS are the bisectors of $\angle Q$ and $\angle R$ then

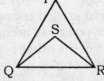

(A) SQ > SR   (B) SQ = SR

(C) SQ < SR   (D) none

39. In the figure, AD is the bisector of $\angle A$ of $\triangle ABC$ then

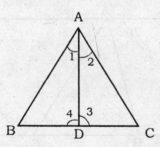

(A) AB > BD   (B) AB = BD

(C) AB < BD   (D) none

40. In $\triangle ABC$ if $\angle B = \angle C = 45^0$, which of the following is the longest side?

(A) AB   (B) AC

(C) BC   (D) None

41. In a $\triangle ABC$ if $\angle A = 45^0$ and $\angle B = 70^0$ then the shortest and the largest sides of the triangle are

(A) AB, BC   (B) BC, AC

(C) AB, AC   (D) none

42. In $\triangle ABC$ $\angle B = 45^0$, $\angle C = 65^0$, and the bisector of $\angle BAC$ meets BC at P. Then the ascending order of sides is

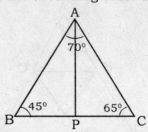

(A) AP, BP, CP   (B) AP, CP, BP

(C) BP, AP, CP   (D) CP, BP, AP

43. In a $\triangle ABC$ if $2\angle A = 3\angle B = 6\angle C$ then $\angle A, \angle B, \angle C$ are

(A) $30^0, 60^0, 90^0$ (B) $90^0, 60^0, 30^0$

(C) $30^0, 90^0, 60^0$ (D) none of these

44. A, B, C are the three angles of a triangle. If $A - B = 15^0$, $B - C = 30^0$ then $\angle A, \angle B, \angle C$ are

(A) $80^0, 65^0, 35^0$ (B) $65^0, 80^0, 35^0$

(C) $35^0, 80^0, 65^0$ (D) $80^0, 35^0, 65^0$

45. Complementary angle of $72\frac{1}{2}^\circ$ is

(A) 17° (B) $18\frac{1}{2}^\circ$

(C) $21\frac{1}{2}^\circ$ (D) $17\frac{1}{2}^\circ$

46. Supplementary angle of 108.5° is

(A) 70.5° (B) 71.5°

(C) 71° (D) 72.5°

47. An angle which measures 90° is called

(A) straight   (B) acute

(C) right   (D) left

48. Measure of an obtuse angle is

(A) > 0°, < 90°   (B) > 90°, < 180°

(C) > 0°, < 270°   (D) > 0°, < 180°

49. An angle which is more than 180° and less than 360° is called

(A) obtuse angle   (B) right angle

(C) reflex angle   (D) complete angle

50. An angle which is equal to 360° is called

(A) right angle
(B) complete angle
(C) acute angle
(D) obtuse angle

51. In the given measure, measure of ∠b and ∠x are

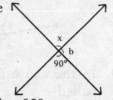

(A) ∠x = 90° ∠b = 60°
(B) ∠x = 90° ∠b = 30°
(C) ∠x = 90° ∠b = 90°
(D) ∠x = 90° ∠b = 180°

52. When two lines meet at a point forming right angles they are said to be _____ to each other.

(A) parallel   (B) perpendicular
(C) adjacent   (D) none

53. At 6 o'clock the angle formed between the hands of a clock is

(A) straight angle (B) right angle
(C) acute angle   (D) obtuse angle

54. Type of angle between the hands of a clock when the time is 5:20 is

(A) right angle
(B) straight angle
(C) obtuse angle
(D) acute angle

55. At 3 o'clock, the angle formed between the hands of a clock is

(A) reflex angle
(B) right angle
(C) straight angle
(D) acute angle

56. At 9 o'clock, the angle formed between the hands of a clock is

(A) complete angle(B) reflex angle
(C) zero angle   (D) none

57. An angle which measures 180° is called a

(A) straight angle
(B) obtuse angle
(C) right angle
(D) complete angle

58. Two adjacent angles whose sum is 180° is called

(A) complementary angles
(B) linear pair
(C) vertically opposite angles
(D) none

59. The measure of angle y in the given figure is _____

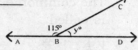

(A) ∠y = 65°   (B) ∠y = 85°
(C) ∠y = 75°   (D) ∠y = 80°

60. If one of the linear pair is acute then the measure of the other angle is

(A) right   (B) obtuse
(C) acute   (D) none

61. A pair of angles with a common vertex and common arm are called

(A) adjacent angles
(B) complementary
(C) supplementary
(D) none

62. Supplement angle of

(A) 122.7°   (B) 131.7°
(C) 132.7°   (D) 132.4°

63. Complement angle of

(A) 77.4°   (B) 67.3°
(C) 76.3°   (D) 77.3°

64. All linear pairs are

(A) supplementary
(B) vertically opposite
(C) right angles
(D) none

65. Supplementary and complementary angles need not be

(A) equal to 180°, 90°
(B) adjacent
(C) angles
(D) none

66. The two rays of an angle are called

(A) lines of the angle
(B) two sides of the angle
(C) two parts of the angle
(D) none

67. The common end point of an angle is called

(A) vertex   (B) zero
(C) end point   (D) none

68. A rotating ray after making a complete rotation coincides with its initial position. The angle formed is

(A) right angle
(B) straight angle
(C) reflex angle
(D) complete angle

69. The maximum number of letters that can be used to represent an angle are

(A) 5   (B) 2
(C) 3   (D) 1

70. Line l is parallel to line m. Symbolically, above statement is written as

(A) $l \perp m$ (B) $l \parallel m$
(C) $l = m$ (D) none

71. If two lines are parallel then the perpendicular distance between them remains

(A) decreasing   (B) increasing
(C) constant   (D) none

72. A line which intersects two or more lines at different points is

(A) perpendicular (B) transversal
(C) parallel   (D) none

73. Number of angles formed by a transversal with a pair of lines

(A) 6   (B) 4
(C) 8   (D) 3

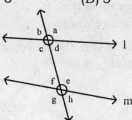

74. In the above figure ∠c and ∠e are called

(A) corresponding
(B) alternate
(C) vertically opposite
(D) none

75. In the above figure ∠a and ∠e are called

(A) corresponding
(B) vertically opposite
(C) alternate
(D) none

76. In the above figure ∠e and ∠g are called

(A) corresponding
(B) vertically opposite
(C) alternate
(D) none

77. In the above figure ∠c + ∠f =

(A) 90°   (B) 120° (C) 180° (D) 160°

78. In the above figure ∠a + ∠b =

(A) 180°   (B) 120° (C) 140° (D) none

79. In the figure ∠a = 115°. Then ∠g =

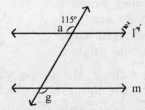

(A) 65°   (B) 75°

(C) 115°   (D) 120°

80. In the figure $\angle b = 70°$. Then $\angle c =$

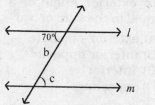

(A) 70°

(B) 110°

(C) 180°

(D) none

81. In the figure $\angle a = 50°$. Then $\angle d =$

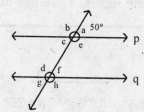

(A) 120° (B) 130° (C) 180° (D) 60°

82. If two lines l and m are perpendicular to each other then they are symbolically written as

(A) $l \parallel m$

(B) $l \perp m$

(C) $l = m$

(D) lm

83. In the given figure $\angle 1 = \angle 5$ because they are

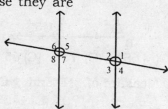

(A) corresponding

(B) alternate

(C) vertically opposite

(D) none

84. Number of pairs of corresponding angles formed when a transversal intersects a pair of line is

(A) 2 pair

(B) 4 pairs

(C) 3 pairs

(D) 8 pairs

85. Number of pairs of alternate angles formed when a transversal intersects a pair of lines is

(A) 2 pair

(B) 4 pairs

(C) 3 pairs

(D) 8 pairs

86. Sum of two interior angles lying on the same side of transversal is _____.

(A) complementary

(B) supplementary

(C) acute angles

(D) right angles

87. In the given figure $\angle 1 = 60°$. Then $\angle 8$ is equal to

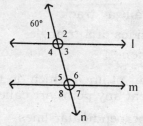

(A) 60° (B) 120° (C) 180° (D) 70°

88. In the given figure, the number of sets of parallel lines are

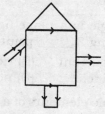

(A) 8 sets

(B) 6 sets

(C) 4 sets

(D) 2 sets

89. Instruments used to draw a pair of parallel lines are

(A) protractor and scale

(B) compass and scale

(C) set square and scale

(D) none

90. If $l \parallel m$ and $m \parallel n$ then

(A) $l \parallel p$

(B) $l \parallel q$

(C) $m \parallel n$

(D) $l \parallel n$

91. p||q, r||s then p is _____
    (A) p||s   (B) p||r
    (C) not parallel to s   (D) none

92. In the figure shown line p is called

    (A) parallel   (B) transversal
    (C) perpendicular (D) none

93. Example for a pair of parallel lines
    (A) corners of a room
    (B) railway track
    (C) sides of a triangle
    (D) none

94. A pair of lines which do not intersect at any point are called
    (A) perpendicular lines
    (B) parallel lines
    (C) concurrent lines
    (D) none

95. A triangle is a plane figure formed by joining 3 _____ points.
    (A) concurrent   (B) noncollinear
    (C) collinear   (D) none

96. The basic elements of a triangle are
    (A) 3 vertices   (B) 3 sides
    (C) 3 angles   (D) all the above

97. The interior and boundary of a triangle is called
    (A) exterior
    (B) interior
    (C) triangular region
    (D) plane

98. Sum of all the three interior angles of a triangle is equal to
    (A) 360° (B) 120° (C) 180° (D) 90°

99. An exterior angle of a triangle is equal to the sum of two _____ angles.
    (A) exterior opposite
    (B) interior opposite
    (C) interior
    (D) opposite

100. In a right angled triangle if an angle measures 35° then the measure of other angle is
    (A) 65° (B) 55°   (C) 45° (D) 30°

101. In the figure, measure of ∠x is

    (A) 65°   (B) 85°   (C) 75° (D) 55°

102. In the following, the set of measures which can form a triangle
    (A) 70°, 90°, 25°   (B) 65°, 85°, 40°
    (C) 65°, 85°, 30°   (D) 45°, 45°, 80°

103. Measure of ∠y is

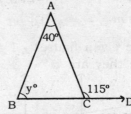

    (A) 65°   (B) 75°   (C) 65°   (D) 55°

104. Measure of ∠B and ∠C are

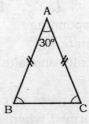

    (A) 75°, 85°
    (B) 75°, 75°
    (C) 55°, 55°
    (D) 65°, 65°

105. Measure of x° in the figure is

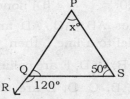

(A) 60° (B) 70° (C) 80° (D) 55°

106. Sum of any two sides of a triangle is always _____ third side in a triangle.

(A) less than   (B) equal to
(C) greater than (D) none

107. Measure of angle ∠ACD in the given figure is

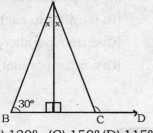

(A) 130° (B) 120° (C) 150° (D) 115°

108. Measure of y° in the given figure is

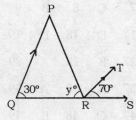

(A) 70°   (B) 75°   (C) 80° (D) 85°

109. Measure of ∠NOP in the given figure is

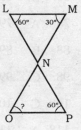

(A) 90°   (B) 30°   (C) 120° (D) 80°

110. The interior opposite angles of the exterior angle ∠ACD are

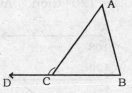

(A) ∠B, ∠C   (B) ∠A, ∠C
(C) ∠A, ∠B   (D) ∠B, ∠E

111. Number of exterior angles formed in a triangle

(A) 5   (B) 3   (C) 6   (D) 8

112. ∠XYW is called _____ angle of the triangle.

(A) interior angle
(B) exterior angle
(C) boundary angle
(D) none

113. A triangle divides the plane into _____ parts.

(A) 4   (B) 2   (C) 3   (D) 6

114. Can 90°, 90° and 20° form a triangle?

(A) Yes   (B) Sometimes
(C) No   (D) None

115. Can 6 cm, 5 cm and 3 cm form a triangle?

(A) Yes   (B) No
(C) Sometimes   (D) None

116. In the adjoining figure, it is given that ∠A = 60°, CE∥BA and ∠ECD = 65° then ∠ACB = _____ .

(A) 60°
(B) 55°
(C) 70°
(D) 90°

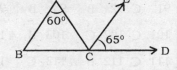

117. In the adjoining figure, it is given that AB||CD. ∠BAO = 108° and ∠OCD = 120° then ∠AOC = ____

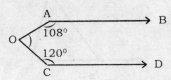

(A) 120°   (B) 72°

(C) 132°   (D) 150°

118. In the adjoining figure, it is given that l||m, t is a transversal. Then the value of x is

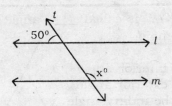

(A) 130°   (B) 50°

(C) 120°   (D) none

119. If lines AB, AC, AD and AE are parallel to a line l, then _____ .

(A) A, B, C, D, E are collinear points

(B) A, B, C, D, E are noncollinear points

(C) AB & AC are parallel and AD & AE are perpendicular

(D) none of these

120. If two lines are perpendicular to the third line, then those two lines are

(A) perpendicular to each other

(B) parallel to each other

(C) either parallel or perpendicular

(D) neither parallel nor perpendicular

Answers

1. C	2. A	3. A	4. C	5. A	6. B	7. C	8. B	9. A	10. B
11. A	12. D	13. B	14. A	15. D	16. C	17. D	18. D	19. A	20. A
21. B	22. A	23. C	24. A	25. A	26. B	27. B	28. A	29. D	30. C
31. D	32. B	33. A	34. B	35. A	36. A	37. A	38. A	39. A	40. C
41. B	42. D	43. B	44. A	45. D	46. B	47. C	48. B	49. C	50. B
51. C	52. B	53. A	54. D	55. B	56. B	57. A	58. B	59. A	60. B
61. A	62. C	63. D	64. A	65. B	66. B	67. A	68. D	69. C	70. B
71. C	72. B	73. C	74. B	75. A	76. B	77. C	78. A	79. C	80. A
81. B	82. B	83. A	84. B	85. A	86. B	87. B	88. B	89. C	90. D
91. C	92. B	93. B	94. B	95. B	96. D	97. C	98. C	99. B	100. B
101. C	102. C	103. B	104. B	105. B	106. C	107. C	108. C	109. B	110. C
111. C	112. B	113. C	114. C	115. A	116. B	117. C	118. A	119. A	120. B

Explanatory Answers

1. (C) $AB = AC - BC$
   $= 15 - 9$
   $AB = 6 \Rightarrow AB^2 = 36.$

2. (A) Let the angles be x, y
   Since x, y are complementary
   $x + y = 90$
   Given that their difference is
   $x - y = 40^0.$

   $x + y = 90$
   $x - y = 40$
   _____
   $2x = 130$

   $\therefore x = 65^0, y = 25.$

3. (A) Let the one angle be 'x' then the other will be 4x.
   Given that $x + 4x = 180$
   $\therefore 5x = 180$
   $x = 36^0, 4x = 4 \times 36 = 144^0.$

5. (A) One angle is $\frac{4}{9} \times 180 = 80^0$

   Second angle is $\frac{5}{9} \times 180 = 100^0.$

6. (B) Complement of 25^0 is
   $90^0 - 25^0 = 65^0.$

7. (C) Sum of $x^0, 2x^0, 3x^0$ is $180^0.$
   $x + 2x + 3x = 180^0.$
   $\therefore 6x^0 = 180^0.$
   $x = 30^0.$

8. (B) $2x + 5y = 180^0.$
   $2(30^0) + 5y = 180^0.$
   $5y = 120^0$
   $y = 24^0.$

9. (A) $b + a = 180^0$
   $a - b = 40^0$
   $a = 110^0, b = 70^0.$

10. (B) $x + y = 180^0 .....(1)$
    $x - y = 34^0 ......(2)$
    $\Rightarrow x = 107^0, y = 73^0.$

11. (A) $x + \dfrac{x}{3} = 180 \Rightarrow \dfrac{4x}{3} = 180$

    $x = 135^0$

    $\dfrac{x}{3} = 45^0.$

12. (D) From the figure
    $\angle BOC = \angle EOF$
    (vertically opposite angles)
    $\angle BOC = \angle EOF = 4y^0$
    $5y + 4y + 9y = 180^0$
    $y = 10^0.$

13. (B) Let the complementary angles be x, y.
    $\therefore x + y = 90^0 ....(1)$
    Given that their difference is $40^0.$
    $\therefore x - y = 40^0 ....(2)$
    By solving (1) & (2) we get
    $x = 65^0, y = 25^0.$

14. (A) Extending the line DC up to some point P
    then $\angle BCP = \angle EDC = x^0$
    $\angle ABC + \angle BCP = 180^0$
    $85^0 + \angle BCP = 180^0$
    $\angle BCP = 95^0$
    $\angle BCP = \angle ECD = 95^0.$
    (Corresponding angles)

15. (D) $x + y + z = 180^0.$
    Given that $x + y = 95,$
    $x - y = 25 \Rightarrow x = 60^0, y = 35^0$
    $60^0 + 35^0 + z = 180^0, z = 85^0.$

16. (C) $180 - x^0 + 180 - y^0 + 180 - z^0$
    $= 360^0$

17. (D) $\angle ECD + \angle CDE = \angle AED$
    $60 + 60 = \angle AED$
    $\therefore \angle AED = 120^0.$

18. (D) From $\triangle ADE$, $\angle CEB = 70^0$

From $\triangle CEB$, $\angle ECB = 90^0$

$\angle ECB + \angle DCB = 180^0$

$90^0 + \angle DCB = 180^0$

$\Rightarrow \angle DCB = 90^0 \therefore x = 90^0$.

19. (A) $\angle 2 + \angle BOC + \angle 4 = 180^0$

$\Rightarrow 2\angle 2 + 2\angle BOC + 2\angle 4 = 360^0$

$\angle BOC = 90 + \dfrac{A}{2}$

20. (A) $\angle A + \angle B = \angle BCQ$

$\angle A + \angle C = \angle CBP$

$\angle A + \angle B + \angle A + \angle C = \angle BCQ + \angle CBP$

$\angle A + 180^0 = \angle 1 + \angle 2 + \angle 3 + \angle 4$

$2\angle 1 + 2\angle 4 = A + 180^0$

$\angle 1 + \angle 4 = \dfrac{A}{2} + 90^0$

$180^0 - \angle BOC = \dfrac{A}{2} + 90^0$

$\therefore \angle BOC = 90^0 - \dfrac{A}{2}$

21. (B) $\angle 2 = 55^0 \Rightarrow \angle 4 = 55^0$

$\angle 4 + \angle 5 = 55^0 + 60^0$

$= 115^0 \Rightarrow$ m, n are not parallel.

22. (A) From the $\triangle ABC$ and $\triangle DEF$

$\angle A + \angle B + \angle C = 180^0$,

$\angle D + \angle E + \angle F = 180^0$.

$\therefore \angle A + \angle B + \angle C + \angle D +$

$\angle E + \angle F = 360^0$.

23. (C) $\angle 1 = \angle 2$, $\angle 3 = \angle 4$

In $\triangle PQR$,

$80^0 + \angle Q + \angle R = 180^0$

$\Rightarrow \angle Q + \angle R = 100^0$

$\angle 2 + \angle 4 = 50^0$

In $\triangle QOR$

$50^0 + \angle QOR = 180^0$

$\angle QOR = 180^0 - 50^0 = 130^0$.

24. (A) $\angle NAB = \angle CAN = \dfrac{1}{2}\angle A$

In $\triangle ABC$

$\Rightarrow \angle A = 75^0 \therefore \dfrac{1}{2}\angle A = 37.5^0$

From $\triangle ABN$, $\angle BAM = 20^0$

$\angle MAN = \angle BAN - \angle BAM$

$\Rightarrow \angle MAN = 37.5^0 - 20^0 = 17.5^0$.

25. (A) $40 + x = 110^0 \Rightarrow x = 70^0$

$\therefore$ angles are 70^0, 70^0.

26. (B) $\triangle BFC$ is

$60^0 + 85 + x = 180^0$

$x = 35^0$.

27. (B) $\angle ABC = \angle BCD \Rightarrow x = \angle BCD$

$\angle BCD = \angle BCE + \angle ECD$

$x = 25^0 + \angle ECD$

$\therefore \angle ECD = \angle GEF = 30^0$

$\therefore \angle ABC = 25 + 30 = 55^0$.

28. (A) Internal and external bisectors

of an angle Q are $\dfrac{\theta}{2}$, $\dfrac{180-\theta}{2}$

Their sum is 90^0

29. (D) Join BD

$\angle A + \angle B + \angle D + \angle C + \angle E = 540^0$

$130^0 + 90^0 + 90^0 + 132^0 + x^0 = 540^0$

$\therefore = 98^0$

30. (C) $\angle B + \angle C = 136^0 ....(1)$

$\angle A + \angle B = \angle BCQ$; $\angle A + \angle C = \angle CBP$

$$\frac{1}{2}(\angle A + \angle B) + \frac{1}{2}(\angle A + \angle C)$$

$$= \frac{1}{2}\angle BCQ + \frac{1}{2}\angle CBP$$

$$\frac{1}{2}(\angle A + \angle A + \angle B + \angle C) =$$

$$\angle OBC + \angle OCB$$

$$= \frac{1}{2}(48^0 + 180^0) = \angle OBC + \angle OCB$$

$$114^0 = = \angle OBC + \angle OCB$$

From $\triangle BOC$

$$\angle OBC + \angle OCB + \angle BOC = 180^0$$

$$\angle BOC = 180^0 - 114^0 = 66^0.$$

31. (D) $AB = AC \Rightarrow \angle C = \angle B$

$$\angle B + \angle C = 140^0$$

$$CB = CH \Rightarrow \angle BHC = \angle HBC = 70^0$$

$$\angle AHK = \angle ABC = 70^0$$

$$\angle BHK = 110^0, \angle CHK = \angle HCK = 40^0.$$

32. (B) In a $\triangle ABC$, $\angle A = 90^0$

$$AB = AC \Rightarrow \angle C = \angle B$$

$$90 + \angle B + \angle B = 180^0 \Rightarrow \angle B = 45^0$$

$$\therefore \angle C = 45^0.$$

33. (A) $AC = AD + DC = 25$ cm
$AC^2 = AB^2 + BC^2$
$AC^2 = AB^2 + BD^2 + CD^2$
$625 = 15^2 + BD^2 + 16^2$
$= 625 - (225 + 256)$
$BD = 12$ cm.

34. (B) The above inequality is possible only in isosceles right angled triangle. Acute angles will be 45^0, 45^0.

35. (A) $PQ||RS$ $\angle PAB = \angle ABC$
(alternate angles)

$$\therefore \angle PAB = \angle ABC = 70^0$$

$$\angle ACB = 180^0 - 110^0 = 70^0$$

$\triangle ABC$, $\angle BAC = 40^0$

$$\therefore \angle A = 40^0.$$

36. (A) Let $\angle 1 = 3x^0$, $\angle 2 = 2x^0$

$$3x^0 + 2x^0 = 180^0 \Rightarrow x = 36^0$$

$AB||CD$ $\angle 2 = \angle 6$
(corresponding angles)

$$\angle 2 = 2(36^0) = 72^0$$

$$\therefore \angle 6 = 72^0$$

37. (A)

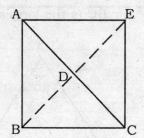

ABCD is a rectangle in which ABC & ADC are right angled triangles and AC, BE are diagonals.

D is the mid point of AC and BD

$$\therefore BD = \frac{1}{2}AC$$

38. (A) $\triangle PQR$, $PQ > PR$

$$\Rightarrow \angle PRQ > \angle PQR$$

$$\frac{1}{2}\angle PRQ > \frac{1}{2}\angle PQR$$

$$\angle SRQ > \angle SQR \Rightarrow SQ > SR.$$

39. (A) In $\triangle ABC$, AD is the bisector of A.

$$\therefore \angle BAD = \angle CAD \Rightarrow \angle 1 = \angle 2$$

In $\triangle ADC$

$$\angle 4 > 2$$

$$AB > CD$$

$$\angle 1 = \angle 2 \Rightarrow \angle 4 > \angle 1$$

$$AB > BD$$

40. (C)

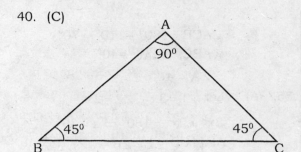

In $\triangle ABC$ given that
$\angle B = \angle C = 45^0$.

$\Rightarrow AC = AB \qquad \Rightarrow \angle A = 90^0$

$\therefore$ BC is the longest side.

41. (B)

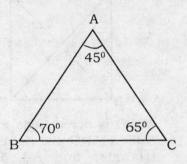

$45^0 + 70^0 + \angle C = 180^0$

$\Rightarrow \angle C = 65^0$

$\Rightarrow$ BC is the shortest and AC is the longest sides of the triangle.

42. (D)

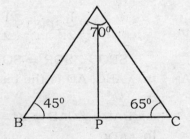

Consider AP, BP, CP

From $\triangle ABP \quad \angle ABP > \angle BAP$

$\qquad\qquad AP > BP$

From $\triangle ACP \quad \angle ACP > \angle CAP$

$\qquad\qquad AP > CP$

Ascending order is CP, BP, AP.

43. (B) $\quad \angle A : \angle B : \angle C = \dfrac{1}{2} : \dfrac{1}{3} : \dfrac{1}{6}$

$\qquad \angle A : \angle B : \angle C = 3 : 2 : 1$

$\qquad \therefore \angle A = 90^0, \ \angle B = 60^0, \ \angle C = 30^0$

44. (A) $\quad 15^0 + B + B + B - 30^0 = 180^0$

$\qquad \Rightarrow B = 65^0$

$\qquad A = 80^0, \ C = 35^0.$

45. (D) $\quad 90° - 72\frac{1}{2} = 17\frac{1}{2}$

46. (B) $\quad 180 - 108.5° = 71.5°$

47. (C) $\quad$ Right angle $= 90°$

48. (B) $\quad$ Obtuse angle is $> 90°$ & $< 180°$

49. (C) $\quad > 180°$ & $< 360°$ Reflex angle

50. (B) $\quad$ Complete angle $= 360°$

51. (C)

$\qquad \angle x = 90°$ is vertically opposite to $90°$.

$\qquad \angle b = 90°$ forms linear pair with $\angle x$.

$\qquad$ So, $\angle x = 90° \ \angle b = 90°$.

52. (B) $\quad$ Perpendicluar - Meeting at right angles

53. (A) $\quad 180° =$ straight angle.

54. (D) $\quad$ Acute angle

55. (B) $\quad$ Right angle

56. (B) $\quad$ Reflex angle

57. (A) $\quad$ Straight angle $= 180°$

58. (B) $\quad$ Adjacent angles whose sum is $180°$ is linear pair.

59. (A) $\quad 115 + 65° = 180°$

$\qquad \angle y = 65°$

60.	(B)	Obtuse	

60. (B)   Obtuse

61. (A)   Common vertex and common arm are called adjacent angles.

62. (C)   180° - 47.3° = 132.7

63. (D)   90 - 12.7 = 77.3

64. (A)   Linear pair are supplementary.

65. (B)   Supplementary and Complementary angles need not be adjacent.

66. (B)   Two sides of the angle

67. (A)   Common end point of an angle is called vertex.

68. (D)   Complete angle

69. (C)   Three letters are used to represent an angle.

70. (B)   l||m

71. (C)   When two lines are parallel $\perp^r$ distance between them remains constant.

72. (B)   Transversal is a line which intersects two or more lines at different points.

73. (C)   8 angles are formed by a transversal with a pair of lines.

74. (B)

75. (A)

76. (B)

77. (C)

78. (A)

79. (C) $\angle g = 115°$

$\angle g$ is alternate to $\angle a$.

80. (A) $\angle b = \angle c$. They are alternate.

81. (B) $\angle a + \angle b = 180°$

$\angle b = 130° = \angle d$

Corresponding angles.

82. (B) $l \perp m$. l is perpendicular to m.

83. (A) $\angle 1$ and $\angle 5$ are corresponding.

84. (B)   4 pairs of corresponding angles

85. (A)   2 pairs of alternate angles

86. (B)   Sum of two interior angles lying on the same side of transversal is supplementary.

87. (B) $\angle 1 = 60°$ $\angle 2 = 120°$ (linear pair)

$\angle 2 = \angle 4 = 120° = \angle 8$ Corresponding vertically opposite angles.

88. (B)   6 sets of parallel lines

89. (C)   setsquare and scale

90. (D)   l||m   m||n   l||n

91. (C)   p||q   r||s

p is not parallel to s.

92. (B)   p is transversal.

93. (B)   railway track

94. (B)   parallel lines

95. (B)   Three noncollinear points joined to form a traingle.

96. (D)   3 sides, 3 angles and 3 vertices are the basic elements of a triangle.

97. (C)   Triangular region

98. (C)   Sum of the interior angles of a triangle is 180°.

99. (B)   Exterior angle = sum of two interior opposite angles

100. (B) $90° + 35° = 125°$

$180° - 125° = 55°$

101. (C) $60^0 + 45^0 = 105^0$
           $180^0 - 105^0 = 75°$

102. (C) $65^0 + 85^0 + 30^0 = 180°$

103. (B) $\angle y = 115^0 - 40^0 = 75°$

104. (B)
           !n Isosceles triangle the base angles are equal.
           $x^0 + x^0 + 30^0 = 180^0$
           $2x^0 = 180^0 - 30^0 = 150°$

105. (B) $x^0 + 50° = 120°$
           $x^0 = 120^0 - 50^0 = 70°$

106. (C) Sum of any two sides is always greater than the third side in any triangle.

107. (C) $90^0 + 30^0 + x^0 = 180°$
           $x^0 = 180^0 - 120^0 = 60°$
           $\angle ACD = x^0 + 90°$
           $= 60^0 + 90^0 = 150°$

108. (C)
           $\angle p = 70°$ Alternate to $\angle TRS$
           $y° + \angle p + \angle Q = 180°$
           $y° = 180^0 - 100^0 = 80°$

109. (B)
           $\angle NOP = \angle NML$ alternate
           $\angle NOP = 30°$

110. (C)
           $\angle ACD = \angle A, \angle B$ Interior opposite angles

111. (C) 6 exterior angles

112. (B) $\angle XYW$ = exterior angle

113. (C) △le divides plane into 3 parts

114. (C) Angle sum property
           $90^0 + 90^0 + 20^0 = 200°$
           Cannot form a triangle.

115. (A)
           $(6 + 5)\ 11 > 3$
           Inequality property
           $(5 + 3)\ 8 > 6$
           $(3 + 6)\ 9 > 5$
           They can form a △le.

116. (B) CE∥BA and AC is a transversal.
           ∴ $\angle ACE = \angle BAC = 60^0$
           (Alternate angles)
           ∴ $\angle ACD = \angle ACE + \angle ECD$
           $= 60^0 + 65^0 = 125^0$
           Now $\angle ACB = 180^0 - \angle ACD$
           (∵ $\angle ACB$ & $\angle ACD$ form a linear pair)
           $= 180^0 - 125^0 = 55^0$.

117. (C) Through O draw a line EOF parallel to AB.

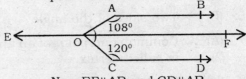

           Now EF∥AB and CD∥AB.
           So, CD∥EF
           ∵ AB∥EF and AO is a transversal.
           We have
           $\angle AOF + \angle OAB = 180^0$
           $\angle AOF + 108^0 = 180^0$
           $\angle AOF = 72^0$
           ∵ EF∥CD and OC is a transversal.
           So,
           $\angle COF + \angle OCD = 180^0$
           $\angle COF + 120^0 = 180^0$
           $\angle COF = 60^0$
           ∴ $\angle AOC = \angle AOF + \angle COF$
           $= 72^0 + 60^0 = 132^0$

118. (A)
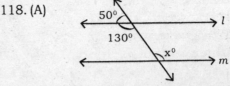

           ∵ alternate interior angles are equal.
           $\Rightarrow x^0 = 130^0$

119. (A) A, B, C, D, E are collinear points.
120. (B) Parallel

Chapter 6

Triangles

6

Synopsis

1. Two figures having exactly the same shape and size are said to be congruent.

2. Two triangles are said to be congruent, if pairs of corresponding sides and the corresponding angles are equal.

3. Two congruent figures are equal in area, but two figures having the same area need not be congruent.

4. The bisector of the vertical angle of an isosceles triangle bisects the base at right angles.

5. Two line segments are congruent, if they have same length.

6. Two circles are congruent, if they have same radius.

7. Two angles are congruent, if they have same measure.

8. Two squares are congruent, if they have same side length.

9. Two rectangles are congruent, if they have the same length and same breadth.

10. *Congruence of Triangles :*
    SSS congruence condition :
    If three sides of a △le are equal to the three sides of another △le, then the two triangles are congruent.

    E.g. :-

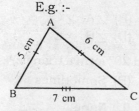 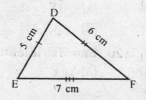

$\therefore \triangle ABC \cong \triangle DEF$

SAS congruence condition :

If two sides and the included angle of a △le are respectively equal to the two sides and the included angle of another △le, then the two triangles are congruent.

E.g. :-

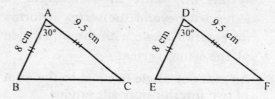

$\therefore \triangle ABC \cong \triangle DEF$

ASA congruence condition :

If two angles and a side of one triangle are respectively equal to the two angles and the corresponding side of another triangle, then the two triangles are congruent.

E.g. :-

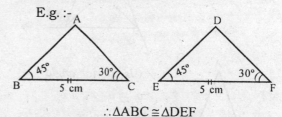

$\therefore \triangle ABC \cong \triangle DEF$

RHS congruence condition :

If the hypotenuse and a side of a right angled triangle are equal to the hypotenuse and a side of another right-angled triangle, then the two triangles are congruent.

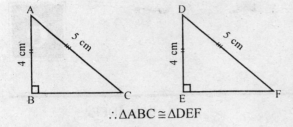

$$\therefore \triangle ABC \cong \triangle DEF$$

Properties of a triangle:

Angle sum Property :- Sum of all the three interior angles of a triangle is 180°.

Inequality Property :- Sum of any two sides of a triangle is always greater than the third side.

When any side of a triangle is extended beyond the vertex it forms an exterior angle with the other side at the same vertex.

An exterior angle is equal to the sum of two interior opposite angles.

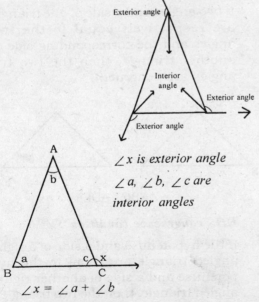

∠x is exterior angle

∠a, ∠b, ∠c are interior angles

∠x = ∠a + ∠b

Exterior angle = sum of two interior opposite angles

Every triangle has six exterior angles and three interior angles.

To get exterior angles the sides of the triangle are to be produced in one direction only either in clockwise or in anticlockwise.

Multiple Choice Questions

1. An exterior angle of a triangle is equal to the sum of two _____ angles.
    (A) exterior opposite
    (B) interior opposite
    (C) interior
    (D) opposite

2. In the following, the set of measures which can form a triangle
    (A) 70°, 90°, 25°

    (B) 65°, 85°, 40°

    (C) 65°, 85°, 30°

    (D) 45°, 45°, 80°

3. Sum of any two sides of a triangle is always _____ third side in a triangle.
    (A) less than   (B) equal to
    (C) greater than (D) none

4. The interior opposite angles of the exterior angle ∠ACD are

    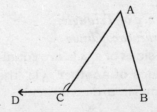

    (A) ∠B, ∠C   (B) ∠A, ∠C
    (C) ∠A, ∠B   (D) ∠B, ∠E

5. Can 90°, 90° and 20° form a triangle?
    (A) Yes   (B) Sometimes

    (C) No   (D) None

6. Can 6 cm, 5 cm and 3 cm form a triangle?

(A) Yes   (B) No
(C) Sometimes (D) None

7. An exterior angle of a triangle is 110⁰ and one of the interior of opposite angles is 40⁰. Then the other two angles of a triangle are

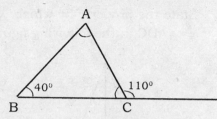

(A) 70⁰, 70⁰   (B) 70⁰, 40⁰
(C) 110⁰, 40⁰   (D) 110⁰, 75⁰

8. In a right angled triangle, the square of the hypotenuse is equal to twice the product of the other two sides. One of the acute angles of the triangle is
(A) 60⁰   (B) 45⁰
(C) 30⁰   (D) 75⁰

9. In the given figure it is given that AB = CF, EF = BD and ∠AFE = ∠DBC

Then △AFE congruent to △CBD by which criterion?

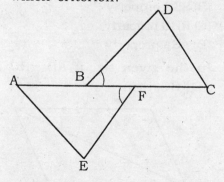

(A) SAS
(B) SSS
(C) ASA
(D) None

10. In the given figure AD is the bisector of ∠A and AB = AC. Then △ACD, △ADB are congruent by which criterion?

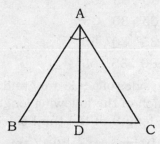

(A) SSS   (B) SAS
(C) ASA   (D) None

11. In △ABC if ∠B = ∠C = 45⁰, which of the following is the longest side?
(A) AB   (B) AC
(C) BC   (D) None

12. In a △ABC if ∠A = 45⁰ and ∠B = 70⁰ then the shortest and the largest sides of the triangle are
(A) AB, BC   (B) BC, AC
(C) AB, AC   (D) none

13. In △ABC ∠B = 45⁰, ∠C = 65⁰, and the bisector of ∠BAC meets BC at P. Then the ascending order of sides is

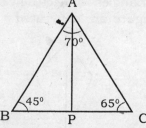

(A) AP, BP, CP   (B) AP, CP, BP
(C) BP, AP, CP   (D) CP, BP, AP

14. In a △ABC if 2∠A = 3∠B = 6∠C then ∠A, ∠B, ∠C are
(A) 30⁰, 60⁰, 90⁰ (B) 90⁰, 60⁰, 30⁰
(C) 30⁰, 90⁰, 60⁰ (D) none of these

15. A, B, C are the three angles of a triangle. If A − B = 15°, B − C = 30° then ∠A, ∠B, ∠C are

(A) 80°, 65°, 35°

(B) 65°, 80°, 35°

(C) 35°, 80°, 65°

(D) 80°, 35°, 65°

16. Two sides of a △le are 7 and 10 units. Which of the following length can be the length of the third side?

(A) 19 cm　　(B) 17 cm

(C) 13 cm　　(D) 3 cm

17. If a, b and c are the sides of a △le, then

(A) a − b > c　　(B) c > a + b

(C) c = a + b　　(D) b < c + a

18. Which of the following statement is correct?

(A) The difference of any two sides is less than the third side

(B) A △le cannot have two obtuse angles

(C) A △le cannot have an obtuse angle and a right angle

(D) All the above

19. By which congruency property, the two triangles connected by the following figure are congruent.

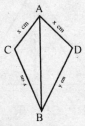

(A) SAS property

(B) SSS property

(C) RHS property

(D) ASA property

20. In △ABC, AB = AC and AD is perpendicular to BC. State the property by which △ADB ≅ △ADC.

(A) SAS property

(B) SSS property

(C) RHS property

(D) ASA property

21. State the property by which △ADB ≅ △ADC in the following figure.,

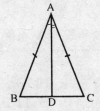

(A) SAS property

(B) SSS property

(C) RHS property

(D) ASA property

22. In △ABC, AD ⊥ BC, ∠B = ∠C and AB = AC. State by which property △ADB ≅ △ADC?

(A) SAS property

(B) SSS property

(C) RHS property

(D) ASA property

23. In the given fig. if AD = BC and AD ∥ BC, then

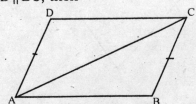

(A) AB = AD

(B) AB = DC

(C) BC = CD

(D) none

24. In the following fig. if AB = AC and BD = DC then ∠ADC =

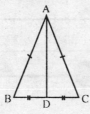

(A) 60°   (B) 120°
(C) 90°   (D) none

25. If two △les have their corresponding angles equal, then they are always congruent.

(A) True
(B) False
(C) Cannot be determined
(D) None

26. If A : Two △les are said to be congruent if two sides and an angle of the one triangle are respectively equal to the two sides and an angle of the other and

R : Two △les are congruent if two sides and the included angle of the one must be equal to the corresponding two sides and included angle of the other, then which of the following statement is correct?

(A) A is false and R is the correct explanation of A
(B) A is true and R is the correct explanation of a A
(C) A is true and R is false
(D) None of these

27. Which of the following statements is true?
(A) Two line segments having the same length are congruent
(B) Two squares having the same side length are congruent.
(C) Two circles having the same radius are congruent.
(D) All the above

28. Which of the following statement(s) is/are false?
(A) Two △les having same area are congruent
(B) If two sides and one angle of a △le are equal to the corresponding two sides and the angle of another △le, then the two △les are congruent
(C) If the hypotenuse of one right triangle is equal to the hypotenuse of another triangle, then the triangles are congruent
(D) All the above

29. If A : If the hypotenuse and an acute angle of one right triangle is equal to the hypotenuse and corresponding acute angle of another right triangle, then those two △les are congruent and

R : By RHS property, the two right △les are congruent, then which of the following statements is true?
(A) A is true and R is the correct explanation of A
(B) A is false and R is the correct explanation of A
(C) A is false and R is false
(D) None of these

30. In the fig. given below, find ∠Z.

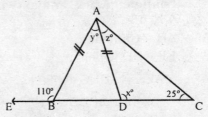

(A) 40°
(B) 110°
(C) 45°
(D) None

1. B	2. C	3. C	4. C	5. C	6. A	7. A	8. B	9. A	10. A
11. C	12. B	13. D	14. B	15. A	16. C	17. D	18. D	19. B	20. C
21. A	22. D	23. B	24. C	25. B	26. A	27. D	28. D	29. A	30. C

Explanatory Answers

1. **(B)** Exterior angle = sum of two interior opposite angles

2. **(C)** $65^0 + 85^0 + 30^0 = 180^0$

3. **(C)** Sum of any two sides is always greater than the third side in any triangle.

4. **(C)** $\angle ACD = \angle A, \angle B$ Interior opposite angles

5. **(C)** Angle sum property
   $90^0 + 90^0 + 20^0 = 200^0$
   Cannot form a triangle.

6. **(A)**
   $(6 + 5)\ 11 > 3$
   Inequality property
   $(5 + 3)\ 8 > 6$
   $(3 + 6)\ 9 > 5$
   They can form a $\triangle$le.

7. **(A)** $40 + x = 110^0 \Rightarrow x = 70^0$
   $\therefore$ angles are $70^0, 70^0$.

8. **(B)** The above inequality is possible only in isosceles right angled triangle. Acute angles will be $45^0, 45^0$.

9. **(A)** AB = CF (side)
   EF = BD (side)
   $\angle AFE = \angle DBC$ (angle)
   $\therefore \triangle AFE \cong \triangle CBD$ (by SAS criterion)

10. **(A)** In $\triangle ABC$, AC = AC $\Rightarrow \angle B = \angle C$
    In $\triangle ABD, ACD$
    AB = AC (side)
    AD is the common side
    BD = CD (side)

11. **(C)**

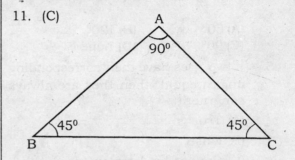

   In $\triangle ABC$ given that $\angle B = \angle C = 45^0$.
   $\Rightarrow AC = AB \qquad \Rightarrow \angle A = 90^0$
   $\therefore$ BC is the longest side.

12. **(B)**

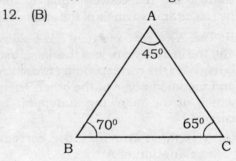

   $45^0 + 70^0 + \angle C = 180^0$
   $\Rightarrow \angle C = 65^0$
   $\Rightarrow$ BC is the shortest and AC is the longest sides of the triangle.

13. **(D)**

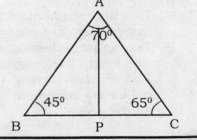

Consider AP, BP, CP

From $\triangle$ABP $\quad \angle$ABP > $\angle$BAP

$\qquad\qquad$ AP > BP

From $\triangle$ACP $\quad \angle$ACP > $\angle$CAP

$\qquad\qquad$ AP > CP

Ascending order is CP, BP, AP.

14. (B) $\quad \angle A : \angle B : \angle C = \dfrac{1}{2} : \dfrac{1}{3} : \dfrac{1}{6}$

$\angle A : \angle B : \angle C = 3 : 2 : 1$

$\therefore \angle A = 90^0, \angle B = 60^0, \angle C = 30^0$

15. (A) $\quad 15^0 + B + B + B - 30^0 = 180^0$

$\Rightarrow B = 65^0$

$A = 80^0, C = 35^0.$

16. (C) Only (C) satisfies the condition, i.e., the sum of any two sides is greater than the third side.

17. (D) $b < c + a$.

$\because$ Sum of any two sides is greater than the third side.

18. (D) $\because$ All the given statements are correct.

19. (B) Separate the given fig. into two $\triangle$les.

$\triangle$ABC and $\triangle$ADB

We can observe that,

AC = AD, BC = BD, AB = AB

So $\triangle$ABC $\cong$ $\triangle$ABD by SSS property.

20. (C) By RHS property

$\triangle$ADB $\cong$ $\triangle$ADC

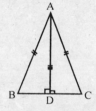

21. (A) $\quad$ AB = AC

$\angle$BAD = $\angle$CAD

AD = AD

$\therefore$ By SAS property $\triangle$ADB $\cong \triangle$ADC.

22. (D)

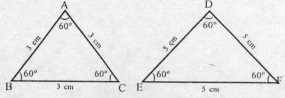

By ASA property

$\triangle$ADB $\cong \triangle$ADC

23. (B) In the give fig.

AD = BC, AC = AC,

$\angle$ADC = $\angle$ABC ($\because$ AD $\parallel$ BC)

By SAS theorem

$\triangle$ABC $\cong \triangle$CDA

So AB = DC.

24. (C) $\quad$ AB = AC

BD = DC and $\qquad$ AD = AD

By SSS property

$\triangle$ADB $\cong \triangle$ADC.

We have

$\angle$ADB + $\angle$ADC = 180°

$\angle$ADB = $\angle$ADC = 90°

$(\because \triangle ADB \cong \triangle ADC)$

25. (B) E. g. :- Take two $\triangle$les as follows.

Even though all angles are same, the two $\triangle$les are not congruent.

26. (A) (See synopsis)

Statement A is false and R is the correct explanation of A.

27. (D)   All the given statements are correct.

28. (D)   All statements are false.

29. (A) $\because$ Statement A is true by RHS property.

30. (C)   We have

$$\angle ABE + \angle ABD = 180°$$

$$\angle ABD = 180 - 110 = 70°$$

so $\angle ABD = \angle ADB = 70°$

$(\because AB = AD)$

$$\angle ADB + \angle ADC = 180°$$

$$\angle ADC = 180° - 70° = 110°$$

$$\Rightarrow x = 110°$$

In $\triangle$ ABD,

$$\angle A + \angle B + \angle D = 180°$$

$$y + 70° + 70° = 180°$$

$$y = 40°$$

In $\triangle$ ADC,

$$\angle A + \angle D + \angle C = 180°$$

$$z + 110° + 25° = 180°$$

$$z = 45°$$

♦ ♦ ♦

Chapter 7

Quadrilaterals

7

1. A quadrilateral in which the measure of each angle is less than 180° is called a convex quadrilateral.

2. A quadrilateral in which the measure of at least one of the angles is more than 180° is known as a concave quadrilateral.

3. In convex quadrilateral both diagonals lie in the interior where as in the case of concave quadrilateral, one diagonal lies in the exterior and the other lies in the interior.

    Eg:- Here AC and BD are diagonals.

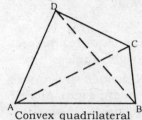

Convex quadrilateral   Concave quadrilateral

4. The sum of the angles of a quadrilateral is 360° (or) 4 right angles.

5. When the sides of a quadrilateral are produced, the sum of the four exterior angles so formed is 360°.

Various Types of Quadrilaterals :

1. Trapezium :

a. A quadrilateral having exactly one pair of parallel sides is called a trapezium

b. A trapezium is said to be an isosceles trapezium if its non-parallel sides are equal.

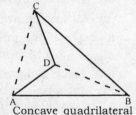

ABCD is a trapezium in which AB||DC.

This trapezium is said to be isosceles trapezium if AB||DC and AD = BC.

2. Parallelogram :

a. A quadrilateral in which both pairs of opposite sides are parallel is called a parallelogram.

ABCD is a parallelogram in which AB||DC and AD||BC.

Properties :

(a) In a parallelogram any two opposite sides are equal.

(b) In a parallelogram any two opposite angles are equal.

(c) In a parallelogram the diagonals bisect each other.

(d) In a parallelogram, each diagonal divides it into two congruent triangles.

(e) In a parallelogram, any two adjacent angles have their sum equal to 180° i.e., supplementary.

3. Rhombus :

A quadrilateral having all sides equal is called a rhombus.

ABCD is a rhombus in which AB||DC, AD||BC and AB = BC = CD = DA.

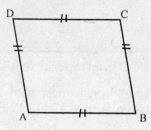

Properties :

(a) The diagonals in a rhombus bisect each other.

(b) Each diagonal of a rhombus divides it into two congruent triangles.

(c) Opposite angles of a rhombus are equal and the sum of any two adjacent angles is 180°.

(d) In a rhombus the diagonals bisect each other at right angles.

(e) The opposite sides of a rhombus are parallel.

(f) All the sides of a rhombus are equal.

4. Rectangle :

A parallelogram whose angles are all right angles is called a rectangle.

E.g. :-

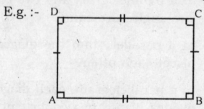

ABCD is a rectangle in which AB||CD, AD||BC and

$\angle A = \angle B = \angle C = \angle D = 90^0$.

Properties :

(a) Opposite sides of a rectangle are equal and opposite angles of a rectangle are equal.

(b) The diagonals of a rectangle bisect each other.

(c) Each diagonal divides the rectangle into two congruent triangles.

(d) The diagonals of a rectangle are equal.

5. Square :

A parallelogram having all sides equal and each angle equal to a right angle is called a square.

E.g. :-

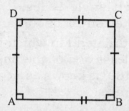

ABCD is a square in which AB||DC, AD||BC, AB = BC = CD = DA and $\angle A$ = $\angle B$ = $\angle C$ = $\angle D$ = 90°.

Properties :

(a) All sides are equal.

(b) All angles are equal.

(c) The diagonals are equal and bisect each other at right angles.

(d) Each diagonal divides the square into two congruent right angled isosceles triangles.

6. Kite :

A quadrilateral having two pairs of equal adjacent sides but unequal opposite sides is called a kite.

E.g. :-

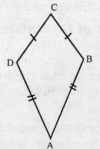

ABCD is a kite in which AB= AD and BC = CD.

Conditions for a quadrilateral to become a parallelogram :

a) Both pairs of opposite sides should be equal (or)

(b) one pair of opposite sides should be equal and parallel (or)

(c) both pairs of opposite angles should be equal (or)

(d) its diagonals should bisect each other.

Conditions for a quadrilateral to become a rectangle :

a) All its angles should be right angles (or)

(b) its diagonals should be equal and bisect each other (or)

(c) both pairs of opposite sides should be equal and one angle must be 90° (or)

(d) both pairs of opposite sides and its diagonals should be equal.

Conditions for a quadrilateral to become a rhombus :

(a) All its sides should be equal (or)

(b) its diagonals should bisect each other at right angles (or)

(c) both pairs of its opposite sides should be equal and the diagonals should intersect at right angles.

Conditions for a quadrilateral to become a square :

(a) All of its sides should be equal and one angle must be 90° (or)

(b) all of its sides and the diagonals should be equal (or)

(c) all its angles should be equal and the diagonals should intersect at right angles.

Number of measurements required to construct different geometrical objects :

1. To construct a quadrilateral 5 independent measurements are needed.

2. To construct a parallelogram only 3 independent measurements are required.

3. To construct a trapezium 4 independent measurements are required.

4. To construct a rhombus 2 independent measurements are required.

5. To construct a rectangle 2 independent measurements are required.

6. To construct a square 1 measurement is required.

Multiple Choice Questions

1. The sides BA and DC of the quadrilateral ABCD are produced as shown in the figure then

(A) $a + x = b + y$
(B) $a + y = b + x$
(C) $a + b = x + y$
(D) $a - b = x - y$

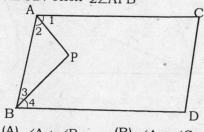

2. In the adjoining figure, AP and BP are angle bisectors of $\angle A$ and $\angle B$ which meet at P of the parallelogram ABCD. Then $2\angle APB =$

(A) $\angle A + \angle B$ (B) $\angle A + \angle C$

(C) $\angle B + \angle D$ (D) $\angle C + \angle D$

3. In the given figure AO and DO are the bisectors of the $\angle A$ and the $\angle D$ of the quadrilateral ABCD. Then the $\angle AOD$ is

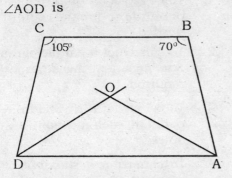

(A) 67.5^0 (B) 77.5^0

(C) 87.5^0 (D) 99.75^0

4. In a parallelogram the sum of the angle bisectors of two adjacent angles is

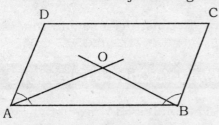

(A) 30^0 (B) 45^0

(C) 60^0 (D) 90^0

5. In a parallelogram ABCD $\angle D = 60^0$ then the measurement of $\angle A$

(A) 120^0 (B) 65^0

(C) 90^0 (D) 75^0

6. In the adjoining figure ABCD, the angles x and y are

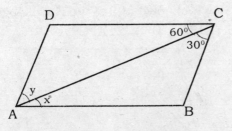

(A) $60^0, 30^0$ (B) $30^0, 60^0$

(C) $45^0, 45^0$ (D) $90^0, 90^0$

7. From the figure parallelogram PQRS, the values of $\angle SQP$ and $\angle QSP$ are

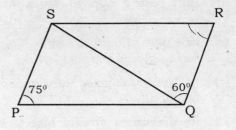

(A) $45^0, 60^0$

(B) $60^0, 45^0$

(C) $70^0, 35^0$

(D) $35^0, 70^0$

8. In the given figure, ABCD is a trapezium in which AB = 7 cm, AD = BC = 5 cm, DC = x cm and the distance between AB and DC is 4 cm. Then the values of x is

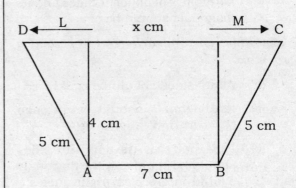

(A) 13 cm

(B) 16 cm

(C) 19 cm

(D) cannot be determined

9. In parallelogram ABCD, AB = 12 cm. The altitudes corresponding to the sides AB and AD are respectively 9 cm and 11 cm. Find AD.

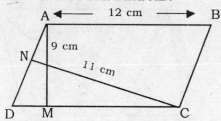

(A) $\dfrac{108}{11}$ cm   (B) $\dfrac{108}{10}$ cm

(C) $\dfrac{99}{10}$ cm   (D) $\dfrac{108}{17}$ cm

10. ABCD is a quadrilateral. If AC and BD bisect each other then ABCD must be

(A) square   (B) rectangle

(C) parallelogram   (D) rhombus

11. ABCD is a parallelogram. The angle bisectors of ∠A and ∠D meet at O. The measure of ∠AOD is

(A) 45^0 (B) 90^0

(C) dependent on the angles A and D

(D) cannot be determined from given data

12. The diameter of circumcircle of a rectangle is 10 cm and breadth of the rectangle is 6 cm. Its length is

(A) 6cm   (B) 5cm

(C) 8cm   (D) none

13. ABCD is a quadrilateral. AB = BC = CD = DA and

∠A = ∠B = ∠C = ∠D = 90^0 Then ABCD can be called

(A) rhombus

(B) square

(C) parallelogram

(D) all of the foregoing

14. The sum of the angles of a quadrilateral is

(A) 180^0

(B) 360^0

(C) 270^0

(D) depends on the quadrilateral

15. RSTU is a parallelogram as shown in the figure below. Then the shown angles x and y are related

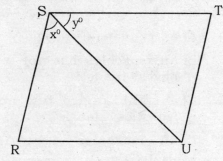

(A) x = y   (B) x < y

(C) x > y

(D) cannot be determined from given data

16. ABCD and MNOP are quadrilaterals as shown in the figure below. Then

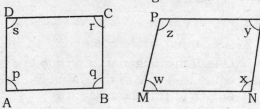

(A) p + q + r + s = w + x + y + z

(B) p + q + r + s < w + x + y + z

(C) p + q + r + s > w + x + y + z

(D) none of the foregoing

17. A parallelogram which has equal diagonals is a

(A) square

(B) rectangle

(C) rhombus

(D) none

18. If ABCD is a parallelogram, then

    $\angle A - \angle C$ is

    (A) 180^0

    (B) 0^0

    (C) 360^0

    (D) 90^0

19. In a square ABCD, the diagonals bisect at O. Then triangle AOB is

    (A) an equilateral triangle

    (B) an isosceles but not a right angled triangle

    (C) a right angled but not an isosceles triangle

    (D) an isosceles right angled triangle

20. The perimeter of a parallelogram is 180 cm. One side exceeds another by 10 cm. The sides of the parallelogram are

    (A) 40 cm, 50 cm

    (B) 45 cm each

    (C) 50 cm each

    (D) cannot be determined

21. One of the diagonals of a rhombus is equal to a side of the rhombus. The angles of the rhombus are

    (A) 60^0 and 80^0

    (B) 60^0 and 120^0

    (C) 120^0 and 240^0

    (D) 100^0 and 120^0

22. In the quadrilateral ABCD, the diagonals AC and BD are equal and perpendicular to each other. Then ABCD is a

    (A) square

    (B) parallelogram

    (C) rhombus

    (D) trapezium

23. ABCD is a parallelogram as shown in figure. If AB = 2AD and P is mid-point of AB, then $\angle CPD$ is equal to

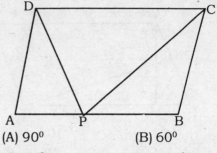

    (A) 90^0 (B) 60^0

    (C) 45^0 (D) 135^0

24. In a parallelogram ABCD, if AB = 2x + 5, CD = y + 1, AD = y + 5 and BC = 3x – 4 then ratio of AB : BC is

    (A) 71 : 21   (B) 12 : 11

    (C) 31 : 35   (D) 4 : 7

25. If ABCD is an isosceles trapezium, $\angle C$ is equal to

    (A) $\angle B$ (B) $\angle A$

    (C) $\angle D$ (D) 90^0

26. The diagonals of a parallelogram ABCD intersect at O. If $\angle BOC = 90^0$ and $\angle BDC = 50^0$, then $\angle AOB$ is

    (A) 10^0 (B) 40^0

    (C) 50^0 (D) 90^0

27. A diagonal of a rectangle is inclined to one side of the rectangle at 25^0. The acute angle between the diagonals is

    (A) 25^0 (B) 40^0

    (C) 50^0 (D) 55^0

28. ABCD is a rhombus. If $\angle ACB = 40^0$, then $\angle ADB$ is

    (A) 40^0 (B) 45^0

    (C) 50^0 (D) 60^0

29. The quadrilateral formed by joining the mid-points of the sides of a quadrilateral PQRS, taken in order, is a rectangle if

(A) PQRS is a rectangle

(B) PQRS is a parallelogram

(C) diagonals of PQRS are perpendicular

(D) diagonals of PQRS are equal

30. The quadrilateral formed by joining the mid-points of the sides of a quadrilateral PQRS, taken in order, is a rhombus if

(A) PQRS is a rhombus

(B) PQRS is a parallelogram

(C) diagonals of PQRS are perpendicular

(D) diagonals of PQRS are equal

31. If angles P, Q, R and S of the quadrilateral PQRS, taken in order, are in the ratio 3 : 7 : 6 : 4 then PQRS is a

(A) rhombus   (B) parallelogram

(C) trapezium   (D) kite

32. If PQ and RS are two perpendicular diameters of a circle, then PRQS is a

(A) rectangle

(B) trapezium

(C) square

(D) rhombus but not square

33. If bisectors of $\angle A$ and $\angle B$ of a quadrilateral ABCD intersect each other at P, of $\angle B$ and $\angle C$ at Q, of $\angle C$ and $\angle D$ and $\angle A$ at S, then PQRS is a

(A) rectangle

(B) rhombus

(C) parallelogram

(D) quadrilateral whose opposite angles are supplementary

34. AB and CD are diameters. Then ACBD is

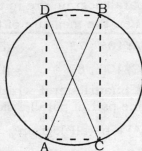

(A) square

(B) trapezium

(C) isosceles trapezium

(D) rectangle

35. ABCD is a square E, F, G, H are the mid-points of the four sides. Then the figure EFGH is

(A) square   (B) rectangle

(C) trapezium   (D) parallelogram

36. If a quadrilateal has two adjacent sides equal and the other two sides equal it is called

(A) parallelogram

(B) square

(C) rectangle

(D) kite

37. Choose the correct statement.

(A) The diagonals of a parallelogram are equal

(B) The diagonals of a rectangle are perpendicular to each other

(C) If the diagonals of a quadrilateral intersect at right angles, it is not necessarily a rhombus.

(D) Every quadrilateral is either a trapezium or a parallelogram or a kite.

38. If two adjacent angles of a parallelogram are in the ratio 3 : 2, then the measure of the angles are

(A) $108^0, 72^0$ (B) $72^0, 36^0$

(C) $100^0, 80^0$ (D) $144^0, 36^0$

39. A quadrilateral which has exactly one pair of parallel sides is called

(A) a parallelogram

(B) a rectangle

(C) a trapezium

(D) a kite

40. Which of the following statements is true?

(A) The diagonals of a rectangle are perpendicular

(B) The diagonals of a rhombus are equal

(C) Every square is a rhombus

(D) None of these

41. The number of measurements required to construct a quadrilateral is

(A) 5   (B) 4

(C) 3   (D) 2

42. To construct a parallelogram, the minimum number of measurements required is

(A) 2   (B) 3

(C) 4   (D) 1

43. In a quadrilateral PQRS, if $\angle P = \angle R = 100^0$ and $\angle S = 75^0$ then $\angle Q = $ _____

(A) 50^0 (B) 85^0

(C) 120^0 (D) 360^0

44. The sum of the angles in a quadrilateral is equal to _____ .

(A) 2 right angles

(B) 3 right angles

(C) 4 right angles

(D) 360 right angles

45. If the lengths of two diagonals of a rhombus are 12 cm and 16 cm, then the length of each side of the rhombus is

(A) 10 cm

(B) 14 cm

(C) cannot be determined

(D) none of these

46. In a quadrilateral the angles are in the ratio 3 : 4 : 5 : 6. Then the difference between the greatest and the smallest angle is

(A) 108°   (B) 54°

(C) 180°   (D) 360°

47. In a quadrilateral ABCD, $\angle A + \angle C = 180°$ then $\angle B + \angle D = $

(A) 360°   (B) 100°

(C) 180°   (D) 80°

48. Which of the following statement(s) is/are false?

(A) Each diagonal of a quadrilateral divides it into two triangles

(B) Each side of a quadrilateral is less than the sum of the remaining three sides

(C) A quadrilateral can utmost have three obtuse angles

(D) A quadrilateral has four diagonals

49. The angles of a quadrilateral are x°, x - 10°, x + 30° and 2x°. Find the greatest angle.

(A) 136°

(B) 180°

(C) 68°

(D) None

50. In a parallelogram ABCD, if $\angle A = 80°$ then $\angle B =$

(A) 80°

(B) 180°

(C) 100°

(D) Data is not sufficient

51. Two adjacent angles of a parallelogram are in the ratio 2 : 3. The angles are

(A) 180°, 180°   (B) 36°, 144°
(C) 72°, 108°   (D) none

52. In a trapezium ABCD, AB||CD. If $\angle A = 50°$ then $\angle D =$ ___

(A) 110°   (B) 130°

(C) 70°   (D) 310°

53. Two adjacent sides of a parallelogram are 5 cm and 7 cm. Its perimeter is

(A) 24 cm   (B) 36 cm
(C) 12 cm   (D) none

54. In a rhombus ABCD, $\angle A = 60°$ and AB = 6 cm. Find the diagonal BD.

(A) $2\sqrt{3}$ cm

(B) 6 cm

(C) 12 cm

(D) Insufficient data

55. Which of the following statement(s) is/are true?

(A) A parallelogram in which two adja- cent angles are equal is a rectangle

(B) A quadrilateral in which both pairs of opposite angles are equal is parallelogram

(C) In a parallelogram the number of acute angles is zero (or) two

(D) All the above

56. Which of the following statement(s) is/are true?

(A) In a trapezium the diagonals bisect each other

(B) In a rectangle diagonals intersect at right angles

(C) The diagonals of a rhombus are equal

(D) None of these

57. In a parallelogram ABCD, diagonals AC and BD intersect at O. If AO = 5 cm then AC = ...

(A) 5 cm   (B) 20 cm
(C) 10 cm   (D) none

58. In a Rhombus ABCD, if AB = AC then $\angle BCD =$ ....

(A) 60° (B) 120° (C) 72° (D) 108°

59. In a rectangle ABCD, the diagonal AC=10 cm then the diagonal BD is ....

(A) 10 cm   (B) 20 cm
(C) 5 cm   (D) none

60. A quadrilateral in which both pairs of opposite sides are parallel is a ....

(A) square   (B) rhombus
(C) rectangle   (D) parallelogram

61. A parallelogram which has equal diagonals is a ....

(A) square

(B) rhombus

(C) rectangle

(D) none

62. If ABCD is a parallelogram, then $\angle A - \angle C =$ ....

(A) 180°

(B) 0°

(C) 360°

(D) 90°

63. A quadrilateral in which diagonals are equal and bisect each other perpendicularly is a ....

(A) square

(B) rhombus which is not a square

(C) rectangle which is not a square

(D) none

64. A quadrilateral is a rhombus but not a square if

(A) its diagonals do not bisect each other

(B) its diagonals are not perpendicular

(C) opposite angles are not equal

(D) the length of diagonals are not equal

65. A quadrilateral is a rectangle but not a square when

(A) its diagonals do not bisect each other

(B) its diagonals are not perpendicular

(C) all angles are not equal

(D) its diagonals are not equal

66. In a parallelogram ABCD, if $\angle A = 50°$, then $\angle B$, $\angle C$ are $\angle D$ are respectively

(A) 50°, 130°, 130°

(B) 130°, 50°, 130°

(C) 130°, 130°, 50°

(D) 130°, 50°, 50°

67. In a parallelogram ABCD, AB = 4 cm and BC = 7 cm. Each of its diagonals is less than ....

(A) 3 cm (B) 4 cm

(C) 7 cm (D) 11 cm

68. In a square ABCD, its diagonals bisect at O. Then the triangle AOB is

(A) an equilateral $\triangle$le

(B) an isosceles but not right angled $\triangle$le

(C) a right angled but not an isosceles $\triangle$le

(D) an isosceles right angled triangle

69. A quadrilateral in which both pairs of opposite sides are equal is a ....

(A) parallelogram (B) square
(C) rhombus   (D) rectangle

70. In which of the following figures the adjacent sides are not necessarily be equal?

(A) Parallelogram (B) Rhombus
(C) Rectangle   (D) Square

71. Which of the following properties are not true for a parallelogram?

(A) Its diagonals are equal

(B) Its diagonals are perpendicular to each other

(C) The diagonals divide the figure into four congruent $\triangle$les

(D) All the above

72. In a rhombus ABCD, the diagonals intersect at O. If AB = 10 cm, diagonal BD = 16 cm, then the length of the diagonal AC is.........

(A) 12 cm   (B) 6 cm

(C) 16 cm   (D) 8 cm

73. The perimeter of a parallelogram is 180 cm. One side exceeds the another by 10 cm. The adjacent sides of the parallelogram are..........

(A) 30 cm, 40 cm
(B) 40 cm, 50 cm
(C) 50 cm, 60 cm
(D) none

74. ABCD is a parallelogram in which $\angle DAO = 40°$, $\angle BAO = 35°$ and $\angle COD = 65°$ then $\angle ODC = $ ....

(A) 80° (B) 105° (C) 25° (D) None

75. ABCD is a parallelogram in which $\angle DAB = 75°$ and $\angle DBC = 60°$ then $\angle CDB = $ ....

(A) 60°   (B) 75°
(C) 45°   (D) 135°

1. C	2. D	3. C	4. D	5. A	6. A	7. A	8. A	9. A	10. C
11. B	12. C	13. D	14. B	15. D	16. A	17. B	18. B	19. D	20. A
21. B	22. A	23. A	24. C	25. C	26. B	27. C	28. C	29. C	30. D
31. C	32. C	33. D	34. D	35. A	36. D	37. C	38. A	39. C	40. C
41. A	42. B	43. B	44. C	45. A	46. B	47. C	48. D	49. A	50. C
51. C	52. B	53. A	54. B	55. D	56. D	57. C	58. B	59. A	60. D
61. C	62. B	63. A	64. D	65. B	66. B	67. D	68. D	69. A	70. A&C
71. D	72. A	73. B	74. A	75. C					

Explanatory Answers

1. **(C)** From the adjoining figure

    $b^0 = y^0, x^0 = a^0$ ....(2)

    $a + b = x + y$.

2. **(D)** $\angle 2 + \angle 3 + \angle APB = 180^0$

    $\angle 1 + \angle 3 + \angle APB = 180^0$

    $2\angle 1 + 2\angle 3 + 2\angle APB = 360^0$ ....(2)

    $2\angle APB = \angle C + \angle D$

3. **(C)** $\angle A + \angle D = 185^0$

    $\dfrac{1}{2}\angle A + \dfrac{1}{2}\angle D = \dfrac{1}{2}\left(185^0\right)$

    $\dfrac{1}{2}\angle A + \dfrac{1}{2}\angle D = 92.5^0$

    From $\triangle AOD$

    $\dfrac{1}{2}\angle A + \dfrac{1}{2}\angle D + \angle AOD = 180^0$

    $\angle AOB = 180 - 92.5 = 87.5^0$

4. **(D)** $\angle A + \angle B = 180^0$

    $\dfrac{\angle A}{2} + \dfrac{\angle B}{2} = 90^0$

5. **(A)** $\angle A + 60^0 = 180^0 \Rightarrow \angle A = 120^0$.

7. **(A)** $\angle QSP = \angle RQS$ [Alternate angles]

    $\therefore \angle QSP = 60^0$

$\angle QSP + \angle P + \angle SQP = 180^0$

$\Rightarrow 60^0 + 75^0 + \angle SQP = 180^0$

$\angle SQP = 180^0 - 135^0 = 45^0$

8. **(A)** $DL = \sqrt{25 - 16} = 3 \, cm.$

    $CM = \sqrt{25 - 16} = 3 \, cm.$

    $\dfrac{4}{2}\{7 + x\} = 6 + 6 + (x - 6)4$

    $\Rightarrow 2x = 26 \Rightarrow x = 13 \, cm.$

9. **(A)** $12 \times 9 = 108 \, cm^2$

    $108 \, cm^2 = AD \times 11 cm$

    $\Rightarrow AD = \dfrac{108}{11} \, cm.$

10. **(C)** Since, diagonals of a parallelogram bisect each other, ABCD must be a parallelogram.

11. **(B)**

As shown in the figure the angle bisectors of $\angle A$ and $\angle D$ meet at O.

Let $\angle A = x^0$ $\angle D = (180 - x)^0$

$\therefore \dfrac{\angle A}{2} = \dfrac{x}{2}$ and

$\dfrac{\angle D}{2} = \dfrac{180 - x}{2} = 90 - \dfrac{x}{2}$.

$\angle AOD = 180 - \left(\dfrac{x}{2} + 90 - \dfrac{x}{2}\right)$

or $\angle AOD = 180 - (90) = 90^0$

12. (C)

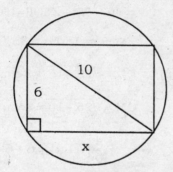

As shown in the diagram, we have a right angled triangle. Let the length of rectangle be x. Then $x^2 + 6^2 = 10^2$ or x = 8 cm.

13. (D)　From definitions, we can clearly see that ABCD can be called a rhombus, square or a parallelogram.

14. (B)

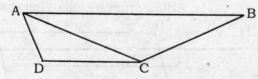

Let us divide a quadrilateral ABCD into two triangles as shown in figure below. Sum of the angles of a triangle is 180^0.

Hence the sum of angles in both triangles = 360^0. Hence sum of angles in a quadrilateral is 360^0.

15. (D)　As seen in the diagram given, triangle RSU and triangle STU are congruent. But x and y are not corresponding angles.

16. (A)　We know that the sum of the angles of a quadrilateral is 360^0.

17. (B)　A square and a rectangle are both parallelograms which have equal diagonals. However (B) is the more appropriate choice since all squares are also rectangles.

18. (B)　We know that opposite angles of a parallelogram are equal. Hence $\angle A - \angle C = 0$.

19. (D)　Since diagonals of a square are equal and bisect at right angles, triangle AOB is an isosceles right angled triangle.

20. (A)　Let one side be x cm. Then adjacent side is (x + 10) cm.
$\therefore$ x + (x + 10) + x + (x + 10)
= 4x + 20 = 180 or x = 40 cm.
$\therefore$ x + 10 = 50 cm.

21. (B)

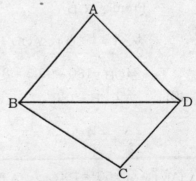

As shown in figure,
let BD = AB = AD. Then ABD is an equilateral triangle and all its angles = 60^0.

$\therefore \angle A = 60^0$. Also $\angle C = 60^0$.

But $\angle B = \angle D$ and

$\angle A + \angle B + \angle C + \angle D = 360^0$

$\therefore \angle B = \angle D = 120^0$.

22. (A) We know that in a square the diagonals are equal and bisect each other at right angles.

23. (A) As shown in the figure, since P is the midpoint of AB and AB = 2AD. We have

AB = 2AP = 2AD

or AP = AD

i.e., triangle ADP is isosceles triangle. $\angle ADP = x$

and $\angle APD = x$ then,

$\angle A = 180 - 2x$

By some argument, since

$\angle B = 2x$,

$\angle CPB = \angle PCB = 90 - x$

Since $\angle APB = 180^0$,

$\angle DPC = 90^0$.

24. (C) We know that in a parallelogram opposite sides are equal.

$\therefore$ AB = CD or 2x + 5 = y + 1

and y + 5 = 3x – 4

or, 2x – y = –4 ....(i)

or, y – 3x = –9 .....(ii)

Adding, –x = – 13 or x = 13 and y = 30.

Substituting we have,

AB = 31 cm and BC = 35 cm.

25. (C)

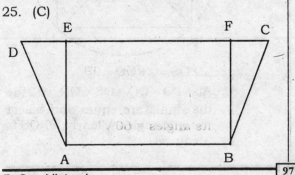

From definition, we know that in an isosceles trapezium the non-parallel sides are equal or AD = BC in the figure. Drop perpendiculars AE and BF to CD. Triangles ADE and BFC are congruent by RHS congruency. Hence $\angle D = \angle C$.

26. (B)

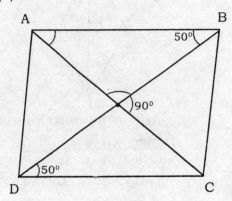

Since alternate angles are equal, we have $\angle DBA = 50^0$.

Also $\angle AOB + \angle BOC = 180^0$ or $\angle AOB = 90^0$. $\therefore$ In triangle OAB, since sum of angles is 180^0, we have $\angle AOB = 40^0$.

27. (C)

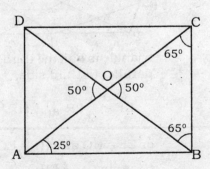

Since $\angle CAB = 25^0$, clearly $\angle OCB = 65^0$. Let diagonals meet at 0. Triangle OCB is an isosceles triangle.

$\therefore \angle OBC = 65^0$

Hence $\therefore \angle BOC = 50^0$.

28. (C)   We know that diagonals of a rhombus bisect each other at right angles. Also AB = BC.

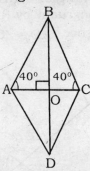

$\therefore$ ABC is an isosceles triangle.

Hence $\angle BAC = 40^0$. Let diagonals meet at O. Then $\angle AOB = 90^0$. $\angle ABO = 50^0$.

But AB = AD and hence ABD is an isosceles triangle.

$\angle ADB = 50^0$

29. (C)   We know that the line joining midpoints of two sides of a

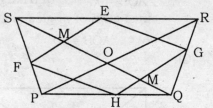

triangle is half the third side and parallel to third side.

$\therefore$ EF = $\frac{1}{2}$PR and HF = $\frac{1}{2}$QS

or EF = HG also HF = EG.

Clearly EFHG is a parallelogram.

If it is to be a rectangle, the diagonals should cut at right angles

$\therefore \angle ROQ = 90^0 \Rightarrow \angle EMO = 90^0$

$\Rightarrow \angle MEG = 90^0$ and

$\angle E = \angle F = \angle G = \angle H = 90^0$.

$\Rightarrow PR \perp QS$

30. (D)   We know from problem 20 (Refer solution 20) that PQRS is a parallelogram. If diagonals of PQRS are equal then

EF = EG = HG = FH or EFGH is a rhombus.

31. (C)   Let the angles be 3x, 7x ,6x and 4x.

$\therefore$ 3x + 7x + 6x + 4x = 360^0 or

20x = 360^0 or x = 18^0. The angles are 54^0, 126^0, 108^0, 72^0. We see that adjacent angles are supplementary but opposite angles are not equal. Clearly, it is a trapezium.

32. (C)   Let the diagonals meet at O as shown in figure.

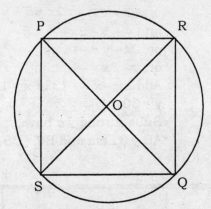

$\angle POS = \angle ROQ = 90^0$.

Also PO = OQ = OS = OR, i.e., the diagonals are equal and bisect at right angles. Clearly, PRQS is a square.

33. (D)

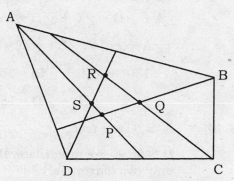

As shown in above figure,

$$\angle S = 180 - \left(\frac{\angle A}{2} + \frac{\angle D}{2}\right) \text{ and}$$

$$\angle Q = 180 - \left(\frac{\angle B}{2} + \frac{\angle C}{2}\right). \text{ Clearly}$$

$$\angle S + \angle Q$$

$$= 360 - \frac{(\angle A + \angle B + \angle C + \angle D)}{2}$$

$$= 360 - \frac{360}{2} = 360^0 - 180^0 = 180^0.$$

34. (D) Since, angle in a semicircle is a right angle. Clearly

$$\angle A = \angle C = \angle B = \angle D = 90^0.$$

The diagonals (diametres) are equal but they are not intersecting (bisecting) at right angles. Hence, it is not a square and can be only a rectangle.

35. (A) We know that the line joining the midpoints of two sides of a triangle is half the third side and parallel to third side.

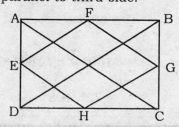

∴ In triangle ADB, $EF = \frac{1}{2}DB$.

Also, $EH = \frac{1}{2}AC$.

But $DB = AC$. ∴ $EF = EH$.

Also, $EF = HG = FG = EH$.

Also, since AEF and BFG are isosceles triangles

$$\angle AEF = \angle AEF - 45^0$$

$$= \angle BFG = \angle FGB.$$

But $\angle AFB = 180^0$ or

$\angle EFG = 90^0$ similarly,

$\angle H = \angle G = \angle E = \angle F = 90^0.$

Hence, EFGH is a square.

36. (D) Hint is sufficient.

37. (C) If the diagonals of a quadrilateral intersect at right angles, it is not necessarily a rhombus.

38. (A) Let the angles be 3x and 2x.

We have,

$$3x + 2x = 180^0$$

$$5x = 180^0$$

$$x = 36^0$$

∴ The angles are 36×3, 36×2

$$= 108^0, 72^0.$$

39. (C) ∵ trapezium having exactly one pair of parallel sides.

40. (C) ∵ every square is a rhombus.

42. (B) To construct a parallelogram minimum 3 measurements are required.

43. (B) We have,

$$\angle P + \angle Q + \angle R + \angle S = 360^0$$

$$100^0 + \angle Q + 100^0 + 75^0 = 360^0$$

$$\angle Q = 360^0 - 275^0 = 85^0.$$

44. (C) Sum of the angles in a quadrilateral $= 360^0$

$$= 4 \times 90^0$$

$$= 4 \text{ right angles.}$$

45. (A) Length of the each side of a rhombus.

$$= \sqrt{\left(\frac{d_1}{2}\right)^2 + \left(\frac{d_2}{2}\right)^2}$$

$$= \sqrt{\left(\frac{12}{2}\right)^2 + \left(\frac{16}{2}\right)^2}$$

$$= \sqrt{6^2 + 8^2}$$

$$= \sqrt{100}$$

$$= 10 \text{ cm.}$$

46. (B) Let the angles be 3x, 4x, 5x and 6x.

We have

$$3x + 4x + 5x + 6x = 360°$$

$$18x = 360°$$

$$x = 20°$$

Difference between greatest and smallest angles
$$= 6x - 3x = 3x$$

$$= 3 \times 18 = 54°.$$

47. (C) We have,

$$\angle A + \angle B + \angle C + \angle D = 360°$$

$$(\angle A + \angle C) + (\angle B + \angle D) = 360°$$

$$180° + (\angle B + \angle D) = 360°$$

$$\angle B + \angle D = 180°$$

48. (D) A, B, C are true.

D is false ∵ a quadrilateral has only two diagonals.

49. (A) We have,

$$x + x - 10 + x + 30 + 2x = 360°$$

$$5x + 20 = 360$$

$$x = \frac{340}{5} = 68°$$

The angles are,

68°, 68 - 10, 68 + 30, 2 × 68

68°, 58°, 98°, 136°

∴ Greatest angle = 136°.

50. (C) ∵ opposite angles in a parallelo gram are equal.

So $\angle A = \angle C = 80°$

∵ $\angle B$ and $\angle D$ are opposite angles, we have $\angle B = \angle D.$

We have

$$\angle B = \angle D = 180° - 80° = 100°.$$

51. (C) The sum of adjacent angles $= 180°$.

The angles are,

$$180° \times \frac{2}{5}, \ 180° \times \frac{3}{5}$$

$$= 72°, 108°.$$

52. (B) ∵ AB||CD.

We have,

∠A + ∠D = 180°

∠D = 180° - 50° = 130°.

53. (A) ∵ Opposite sides of a parallelo gram are equal.

So perimeter = 5 + 7 + 5 + 7

= 24 cm.

54. (B) ∵ All sides of a Rhombus are equal

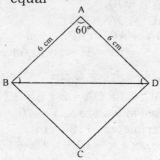

So AB = AD = 6 cm.

Since AB = AD, we have ∠B = ∠D.

In △ABD,

∠A + ∠B + ∠D = 180°

60° + ∠B + ∠B = 180°

∠B = 60° = ∠D

So △ABD is an equilateral △le.

Hence BD = 6 cm.

55. (D) All given statements are true.

(See synopsis)

56. (D) All given statements are false.

(See synopsis)

57. (C) Diagonals bisect each other.

We have

AC = 2 × AO = 2 × 5

= 10 cm.

58. (B) ∵ AB = AC

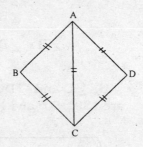

△ABC is an equilateral △le.

So ∠BCA = 60°, also ∠ACD = 60°.

∴ ∠BCD = 60° + 60° = 120°.

59. (A) ∵ In a rectangle the diagonals are equal.

So AC = BD = 10 cm.

60. (D) Parallelogram (See synopsis)

61. (C) Rectangle (See synopsis)

62. (B) In a parallelogram opposite angles are equal.

So ∠A = ∠C

⇒ ∠A - ∠C = 0°.

63. (A) Square (See synopsis)

64. (D) (See synopsis)

65. (B) If diagonals are not perpendicular.

(See synopsis)

66. (B) ∵ In a parallelogram opposite angles are equal.

So ∠A = ∠C = 50°

Aslo ∠B = ∠D

We have

$$\angle A + \angle B + \angle C + \angle D = 360°$$

$$50° + \angle B + 50° + \angle B = 360°$$

$$2\angle B = 260°$$
$$\angle B = 130°$$

$$\angle B = \angle D = 130°$$

$\angle B$, $\angle C$ and $\angle D$ respectively are 130°, 50° and 130°.

67. (D)

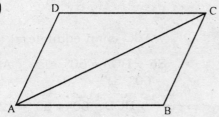

Diagonals divide the parallelogram into two congruent $\triangle$les.

In a $\triangle$le the sum of any two sides must be greater than the third side.
So, the length of the diagonal must be less than 7 cm + 4 cm = 11 cm.

68. (D)

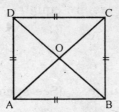

$\triangle$AOB is an isosceles right angled $\triangle$le.

(See synopsis)

69. (A)   Parallelogram (See synopsis)

70. (A) & (C)

Both parallelogram and Rectangle. (See synopsis)

71. (D) All the given statements are false.

72. (A)

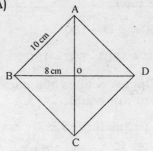

$\because$ BD = 16 cm
BO = OD = 8 cm
In $\triangle$AOB,
$AB^2 = OA^2 + OB^2$
$OA^2 = AB^2 - OB^2$
$\qquad = 10^2 - 8^2 = 100 - 64 = 36$

$OA = \sqrt{36} = 6$ cm

AC = 2 × OA = 2 × 6 = 12 cm.

73. (B) Two sides are x, x + 10
Perimeter = 180 cm
i.e., x + x + 10 + x + x + 10 = 180
$\qquad\qquad$ 4x + 20 = 180
$\qquad\qquad\qquad$ x = 40 cm.

The sides are 40 cm, 50 cm.

74. (A)

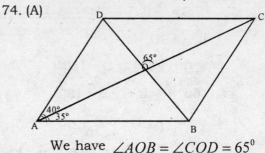

We have $\angle AOB = \angle COD = 65^0$

In $\triangle AOB$, $\angle A + \angle O + \angle B = 180°$

$$35° + 65° + \angle B = 180°$$

$$\angle B = 180 - 100 = 80°$$

$$\therefore \angle ABO = 80°$$

$$\angle ODC = \angle ABO = 80°$$

(alternate interior angles)

75. (C)

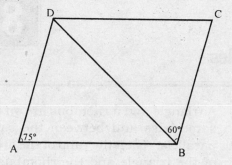

We have

∠ADB = ∠CBD = 60°

In △ADB,

∠A + ∠D + ∠B = 180°

75° + 60° + ∠B = 180°

∠B = 45°

∴ ∠ABD = 45°

∴ ∠CDB = ∠ABD = 45° (alternate
interior angles)

◆ ◆ ◆

Chapter 8

Areas of Parallelograms and Triangles

8

Synopsis

1. Parallelograms on the same base and between the same parallel lines are equal in area.

2. Parallelograms on equal bases and between the same parallel lines are equal in area.

3. Triangles on the same base and between the same parallel lines are equal in area.

4. If a triangle and a parallelogram are on the same base and between the same parallel lines, the area of the triangle is equal to half that of the parallelogram.

5. Triangles with equal areas and having one side of one triangle, equal to one side of the other, have their corresponding altitudes equal.

Multiple Choice Questions

1. Two parallelograms are on the same base and between the same parallels. The ratio of their areas is _____

   (A) 2 : 1   (B) 1 : 2

   (C) 1 : 1   (D) 3 : 1

2. ABCD is a parallelogram and 'O' is the point of intersection of its diagonals $\overline{AC}$ and $\overline{BD}$. If the area of $\triangle AOD = 8cm^2$, the area of the parallelogram is _____.

   (A) 2 cm²   (B) 4 cm²

   (C) 16 cm²   (D) 32 cm²

3. A triangle and a rhombus are on the same base and between the same parallels. Then the ratio of the areas of the triangle and the rhombus is _____.

   (A) 1 : 1   (B) 1 : 2

   (C) 1 : 3   (D) 1 : 4

4. The area of a trepezium is 24cm². The distance between its parallel sides is 4 cm. If one of the parallel sides is 7 cm, the other parallel side is _____

   (A) 5cm   (B) 8cm

   (C) 12cm   (D) 7cm

5. The area of a square is 16cm². Its perimeter is _____.

   (A) 4cm   (B) 8cm

   (C) 112cm   (D) 16cm

6. The ratio of the areas of two squares is 4 : 9. The ratio of their perimeters in the same order is _____

   (A) 3 : 2   (B) 2 : 3

   (C) 9 : 4   (D) 4 : 9

7. In the given figure, P is a point in the interior of parallelogram ABCD. If the area of parallelogram ABCD is 60cm²,

   area of $\triangle ADP$ + area of $\triangle BPC$ = _____.

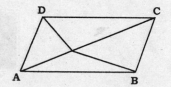

(A) 15cm²   (B) 30cm²

(C) 45cm²   (D) 20cm²

8. A parallelogram and a rectangle are on the same base and between the same parallel lines. Then the perimeter of the rectangle is _____.

(A) equal to the perimeter of the parallelogram

(B) greater than the perimeter of the parallelogram

(C) less than the perimeter of the parallelogram

(D) none of these

9. The area of a rhombus is 20cm². If one of its diagonals is 5cm, the other diagonal is _____.

(A) 4cm

(B) 8cm

(C) 10cm

(D) 16cm

10. The diagonal of a square is 8cm. Its area is _____.

(A) 4cm²

(B) 16cm²

(C) 24cm²

(D) 32cm²

Answers

1. C   2. D   3. B   4. A   5. D   6. B   7. B   8. C   9. B   10. D

✦ ✦ ✦

Chapter 9

Circles

Synopsis

1. A line segment with its end points lying on a circle is called a chord of the circle.

2. A secant is a line that intersects a circle in two distinct points.

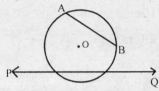

   In this circle, AB is a chord and PQ is a secant.

3. A line that intersects a circle at exactly one point is called a tangent to the circle.

4. A chord AB of a circle with centre O divides the circular region into two parts. Each part is called a segment of the circle.

   The segment containing the centre of the circle is called the major segment and that which does not is called the minor segment of the circle.

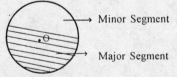

5. If all the four vertices of a quadrilateral lie on a circle then it is called a cyclic quadrilateral.

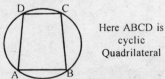

   Here ABCD is cyclic Quadrilateral

6. In a circle, the perpendicular from the centre to a chord bisects the chord.

7. In a circle, the line segment joining the centre to the midpoint of a chord is perpendicular to the chord.

8. The angle subtended by an arc of a circle at the centre is double the angle subtended by it at any point on the remaining part of the circle.

$$\angle AOB = 2\angle ACB$$

9. Angle in a semicircle is a right angle.

10. The angles formed at a point in the arc of a segment by joining the point to the end points of the chord is called an angle of the segment.

11. Angles in the same segment of a circle are equal.

12. The sum of the opposite angles of a cyclic quadrilateral is 180°.

13. If one side of a cyclic quadrilateral is produced, the exterior angle so formed is equal to the interior opposite angle.

14. A cyclic parallelogram is a rectangle.

15. In a circle, the perpendicular from the centre to a chord bisects the chord.

16. In a circle, the line joining the centre to the midpoint of a chord is perpendicular to that chord.

17. In a circle, equal chords subtend equal angles at the centre.

18. In a circle, chords which subtend equal angles at the centre are equal.

19. An arc of a circle is intercepted by an angle if
    (a) the end-points of the arc lie on the arms of the angle and
    (b) each arm of the angle contains at least one end-point.

20. An angle with its vertex at the centre of a circle is called a central angle of the circle.

21. In a circle, if two central angles are equal, then the intercepted arcs are congruent.

22. In a circle, with centre O
    (i) degree measure of minor $\overline{MN}$ is the measure of the central angle MON, that is,
    $$m\ (minor\ \overline{MN}\ ) = \angle MON\ ,$$
    (ii) degree measure of major $\overline{MN}$ is $360^0 - m\ (minor\ \overline{MN}\ )$ and
    (iii) degree measure of a semi-circle is 180^0.

23. Degree measure of a whole circle is 360^0.

24. To each $\angle AOB$, there exists at O, another angle called, reflex $\angle AOB$, such that reflex $\angle AOB = 360^0$.

25. An angle is said to be inscribed in a circle if
    (i) its vertex lies on the circle and
    (ii) each of its arms intersects the circle in two distinct points.

26. In a circle, the measure of an inscribed angle is half the measure of its intercepted arc.

27. The angle an arc subtends at the centre is twice the angle it subtends at any point on the remaining part of the circle.

28. Two angles are said to be inscribed in the same arc (or the same segment) of a circle, if they intercept the same arc.

29. Angles inscribed in the same arc of a circle are equal.

30. Angle in a semicircle is a right angle.

31. A quadrilateral is said to be a cyclic quadrilateral, if its vertices lie on a circle.

32. Opposite angles of a cyclic quadrilateral are supplementary.

33. A secant line of a circle is a line that intersects the circle at two distinct points.

34. A tangent line to a circle is a line in its plane that intersects the circle at exactly one point.

35. The point common to a circle and its tangent is called the point of contact.

36. In a circle, the tangent at a point and the radius through the point of contact are perpendicular to each other.

37. A line through the end-point of a radius of a circle, perpendicular to the radius, is tangent to the circle at that point.

38. At each point of a circle, there is one and only one tangent to the circle.

39. If the line PA is tangent to a circle, at the point A on it, then the line

segment PA is called the tangent segment from P to the circle.

40. The length of the tangent segment from a point P to a circle, is called the length of the tangent from P to the circle.

41. Lengths of the two tangents to a circle from an external point are equal.

42. The two tangents to a circle from an external point are equally inclined to the line joining the point to the centre of the circle.

Multiple Choice Questions

1. AB is a chord of a circle with centre O and radius 17 cm. If OM $\perp$ AB and OM = 8 cm, find the length of chord AB.

   (A) 12 cm   (B) 30 cm

   (C) 15 cm   (D) 24 cm

2. AB is a chord of length 24 cm of a circle with centre O and radius 13 cm. Find the distance of the chord from the centre.

   (A) 5 cm   (B) 6 cm

   (C) $\sqrt{407}$ (D) None

3. 48 cm long chord of a circle is at a distance of 7 cm from the centre. Find the radius of the circle.

   (A) 5 cm   (B) 17 cm
   (C) 25 cm   (D) None

4. A chord of a circle is 12 cm in length and its distance from the centre is 8 cm. Find the length of the chord of the same circle which is at a distance of 6 cm from the centre.

   (A) 30 cm   (B) 24 cm
   (C) 16 cm   (D) 18 cm

5. Which of the following statement(s) is/are true?

   (A) Two chords of a circle equidistant from the centre are equal
   (B) Equal chords in a circle subtend equal angles at the centre
   (C) Angle in a semicircle is a right angle
   (D) All the above

6. In the following figure, find the value of x.

   (A) 68°

   (B) 63°

   (C) 252°

   (D) None

7. In the given figure, $\triangle$ABC is inscribed in a circle with centre O. If $\angle$ACB = 65°, find $\angle$ABC.

   (A) 25°
   (B) 35°
   (C) Cannot be determined
   (D) None

8. In the following figure if O is the centre of the circle, then find x.

   (A) 55°   (B) 208°
   (C) 52°   (D) None

9. An equilateral △le PQR is inscribed in a circle with centre O. Find ∠QOR.

(A) 60°   (B) 120°
(C) 30°   (D) None

10. In the given figure, △XYZ is inscribed in a circle with centre O. If the length of the chord YZ is equal to the radius of the circle OY then ∠YXZ = _____

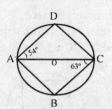

(A) 60°   (B) 30°
(C) 80°   (D) 100°

11. In the given figure, O is the centre of a circle. If ∠DAC = 54° and ∠ACB = 63° then ∠BAC = _____

(A) 72°   (B) 54°

(C) 27°   (D) 90°

12. In the given figure, AOB is a diameter of a circle with centre O. If ∠BOD = 120°, find ∠ACD.

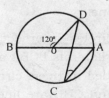

(A) 30°   (B) 40°
(C) 60°   (D) 90°

13. In the following figure, O is the centre of the circle. Find the value of x.

(A) 30°   (B) 45°
(C) 60°   (D) 75°

14. In the given figure, ABCD is a quadrilateral inscribed in a circle. Diagonals AC and BD are joined. If ∠CAD = 50° and ∠BDC = 45°. Find ∠BCD.

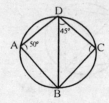

(A) 75°   (B) 105°
(C) 85°   (D) 60°

15. Find the value of x in the following figure.

(A) 45°   (B) 35°
(C) 60°   (D) 55°

16. In the given figure, two chords AB and CD of a circle intersect each other at a point E such that ∠BAC = 45°, ∠BED = 120°. Then find ∠ABD.

(A) 15°   (B) 30°
(C) 45°   (D) 60°

17. In the given figure, AOB and COD are two diameters of a circle with centre O. If ∠OAC = 60°. Find ∠ABD.

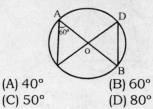

(A) 40°   (B) 60°
(C) 50°   (D) 80°

18. In the given figure, ABCD is a quadrilateral inscribed in a circle. Diagonals AC and BD are joined. If ∠CAD = 40° and ∠BDC = 25° Find ∠BCD.

(A) 85°   (B) 120°
(C) 115°   (D) 95°

19. Two chords AB and CD of a circle cut each other when produced outside the circle at P. AD and BC are joined.

If ∠PAD = 30° and ∠CPA = 45°. Find ∠CBP.

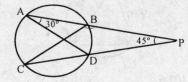

(A) 105°   (B) 115°
(C) 135°   (D) None

20. In the given figure, △ABC is inscribed in a circle. The bisector of ∠BAC meets BC at D and the circle at E. If EC is joined then ∠ECD = 30°. Find ∠BAC.

(A) 30°
(B) 40°
(C) 50°
(D) 60°

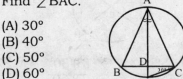

21. In the given figure, ABCD is a cyclic quadrilateral in which ∠BAD = 120°. Find ∠BCD.

(A) 240° (B) 60° (C) 120° (D) 180°

22. In the given figure, POQ is a diameter of a circle with centre O and PQRS is a cyclic quadrilateral. SQ is joined. If ∠R=138°, find ∠PQS.

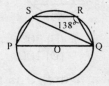

(A) 90°   (B) 42°
(C) 48°   (D) 38°

23. In the given figure, PQRS is a cyclic trapezium in which PQ||SR. If ∠P = 82°. Find ∠S.

(A) 98°

(B) 108°

(C) Data not sufficient

(D) None

24. Two circles intersect in A and B. Quadrilaterals PCBA and ABDE are inscribed in these circles such that PAE and CBD are line segments. If ∠P = 95° and ∠C = 40°. Find the value of Z.

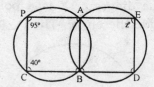

(A) 65°   (B) 105°
(C) 95°   (D) 85°

25. Which of the following statement(s) is/are true?

(A) Sum of the opposite angles of a cyclic quadrilateral is 180°

(B) If one side of a cyclic quadrilateral is produced, the exterior angle soformed is equal to the interior opposite angle

(C) A cyclic parallelogram is a rectangle

(D) All the above

26. The circumference of a circle is 60 cm. The length of an arc of 90° is

(A) 10 cm   (B) 15 cm
(C) 20 cm   (D) none

27. A circle is divided into 12 equal parts. The number of degrees in each arc is

(A) 30°   (B) 60°
(C) 45°   (D) none

28. An equilateral triangle XYZ is inscribed in a circle with centre O. The measure of XOY is

(A) 60°   (B) 120°
(C) 45°   (D) 75°

29. A diameter of a circle is also a

(A) tangent   (B) chord
(C) secant   (D) radius

30. The number of tangents that can be drawn to a circle at a given point on it is

(A) two   (B) one
(C) zero   (D) three

31. In a circle, the major arc is twice the minor arc. The corresponding central angles and the degree measures of the two arcs are

(A) 90° and 270° (B) 60° and 300°
(C) 240° and 120°(D) 120° and 240°

32. AB, BC and CD are equal chords of a circle with O as the centre. ∠AOB is

(A) 60°

(B) 120°

(C) 90°

(D) not necessarily any of the foregoing

33. One side of a regular polygon with vertices on a circle subtends an angle of 20° at the centre of this circle. This polygon is

(A) 20–sided   (B) 18–sided
(C) 9–sided   (D) 6–sided

34. In the figure drawn below if ∠C = 30°, then ∠A and ∠B are respectively

(A) 60° and 90°

(B) 90° and 60°

(C) 45° and 105°

(D) 75° and 75°

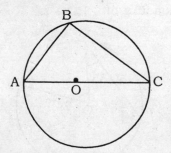

35. The least number of noncollinear points required to draw a circle passing through them is

(A) two   (B) three
(C) four   (D) nine

36. A circle with radius 2 units is intersected by a line at points R and T. The maximum possible distance between R and T is

(A) 1 unit (B) 2π units

(C) 4π units (D) 4 units

37. P, Q, R, S, T and U are points on the circle shown below and the length of arc PQR is 6 cm. Then length of arc STU is

(A) 12 cm

(B) 6π cm

(C) 6 cm

(D) cannot be determined from the given data

38. O is the centre of the circle as shown in the diagram. The distance between P and Q is 4 cm. Then the measure of $\angle$ROQ is

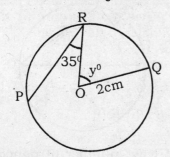

(A) y^0

(B) 35^0

(C) 105^0

(D) 70^0

39. RS is a diameter of circle as shown in the diagram. X is a point lying outside the circle. Then $\angle$RXS is

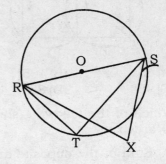

(A) 90^0

(B) greater than 90

(C) lesser than 90^0

(D) cannot be determined from given data

40. C is the centre of the circle as shown in the diagram below. Then x + y is equal to

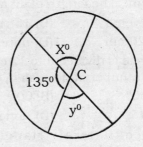

(A) 90^0 (B) 100^0

(C) 130^0 (D) 45^0

41. E and F are two points on a circle O. Point G is inside circle O and point H is outside circle O. The degree measure of $\angle$EHF is

(A) 60^0

(B) greater than 60^0

(C) less than 60^0

(D) cannot be determined from given data

42. Given a circle as shown in figure below. If the length of arc ABC is 12 cm then length of arc ADC is

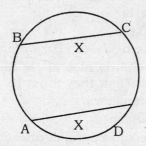

(A) 12 cm

(B) 8 cm

(C) 16 cm

(D) cannot be determined from given data

43. Triangle PQR is inscribed in a circle. If PQ = 4 cm then QR is equal to

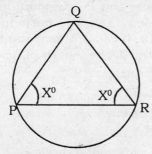

(A) 4 cm

(B) 8 cm

(C) 6 cm

(D) cannot be determined from given data

44. In the figure given below O is the centre of the circle. Line AB intersects the circle only at point B, and line DC intersects the circle only at point C. If the circle has a radius of 2 cm, then AC is

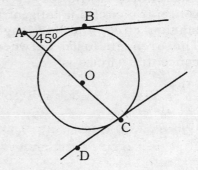

(A) 4 cm

(B) $2 + \sqrt{2}$ cm

(C) $4 + \sqrt{2}$ cm

(D) $2 + 2\sqrt{2}$ cm

45. The length l of a tangent, drawn from a point A to a circle is $\dfrac{4}{3}$ of the radius r. The shortest distance from A to the circle is

(A) $\dfrac{1}{2}$ r   (B) r

(C) $\dfrac{1}{2} l$ (D) $\dfrac{2}{3} l$

46. A triangle ABC is inscribed in a circle, and the bisectors of the angles meet the circumference at X, Y, Z. The angles of the triangle X, Y, Z are respectively

(A) $90^0 - \dfrac{A}{2}, 90^0 - \dfrac{B}{2}, 90^0 - \dfrac{C}{2}$

(B) $90^0, 60^0, 30^0$

(C) $\dfrac{A}{2}, \dfrac{B}{2}, \dfrac{C}{2}$

(D) $\dfrac{B}{2}, \dfrac{A}{2}, \dfrac{A}{2} - \dfrac{B}{2}$

47. The chord of the larger of two concentric circles is tangent to the smaller circle and has length 'a'. The area enclosed between the concentric circles is

(A) πa^2

(B) $\dfrac{\pi a^2}{2}$

(C) $\dfrac{\pi a^2}{4}$

(D) cannot be determined from given data

48. A regular decagon (10 sides) is inscribed in a circle. The angle that each side of the decagon subtends at the centre is

(A) 100^0 (B) 42^0

(C) 36^0 (D) 24^0

49. A circle has

(A) 10 sides   (B) 20 sides

(C) 3000 sides   (D) infinite sides

50. The length of a chord of a circle is equal to the radius of the circle. The angle which this chord subtends on the longer segment of the circle is equal to

(A) 30^0 (B) 45^0

(C) 60^0 (D) 90^0

51. In the given circle ABCD, O is the centre and $\angle BDC = 42^0$. Then $\angle ACB$ is equal to

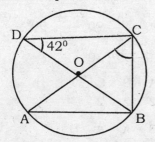

(A) 42^0 (B) 45^0

(C) 48^0 (D) 60^0

52. Two parallel chords on the same side of the centre of a circle are 10 cm and 24 cm long and their distance apart is 7 cm. The radius of the circle is

(A) 13 cm   (B) 8 cm

(C) 5 cm   (D) 7 cm

53. Two chords of a circle bisect each other. Then they must be

(A) diameters

(B) tangents

(C) secants parallel to each other

(D) none of the foregoing

54. A telegraph wire spans 20 m with a dip at the centre of 10 cm. Assuming the wire is in the form of a circular arc, its radius is

(A) 45 m   (B) 116 m

(C) 208 m   (D) 500.05 cm

55. AB is a chord of a circle of radius 4.3 cm and P is a point on it which divides it into two parts in the ratio 7 : 10. If P is 2.7 cm distant from the centre O, the length of AB is

(A) 5 cm

(B) 6.8 cm

(C) 6.4 cm

(D) 6.1 cm

56. The radius of a circle is 2.5 cm. AB and CD are two parallel chords 2.7 cm apart. If AB = 4.8 cm then CD is equal to

(A) 4.8 cm

(B) 2.4 cm

(C) 3 cm

(D) 4 cm

57. The diameter is

(A) smallest chord of a circle

(B) greatest chord of a circle

(C) three times radius of circle

(D) none of the foregoing

58. Given a circle and a quadrilateral ABCD inscribed in it as shown. If $\angle B = 125^0$, $\angle E$ is equal to

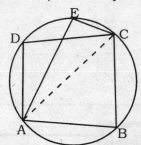

  (A) 55^0 (B) 125^0

  (C) 130^0 (D) 62.5^0

59. Given a chord AB in a circle as shown. If two more chords AD and BE are drawn perpendicular to AB then

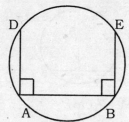

  (A) AD = BE

  (B) AD = 2BE

  (C) 2AD = BE

  (D) none of these

60. PQ, PR are tangents to a circle and QS is a diameter. Then

  (A) $\angle QPR = \dfrac{1}{2}\angle RQS$

  (B) $\angle QPR = 2\angle RQS$

  (C) $\angle QPR = \angle RQS$

  (D) none of the foregoing

61. ABCD is a quadrilateral. If $\angle ACB = \angle ADB$ then
  (A) ABCD is a cyclic quadrilateral
  (B) ABCD is a parallelogram
  (C) ABCD is a square
  (D) ABCD is not a cyclic quadrilateral

62. As shown in figure, ABC is a triangle inscribed in a circle with centre O. If $\angle OBC = 30^0$ then $\angle A$ is equal to

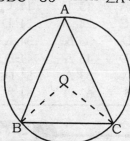

  (A) 30^0 (B) 60^0

  (C) 45^0 (D) 75^0

63. Which of the following is a cyclic quadrilateral?
  (A) Trapezium

  (B) Parallelogram

  (C) Rhombus

  (D) Rectangle

64. O is the centre of a circle and if $\angle A + \angle BOC = 120^0$ then $\angle BOC$ is equal to

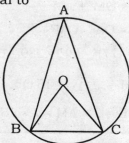

  (A) 80^0 (B) 30^0

  (C) 60^0 (D) 100^0

65. $\overline{AB}$, $\overline{CD}$, $\overline{EF}$ and $\overline{GH}$ are chords of a circle. If $\overline{AB} = 3.5$ cm, CD = 4 cm, EF = 3 cm and GH= 5 cm then the chord nearest to the centre of the circle is

  (A) $\overline{AB}$ (B) $\overline{CD}$

  (C) $\overline{EF}$ (D) $\overline{GH}$

1. B	2. A	3. C	4. C	5. D	6. B	7. A	8. C	9. B	10. B
11. C	12. A	13. D	14. C	15. B	16. A	17. B	18. C	19. A	20. D
21. B	22. C	23. A	24. D	25. D	26. B	27. A	28. B	29. B	30. B
31. C	32. D	33. B	34. A	35. B	36. D	37. D	38. D	39. C	40. A
41. D	42. D	43. A	44. D	45. C	46. A	47. C	48. C	49. D	50. A
51. C	52. A	53. A	54. D	55. B	56. C	57. B	58. A	59. A	60. B
61. A	62. B	63. D	64. A	65. D					

Explanatory Answers

1. (B)

OA = 17 cm; OM = 8 cm.

In $\triangle$ OMA we have,

$OA^2 = OM^2 + AM^2$

$AM^2 = OA^2 - OM^2$

$= (17)^2 - (8)^2 = 289 - 64 = 225$

$AM = \sqrt{225} = 15$ cm.

So AB = 2 × AM = 2 × 15 = 30 cm.

2. (A)

AB = 24 cm.

So AM = MB = 12 cm, OA = 13 cm.

In $\triangle$ OMA,

$OA^2 = OM^2 + AM^2$

$OM^2 = OA^2 - AM^2$

$= (13)^2 - (12)^2$

$= 169 - 144 = 25$

$OM = \sqrt{25} = 5$ cm.

3. (C)

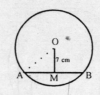

OM = 7 cm.

AB = 48 cm.

AM = MB = 24 cm.

In $\triangle$ OAM,

$OA^2 = OM^2 + AM^2$

$= 7^2 + 24^2$

$= 49 + 576 = 625$

$OA = \sqrt{625} = 25$ cm.

4. (C)

AB = 12 cm.

AM = MB = 6 cm.

In $\triangle$ OMA,

$OA^2 = OM^2 + AM^2$

$\quad = 8^2 + 6^2$

$\quad = 64 + 36 = 100$

$OA = \sqrt{100} = 10$ cm.

$\therefore$ Radius = OA = OC = 10 cm.

In $\triangle$ ONA,

$OC^2 = ON^2 + NC^2$

$NC^2 = OC^2 - ON^2$

$\quad = 10^2 - 6^2$

$\quad = 100 - 36 = 64$

$NC = \sqrt{64} = 8$ cm.

Length of the chord = 2 × NC

$\quad = 2 \times 8$

$\quad = 16$ cm.

5. (D) $\because$ All the given statements are true.

6. (B) $\angle AOB = 2 \times \angle ACB$

$\angle ACB = \dfrac{\angle AOB}{2} = \dfrac{126°}{2} = 63°$.

7. (A) Angle in a semicircle is a right angle.

So $\angle BAC = 90°$.

In $\triangle$ ABC,

$\angle A + \angle B + \angle C = 180°$

$90° + \angle B + 65° = 180°$

$\angle B = 180° - 155° = 25°$.

8. (C) We have,

$2x° = 104°$

$x = \dfrac{104}{2} = 52°$.

9. (B)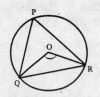

$\because$ $\triangle$ PQR is equilateral

$\angle P = \angle Q = \angle R = 60°$

$\angle QOR = 2 \angle QPR = 2 \times 60°$

$\quad = 120°$.

10. (B) $\because$ OY = OZ = YZ

So $\triangle$ OYZ is an equilateral $\triangle$le.

$\therefore$ $\angle YOZ = 60°$

$\angle YXZ = \dfrac{1}{2} \angle YOZ = \dfrac{1}{2} \times 60° = 30°$.

11. (C) Angle in a semi circle is a right angle.

So $\angle ABC = 90°$

In $\triangle$ ABC,

$\angle A + \angle B + \angle C = 180°$

$\angle A + 90° + 63° = 180°$

$\angle A = 27°$

$\therefore$ $\angle BAC = 27°$.

12. (A) $\because$ $\angle AOB = 180°$

$\angle BOD + \angle AOD = 180°$

$\angle AOD = 180° - \angle BOD$

$\quad = 180° - 120° = 60°$.

We have,

$\angle ACD = \dfrac{1}{2} \angle AOD$

$\quad = \dfrac{1}{2} \times 60° = 30°$.

13. (D) ∵ Angles in the same segment of a circle are equal.

$\angle BAC = \angle BDC = 45°$

In $\triangle BCD$,

$\angle B + \angle C + \angle D = 180°$.

$60° + x° + 45° = 180°$

$x = 180 - 105$

$= 75°$.

14. (C) We have

$\angle CBD = \angle CAD = 50°$

(Angles in same segment)

Now in $\triangle BCD$

$\angle B + \angle C + \angle D = 180°$

$50° + 45° + \angle C = 180°$

$\angle C = 180 - 95° = 85°$

∴ $\angle BCD = 85°$.

15. (B) Angles in the same segment are equal

So $\angle BAC = \angle BDC = 45°$

In $\triangle ABC$,

$\angle A + \angle B + \angle C = 180°$

$45° + 100° + \angle C = 180°$

$\angle C = 180° - 145° = 35°$

∴ $x = 35°$.

16. (A) Angles in the same segment are equal.

$\angle BAC = \angle BDC = 45°$

In $\triangle BED$,

$\angle B + \angle E + \angle D = 180°$

$\angle B + 120° + 45° = 180°$

$\angle B = 180 - 165 = 15°$

∴ $\angle ABD = 15°$.

17. (B) Angles in the same segment are equal.

$\angle CAB = \angle BDC = 60°$

We have,

$\angle COB = 2 \angle CAB = 2 × 60° = 120°$

So $\angle BOD = 180° - 120° = 60°$

In $\triangle BOD$,

$\angle B + \angle O + \angle D = 180°$

$\angle B + 60° + 60° = 180°$

$\angle B = 60°$

∴ $\angle ABD = 60°$.

18. (C) Angles in a same segments are equal.

$\angle BDC = \angle BAC = 25°$

So $\angle BAD = 25° + 40° = 65°$

Here ABCD is a cyclic quadrilateral.

So the sum of opposite angles $= 180°$

$\angle BAD + \angle BCD = 180°$

$\angle BCD = 180° - \angle BAD$

$= 180° - 65° = 115°$.

19. (A) Angles in a same segment are equal.

$\angle BAD = \angle BCD = 30°$

In $\triangle CBP$,

$\angle C + \angle B + \angle P = 180°$

$30° + \angle B + 45° = 180°$

$\angle B = 180° - 75° = 105°$

∴ $\angle CBP = 105°$.

20. (D) ∵ Angle in same segment are equal

∠BCE = ∠BAE = 30°

∵ AD is a bisector,

So ∠BAE = ∠CAE = 30°

∴ ∠BAC = 30° + 30°

= 60°.

21. (B) Sum of the opposite angles in a cyclic quadrilateral = 180°.

∠BAD + ∠BCD = 180°

∠BCD = 180° - ∠BAD

= 180° - 120° = 60°.

22. (C) ∵ PQRS is a cyclic quadrilateral.

∠P + ∠R = 180°

∠P + 138° = 180°

∠P = 180° - 138° = 42°

Angle in a semicircle is a right angle.

So ∠PSQ = 90°

In △PQS,

∠P + ∠Q + ∠S = 180°

42° + ∠Q + 90 = 180°

∠Q = 180° - 132° = 48°

∴ ∠PQS = 48°.

23. (A) PQ||RS and PS is a transversal. We have

∠P + ∠S = 180°

∠S = 180° - ∠P = 180° - 82° = 98°.

24. (D) In PACB,

∠P + ∠B = 180° ⇒ ∠B

= 180° - 95° = 85°

∠CBD = 180° ⇒ ∠ABD

= 180° - 85° = 95°

In ABDE,

∠B + ∠E = 180° ⇒ ∠E = Z°

= 180° - 95° = 85°.

25. (D) All the given statements are true.

26. (B) Since the arc subtends 90° at centre it is a quadrant and is equal

to $\frac{1}{4}$ circumference.

$= \frac{1}{4} \times 2\pi r = \frac{1}{4} \times 60 = 15$ cm.

27. (A) A circle contains 360°.

∴ each $\frac{1}{12}$ th part subtends

$\frac{1}{12} \times 360 = 30°$

28. (B) XYZ is an equilateral triangle. We know that O is circu-mcentre, as well as incentre for an equilateral triangle.

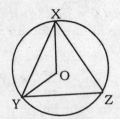

∴ ∠XYO = ∠YXO = 30°

∴ ∠XOY = 180° − (30° + 30°)

= 120°

29. (B) We know that the diametre is the largest chord of a circle.

30. (B) Clearly only one tangent can be drawn to a circle at a point on the circle.

31. (C) Let the major arc subtend x° at centre. Since it is twice the minor

arc, the minor arc subtends $\frac{x°}{2}$

at centre. But $x^0 + \dfrac{x^0}{2} = 360^0$

or $x = 240^0$ and $\dfrac{x}{2} = 120^0$

32. (D) Clearly, as shown in the figure, triangle AOB, OBC and OCD are congruent by SSS congruency.

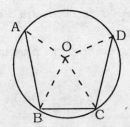

Let $\angle AOB = x$ then

$\angle AOB = \angle BOC = \angle COD = x$

Let $\angle AOD = y$. Clearly,

$3x + y = 360^0$ is an equation which is satisfied for an infinite values of x.

33. (B) Clearly, $\dfrac{360}{n} = 20^0$ or n = 18. Hence the polygon is 18–sided.

34. (A) We know that angle in a semi-circle is a right angle.
Hence, $\angle B = 90^0$. Also

$\angle A + \angle B + \angle C = 180^0$

$\therefore \angle A = 60^0$

35. (B) We know that there is exactly one circle passing through three given noncollinear points.

36. (D) Clearly RT is any chord. RT is maximum, if it is the diametre = 2 × radius = 4 units.

37. (D) First we cannot assume that PS and RU are diametres.

$\angle PXR = \angle UXS$. But X is not the centre of the circle.

38. (D) Since PQ = 4 cm = 2 × OQ

= 2 × radius, PQ is the diametre of circle. Join RQ. $\angle PRQ = 90^0$

$\therefore \angle ORQ = 90 - 35 = 55^0$
But OR = OQ.

$\therefore \angle ORQ = \angle OQR = 55^0$

$\therefore y = 180 - (55 + 55) = 70^0$

39. (C) Let SX cut the circle at Y. Join RY.
$\angle RYS = 90^0$. But in triangle RYX,

$\angle RYX = \angle RXY + \angle YRX$

or $\angle RXY = \angle RYX - \angle YRX$

or $\angle RXS = \angle RYX - \angle YRX$

$= 90^0 - \angle YRX$

i.e., $\angle RXS$ is less than 90^0.

40. (A) Vertically opposite angles are equal.
Hence $\angle X = \angle Y$. Also

$\angle X + \angle Y + 135^0 + 135^0 = 360^0$

$\therefore 2\angle X = 90^0$ or $\angle x = 45^0$

or $\angle x + \angle y = 90^0$

41. (D) As shown in figure, join F to point J where EH intersects the circle. Clearly, EGFJ is a cyclic quadrilateral.

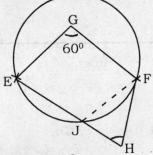

Hence, $\angle EJF = 120^0$.

Also in triangle FJH, $\angle FJE = 120^0$

$= \angle JFH + \angle JHF$

Clearly $\angle EHF$ can be less than, equal to or less than 60^0.

42. (D) Since the chords AD and BC need not necessarily be parallel, D is the correct option.

43. (A) Since base angles are equal, it is an isosceles triangle.
Hence PQ = QR = 4 cm.

44. (D) Join OB. $\angle OBA = 90^0$. By Pythagorus theorem,
$AB^2 + OB^2 = AO^2$ also, OBA is an isosceles right angled triangle.
$\therefore$ OB = AB = 2 cm.
Hence $AO^2 = 2^2 + 2^2$ or
$AO = 2\sqrt{2}$ cm.
$\therefore$ AC = AO + OC = $\left(2\sqrt{2} + 2\right)$ cm.

45. (C) Join AO. Let AO intersect the circle at X. Since $\angle ABO = 90^0$.

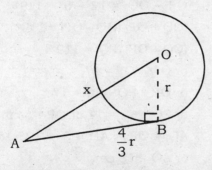

$$AO^2 = AB^2 + OB^2$$

$$= \left(\frac{4}{3}r\right)^2 + r^2 = \frac{25r^2}{9}$$

$$AO = \frac{5}{3}r$$

$$(AX + r)^2 = \left(\frac{5}{3}r\right)^2 = \frac{25}{9}r^2$$

$$AX + r = \frac{5}{3}r \text{ or}$$

$$AX = \frac{2}{3}r = \frac{1}{2}l$$

46. (A) Clearly, $\angle BYX = \angle BAX = \dfrac{\angle A}{2}$

Also $\angle ZYB = \angle ZCB = \dfrac{\angle C}{2}$ are angles in same segment.

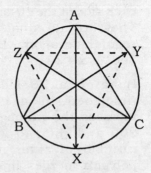

Hence, $\angle ZYX = \angle ZYB + \angle BYX$

$$\angle ZYX = \frac{\angle C}{2} + \frac{\angle A}{2} = \frac{\angle A + \angle C}{2}$$

$$\frac{180 - \angle B}{2} = 90^0 - \frac{\angle B}{2}$$

Similarly, other angles are

$$90^0 - \frac{A}{2} \text{ and } 90^0 - \frac{C}{2}.$$

47. (C)

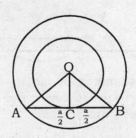

Let the radius of smaller circle be 'r' and that of outer circle be R.

In $\triangle OAB$, $r^2 + \left(\dfrac{a}{2}\right)^2 = OB = R^2$

$\therefore$ area enclosed between concentric circles

$$= \pi R^2 - \pi r^2 = \pi \left(r^2 + \frac{a^2}{4} \right) - \pi r^2$$

$$= \frac{\pi a^2}{4}$$

48. (C) Let x^0 be the angle subtended by each side of the 10–sided decagon. They are all equal since it is a regular decagon. Hence, $10x = 360^0$ or $x = 36^0$.

49. (D) Imagine a 20–sided polygon inscribed in a circle. Now, increase the number of sides to 200 and then to 2000. As the number of sides increase the polygon merges into the circle. Hence we can say that a circle is a polygon with an infinite number of sides.

50. (A) Clearly, OAB is an equilateral triangle. Hence $\angle AOB = 60^0$. Take any point P on longer

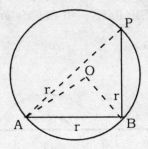

segment of circle. The angle at centre is twice the angle at the circumference.

51. (C) $\angle BAC = 42^0$ (Angles in the same segment)

$\angle ABC = 90^0$ (Angle in a semi-circle)

$\therefore \angle ACB = 180^0 - \left(90^0 + 42^0 \right) = 48^0$

52. (A) AP = 12 cm and CQ = 5 cm.

AB = 24 cm and CD = 10 cm.

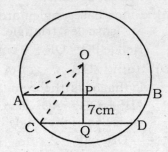

Since the perpendicular to the chord bisects the chord.

$AO^2 = AP^2 + OP^2 = 12^2 + OP^2$

$OC^2 = CQ^2 + OQ^2 = 5^2 + OQ^2$

Subtracting, we have,

$OP^2 - OQ^2 = 12^2 - 5^2 = 119$

$(OQ + OP)(OQ - OP) = 119$

$(OQ + OP)(PQ) = 119$

or OQ + OP = 17

or OP + PQ + OP = 17

or 2OP + 7 = 17 or OP = 5 cm.

$AO^2 = OP^2 + AP^2 = 5^2 + 12^2 = 169$

or AO = 13 cm,
    i.e., radius =13 cm.

53. (A) We know that perpendicular drawn from the centre bisects the chord and line that bisects the chord is the perpendicular drawn from the centre. Hence if the chords bisect each other, both must pass through the centre, i.e., both are diametres.

54. (D) $AO^2 = AP^2 + OP^2$ or

$r^2 = 10^2 + OP^2$

OQ = r (OP + 0.1)

$(OP + 0.1)^2 = 10^2 + OP^2$

$OP^2 + 0.01 + 0.2OP = 10^2 + OP^2$

or OP = $\dfrac{99.99}{.2}$ = 499.95m

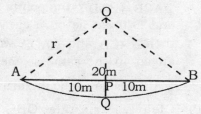

Hence r = OP + PQ = 499.95 + .1
= 500.05 m.

55. (B) As shown in the diagram below, OP = 2.7cm and OA = 4.3 cm. Draw a perpendicular OQ to the chord AB. Clearly, AQ = QB since P divides AB in the ratio 7:10. let AP = 7x and PB = 10x.

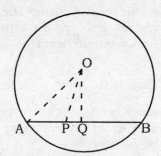

Also, PQ = AQ – AP = $\dfrac{AB}{2}$ – AP

= $\dfrac{17x}{2}$ – 7x = 1.5x.

By Pythagorus theorem, we have,
AQ^2 + OQ^2 = AO^2

Also, OP^2 = PQ^2 + OQ^2

AQ^2 + OQ^2 = AO^2

PQ^2 + OQ^2 = OP^2

AQ^2 – PQ^2 = AO^2 – OP^2

or (8.5x)^2 – (1.5x)^2 = (4.3)^2 – (2.7)^2

(10x) (7x) = 7(1.6)

x^2 = 16 or x = 4 cm.

∴ AB = 17x = 17 × .4 = 6.8 cm.

56. (C)

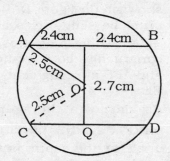

From the above diagram, it is clear that,

AP^2 + PO^2 = AO^2 or

OP^2 = 2.5^2 – 2.4^2 = 0.49

or OP = 0.7 cm

or OQ = PQ – OP = 2 cm.

Also, CO^2 = OQ^2 + CQ^2

2^2 + CQ^2 = 2.5^2

or CQ = 1.5 cm

∴ CD = 3 cm

57. (B) The diameter is the greatest chord in a circle.

58. (A) ∠B = 125^0

∴ ∠D = 180^0 – 125^0 = 55^0

Since opposite angles of a cyclic quadrilateral are supplementary.

But ∠D = ∠E (Angles in same segment)

∴ ∠E = 55^0

59. (A) Join BD and AE as shown in the diagram.

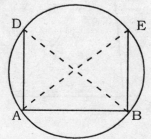

Since ∠DAB = ∠ABE = 90^0 as

shown in the figure, DAB and DEB must be semicircles and AE = BD are diametres. By RHS congruency both triangles ADB and AEB are congruent. Hence BE = AD.

60. (B) As shown in the figure below, $\angle ROS = 2\angle RQS$ because the angle at the centre is twice the angle formed at any remaining part of circumference.

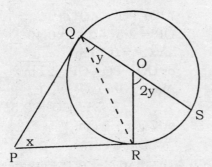

But $\angle ROQ = 180 - 2y$. Also PQOR is a quadrilateral and $\angle P + \angle Q + \angle R + \angle O = 360^0$

$\therefore x + 90^0 + 90^0 + 180 - 2y$

$= 360^0$

$\therefore \angle QPR = 2\angle RQS$

61. (A)

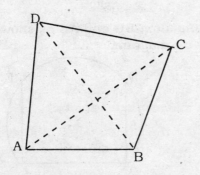

ABCD is a quadrilateral and $\therefore \angle ACB = \angle ADB$. But since $\angle ACB = \angle ADB$ the points A, B, C and D must lie on a circle since then $\angle ACB$ and $\angle ADB$ would be angles in the same segment.

$\therefore$ ABCD is a cyclic quadrilateral.

62. (B) Clearly, triangle OBC is an isosceles triangle. OB = OC.

$\therefore \angle OBC = \angle OCB = 30^0$

$\therefore \angle BOC = 120^0 \therefore \angle A = 60^0$ Since the angle at the centre is twice the angle formed at the remaining part of the boundary of the circle.

63. (D) As a rectangle can be inscribed in a circle and since the opposite angles are supp-lementary, it is a cyclic quadrilateral.

64. (A) Clearly if $\angle BOC = x$ then $\angle A = \dfrac{x}{2}$ since angle at centre is twice the angle at remaining part of circumference.

$\therefore x + \dfrac{x}{2} = 120^0$ or $x = 80^0$.

65. (D) We know that the greater chord is nearer the centre. Hence GH = 5 cm is nearest to centre.

❖ ❖ ❖

Chapter 10

Constructions

Synopsis

1. *A triangle is said to be :*

    (a) an equilateral triangle, if all of its sides are equal.

    (b) an isosceles triangle, if any two of its sides are equal.

    (c) a scalene triangle, if all of its sides are of different lengths.

2. *A triangle is said to be :*

    (a) an acute angled triangle, if each one of its angles measure less than 90°.

    (b) a right angled triangle, if any one of its angles measure 90°.

    (c) an obtuse angled triangle, if any one of its angles measure more than 90°.

3. The sum of the angles of a triangle is 180°.

4. The sum of any two sides of a triangle is greater than the third side.

5. The difference of any two sides is less than the third side.

6. If a side of a triangle is produced, the exterior angle so formed is equal to the sum of interior opposite angles.

    E.g. :-

    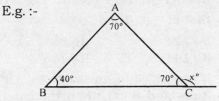

    Exterior angle
    $X° = \angle A + \angle B = 70° + 40° = 110°$

7. *Pythagoros theorem :*

    In a right angled triangle, the square of the hypotenuse is equal to the sum of the squares of the remaining two sides.

    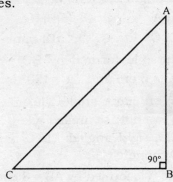

    Here $AC^2 = AB^2 + BC^2$

8. In a right angled triangle hypotenuse is the longest side.

9. Of all the line segments that can be drawn to a given line from a point outside it, the perpendicular line segment is the shortest.

10. Three positive integers a, b and c are said to form a Pythagorean triplet in the same order if $c^2 = a^2 + b^2$.

    E.g. :- 3, 4, 5; 5, 12, 13; 7, 24, 25; 8, 15, 17; 12, 35, 37; ...... etc. are called Pythagorean triplets.

11. All the three angles of a scalene triangle are of different measures.

12. The angles opposite to the equal sides of an isosceles triangle are equal.

13. Each angle of an equilateral triangle measures 60°.

1. The triangle formed by BC = 5 cm, AC = 3 cm, AB = 5.8 cm is

   (A) a right angled $\triangle$le
   (B) an isosceles $\triangle$le
   (C) an equilateral $\triangle$le
   (D) a scalene $\triangle$le

2. In a $\triangle$ABC, if $AB^2 = BC^2 + AC^2$, then the right angle is at

   (A) A   (B) B
   (C) C   (D) none

3. The $\triangle$le formed by BC = 7.2 cm, AC = 6 cm and $\angle$C =120° is

   (A) an acute angle $\triangle$le
   (B) an obtuse angled $\triangle$le
   (C) a right angled $\triangle$le
   (D) none

4. The $\triangle$le formed by AB = 3 cm, BC = 4 cm, AC = 8 cm is

   (A) a scalene $\triangle$le
   (B) an isosceles $\triangle$le
   (C) an equilateral $\triangle$le
   (D) no triangle is formed

5. If two angles in a $\triangle$le are 65° and 85°, then the third angle is

   (A) 30°   (B) 45°   (C) 60°   (D) 90°

6. If one angle is the average of the other two angles and the difference between the greatest and least angles is 60°, then the formed $\triangle$le is

   (A) an isosceles $\triangle$le
   (B) an equilateral $\triangle$le
   (C) a right angled $\triangle$le
   (D) a right angled isosceles $\triangle$le

7. In $\triangle$ABC, if AB = BC and $\angle$B = 80° then $\angle$C =

   (A) 50°   (B) 100°
   (C) 130°   (D) none

8. The $\triangle$le formed by BC = AC = 7.2 cm and $\angle$C = 90° is

   (A) a right angled $\triangle$le
   (B) an isosceles $\triangle$le
   (C) a right angled isosceles $\triangle$le
   (D) no $\triangle$le is formed

9. Which of the following statement is false?

   (A) The sum of two sides of a $\triangle$le is greater than the third side
   (B) In a right angled $\triangle$le hypotenuse is the longest side
   (C) A, B, C are collinear if AB + BC=AC
   (D) None of these

10. The length of the hypotenuse of a right angled $\triangle$le whose two legs measure 12 cm and 0.35 m is

    (A) 37 cm   (B) 3.72 cm
    (C) 0.372 cm   (D) 37 m

11. If the two legs of a right angled $\triangle$le are equal and the square of the hypotenuse is 100 then the length of each leg is

    (A) 10   (B) $5\sqrt{2}$
    (C) $10\sqrt{2}$ (D) none

12. Two sides of an isosceles $\triangle$le are 5 cm and 6 cm. Then the length of the third side is

    (A) 5 cm   (B) 6 cm
    (C) 5 cm or 6 cm   (D) none

13. In a $\triangle$PQR, PQ = PR and $\angle$Q is twice that of $\angle$P. Then $\angle$Q =

    (A) 72 °   (B) 36°
    (C) 144°   (D) 108°

14. If two sides of an isosceles $\triangle$le are 3 cm and 8 cm, then the length of the third side is

    (A) 3 cm   (B) 8 cm
    (C) 3 cm or 8 cm   (D) none

15. If in a △ABC, ∠A = 60° and AB = AC then △ABC is

(A) an isosceles △le
(B) a right angled △le
(C) an isosceles right angled △le
(D) an equilateral △le

16. Two sides of a △le are 7 and 10 units. Which of the following length can be the length of the third side?

(A) 19 cm   (B) 17 cm
(C) 13 cm   (D) 3 cm

17. In a △ABC, if AB + BC = 10 cm, BC + CA = 12 cm, CA + AB = 16 cm, then the perimeter of the △le is

(A) 19 cm   (B) 17 cm
(C) 38 cm   (D) none

18. In the following figure if AB = AC then find ∠x.

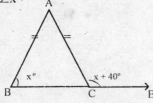

(A) 80°   (B) 70°
(C) 60°   (D) 110°

19. The angles in a right angled △le other than the right angle are

(A) acute   (B) obtuse
(C) right   (D) none

20. In a △ABC, if ∠A = ∠B + ∠C then ∠A = _____

(A) 60°   (B) 45°
(C) 90°   (D) none

21. If a, b and c are the sides of a △le, then

(A) a - b > c
(B) c > a + b
(C) c = a + b
(D) b < c + a

22. If the angles of a △le are in the ratio 1 : 2 : 7 then the △le is

(A) acute angled
(B) obtuse angled
(C) right angled
(D) right angled isosceles

23. A triangle always has

(A) exactly one acute angle
(B) exactly two acute angles
(C) at least two acute angles
(D) none of these

24. The number of independent measurements required to construct a △le is
(A) 3   (B) 4   (C) 2   (D) 5

25. In a △ABC, if ∠B is an obtuse angle, then the longest side is

(A) AB   (B) BC
(C) AC   (D) none

26. If A : An isosceles △le is right angled

R : ∠A = ∠B = 45° and ∠C = 90°

then which of the following statement is true?

(A) A is true and R is the correct explanation of A
(B) A is true and R is not the correct explanation of A
(C) A is false
(D) None of these

27. An isosceles △le can be obtuse angled.
(A) False
(B) True
(C) Cannot be determined
(D) None

28. Which of the following statement is correct?
(A) The difference of any two sides is less than the third side
(B) A △le cannot have two obtuse angles
(C) A △le cannot have an obtuse angle and a right angle
(D) All the above

29. Two chimneys 18 m and 13 m high stand upright in a ground. If their feet are 12 m apart, then the distance between their tops is

(A) 5 m   (B) 31 m

(C) 13 m   (D) 18 m

30. The top of a broken tree touches the ground at a distance of 15 m from its base. If the tree is broken at a height of 8 m from the ground, then the actual height of the tree is

(A) 20 m   (B) 25 m

(C) 30 m   (D) 17 m

Answers

1. D	2. C	3. B	4. D	5. A	6. C	7. A	8. C	9. D	10. A
11. B	12. C	13. A	14. B	15. D	16. C	17. A	18. B	19. A	20. C
21. D	22. B	23. C	24. A	25. C	26. A	27. B	28. D	29. C	30. B

Explanatory Answers

1. (D) Given three lengths are different.

2. (C) $\angle C = 90°$

3. (B) $\because \angle C = 120° > 90°$

4. (D) $\because AB + BC < AC$

The sum of any two sides is greater than the third side.

5. (A) $\because$ sum of the angles in a $\triangle$le = $180°$

i.e., $65° + 85° + x = 180° \Rightarrow x = 30°$

$\therefore$ Third angle = $30°$.

6. (C) Let least angle be x°.

Greatest angle = x° + 60°

Third angle = $\dfrac{x + x + 60}{2}$ = x + 30°

We have,

$x + x + 30 + x + 60 = 180°$

$3x + 90 = 180°$

$x = 30°$

The angles are 30°, 60°, 90°.

$\because$ one of the angle is 90°, so the $\triangle$le formed is a right angled $\triangle$le.

7. (A) $\because$ AB = AC

$\Rightarrow \angle A = \angle C$

$\angle A + \angle B + \angle C = 180°$

$2\angle C + 80° = 180°$

$\angle C = 50°$.

8. (C) $\because$ BC = AC   isosceles

$\because \angle C = 90°$ right angled

So $\triangle$ABC is right angled isosceles $\triangle$le.

9. (D) $\because$ All given statements are true.

10. (A) 0.35m = 0.35 x 100 cm = 35 cm.

We have,

(Hypotenuse)² = (side)² + (side)²

= (12)² + (35)²

= 144 + 1225

= 1369

Hypotenuse = $\sqrt{1369}$ = 37 cm.

11. (B) We have

$x^2 + x^2 = 100$

$2x^2 = 100$

$x^2 = 50$

$x = \sqrt{50} = \sqrt{25 \times 2} = 5\sqrt{2}$.

12. (C) ∵ In an isosceles Δle lengths of any two sides must be equal. So the length of the third side may be either 5cm or 6cm.

13. (A) ∵ PQ = PR

$\Rightarrow \angle Q = \angle R$

Given that $\angle Q = 2\angle P$

We have

$\angle P + \angle Q + \angle R = 180°$

$\dfrac{\angle Q}{2} + \angle Q + \angle Q = 180°$

$\dfrac{5}{2}\angle Q = 180°$

$\angle Q = 72°$.

14. (B) Length of the third side should be 8 cm. Because if we take third side as 3 cm, then the sum of two sides 3 cm + 3 cm = 6 cm is less than third side.

15. (D) $\angle A = 60°$

$AB = AC \Rightarrow \angle B = \angle C = 60°$

∴ Δle ABC is an equilateral Δle.

16. (C) Only (C) satisfies the condition, i.e., the sum of any two sides is greater than the third side.

17. (A) AB + BC = 10

BC + CA = 12

CA + AB = 16

_____

2(AB + BC + CA) = 38

AB + BC + CA = 19 cm

∴ Perimeter = 19 cm

18. (B) ∵ AB = AC

$\Rightarrow \angle B = \angle C = x°$

$\angle A + \angle B + \angle C = 180°$

$\angle A + X + X = 180°$

$\angle A = 180° - 2x$

∵ Exterior angles is equal to the sum of opposite interior angles.

$180° - 2x° + x° = x + 40$

$2x = 140°$

$x = 70°$

19. (A) ∵ one of the angle is 90° and the sum of other two angles is 90°. So they are acute.

20. (C) We have,

$\angle A + \angle B + \angle C = 180°$

$(\angle B + \angle C) + (\angle B + \angle C) = 180°$

$2(\angle B + \angle C) = 180°$

$\angle B + \angle C = 90°$

So $\angle A = 90°$

21. (D) b < c + a.

∵ Sum of any two sides is greater than the third side.

22. (B) Let the angles be 1x, 2x, 7x.

We have,

$1x + 2x + 7x = 180°$

$x = 18°$

The angles are 18°, 36° and 126°.

∴ The Δle is obtuse angled.

23. (C) ∵ the sum of the angles in a Δle is 180°.

So at least two angles must be acute.

24. (A) We have three measurements to construct a Δle.

25. (C)

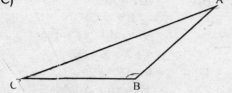

Clearly AC is longest side.

26. (A) ∵ If $\angle A = \angle B = 45°$ and $\angle C = 90°$,

$\triangle ABC$ is isosceles as well as right angled.

27. (B) E.g.:- Take the angles as 100°, 40°, 40°.

28. (D) ∵ All the given statements are correct.

29. (C)

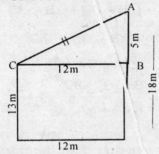

We have to find AC.

$AC^2 = AB^2 + BC^2$ (∵ $\triangle ABC$ is right $\triangle$le)

$AC^2 = 5^2 + 12^2$

$= 25 + 144 = 169$

$AC = \sqrt{169} = 13$ m.

30. (B)

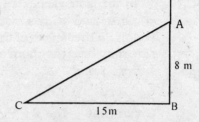

∵ $\triangle ABC$ is right angled

$AC^2 = AB^2 + BC^2$

$AC^2 = 8^2 + 15^2$

$= 64 + 225$

$= 289.$

$AC = \sqrt{289} = 17$ m.

∴ Actual length of tree $= AB + AC$

$= 8 + 17$

$= 25$ m.

❖ ❖ ❖

Chapter 11

Heron's Formula

Synopsis

1. Area of a triangle $= \dfrac{1}{2} \times$ base $\times$ height

2. *Heron's Formula :*

   Area of a triangle

   $$= \sqrt{s(s-a)(s-b)(s-c)}$$

   Where a, b and c are the sides of the triangle, and s = semi-perimeter i.e. half the perimeter of the triangle

   $$= \dfrac{a+b+c}{2}$$

3. Area of a quadrilateral whose sides and one diagonal are given, can be calculated by dividing the quadrilateral into two triangles and using the Heron's formula.

Multiple Choice Questions

1. The perimeter of a triangular field is 144 m and ratio of the sides is 3 : 4 : 5. Then the area of the field is

   (A) 864 sq m

   (B) 764 sq m

   (C) 854 sq m

   (D) 754 sq m

2. One side of an equilateral triangle is 8 cm. Its area is

   (A) $16\sqrt{3}$ cm²   (B) $12\sqrt{3}$ cm²

   (C) $8\sqrt{3}$ cm²   (D) $4\sqrt{3}$ cm²

3. The base of an isosceles triangle is 12 cm and its perimeter is 32 cm. Then its area is

   (A) 48 sq cm   (B) 36 sq cm

   (C) 24 sq cm   (D) 12 sq cm

4. The area of a triangle whose sides are 13 cm, 14 cm and 15 cm.

   (A) 84 sq cm   (B) 64 sq cm

   (C) 825 sq cm   (D) none

5. Two adjacent sides of a parallelogram are 5 cm and 3.5 cm. One of its diagonals is 6.5 cm. Then the area of parallelogram is

   (A) $5\sqrt{3}$ cm²   (B) $10\sqrt{3}$ cm²

   (C) $15\sqrt{3}$ cm²   (D) $20\sqrt{3}$ cm²

6. Two adjacent sides of a parallelogram are 51 cm and 37 cm. One of its diagonals is 20 cm, then the its area is

   (A) 412 cm²   (B) 512 cm²

   (C) 612 cm²   (D) 712 cm²

7. The sides of a triangle are in the ratio of 13 : 14 : 15 and its perimeter is 84 cm. Then the area of the triangle is

   (A) 136 cm²   (B) 236 cm²

   (C) 336 cm²   (D) 436 cm²

8. The area of a parallelogram whose diagonal is 6.8 cm and the perpendiculr distance of this diagonal from an opposite vertex is 7.5 cm is

   (A) 25.5 cm²   (B) 11.9 cm²

   (C) 12.5 cm²   (D) 51 cm²

9. The adjacent sides of a parallelogram are 4 cm and 9 cm. The ratio of its altitudes is

(A) 16 : 81   (B) 9 : 4

(C) 2 : 3   (D) 3 : 2

10. The perimeter of a rhombus is 52 cm and one of its diagonals is 24 cm. The length of the other diagonal is

(A) 24 cm   (B) 10 cm

(C) $2\dfrac{1}{6}$ cm   (D) 12 cm

11. In quadrilateral ABCD given that AB = 7 cm, BC = 12 cm, CD = 12 cm, DA = 9 cm and diagonal AC = 15 cm. It's area is

(A) $\left(10\sqrt{34}+54\right)$ sq cm

(B) $\left(10\sqrt{34}-54\right)$ sq cm

(C) data insufficient

(D) none of these

12. Adjacent sides of a parallelogram are 5 cm and 3.5 cm. One of its diagonals is 6.5 cm. Then the area of parallelogram is

(A) $8\sqrt{3}$ cm^2 (B) $9\sqrt{3}$ cm^2

(C) $10\sqrt{3}$ cm^2 (D) $12\sqrt{3}$ cm^2

13. The perimeter of a rhombus is 146 cm. One of its diagonals is 55 cm. Then the length of the other diagonal and the area of the rhombus is

(A) 48 cm, 1320 sq cm

(B) 45 cm, 660 sq cm

(C) 27.5 cm, 660 sq cm

(D) none of these

14. In a quadrilateral the sides are 9, 40, 28, 15 units and the angle between first sides is a right angle. The area of quadrilateral is

(A) 106 sq units   (B) 206 sq units

(C) 306 sq units   (D) 406 sq units

15. In a quadrilateral ABCD, AB = 7 cm, BC = 6 cm, CD = 12 cm, DA =15 cm, AC = 9 cm. Its area is

(A) $\left(\sqrt{440}+54\right)$ sq cm

(B) $\left(\sqrt{440}+44\right)$ sq cm

(C) $\left(\sqrt{110}+44\right)$ sq cm

(D) $\left(\sqrt{340}+64\right)$ sq cm

16. The area of a rhombus is 28 cm^2 and one of its diagonals is 4 cm. Its perimeter is

(A) $4\sqrt{53}$ cm   (B) 36 cm

(C) $2\sqrt{53}$ cm   (D) none

17. The adjacent sides of a parallelogram are 8 cm and 9 cm. The diagonal joining the ends of these sides is 13 cm. Its area is

(A) 72 cm^2 (B) $12\sqrt{35}$ cm^2

(C) $24\sqrt{35}$ cm^2 (D) 150 cm^2

18. The sides of a triangle are 11 cm, 15 cm and 16 cm. The altitude to largest side is

(A) $30\sqrt{7}$ cm   (B) $\dfrac{15\sqrt{7}}{2}$ cm

(C) $\dfrac{15\sqrt{7}}{4}$ cm   (D) 30 cm

19. The perimeter of a triangular field is 144 m and the ratio of the sides is 3 : 4 : 5. The area of the field is

(A) 864 m²   (B) 468 m²

(C) 824 m²   (D) none

20. If the altitude of an equilateral triangle is $\sqrt{6}$ cm, its area is

(A) $2\sqrt{3}$ cm²   (B) $2\sqrt{2}$ cm²

(C) $3\sqrt{3}$ cm²   (D) $6\sqrt{2}$ cm²

Answers

1. A	2. A	3. A	4. A	5. B	6. C	7. C	8. D	9. B	10. B
11. A	12. C	13. A	14. C	15. A	16. A	17. B	18. C	19. A	20. A

Explanatory Answers

1. (A) Let the length of the sides be 3x, 4x, 5x meters.

$144 = 12x \Rightarrow x = 12$

∴ sides are 36, 48, 60 units.

$\Delta = \sqrt{72(72-36)(72-48)(72-60)}$

= 864 sq m.

2. (A) If 8 is the length of a side of an equilateral triangle then its area is $\dfrac{\sqrt{3}}{4} \times (8)^2 = 16\sqrt{3}$ cm².

3. (A) Let the side of an isosceles triangle is x cm. It's perimeter is $x + x + 12 = 32 \Rightarrow x = 10$ cm.

Area of a triangle is

$\Delta = \sqrt{16(16-12)(16-10)(16-10)}$

$= \sqrt{16 \times 4 \times 6 \times 6}$

$= 8 \times 6$

= 48 sq cm.

4. (A) Apply Heron's formula

$\Delta = \sqrt{s(s-a)(s-b)(s-c)}$

5. (B) Diagonal divides the parallelogram into two triangles of equal area.

$\therefore \Delta = \sqrt{\dfrac{15}{2}\left(\dfrac{5}{2}\right)\left(\dfrac{8}{2}\right)(11)}$

$= 5\sqrt{3}$

$= 2 \times 5\sqrt{3} = 10\sqrt{3}.$

6. (C) $\Delta = \sqrt{54 \times 3 \times 17 \times 34} = 306$

Area of parallelogram

$= 2 \times 306 = 612$ cm².

7. (C) Let the sides 13x, 14x, 15x

$13x + 14x + 15x = 84$

$\Rightarrow x = \dfrac{84}{42} = 2$

Sides are 26, 28, 30 cm.

Area of the triangle

$\Delta = \sqrt{42(42-26)(42-28)(42-30)}$

= 336 cm².

8. (D)

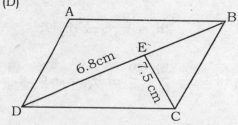

Area $\triangle$ BDC is $\frac{1}{2} \times BD \times CE$

$$= \frac{1}{2} \times 6.8 \times 7.5$$

$$= 25.5 \text{ cm}^2$$

Area of parallelogram ABCD

$= 2 \times$ area $\triangle$ BDC

$= 2 \times 25.5$

$= 51 \text{ cm}^2.$

9. (B) Diagonal divides parallelogram into two triangles of equal area.

BD is the diagonal.

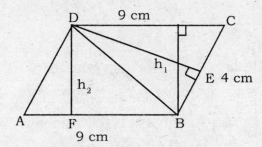

Area $\triangle$ BDC is $\frac{1}{2} \times BC \times DE$

$$= \frac{1}{2} \times 4 \times h_1 = 2h_1$$

Area $\triangle$ BAD is $\frac{1}{2} \times AB \times DF$

$$= \frac{1}{2} \times 9 \times h_2 = \frac{9h_2}{2}$$

$2h_1 = \frac{9h_2}{2} \Rightarrow 4h_1 = 9h_2$

$\frac{h_1}{h_2} = \frac{9}{4}$ or $h_1 : h_2 = 9 : 4$

10. (B)

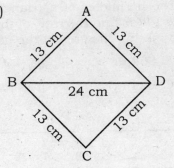

Area of rhombus ABCD

= area of $\triangle$ ABD+ area of $\triangle$ BCD

$$= \sqrt{25(25-24)(25-13)(25-13)}$$

$$+ \sqrt{25(25-24)(25-13)(25-13)}$$

$$= \sqrt{25 \times 1 \times 12 \times 12} + \sqrt{25 \times 1 \times 12 \times 12}$$

$$= 5 \times 12 + 5 \times 12$$

$$= 60 + 60$$

$$= 120 \text{ sq cm.}$$

$\frac{1}{2} \times$ product of diagonals

$120 = \frac{1}{2} \times 24 \times d$

$d = 10 \text{ cm.}$

∴ the other diagonal is 10 cm.

11. (A)

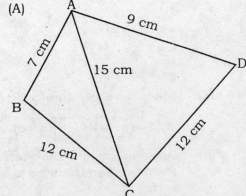

$$= \sqrt{17(17-12)(17-15)(17-7)}$$

$$+ \sqrt{18(18-15)(18-12)(18-9)}$$

$$= 10\sqrt{34} + 54$$

12. (C) Diagonal divides the parallelogram into two triangles of equal area.

Area of ▱ABCD

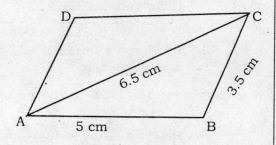

$$= 2 \times \text{area of } \triangle ABC$$

$$= 2 \times \sqrt{7.5(7.5-5)(7.5-3.5)(7.5-6.5)}$$

$$= 10\sqrt{3} \text{ sq cm.}$$

13. (A)

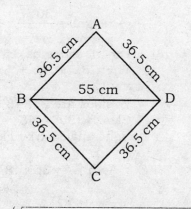

$$= \left(\sqrt{64(64-36.5)(64-36.5) \times (64-55)} \right) 2$$

$$= \left(\sqrt{64(27.5) \times (27.5)(9)} \right) 2$$

$$= \left(\sqrt{1760 \times 247.5} \right) 2$$

$$= \left(\sqrt{455600} \right) 2 = 660 \times 2 \text{ sq cm.}$$

$$= 1320 \text{ sq cm.}$$

Length of the other diagonal (d_2)

$$\frac{2 \times \text{area of rhombus}}{d_1} = 48 \text{ cm.}$$

14. (C)

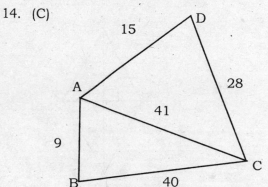

Area of quadrilateral

ABCD = area of △ABC +area of △ADC

$$= \frac{1}{2} \times BC \times AB + \text{area of } \triangle ADC$$

$$= \frac{1}{2} \times 40 \times 9 + \sqrt{42(42-14)(42-28)(42-15)}$$

$$= 180 + 126 = 306 \text{ sq units.}$$

15. (A)

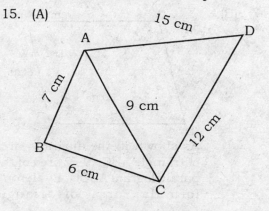

Area of ABCD =

area of $\triangle$ ABC + area of $\triangle$ ADC

$= \sqrt{11(11-7)(11-6)(11-9)}$

$+\sqrt{18(18-9)(18-12)(18-15)}$

$= \left(\sqrt{440} + 54\right)$ sq cm.

16. (A)   Let AD = x and BC = 4 cm (given)

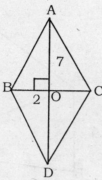

Then $\frac{1}{2} \times x \times 4 = 28$ or x = 14 cm.

Clearly, AO = $\frac{14}{2}$ = 7 cm.

By Pythagorus theorem,

AO² + BO² = AB²

or $7^2 + 2^2 = 53$ or AB = $\sqrt{53}$

∴ perimeter = 4AB = $4\sqrt{53}$.

17. (B)

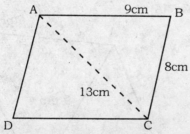

As shown in the diagram, area of triangle ABC = 1/2 area of the parallelogram ABCD. By Heron's formula, area of triangle

$= \sqrt{S(S-a)(S-b)(S-C)}$

Here S = $\frac{9+8+13}{2}$ = 15

∴ Area of ABC = $\sqrt{15(6)(2)(7)}$

$\sqrt{180 \times 7} = \sqrt{1260} = \sqrt{6 \times 210}$

$\sqrt{6 \times 7 \times 30} = 6\sqrt{35}$ sq cm.

Hence, area of ABCD

$= 2 \times 6\sqrt{35} = 12\sqrt{35}$ sq cm.

18. (C)   By Heron's formula, we have area of triangle

$= \sqrt{S(S-a)(S-b)(S-c)}$

Here, S = $\frac{11+15+16}{2} = \frac{42}{2}$

$= 21$ cm.

∴ Area = $= \sqrt{21(10)(6)(5)}$

$= 30\sqrt{7}$ sq cm.

∴ height $= \frac{30\sqrt{7}}{8} = \frac{15\sqrt{7}}{4}$ cm.

19. (A)   Let the sides be 3x, 4x and 5x. Then 3x + 4x + 5x = 144 or x = 12.

∴ sides are 36, 48 and 60 cm. Clearly, $36^2 + 48^2 = 60^2$. It is a right angled triangle.

∴ Area $= \frac{1}{2} \times 36 \times 48 = 864$ cm².

20. (A) $\frac{\sqrt{3}}{2} \times$ side = $\sqrt{6}$

Side = $2\sqrt{2}$ cm.

area $= \frac{\sqrt{3}}{4} \times (\text{side})^2 = \frac{\sqrt{3}}{4} \times \left(2\sqrt{2}\right)^2$

$= 2\sqrt{3}$ cm².

Chapter 12

Surface areas and volumes

Synopsis

1. Cube :

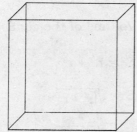

If 'a' be the edge of a cube, then

volume = a³

total surface area = 6a²

diagonal of a cube = $\sqrt{3} \times$ edge = $\sqrt{3}$ a

edge of a cube = $\sqrt[3]{\text{volume}}$

2. Cuboid :

If '*l*' be the length, 'b' be the breadth and 'h' be the height or depth of a cuboid, then

(i) volume = length × breadth × height

$$= l \times b \times h$$

length $l = \dfrac{\text{volume}}{b \times h}$

breadth (b) = $\dfrac{\text{volume}}{l \times h}$

height (h) = $\dfrac{\text{volume}}{l \times b}$

(ii) Total surface area

$$= 2(lb + bh + hl)$$

(iii) Diagonal of a cuboid

$$= \sqrt{l^2 + b^2 + h^2}$$

3. Cylinder :

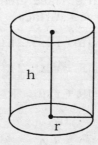

If 'r' is the radius of the base

'h' is the height of the cylinder

'd' is the diameter of the base

(i) Area of curved surface

$$= 2\pi rh = \pi dh$$

(ii) Total surface area

$$= 2\pi r(h + r) = \pi d \left(\dfrac{d}{2} + h\right)$$

(iii) Volume of the cylinder $= \pi r^2 h$

4. Hollow Cylinder :

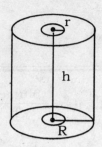

(i) Volume of the hollow cylinder

$$= (\pi R^2 - \pi r^2)h$$

$$= \pi (R^2 - r^2) h$$

(ii) Area of the curved surface

$$= 2\pi Rh + 2\pi rh$$

$$= 2\pi (R + r)h$$

(iii) Total surface area = area of curved surface + 2(area of base)

$$= 2\pi (R + r)h + 2\pi (R^2 - r^2)$$

$$= 2\pi (R + r)h + 2\pi (R + r) (R - r)$$

$$= 2\pi (R + r) (h + R - r)$$

5. Cone :

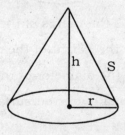

If 'S' is the slant height, 'r' is the radius of the base 'h' is the vertical height.

(i) Area of curved surface $= \pi rs$

$$= \pi r\left(\sqrt{h^2 + r^2}\right)$$

(ii) Total surface area = curved surface area + area of the base

$$= \pi rs + \pi r^2$$

$$= \pi r(s + r)$$

(iii) Volume of the cone $= \dfrac{1}{3}\pi r^2 h$

$$S^2 = h^2 + r^2$$

$$S = \sqrt{h^2 + r^2}$$

$$h = \sqrt{S^2 - r^2}$$

$$r = \sqrt{S^2 - h^2}$$

6. Sphere :

If 'r' is the radius of the sphere and 'd' is the diameter of the sphere, then

(i) Surface Area (A) $= 4\pi r^2 = \pi d^2$

(ii) Volume of the sphere (V) $= \dfrac{4}{3}\pi r^3$

$$= \dfrac{\pi}{6}d^3$$

$$r = \sqrt[3]{\dfrac{3v}{4\pi}}$$

1. The lateral surface area of a right circular cylinder with base radius 7 cm and height 10 cm is
   (A) 440 cm^2 (B) 404 cm^2
   (C) 240 cm^2 (D) none

2. Ratio of lateral surface areas of two cylinders with equal heights is
   (A) H : h   (B) R : r
   (C) 1 : 2   (D) none

3. Ratio of volumes of two cylinders with equal heights is
   (A) R : r   (B) H : h
   (C) R^2 : r^2 (D) none

4. Ratio of curved surface areas of two cylinders with equal radii is
   (A) R : r   (B) R^2 : r^2
   (C) H : h   (D) none

5. Ratio of volumes of two cylinders with equal radii are
   (A) R : r   (B) H : h
   (C) R^2 : r^2 (D) none

6. The base radius of a cylinder is $1\frac{2}{3}$ times its height. The cost of painting its CSA at 2 paise/cm^2 is Rs. 92.40. The volume of the liquid is _____
   (A) 80850 cm^3 (B) 80580 cm^3
   (C) 80508 cm^3 (D) none

7. The total surface area of a cylinder is 220 sq cm with height 6.5 cm. Then its volume is _____
   (A) 25.025 cm^3 (B) 2.5025 cm^3
   (C) 2502.5 cm^3 (D) 250.25 cm^3

8. The lateral surface area of cylinder is 176 cm^2 and base area 38.5 cm^2. Then its volume is _____
   (A) 830 cm^3 (B) 380 cm^3
   (C) 308 cm^3 (D) 803 cm^3

9. A cylindrical vessel contains 49.896 litres of liquid. Cost of painting its CSA at 2 paise/sq cm is Rs. 95.04. Then its total surface area is _____
   (A) 5724 cm^2 (B) 7524 cm^2
   (C) 5742 cm^2 (D) none

10. Ratio of volumes of two cones with same radii is
    (A) $h_1 : h_2$ (B) $r_1 : r_2$
    (C) $s_1 : s_2$ (D) none

11. Ratio of volumes of two cones with same height is
    (A) $r_1 : r_2$ (B) $r_1{}^2 : r_2{}^2$
    (C) $h_1{}^2 : h_2{}^2$ (D) none

12. The area of the base of a cone is 616 sq cm. Its height is 48 cm. Then its total surface area is _____
    (A) 2816 cm^2 (B) 2861 cm^2
    (C) 2618 cm^2 (D) 2681 cm^2

13. The ratio of base radius and height of a cone is 3 : 4. If the cost of smoothening the CSA at 5 paise/sq cm is Rs. 115.50. Then volume of liquid is _____
    (A) 12963 cm^3 (B) 12693 cm^3
    (C) 12936 cm^3 (D) none

14. The cost of painting the CSA of cone at 5 ps/cm^2 is Rs.35.20. The volume of the cone its slant height being 25 cm is
    (A) 1223 cm^2
    (B) 1232 cm^2
    (C) 1323 cm^2
    (D) 1332 cm^2

15. A vessel is in conical shape. If its volume is 33.264 litres and height is 72 cm, the cost of repairing its CSA at Rs.12/sq m is
    (A) 5.94   (B) 6.94
    (C) 7.95   (D) none

16. From a circle of radius 15 cm a sector with 216° angle is cut out and its bounding radii are bent so as to form a cone. Then its volume is
(A) 1081.3 cm³   (B) 1071.3 cm³
(C) 1018.3 cm³   (D) none

17. A hemispherical bowl is made of steel of 0.25 cm thickness. The inner radius of the bowl is 5 cm. The volume of steel used is _____
(A) 42.15 cm³   (B) 41.52 cm³
(C) 41.25 cm³   (D) none

18. A cuboidal metal of dimensions 44 cm × 30 cm × 15 cm was melted and cast into a cylinder of height 28 cm. Its radius is _____
(A) 20 cm   (B) 15 cm
(C) 10 cm   (D) none

19. A cylindrical vessel of diameter 9 cm has some water in it. A cylindrical iron piece of diameter 6 cm and height 4.5 cm is dropped in it. After it was completely immersed, the raise in the level of water is _____
(A) 0.8 cm   (B) 0.5 cm
(C) 0.1 cm   (D) none

20. A piece of metal pipe is 77 cm long with inside diameter of the cross section as 4 cm. If the outer diameter is 4.5 cm and the metal weighs 8 gm/cu cm, the weight of pipe is _____
(A) 2.057 kg   (B) 20.57 kg
(C) 205.7 kg   (D) none

21. With a bucket of radius 14 cm and height 16 cm, 27 buckets of lime was poured to form a conical heap. If its area is 5544 cm², the canvas required to cover it is _____
(A) 1980 cm²   (B) 19800 cm²
(C) 198 cm²   (D) none

22. A circus tent is in the form of a cone over a cylinder. The diameter of the base is 9 m, the height of cylindrical part is 4.8 m and the total height of the tent is 10.8 m. The canvas required for the tent is _____
(A) 24.184 sq m   (B) 2418.4 sq m
(C) 241.84 sq m   (D) none

23. A top is of the shape of a cone over a hemisphere. The radius of the hemisphere is 3.5 cm. The total height of the top is 15.5 cm. The total area of top is _____
(A) 214.5 sq cm   (B) 21.45 sq cm
(C) 215.4 sq cm   (D) none

24. The diameter of a copper sphere is 6 cm. It is beaten and drawn into a wire of diameter 0.2 cm. The length of wire is _____
(A) 36 cm   (B) 360 cm
(C) 3600 cm   (D) none

25. A cylindrical vessel of diameter 4 cm is partly filled with water. 300 lead balls are dropped in it. The raise in water level is 0.8 cm. The diameter of each ball is _____
(A) 0.8 cm   (B) 0.4 cm
(C) 0.2 cm   (D) none

26. Liquid is full in a hemisphere of inner diameter 9 cm. This is to be poured into cylindrical bottles of diameter 3 cm and height 4 cm. The number of bottles required are

_____
(A) 50   (B) 54   (C) 45   (D) none

27. A hollow sphere of internal and external diameters 4 cm and 8 cm respectively is melted into a cone of base diameter 8 cm. Find the height of the cone.
(A) 14 cm   (B) 12 cm
(C) 16 cm   (D) none

28. If the radii of the circular ends of a conical bucket are 28 cm and 7 cm and the height is 45 cm. The capacity of the bucket is _____

(A) 48150 cm³   (B) 48510 cm³
(C) 48105 cm³   (D) none

29. The height of a cone is 30 cm. A small cone is cut off at the top by a plane parallel to the base. If its volume is $\frac{1}{27}$ th the volume of cone, the height at which the section is made is _____

(A) 10 cm   (B) 15 cm
(C) 20 cm   (D) none

30. A cone of radius 10 cm is divided into two parts by drawing a plane through the midpoint of its axis, parallel to its base. The ratio of volumes of the two parts formed is _____

(A) 1 : 7   (B) 2 : 7

(C) 3 : 7   (D) none

31. The radius of the cylinder whose lateral surface area is 704 cm² and height 8 cm is

(A) 6 cm   (B) 4 cm
(C) 8 cm   (D) 14 cm

32. The radius of a sphere is increased by P%. Its surface area increases by

(A) P%   (B) P²⁰%

(C) $\left(2P + \frac{P^2}{100}\right)\%$ (D) $\frac{P^2}{2}\%$

33. The radius of a cylinder is doubled but its lateral surface area is unchanged. Then its height must be

(A) doubled   (B) halved
(C) trebled   (D) constant

34. The height and radius of a cone are 3 cm and 4 cm respectively. Its curved surface area must be is

(A) $62\frac{6}{7}$ sq cm

(B) $57\frac{3}{4}$ sq cm

(C) 6 cm²
(D) 12 cm²

35. The ratio of the volume and surface area of a sphere of unit radius

(A) 4 : 3   (B) 3 : 4
(C) 1 : 3   (D) 3 : 1

36. A cylindrical rod whose height is 8 times of its radius is melted and recast into spherical balls of same radius. The number of balls will be

(A) 4   (B) 3
(C) 6   (D) 8

37. Two identical right circular cones each of height 2 cm are placed as shown in diagram (each is vertical, apex downward). At the start, the upper cone is full of water and lower cone is empty.

Then water drips down through a hole in the apex of upper cone into the lower cone. The height of water in the lower cone at the moment when height of water in upper cone is 1 cm is

(A) 1 cm

(B) $\sqrt{\dfrac{1}{2}}$ cm

(C) $\sqrt[3]{\dfrac{1}{4}}$ cm

(D) $\sqrt[3]{7}$ cm

NOTE : Height is measured from apex of cone.

38. A sphere and a cube are of the same height. The ratio of their volume is

(A) 3 : 4

(B) 21 : 11

(C) 4 : 3

(D) 11 : 21

39. The largest sphere is cut off from a cube of side 5 cm. The volume of the sphere will be :

(A) 27π cm³

(B) 30π cm³

(C) 108π cm²

(D) $\dfrac{125\pi}{6}$ cm³

40. Vertical and horizontal cross-sections of a right circular cylinder are always respectively

(A) rectangle, square

(B) rectangle, circle

(C) square, circle

(D) rectangle, ellipse

41. The slant height of a cone is increased by P%. If radius remains same, the curved surface area is increased by

(A) P%

(B) P²%

(C) 2P%

(D) None

42. The volumes of two spheres are in the ratio 64 : 27. Find the difference of their surface areas, if the sum of their radii is 7 units.

(A) 28π sq units

(B) 88 sq units

(C) 88π sq units

(D) 4π sq units

43. In the figure below, LMNO and GHJK are rectangles where $GH = \dfrac{1}{2}LM$ and $HJ = = \dfrac{1}{2}MN$. What fraction of the region is bounded by LMNO that is not shaded?

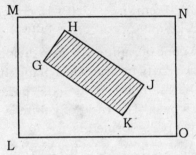

(A) $\dfrac{1}{4}$

(B) $\dfrac{1}{3}$

(C) $\dfrac{1}{2}$

(D) $\dfrac{3}{4}$

44. In the figure below, RSTV is a square inscribed in a circle with centre O and radius r. The total area of shaded region is

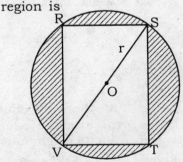

(A) $r^2(\pi - 2)$

(B) $2r(2 - \pi)$

(C) $\pi(r^2 - 2)$

(D) $\pi r^2 - 8r$

45. A right circular cone of diameter K cm and height 12 cm rests on the base of a right circular cylinder of radius K cm (their bases lie in the same plane, as shown in figure). The cylinder is filled with water to a height of 12 cm. If the cone is then removed, the height to which water will fall is

(A) 11 cm

(B) 10 cm

(C) 8 cm

(D) cannot be determined from given data

46. The ratio of radii of two cylinders is $1 : \sqrt{3}$ and heights are in the ratio $2 : 3$. The ratio of their volumes is

(A) 1 : 9

(B) 2 : 9

(C) 4 : 9

(D) 5 : 9

47. The dimensions of a hall are 40 m, 25 m and 20 m. If each person requires 200 cubic metre, then the number of persons who can be accomodated in the hall are

(A) 120   (B) 150

(C) 140   (D) 100

48. Correct the perimeter of the figure given below to one decimal place.

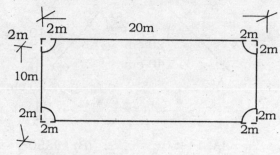

(A) 56.0 m

(B) 56.6 m

(C) 57.2 m

(D) 57.9 m

49. A hollow spherical ball whose inner radius is 4 cm is full of water. Half of the water is transferred to a conical cup and it completely filled the cup. If the height of the cup is 2 cm, then the radius of the base of cone, in cm is

(A) 4   (B) 8π

(C) 8   (D) 16

50. The largest volume of a cube that can be enclosed in a sphere of diameter 2 cm is (in cm³)

(A) 1

(B) $2\sqrt{2}$

(C) π

(D) $\dfrac{8}{3\sqrt{3}}$

51. A cooking pot has a spherical bottom, while the upper part is a truncated cone. Its vertical cross-section is shown in the figure. If the volume of food increases by 15% during cooking, the maximum initial

volume of food that can be cooked without spilling is (in cc)

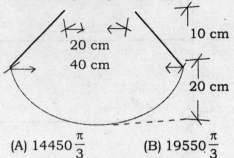

(A) $14450\dfrac{\pi}{3}$ 　　　(B) $19550\dfrac{\pi}{3}$

(C) $\dfrac{340000}{69}\pi$ 　　(D) $\dfrac{20000}{3}\pi$

52. Each side of a cube is increased by 50%. Then the surface area of the cube increases by
(A) 50%　　　　　(B) 100%
(C) 125%　　　　(D) 150%

53. Three cylinders each of height 16 cm and radius of base 4 cm are placed on a plane so that each cylinder touches the other two. Then the volume of region enclosed between the three cylinders in cm³ is

(A) $98\left(4\sqrt{3}-\pi\right)$ 　(B) $98\left(2\sqrt{3}-\pi\right)$

(C) $98\left(\sqrt{3}-\pi\right)$ 　(D) $128\left(2\sqrt{3}-\pi\right)$

54. Instead of walking along two adjacent sides of a rectangular field, a boy took a short cut along the diagonal and saved a distance equal to half the longer side. Then the ratio of the shorter side to the longer side is

(A) $\dfrac{1}{2}$ 　　　　(B) $\dfrac{2}{3}$

(C) $\dfrac{1}{4}$ 　　　　(D) $\dfrac{3}{4}$

55. The number of surfaces in right circular cylinder is
(A) 1　　　　　(B) 2
(C) 3　　　　　(D) 4

56. Fields X and Y are to be enclosed with a fencing at the cost of Rs 40 per meter. If the cost on field X is denoted by C_x and that on field Y is denoted by C_y we have

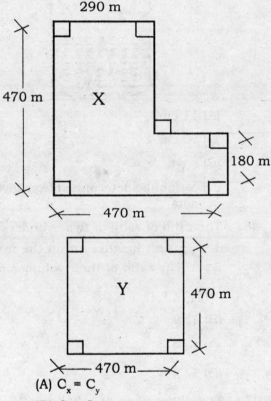

(A) $C_x = C_y$
(B) $C_x < C_y$
(C) $C_x > C_y$
(D) cannot be determined

57. A covered wooden box has the inner measures as 115 cm, 75 cm and 35 cm and the thickness of wood is 2.5 cm. Find the volume of the wood.
(A) 80,000 cu cm　　(B) 82,125 cu cm
(C) 84,000 cu cm　　(D) 85,000cu cm

58. The edge of a cube is 20 cm. How many small cubes of 5 cm edge can be formed from this cube?

(A) 4   (B) 32

(C) 64   (D) 100

59. Two cylinders of same volume have their heights in the ratio 1 : 3. Find the ratio of their radii.

(A) $\sqrt{3}:1$ (B) $\sqrt{2}:1$

(C) $\sqrt{5}:2$ (D) $2:\sqrt{5}$

60. A metallic right circular cone of height 9 cm and base radius 7 cm is melted into a cuboid whose two sides are 11 cm and 6 cm. What is the third side of the cuboid?

(A) 5 cm   (B) 6 cm

(C) 7 cm   (D) 10 cm

Answers

1. A	2. B	3. C	4. C	5. B	6. A	7. D	8. C	9. B	10. A
11. B	12. A	13. C	14. B	15. A	16. C	17. C	18. B	19. B	20. A
21. B	22. C	23. A	24. C	25. B	26. B	27. A	28. B	29. C	30. A
31. D	32. C	33. B	34. A	35. C	36. C	37. D	38. D	39. D	40. B
41. A	42. A	43. D	44. A	45. A	46. B	47. D	48. B	49. C	50. B
51. D	52. C	53. D	54. D	55. C	56. A	57. B	58. C	59. A	60. C

Explanatory Answers

1. (A) LSA $= 2\pi rh$

$= 2 \times \dfrac{22}{7} \times 7 \times 10$

$= 440$ cm^2.

2. (B) $2\pi Rh : 2\pi rh$

$= R : r$

3. (C) $\pi R^2 h : \pi r^2 h$

$= R^2 : r^2$

4. (C) $2\pi RH : 2\pi Rh$

$= H : h$

5. (B) $\pi R^2 H : \pi R^2 h$

$= H : h$

6. (A) CSA $= 2 \times \dfrac{22}{7} \times h \times \dfrac{5h}{3} = \dfrac{220h^2}{21}$

$\therefore \dfrac{9240}{2} = \dfrac{220h^2}{21}$

$\therefore h = 21 \Rightarrow r = 35$

$\therefore v = \pi r^2 h$

$= 80850$ cm^3.

7. (D) $220 = 2 \times \dfrac{22}{7} \times r \left(r + \dfrac{13}{2}\right)$

$\Rightarrow 2r^2 + 13r - 70 = 0$

$\Rightarrow r = \dfrac{7}{2}$

$\therefore V = \pi r^2 h$

$$= \frac{22}{7} \times \left(\frac{7}{2}\right)^2 \times \frac{13}{2}$$

$$= 250.25 \text{ cm}^3.$$

8. (C) $\pi r^2 = 38.5$

$$\Rightarrow r = \frac{7}{2} \text{ cm}$$

$2\pi rh = 176$

$\Rightarrow h = 8$ cm

$\therefore V = \pi r^2 h$

$$= 308 \text{ cm}^3.$$

9. (B) $V = 49.896 \times 10000 \text{ cm}^3$

$\therefore \pi r^2 h = 49896 \text{ cm}^3$

$$\text{CSA} = \frac{9504}{2} \text{ cm}^2$$

$\therefore 2\pi rh = 4752$

$$\frac{\pi r^2 h}{2\pi rh} = \frac{49896}{4752}$$

$\Rightarrow r = 21$

$h = 36$

TSA $= 2\pi r(h+r)$

$$= 7524 \text{ cm}^2.$$

10. (A) $\frac{1}{3}\pi r_1^2 h_1 : \frac{1}{3}\pi r_2^2 h_2 \ (r_1 = r_2)$

$h_1 : h_2$

11. (B) $\frac{1}{3}\pi r_1^2 h_1 : \frac{1}{3}\pi r_2^2 h_2 \ (h_1 = h_2)$

$r_1^2 : r_2^2$

12. (A) $\pi r^2 = 616$

$\Rightarrow r = 14$

$l = \sqrt{h^2 + r^2} = 50$

$\therefore$ TSA $= \pi r(l+r)$

$= 2816$ sq cm.

13. (C) CSA $= \pi r l = \dfrac{11550}{5} = 2310 \text{ cm}^2$

$l = \sqrt{h^2 + r^2} = 5x$

$\therefore \dfrac{22}{7} \times 3x \times 5x = 2310$

$\Rightarrow x = 7$

$\therefore V = \dfrac{1}{3}\pi r^2 h = 12936 \text{ cm}^3.$

14. (B) TSA $= \dfrac{3520}{5} = 704 \text{ cm}^2$

$\pi r(l+r) = 704$

$\therefore r = 7$

$h = \sqrt{l^2 - r^2} = 24$

$V = \dfrac{1}{3}\pi r^2 h$

$= 1232 \text{ cm}^3.$

15. (A) $V = 33264 \text{ cm}^3$

$\therefore \dfrac{1}{3}\pi r^2 h = 33264$

$\Rightarrow r = 21$

$$l = \sqrt{h^2 + r^2}$$

$$= 75$$

$$\text{CSA} = \pi rl = \frac{22}{7} \times 21 \times 75$$

$$1 \text{ sq m} = 10000 \text{ cm}^2$$

$$\therefore \text{ cost} =$$

$$\frac{12 \times 22 \times 21 \times 75}{7 \times 10000}$$

$$= \text{Rs. } 5.94$$

16. (C) $\text{CSA} = \pi rl$

$$= \frac{22}{7} \times r \times 15 = \frac{216}{360} \times \frac{22}{7} \times (15)^2$$

$$\Rightarrow r = 9$$

$$h = \sqrt{s^2 - r^2} = 12$$

$$\therefore V = \frac{1}{3}\pi r^2 h = 1018.3 \text{ cm}^3.$$

17. (C) $R = 5 + 0.25 = 5.25$

Volume of metal used

$$= \frac{2}{3} \times \frac{22}{7}((5.25)^3 - (5)^3)$$

$$= 41.25 \text{ cm}^3.$$

18. (B) Volume of cuboid = volume of cylinder

$$\pi r^2 h = l \times b \times h$$

$$\Rightarrow r^2 = \frac{44 \times 30 \times 15 \times 7}{22 \times 28}$$

$$\therefore r = 15 \text{ cm}.$$

19. (B) Let height raised be 'x'.

Volume of water raised
= volume of piece droped

$$\frac{22}{7} \times (4.5)^2 \times x = \frac{22}{7} \times (3)^2 \times 4.5$$

$$x = 0.5 \text{ cm}.$$

20. (A) Mass $= D \times V = \pi(R+r)(R-r)h \times D$

$$= \frac{22}{7}\left(\frac{4.5}{2} + 2\right)\left(\frac{4.5}{2} - 2\right)77 \times 8 \text{gm/cc}$$

$$= 2.057 \text{ kg}.$$

21. (B) Volume of bucket $= \pi r^2 h = 9856$ cm^3

Volume of 27 buckets $= 27 \times 9856$

$$\therefore \frac{1}{3}\pi r^2 h = 27 \times 9856$$

$$h = 144 \text{ cm}.$$

$$\pi r^2 = 5544 \Rightarrow r = 42 \text{ cm}.$$

$$l = \sqrt{h^2 + r^2} = 150$$

Canvas required = CSA

$$= \pi rl$$

$$= 19800 \text{ cm}^2.$$

22. (C) $l = \sqrt{h^2 + r^2}$

$$= \sqrt{(6)^2 + (4.5)^2}$$

$$= 7.5 \text{ m}$$

Total canvas required

$$= \pi rl + 2\pi rh$$

$$= \frac{22}{7} \times 4.5 \times 7.5 + 2 \times \frac{22}{7} \times 4.5 \times 4.8$$

$$= 241.84 \text{ sq m.}$$

23. (A) Height of cone = 15.5 - 3.5 = 12 cm.

$$l = \sqrt{h^2 + r^2}$$

$$= \sqrt{(3.5)^2 + (12)^2}$$

$$= 12.5 \text{ cm.}$$

CSA $= \pi r l$

$$= 137.5 \text{ sq cm.}$$

CSA of hemisphere $= 2\pi r^2$

$$= 77 \text{ sq cm.}$$

$\therefore$ total area of top = 214.5 sq cm.

24. (C) Volume of cylindrical wire = volume of sphere.

$$\pi r^2 h = \frac{4}{3} \pi r^3$$

$$\Rightarrow l = \frac{4}{3} \times \frac{22}{7} \times 3 \times 3 \times 3 \times \frac{7}{22} \times \frac{1}{0.01}$$

$$= 3600 \text{ cm.}$$

25. (B) Volume of 300 spherical balls = Volume of water raisen

$$\therefore 300 \times \frac{4}{3} \times \frac{22}{7} \times \left(\frac{d}{2}\right)^3 = \frac{22}{7} \times 2 \times 2 \times \frac{4}{5}$$

$$\Rightarrow d = \frac{2}{5} = 0.4 \text{ cm.}$$

26. (B) Bottles required

$$= \frac{\text{vol. of one bottle}}{\text{vol. of liquid in vessel(hemispherical)}}$$

$$= \frac{\frac{22}{7} \times \frac{3}{2} \times \frac{3}{2} \times 4}{\frac{2}{3} \times \frac{22}{7} \times (9)^3}$$

$$= 54.$$

27. (A) Volume of cone = volume of hollow sphere

$$\frac{1}{3} \pi r^2 h = \frac{4}{3} \pi [R^3 - r^3]$$

$$h = \frac{4}{3} \times \frac{22}{7} \times [(4)^3 - (2)^3] \times 3 \times \frac{7}{22} \times \frac{1}{16}$$

$$= 14 \text{ cm.}$$

28. (B) Capacity of bucket = volume of frustum

$$= \frac{\pi h}{3} [R^2 + r^2 + Rr]$$

$$= \left[\frac{1}{3} \times \frac{22}{7} \times 45\right]\left[(28)^2 + (7)^2 + (28 \times 7)\right]$$

$$= 48510 \text{ cm}^3.$$

29. (C) Volume of given cone $= \frac{1}{3} \pi R^2 \times 30$

$$= 10\pi R^2$$

Volume of smaller cone

$$= \frac{1}{3} \pi r^2 h$$

$\therefore \dfrac{1}{3}\pi r^2 h = \dfrac{1}{27} \times 10\pi R^2$

$\Rightarrow \left(\dfrac{R}{r}\right)^2 = \dfrac{9}{10}h$

From figure, $\dfrac{R}{r} = \dfrac{30}{h}$

$\therefore \left(\dfrac{30}{h}\right)^2 = \left(\dfrac{9}{10}\right)h$

$\Rightarrow h = 10$ cm.

$\therefore$ height of the section

$= 30 - h = 20$ cm.

30. **(A)** Ratio of volumes

$= \dfrac{\text{volume of smaller cone}}{\text{volume of frustum}}$

$= \dfrac{\dfrac{1}{3}\pi r^2 (h/2)}{\dfrac{1}{3}\pi h/2[R^2 + r^2 + Rr]}$

$= \dfrac{5 \times 5}{(10)^2 + (5)^2 + 10 \times 5}$

$= \dfrac{1}{7}$

$= 1 : 7$

31. **(D)** Lateral surface area of a cylinder
$= 2\pi rh = 704$ cm^2.

$\therefore r = \dfrac{704}{2\pi h} = \dfrac{704}{2 \times \dfrac{22}{7} \times 8} = 14$ cm.

32. **(C)** Surface area of sphere of radius
$r = 4\pi r^2$

After increase of P% the radius

becomes $= r + \dfrac{Pr}{100}$

Hence new surface area

$= 4\pi\left(r + \dfrac{Pr}{100}\right)^2 = 4\pi r^2\left(1 + \dfrac{P}{100}\right)^2$

Percentage increase

$= \dfrac{\text{final} - \text{initial}}{\text{initial}} \times 100$

$= \left[\dfrac{4\pi r^2\left(1 + \dfrac{P}{100}\right)^2 - 4\pi r^2}{4\pi r^2}\right] \times 100$

$= \left[1 + \dfrac{P^2}{100^2} + \dfrac{2P}{100} - 1\right] \times 100$

$= \left(\dfrac{P^2}{100} + 2P\right)\%$

33. **(B)** Lateral surface area of a cylinder
$= 2\pi rh$. Let h_1 and h_2 be the
heights.

Then $2 \times \dfrac{22}{7} \times r \times h_1$

$= 2 \times \dfrac{22}{7} \times 2r \times h_2$

Clearly $h_2 = \dfrac{h_1}{2}$.

34. **(A)**

Curved surface area of a cone
$= \pi rl$. Also, as shown in diagram,
$l^2 = r^2 + h^2 = 3^2 + 4^2$ or $l = 5$ cm.

$\therefore$ CSA $= \dfrac{22}{7} \times 4 \times 5 = \dfrac{440}{7}$

$$= 62\frac{6}{7} \text{ sq cm.}$$

35. (C) Volume of sphere = $\frac{4}{3}\pi r^3$ and

it's surface area = $4\pi r^2$.

ratio = $\frac{4}{3}\pi r^3 : 4\pi r^2 = \frac{r}{3} : 1$

But r = 1 unit (unit radius)

∴ ratio = $\frac{1}{3} : 1$ or 1 : 3.

36. (C) The volume of the cylindrical rod is now occupied by the spherical balls.

∴ $\pi R^2 H = \frac{4}{3}\pi R^3 \times n$ where n is

the number of balls.

$n = \frac{3H}{4R} = \frac{3 \times 8R}{4R} = 6.$

37. (D) As given in the hint, the loss of water in the upper cone is exactly equal to the gain of water in lower cone.

Let the height of water in lower cone be h cm at the time when height of water in upper cone is 1 cm.

Now volume of water in upper cone

$= \frac{1}{3}\pi r^2 h$ (Here h = 1 cm and

r = CD)

By similar triangles, $\frac{OB}{CD} = \frac{AB}{AC}$

$CD = \frac{R \times 1}{2} = \frac{R}{2}$

∴ Volume of the water in upper

cone = $\frac{1}{3}\pi\left(\frac{R}{2}\right)^2 h$

$= \frac{\pi}{3}\frac{R^2}{4} \times 1 = \frac{\pi R^2}{12}$

Volume of water lost in the upper cone =

$\frac{1}{3}\pi R^2 \times 2 = \frac{\pi R^2}{12} = \frac{7\pi R^2}{12}$

Since water lost by upper cone

= water gained by lower cone

$\frac{7\pi R^2}{12} = \frac{1}{3}\pi R^2 h$

But $\frac{r}{h} = \frac{R}{2}$ or $r = \frac{Rh}{2}$

or $\frac{7\pi R^2}{12} = \frac{1}{3}\pi\frac{R^2 h^2}{4} \times h$

or $h^3 = 7$ or $h = \sqrt[3]{7}$ cm.

38. (D) Since the sphere and cube are of same height, diameter of sphere = length of cube.

∴ $2R = l$

Ratio of volumes = $\frac{4}{3}\pi R^3 : l^3$

or $\frac{4}{3}\pi R^3 : 8R^3$

or $\pi : 6$ or $\frac{22}{7} : 6$ or 11 : 21

39. (D)

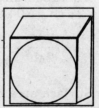

As shown in figure, the largest sphere is such that its diameter is equal to length of cube or 2R = 5 cm.

$$R = \frac{5}{2} \text{ cm.}$$

$$\therefore \text{ volume } = \frac{4}{3}\pi \times \left(\frac{5}{2}\right)^3$$

$$= \frac{125\pi}{6} \text{ cm}^3.$$

40. (B) The vertical section of a right circular cylinder is a rectangle and the horizontal section is always a circle.

41. (A) Curved surface area = $\pi r l$. New curved surface area

$$= \pi r \left(l + \frac{Pl}{100}\right)$$

Percentage increase

$$= \frac{\pi r \left(l + \dfrac{Pl}{100}\right) - \pi r l}{\pi r l} \times 100 = P\%$$

42. (A) Let the radii of the spheres be R_1

and R_2. Then $\dfrac{\dfrac{4}{3}\pi R_1^{\,3}}{\dfrac{4}{3}\pi R_2^{\,3}} = \dfrac{64}{27}$

or $\dfrac{R_1^{\,3}}{R_2^{\,3}} = \dfrac{64}{27}$ or $\dfrac{R_1}{R_2} = \dfrac{4}{3}$

Let $R_1 = 4x$ and $R_2 = 3x$
Then $R_1 + R_2 = 7$
or $4x + 3x = 7$ or $x = 1$
$\therefore R_1 = 4$ and $R_2 = 3$ units
$\therefore$ Difference of their surface areas = $4\pi(4^2 - 3^2)$
$\qquad = 28\pi$ sq units.

43. (D) Area of rectangle GHKJ

$$= \text{GH} \times \text{HJ} = \frac{1}{2}\text{LM} \times \frac{1}{2}\text{MN}$$

$$= \frac{1}{4}\text{LM} \times \text{MN} = \frac{1}{4}\text{ rectangle LMNO}$$

Hence, unshaded region
= rectangle LMNO – rectangle GHKJ

$$= \frac{3}{4}\text{ rectangle LMNO.}$$

44. (A) Clearly, area of shaded region
= area of circle – area of square RSTV
But, diameter of circle
= diagonal of square

or $2R = \sqrt{2}l$ or $R = \dfrac{l}{\sqrt{2}}$ or $l = R\sqrt{2}$

Area of shaded Region
$= \pi R^2 - l^2 = \pi R^2 - (R\sqrt{2})^2$
$= \pi R^2 - 2R^2 = R^2(\pi - 2)$ sq units.

45. (A) As shown in figure, the volume occupied by the cone will be occupied by water when the cone is removed.

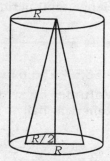

Before the removal of cone, volume of water in cylinder

$$= \pi R^2 (12) - \frac{1}{3}\pi \left(\frac{R}{2}\right)^2 \times 12$$

$$= 12\pi R^2 - \pi R^2 = 11\pi R^2$$

Then $\pi R^2 h = 11\pi R^2$ or
$h = 11$ cm.

46. (B) The radii are x and $\sqrt{3}x$ and heights be 2y and 3y.

The ratio of volumes

$\pi x^2(2y) : \pi\left(\sqrt{3}x\right)^2(3y)$

$= \pi x^2(2y) : \pi\left(3x^2\right)(3y)$

or 2 : 9

47. (D) The volume of the hall is

40 × 25 × 20 cu m.

Since each person needs 200 cu m, number of persons

$= \dfrac{40 \times 25 \times 20}{200} = 100.$

48. (B) The corners are quadrants, i.e.,

$\dfrac{1}{4} \times 2 \times \pi \times 2 = \pi$

For 4 corners, we have perimeter of quadrants = 4π

Perimeter of horizontal portions = 2(20 – 4) = 32 m.

Perimeter of vertical portions = 2(14 – 4) = 12 m.

Hence total perimeter = 44 + 4π

$= 44 + \dfrac{88}{7} = \dfrac{154 + 88}{7}$

= 56.57. ≈ 56.6 m.

49. (C) Volume of water in hollow spherical ball

$= \dfrac{4}{3}\pi R^3 = \dfrac{4}{3} \times \dfrac{22}{7} \times 64$

Half the water = $\dfrac{44 \times 64}{21}$ cm^3.

Volume of cone = $\dfrac{1}{3}\pi r^2 h$

$= \dfrac{1}{3} \times \dfrac{22}{7} \times r^2 \times 2 = \dfrac{44r^2}{21}$

Hence, $\dfrac{44 \times 64}{21} = \dfrac{44r^2}{21}$ or

$r^2 = 64$ or r = 8cm.

50. (B) When the enclosed cube is largest, we have, diameter of sphere = diagonal of cube.

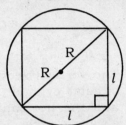

or 2R = $\sqrt{2}\,l$ or $l = \sqrt{2}\,R$

∴ volume of cube = $l^3 = 2\sqrt{2}\,R^3$

2R = 2 cm or R = 1 cm.

Volume of cube = $2\sqrt{2}$ cm^3.

51. (D) Let us estimate the volume of cooking pot.

Hemi-spherical bottom

$= \dfrac{\dfrac{4}{3}\pi R^3}{2} = \dfrac{2}{3} \times \pi \times 20^3$

$= \dfrac{16000\,\pi}{3}$ cm^3

Volume of truncated cone

$= \dfrac{1}{3}(20)^2(10 + \pi) - \dfrac{\pi}{3}(10)^2 h$

By similar triangles,

$\dfrac{10}{h} = \dfrac{20}{10 + h}$

or h = 10 cm.

$= \dfrac{\pi}{3}\left(20^2(20) - 10^3\right) = \dfrac{\pi}{3}\left(20^3 - 10^3\right)$

$= \dfrac{\pi}{3}(10).\left(20^2 + 200 + 10^2\right)$

$= \dfrac{10\pi}{3}(700) = \dfrac{7000\,\pi}{3}$ cm³

∴ total volume $= \dfrac{23000\,\pi}{3}$

Let maximum initial volume of food before spilling be x.

After 15% increase it is equal to total volume

∴ $x + \dfrac{15}{100}x = \dfrac{23000\pi}{3}$ cm³

or $x = \dfrac{20000\,\pi}{3}$ cm³.

52. (C) Let each side be $1.5l$ (after increase). Then % increase in surface area

$= \dfrac{6(1.5l)^2 - 6l^2}{6l^2} \times 100$

$= \dfrac{13.5l^2 - 6l^2}{6l^2} \times 100 = 125\%$

53. (D)

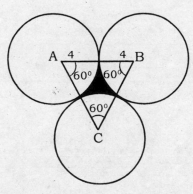

Required area is darkened.
The required area
= area of ABC – 3 × area of 60° sectors

$= \dfrac{\sqrt{3}}{4} \times 8^2 - 3 \times \dfrac{60}{360} \times \pi \times 4^2$

$= 16\sqrt{3} - 8\pi = 8\left(2\sqrt{3} - \pi\right)$ cm²

Hence, required volume

$= 16(8)\,(2\sqrt{3} - \pi)$

$= 128\,(2\sqrt{3} - \pi)$ cm³.

54. (D) As shown in hint, distance saved

$= (l + b) - \sqrt{l^2 + b^2} = \dfrac{l}{2}$

or $\dfrac{l}{2} + b = \sqrt{l^2 + b^2}$ or

$\dfrac{l^2}{4} + b^2 + lb = l^2 + b^2$

or $l^2 + 4lb = 4l^2$ or $3l^2 = 4lb$

or $3l = 4b$ or $\dfrac{b}{l} = \dfrac{3}{4}$

55. (C) The number of surfaces in a right circular cylinder = 3.

56. (A) Perimetre of field X = 470 + 290
+ (470 − 180) + 180
+ (470 − 290) + 470
= 4 × 470 = 1880 m.

Perimetre of field Y
= 4 × 470 = 1880 m.

Hence C_x = 1880 × 40
and Cy = 1880 × 40
or $C_x = C_y$.

57. (B) Internal volume
= 115 × 75 × 35 = 301875 cu cm.

External measurements are

length = 115 + 2 × 2.5 = 120 cm.

breadth = 75 + 2 × 2.5 = 80 cm.

height = 35 + 2 × 2.5 = 40 cm.

External volume
= 120 × 80 × 40 = 384000 cu cm.

Volume of wood

= 384000 – 301875

= 82,125 cu cm.

58. (C) Number of cubes = $\dfrac{(20)^3}{(5)^3}$

$= \dfrac{8000}{125} = 64$.

59. (A) Given that $h_1 : h_2 = 1 : 3$
We have,

$\pi r_1^2 h_1 = \pi r_2^2 h_2$

$\dfrac{r_1^2}{r_2^2} = \dfrac{\pi h_2}{\pi h_1} = \dfrac{h_2}{h_1} = \dfrac{3}{1}$

$\dfrac{r_1}{r_2} = \dfrac{\sqrt{3}}{1}$

$\therefore r_1 : r_2 = \sqrt{3} : 1$

60. (C) Let the third side of cuboid be x cm.
We have,

$11 \times 6 \times x = \dfrac{1}{3} \times \dfrac{22}{7} \times 7^2 \times 9$

$66x = 462$

$x = \dfrac{462}{66} = 7$ cm.

✦ ✦ ✦

Chapter 13

Statistics

13

Statistics, a branch of mathematics is useful in the collection, classification and interpretation of data.

The word statistics is used in two different senses:

i. In plural sense, statistics means data

ii. In singular sense, statistics is the science which deals with the collection, presentation, analysis and interpretation of some numerical data.

1. Data :

The word data means information in the form of numerical figures or a set of given facts.

Ex : The marks obtained by 10 pupils of a class in a monthly test are

21, 27, 28, 17, 11, 26, 27, 17, 30

2. Raw data :

Data obtained in original form is called a raw data

3. Tabulation :

Arranging the data in a systematic form in tabular form.

4. Observation :

Each numerical figure in a data.

5. Frequency

The number of times a particular observation occurs is called its frequency.

6. Range :

The difference between the maximum value and the minimum value of the observation is called its range.

7. Graphical Representation of Statistical Data :

There are three types of graphs to represent the statistical data.

(i) Bar Graphs

(ii) Histogram

(iii) Frequency Polygon

(i) Bar Graph :

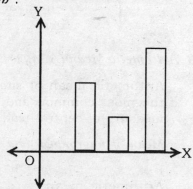

(ii) Histogram :

A histogram is a graphical representation of frequency distribution in the form of rectangles with class intervals as bases and the corresponding frequencies as heights

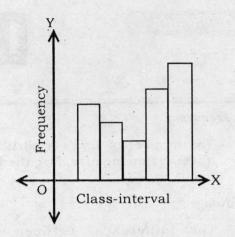

Class-interval

(iii) Frequency Polygon :

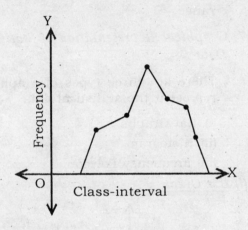

Class-interval

8. Arithmetic Mean (A.M.) or Mean :

Arithmetic mean or simply mean is the most common and widely used measure of central tendency.

Mean of ungrouped data :

If x_1, x_2 . . . . .x_n are 'n' items, then Arithmetic mean

$$\text{A.M.} (\bar{x}) = \frac{x_1 + x_2 + x_3 + \dots x_n}{n}$$

9. MEDIAN :

Median of ungrouped data :

If the observations are arranged in increasing or decreasing order, the median is defined as the middle observation.

If the number of observations is even then the median is the arithmetic mean of middle two terms.

Ex : 4, 7, 2, 1, 9, 3

Ascending order is,

1, 2, 3, 4, 7, 9

$$\text{Median} = \frac{3+4}{2} = 3.5$$

Ex : 3, 9, 11, 17, 1

Ascending order is,

1, 3, 9, 11, 17   Median = 9

10. MODE :

An observation with the highest frequency is called the mode

Mode of Ungrouped Data :

The item which repeats more is the mode.

Note : (i) For a given data, mode may or may not exist.

(ii) If mode exists for a given data, it may or may not be unique.

(iii) Data having unique mode is called uni–model.

(iv) Data having two modes is called bi–model

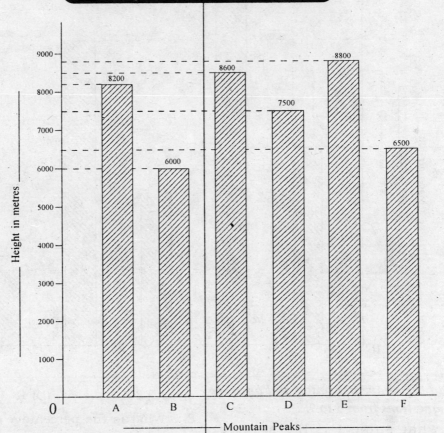

Given above is a bar graph showing the heights of six mountain peaks.

Read the above diagram and answer the questions from 1 to 4.

1. Which is the highest peak?

    (A) A   (B) E

    (C) C   (D) B

2. Write the ratio of the heights of highest peak and the lowest peak.

    (A) 22 : 15

    (B) 15 : 22

    (C) 20 : 13

    (D) 13 : 22

3. Which peak is second highest?

    (A) B

    (B) A

    (C) C

    (D) E

4. When the heights of the given peaks are written in ascending order, then what is the average of the middle two peaks?

    (A) 7950 m

    (B) 7560 m

    (C) 7650 m

    (D) 7850 m

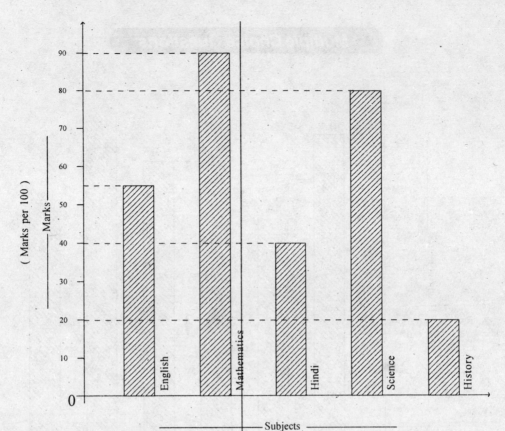

Read the above bar graph and answer the questions from 5 to 9.

5. At what subject is the student sharp?
   (A) English
   (B) Mathematics
   (C) Science
   (D) History

6. In which subject is the student poor?
   (A) English
   (B) Mathematics
   (C) Science
   (D) History

7. What are the average marks obtained by the student?
   (A) 57   (B) 63

(C) 80   (D) 48

8. What is the percentage obtained by the student?
   (A) 80%
   (B) 63%
   (C) 57%
   (D) 90%

9. What is the ratio of the highest marks to the lowest marks obtained by the student?
   (A) 2 : 11   (B) 9 : 2
   (C) 2 : 9   (D) 11 : 2

A car is going on a long journey for 16 hours, starting at 5-00 hrs. The speed of the car at different hours is given below.

Time (in hrs.)	Speed (in kmph)
5	40
7	50
9	60
11	80
13	70
17	65
15	75
19	60
21	50

The temperature chart of a patient is given below :

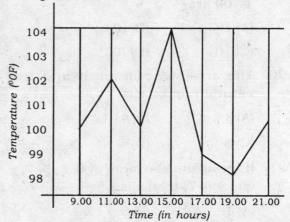

Read the above table and answer the questions from 10 to 13.

10. Average speed of the car during 5.00, 7.00 hrs. is

(A) 40   (B) 50

(C) 45   (D) 55

11. What is the percentage increase in speed during 9.00 hrs and 11.00 hrs?

(A) $33\frac{1}{3}\%$ (B) 35%

(C) $23\frac{1}{3}\%$ (D) 45%

12. What is the percentage of decrease in speed during 19.00 hrs and 21.00 hrs?

(A) $16\frac{1}{3}\%$ (B) $16\frac{2}{3}\%$

(C) $17\frac{2}{3}\%$ (D) $18\frac{2}{3}\%$

13. What is the average speed between 5.00, 7.00 and 9.00 hrs?

(A) 50   (B) 55

(C) 60   (D) 65

Read the above temperature chart and answer the questions from 14 to 19.

14. The temperature of patient at 21.00 hrs. is

(A) 100   (B) 101

(C) 102   (D) 103

15. At what time is the temperature highest?

(A) 9.00 hrs   (B) 15.00 hrs

(C) 17.00 hrs   (D) 21.00 hrs

16. At what time is the temperature lowest?

(A) 9.00 hrs   (B) 13.00 hrs

(C) 19.00 hrs   (D) 21.00 hrs

17. What is the percentage increase in temperature between 9.00 hrs and 15.00 hrs?

(A) 4%   (B) 3%

(C) 2%   (D) 1%

18. What is the percentage decrease in temperature between 17.00 hrs and 19.00 hrs?

(A) 1.02%   (B) 1.03%

(C) 1.04%   (D) 1.01%

19. What is the average temperature of the patient between 13.00, 15.00, 17.00 hrs?

   (A) 103   (B) 102

   (C) 101   (D) 100

20. The arithmetic mean of first five natural numbers is

   (A) 3   (B) 4

   (C) 5   (D) 6

21. If the arithmetic mean of 6, 8, 5, 7, x and 4 is 7, then x is

   (A) 12   (B) 6

   (C) 8   (D) 4

22. The arithmetic mean of first ten natural numbers is

   (A) 5.5   (B) 6

   (C) 7.5   (D) 10

23. The weight (in kg) of 5 men are 62, 65, 69, 66 and 61. The median is

   (A) 45 kg

   (B) 66 kg

   (C) 65 kg

   (D) 55 kg

24. If in a data, 10 numbers arranged in increasing order. If the 7th entry is increased by 4, then the median increases by

   (A) zero   (B) 4

   (C) 6   (D) 5

25. The mean of x, x + 3, x + 6, x + 9 and x + 12 is

   (A) x + 6   (B) x + 3

   (C) x + 9   (D) x + 12

26. 20 years ago, when my parents got married, their average age was 23 years, now the average age of my family, consisting of myself and my parents only is 35 years. My present age is

   (A) 34 years

   (B) 42 years

   (C) 24 years

   (D) 16 years

27. The daily sale of kerosene (in litres) in a ration shop for six days is as follows :

   75, 120, 12, 50, 70.5 and 140.5

   The average daily sale is

   (A) 150   (B) 10

   (C) 142   (D) 78

28. The mean of five numbers is 27. If one of the numbers is excluded the mean gets reduced by 2. The excluded number is

   (A) 35   (B) 27

   (C) 25   (D) 40

29. The median of the following data

   46, 64, 87, 41, 58, 77, 35, 90, 55, 33, 92 is

   (A) 87

   (B) 77

   (C) 58

   (D) 60.2

30. The mean of 10 observation is 25. If one observation, namely 25, is deleted, the new mean is

   (A) 25   (B) 20

   (C) 28   (D) 22

31. Mean of a set of observations is the value which

    (A) occurs most frequently

    (B) divides observations into two equal parts

    (C) is a representative of whole group

    (D) is the sum of observations

32. If each entry of a data is increased by 5, then the arithmetic mean

    (A) remains the same

    (B) increases by 5

    (C) decreases by 5

    (D) none of the foregoing

33. The arithmetic mean of five given numbers is 85. Their sum is

    (A) 425

    (B) 85

    (C) between 85 and 425

    (D) more than 425

34. The daily earnings (in rupees) of 10 workers in a factory are 8, 16, 19, 8, 16, 19, 16, 8, 19, 16. The median wage is

    (A) Rs. 17.50   (B) Rs. 8.00

    (C) Rs. 19.00   (D) Rs. 16.00

35. The average weight of sample of 10 apples is 52 g. Later it was found that the weighing machine had shown the weight of each apple 10 g less. The correct average weight of an apple is

    (A) 62 g   (B) 54 g

    (C) 56 g   (D) 52 g

36. The mean of 6, y, 7, x and 14 is 8. Then

    (A) x + y = 13   (B) x – y = 13

    (C) 2x + 3y = 13 (D) $x^2 + y^2 = 15$

37. The mean of 994, 996, 998, 1000 and 1002 is

    (A) 992   (B) 1004

    (C) 998   (D) none

38. The mode of a set of observations is the value which

    (A) occurs most frequently

    (B) is central

    (C) is between maximum and minimum

    (D) none of the foregoing

39. The runs scored by Sachin in 5 test matches are 140, 153, 148, 150 and 154 respectively. Find his mean.

    (A) 150   (B) 149
    (C) 148   (D) None

40. The mean of first six multiples of 4 is

    (A) 13.5   (B) 14.5
    (C) 14   (D) 16

41. The mean of first five prime numbers is

    (A) 5.6   (B) 3.6
    (C) 6.83   (D) 5.2

42. The mean of x-5y, x-3y, x-y, x+y, x+3y and x+5y is 12. Then the value of x is

    (A) 18
    (B) 12
    (C) cannot be determined
    (D) data is not sufficient

43. The mean of 7, 9, 11, 13, x, 21 is 13. Then the value of x is

    (A) 18   (B) 19
    (C) 15   (D) 17

44. If 6, 4, 8 and 3 occur with frequencies 4, 2, 5 and 1 respectively, then the arithmetic mean is

    (A) 6.25   (B) 6.75
    (C) 6.5   (D) 6

45. The mean of $\dfrac{1}{3}, \dfrac{3}{4}, \dfrac{5}{6}, \dfrac{1}{2}$ and $\dfrac{7}{12}$ is

(A) $\dfrac{2}{5}$ (B) $\dfrac{3}{5}$

(C) $\dfrac{1}{5}$ (D) none

46. The sum of 15 numbers is 420. The mean of those numbers is

(A) 25   (B) 30
(C) 28   (D) none

47. The mean of a data is 'p'. If each observation is multiplied by 3 and then 1 is added to each result, then the mean of the new observations so obtained is

(A) p   (B) 3p
(C) p+1   (D) 3p+1

48. The mean of 20 observations is 12.5. By error, one observation was noted as −15 instead of 15. Then the correct mean is

(A) 11.75   (B) 11
(C) 14   (D) none

49. The mean of 11 observations is 17.5. If an observation 15 is deleted, the mean of the remaining observations is

(A) 16   (B) 17.75
(C) 17.5   (D) 17.25

50. The mean of 67, 79, 15, 0, 93, 44, 17 is

(A) 52.5
(B) 45
(C) 50
(D) none

51. The arithmetic mean of a-2, a and a+2 is

(A) a+2   (B) a-2
(C) a   (D) 3a

52. The sum of the deviations of the variable values 6, 8, 9, 13, 14 from 10 is

(A) 0   (B) 1
(C) 10   (D) none

53. The sum of the deviations of a set of values $x_1, x_2, \ldots, x_n$ measured from 50 is -10 and the sum of deviations of the values from 46 is 70. The mean is

(A) 49   (B) 49.5
(C) 49.75   (D) none

54. The mean of all factors of 24 is

(A) 7   (B) 7.75
(C) 7.25   (D) 7.5

55. The mean of 20 numbers is 15. If 2 is added to each of the first ten numbers, then the mean of the new set of 20 numbers is

(A) 17
(B) 16
(C) 30
(D) 13

56. The mean of the six numbers is 43. If one of the numbers is excluded, the mean of the remaining numbers is 41. Then the excluded number is

(A) 53
(B) 84
(C) 12
(D) none

57. The average age of 5 teachers is 28 years. If one teacher is excluded the mean gets reduced by 2 years. The age of the excluded teacher is

(A) 26 years   (B) 33 years
(C) 36 years   (D) none

58. The mean of 9 observations is 36. If the mean of the first 5 observations is 32 and that of the last 5 observations is 39, then the fifth observation is

(A) 28   (B) 31
(C) 43   (D) 37

59. The average temperatures of Tuesday, Wednesday and Thursday was 42°C. The average temperature of Wednesday, Thursday and Friday was 47°C. If the temperature on Tuesday was 43°C, then the temperature on Friday was

(A) 58°C   (B) 50°C
(C) 53°C   (D) 49°C

60. The average of A & B is 25, B & C is 28 and C & A is 21. Then the average of A, B & C (approximately) is

(A) 23   (B) 24
(C) 25   (D) none

Answers

1. B	2. A	3. C	4. D	5. B	6. D	7. A	8. C	9. B	10. C
11. A	12. B	13. A	14. A	15. B	16. C	17. A	18. D	19. C	20. A
21. A	22. A	23. C	24. A	25. A	26. D	27. D	28. A	29. C	30. A
31. C	32. B	33. A	34. D	35. A	36. A	37. C	38. A	39. B	40. C
41. A	42. B	43. D	44. A	45. B	46. C	47. D	48. C	49. B	50. B
51. C	52. A	53. B	54. D	55. B	56. A	57. C	58. B	59. A	60. C

Explanatory Answers

1. (B) E is the highest peak.

2. (A) Height of highest peak
   = 8800 m
   Height of lowest peak = 6000 m
   Ratio   = 8800 : 6000
               = 22   : 15

3. (C) Second highest peak is C.

4. (D) The ascending order of heights is,
   6000 m < 6500 m < 7500 m < 8200 m < 8600 m < 8800 m.

   The two middle peaks are 7500 m and 8200 m.

Average $= \dfrac{7500 + 8200}{2}$

$= \dfrac{15700}{2} = 7850$ m.

5. (B) Mathematics

6. (D) History

7. (A) Total marks
   = 55 + 90 + 40 + 80 + 20
   = 285.

∴ Average $= \dfrac{285}{5} = 57$.

8. (C) Percentage = $\frac{285}{500} \times 100 = 57\%$

9. (B) Highest marks = 90

    Lowest marks = 20

    Ratio = 90 : 20

    = 9 : 2

11. (A) $\frac{100}{60} \times 20 = \frac{100}{3} = 33\frac{1}{3}\%$

12. (B) $\frac{100}{60} \times 10 = \frac{50}{3} = 16\frac{2}{3}\%$

13. (A) $\frac{40 + 50 + 60}{3} = \frac{150}{3} = 50$

18. (D) $\frac{100}{99} \times 1 = \frac{100}{99} = 1.01\%$

    approximately.

20. (A) By definition,

    $$AM = \frac{1 + 2 + 3 + 4 + 5}{5} = 3$$

    Short cut : Take the average of last number and first number.

    i.e., $\frac{5 + 1}{2} = 3$

21. (A) By definition,

    $$AM = \frac{6 + 8 + 5 + 7 + x + 4}{6} = 7$$

    or x = 12.

22. (A) By definition,

    $$AM = \frac{1 + 2 + 3 + ... + 10}{6} = 5.5$$

    By shortcut, $AM = \frac{10 + 1}{2} = 5.5$

23. (C) Arranging in the ascending order we have 61, 62, 65, 66, 69.

    Hence median = 65 kg.

24. (A) The median would be average of the 5th and 6th observations. Since they are unaffected by increase in 7th entry, the median will be unchanged.

25. (A) By definition,

    $$\text{Average} = \frac{x + (x+3) + (x+6) + (x+9) + (x+12)}{5}$$

    $$= \frac{5x + 30}{5} = x + 6$$

26. (D) Let my age be x years. Sum of ages of my parents 20 years ago

    = 46.

    Sum of present ages

    = 46 + 20 + 20 = 86 (since both mother's and father's ages increase by 20 years each)

    ∴ present average

    $$= \frac{86 + x}{3} = 34 \text{ or } x = 16 \text{ years.}$$

27. (D) By definition of average

    $$= \frac{75 + 120 + 12 + 50 + 70.5 + 140.5}{5}$$

    However, without calculating we can say that the answer is D since the average lies between the maximum and the minimum.

28. (A) Let the sum of four numbers be y and the excluded number be x.

    Then $\frac{y + x}{5} = 27$ and $\frac{y}{4} = 25$

    or x + y = 135 and

    y = 100 or x = 35.

29. (C) Arrange the given data in ascending order.

We have, 33, 35, 41, 46, 55, 58, 64, 77, 87, 90 and 92.

The sixth entry is 58.

Median is 58.

30. (A) The sum of 10 observations is 250.

∴ new mean

$$= \frac{250 - 25}{9} = \frac{225}{9} = 25 \, .$$

31. (C) Mean is representative of whole group.

32. (B) Let the observations be $x_1, x_2, \ldots x_n$.

After the increase they are $x_1 + 5$, $x_2 + 5, \ldots, x_n + 5$.

$$AM = \frac{x_1 + 5 + x_2 + 5 + \ldots + x_n + 5}{n}$$

$$= \frac{x_1 + x_2 + \ldots + x_n}{n} + \frac{5n}{n}$$

$$= \text{old AM} + 5$$

33. (A) By definition

$$\frac{x_1 + x_2 + x_3 + x_4 + x_5}{5} = 85 \text{ or}$$

$$\sum_{i=1}^{5} X_i = 425 \, .$$

34. (D) Arranging the daily earnings in ascending order, we have 8, 8, 8, 16, 16, 16, 16, 19, 19, 19. The median is average of 5th and 6th wages, i.e., $\frac{16 + 16}{2} = 16$.

35. (A) The sum of weights of 10 apples before the error was detected is 520 g. Increase in the weight after the correction

(a) 10g per apple

$$= 10 \times 10 \text{ g} = 100 \text{ g}.$$

∴ correct sum of weight

$$= 520 + 100 = 620 \text{ g}.$$

Hence, correct average weight

$$= \frac{620}{10} = 62 \text{ g}.$$

36. (A) By definition,

$$\frac{6 + y + 7 + x + 14}{5} = 8 \text{ or}$$

$$27 + x + y = 40$$

or $x + y = 13$.

37. (C) We know that the average lies between maximum and minimum. This fact helps us to eliminate (A) and (B).

But to decide between (C) and (D) we need calculate using formula.

$$AM = \frac{994 + 996 + 998 + 1000 + 1002}{5} = 998$$

38. (A) By definition, mode is the value which occurs most frequently.

39. (B) Mean

$$= \frac{140 + 153 + 148 + 150 + 154}{5}$$

$$= \frac{745}{5} = 149.$$

40. (C) Mean

$$= \frac{4 + 8 + 12 + 16 + 20 + 24}{6}$$

$$= 14.$$

41. (A) Mean

$$= \frac{2 + 3 + 5 + 7 + 11}{5}$$

$= \dfrac{28}{5} = 5.6$

42. (B) Mean

$$=\dfrac{(x-5y)+(x-3y)+(x-y)+(x+y)+(x+3y)+(x+5y)}{6}$$

$$12 = \dfrac{6x}{6}$$

$$\Rightarrow \quad x = 12.$$

43. (D) Mean $\quad =$

$$\dfrac{7+9+11+13+x+21}{6}$$

$$13 = \dfrac{61+x}{6}$$

$$x = 78-61 = 17.$$

44. (A) Mean $= \dfrac{(6\times4)+(4\times2)+(8\times5)+(3\times1)}{4+2+5+1}$

$$= \dfrac{75}{12}$$

$$= 6.25$$

45. (B) Mean $= \dfrac{\dfrac{1}{3}+\dfrac{3}{4}+\dfrac{5}{6}+\dfrac{1}{2}+\dfrac{7}{12}}{5}$

$$= \dfrac{3}{5}$$

46. (C) Mean $= \dfrac{420}{15}$

$$= 28.$$

47. (D) (See synopsis)

Mean $= 3p+1.$

48. (C) Sum of 20 observations $= 20\times12.5$
$= 250$

Correct sum $= 250-(-30) = 280$

$\therefore$ Mean $= \dfrac{280}{20} = 14.$

49. (B) Sum of 11 observations
$= 17.5 \times11$

$= 192.5$

After deleting 15, the sum of remaining 10 observations
$= 192.5 - 15$

$= 177.5$

$\therefore$ Mean $= \dfrac{177.5}{10}$

$= 17.75$

50. (B) Mean

$$= \dfrac{67+79+15+0+93+44+17}{7}$$

$$= \dfrac{315}{7}$$

$$= 45.$$

51. (C) Mean $= \dfrac{(a-2)+a+(a+2)}{3}$

$$= a.$$

52. (A) Mean $= \dfrac{6+8+9+13+14}{5}$

$$= \dfrac{50}{5} = 10$$

The sum of the deviations from their mean is zero.

53. (B) $(x_1-50)+(x_2-50)+\ldots\ldots+(x_n-50) = -10$

$(x_1+x_2+\ldots\ldots+x_n)-50n = -10$ -----(1)

$(x_1-46)+(x_2-46)+\ldots\ldots(x_n-46) = 70$

$(x_1+x_2+\ldots\ldots+x_n)-46n = 70$ -----(2)

By solving (1) & (2) we get

$n = 20$ and $x_1+x_2+\ldots\ldots+x_n = 990$

$\therefore$ mean $= \dfrac{x_1+x_2+\ldots\ldots+x_n}{n}$

$= \dfrac{990}{20}$

$= 49.5$

54. (D) The factors of 24 are,

1, 2, 3, 4, 6, 8, 12 and 24.

$\therefore$ mean

$= \dfrac{1+2+3+4+6+8+12+24}{8}$

$= \dfrac{60}{8}$

$= 7.5$

55. (B) Sum of 20 numbers $= 20 \times 15 = 300$

Sum of new set of 20 numbers
$= 300 + 10 \times 2 = 320$

$\therefore$ mean $= \dfrac{320}{20} = 16$.

56. (A) Excluded number $= (43 \times 6)-(41 \times 5)$

$= 258-205$

$= 53$.

57. (C) The age of excluded teacher

$= (28 \times 5)-(26 \times 4)$

$= 140-104$

$= 36$ years.

58. (B) Sum of 9 observations

$= 9 \times 36 = 324$

Sum of first 5 observaions

$= 5 \times 32 = 160$

Sum of last 5 observaions

$= 5 \times 39 = 195$

5th observation

$= 160 + 195 - 324$

$= 31$.

59. (A) $W + Th + F = 47 \times 3 = 141$------(1)

$T+W+Th = 42 \times 3 = 126$------(2)

(1) - (2) $\Rightarrow$

$F - T = 15$

$F = 15 + 43 = 58°C$

$\therefore$ temperature on Friday $= 58°C$.

60. (C) $A + B \qquad\qquad = 50$

$B + C \qquad\qquad = 56$

$C + A \qquad\qquad = 42$

$2(A + B + C) \qquad = 148$

$A + B + C = \dfrac{148}{2} = 74$

$\therefore$ average of A, B & C $= \dfrac{74}{3} \sim 25$.

Chapter 14

Probability

1. Random experiment :

An experiment in which all possible outcomes are known and the exact outcome cannot be predicted in advance is called a random experiment.

Eg:- (1) Tossing a coin.

(2) Rolling an unbiased die.

2. Sample space :

The set S of all possible outcomes of a random experiment is called the sample space.

Eg:- (1) In tossing a coin,

sample space (S) = { H, T}

(2) In rolling a die, sample space (S) = {1,2,3,4,5,6}

3. Probability :

Probability is a concept which numerically measures the degree of certainity of the occurence of events.

4. Definition of probability :

In a random experiment, let S be the sample space and let E be the event. Then probability of occurence of

$$E = P(E) = \frac{n(E)}{n(S)}$$

n(E)-number of elements favourable in E

n(S)-number of distinct elements in S

5. Some details about these experiments :

(a) A coin has 2 sides - one side is head (H) and the other side is tail (T).

(b) A die is a cube with 6 faces - on 1st face 1 dot, on the 2nd face 2 dots, on the 3rd face 3 dots, ... and on the 6th face 6 dots.

(c) Description of normal pack of cards (52):

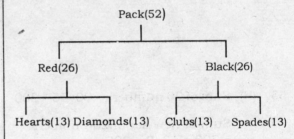

The 13 cards are,

2, 3, 4, 5, 6, 7, 8, 9, 10, A, K, Q, J.

Note : (1) $0 \leq P(E) \leq 1$

(2) If P(E) = 1, the event E is called a certain event and if P(E) = 0, the event E is called an impossible event.

1. In a throw of a dice, the probability of getting a prime number is

    (A) 2.

    (B) $\dfrac{1}{2}$

    (C) $\dfrac{3}{2}$

    (D) 6

2. The probability that a vowel selected at random in English language is an "i" is

    (A) $\dfrac{1}{5}$

    (B) $\dfrac{1}{26}$

    (C) $\dfrac{1}{6}$

    (D) none

3. The probability of three coins falling all heads up when tossed simultaneously is

    (A) $\dfrac{1}{2}$

    (B) $\dfrac{1}{6}$

    (C) $\dfrac{1}{8}$

    (D) none

4. When two dice are thrown, the probability of getting a number always greater than 4 on the second dice is

    (A) $\dfrac{1}{6}$

    (B) $\dfrac{1}{3}$

    (C) $\dfrac{1}{36}$

    (D) none

5. The probability for a leap year to have 52 mondays and 53 sundays is

    (A) $\dfrac{1}{366}$

    (B) $\dfrac{1}{52}$

    (C) $\dfrac{2}{7}$

    (D) $\dfrac{1}{7}$

6. When two dice are thrown, the probability of getting equal numbers is

    (A) $\dfrac{1}{36}$

    (B) $\dfrac{1}{6}$

    (C) 1

    (D) none

7. In a single throw of two dice, the probability of getting a sum of 10 is

    (A) $\dfrac{1}{12}$

    (B) $\dfrac{1}{36}$

    (C) $\dfrac{1}{6}$

    (D) none

8. Three letters, to each of which corresponds an addressed envelope are placed in the envelopes at random. The probability that all letters are placed in the right envelopes is

    (A) $\dfrac{1}{3}$

    (B) 1

    (C) $\dfrac{1}{6}$

    (D) 0

9. From a normal pack of cards, a card is drawn at random. The probability of getting a jack or a king is

    (A) $\dfrac{2}{52}$

    (B) $\dfrac{1}{52}$

    (C) $\dfrac{2}{13}$

    (D) none

10. Two numbers are chosen from 1 to 5. The probability for the two numbers to be consecutive is

    (A) $\dfrac{1}{5}$

    (B) $\dfrac{2}{5}$

    (C) $\dfrac{1}{10}$

    (D) $\dfrac{2}{10}$

11. Two dice are thrown at a time. The probability that the difference of the numbers shown on the dice is 1 is

(A) $\dfrac{5}{18}$ (B) $\dfrac{1}{36}$

(C) $\dfrac{1}{6}$ (D) none

12. A bag contains 3 white and 5 red balls. If a ball is drawn at random, the probability that the drawn ball to red is

(A) $\dfrac{3}{8}$ (B) $\dfrac{5}{8}$

(C) $\dfrac{3}{15}$ (D) $\dfrac{5}{15}$

13. The probability of getting an even number when a die is rolled is

(A) $\dfrac{1}{6}$ (B) $\dfrac{1}{36}$

(C) $\dfrac{1}{2}$ (D) none

14. A card is drawn from a packet of 100 cards numbered 1 to 100. The probability of drawing a number which is a square is

(A) $\dfrac{1}{10}$ (B) $\dfrac{9}{100}$

(C) $\dfrac{1}{100}$ (D) $\dfrac{2}{100}$

15. The probability for a randomly selected number out of 1, 2, 3, 4, ..., 25 to be a prime number is

(A) $\dfrac{2}{25}$ (B) $\dfrac{23}{25}$

(C) $\dfrac{10}{25}$ (D) $\dfrac{9}{25}$

16. A book containing 100 pages is opened at random. The probability that a doublet page is found is

(A) $\dfrac{9}{100}$ (B) $\dfrac{90}{100}$

(C) $\dfrac{10}{100}$ (D) $\dfrac{20}{100}$

17. If a coin is tossed twice, the probability of getting at least one head is

(A) $\dfrac{1}{2}$ (B) $\dfrac{1}{4}$

(C) $\dfrac{3}{4}$ (D) none

18. The probability of getting a number greater than 2 or an even number in a single throw of a fair die is

(A) $\dfrac{1}{3}$ (B) $\dfrac{2}{3}$

(C) $\dfrac{5}{6}$ (D) none

19. The probability that in a family of 3 children, there will be at least one boy is

(A) $\dfrac{7}{8}$ (B) $\dfrac{1}{8}$

(C) $\dfrac{4}{8}$ (D) $\dfrac{6}{8}$

20. The chance that a non-leap year contains 53 saturdays is

(A) $\dfrac{2}{7}$ (B) $\dfrac{1}{7}$

(C) $\dfrac{2}{365}$ (D) $\dfrac{1}{365}$

Answers

1. B	2. A	3. C	4. B	5. D	6. B	7. A	8. C	9. C	10. B
11. A	12. B	13. C	14. A	15. D	16. A	17. C	18. C	19. A	20. B

Explanatory Answers

1. (B) E = {2, 3, 5}

   n(E) = 3

   S = {1, 2, 3, 4, 5, 6}

   n(S) = 6

   $\therefore P(E) = \dfrac{n(E)}{n(S)} = \dfrac{3}{6} = \dfrac{1}{2}$

2. (A) E = {i}

   n(E) = 1

   S = {a, e, i, o, u}

   n(S) = 5

   $\therefore P(E) = \dfrac{n(E)}{n(S)} = \dfrac{1}{5}$

3. (C) E = {HHH}, n(E) = 1

   S = {HHH, HHT, HTH, HTT, THH, THT, TTH, TTT}

   n(S) = 8

   $p(E) = \dfrac{n(E)}{n(S)} = \dfrac{1}{8}$

4. (B) E = {(1,5), (2,5), (3,5), (4,5), (5,5), (6,5), (1, 6), (2, 6), (3, 6), (4, 6), (5, 6), (6, 6)}

   n(E) = 12

   n(S) = 6×6 = 36

   $P(E) = \dfrac{n(E)}{n(S)} = \dfrac{12}{36} = \dfrac{1}{3}$

5. (D) A leap year has 366 days, i.e., 52 weeks and 2 days. The 2 days can be chosen in 7 ways. They are (i) M & Tu (ii) Tu & W (iii) W & Th (iv) Th & F (v) F & Sa (vi) Sa & S (vii) S & M

   n(E) = 1 (Sa & S)

   n(S) = 7

   $\therefore P(E) = \dfrac{1}{7}$

6. (B) E = {(1, 1), (2, 2), (3, 3), (4, 4), (5, 5), (6, 6)}

   n(E) = 6

   n(S) = 6×6 = 36

   $P(E) = \dfrac{n(E)}{n(S)} = \dfrac{6}{36} = \dfrac{1}{6}$

7. (A) E = {(4, 6), (5, 5), (6, 4)}

   n(E) = 3

   n(S) = 6×6 = 36

   $P(E) = \dfrac{n(E)}{n(S)} = \dfrac{3}{36} = \dfrac{1}{12}$

8. (C) n(E) = 1

$$n(S) = 3 \times 2 \times 1 = 6$$

$$P(E) = \frac{n(E)}{n(S)} = \frac{1}{6}$$

9. (C) $n(E) = 4+4 = 8$

$$n(S) = 52$$

$$P(E) = \frac{n(E)}{n(S)} = \frac{8}{52} = \frac{2}{13}$$

10. (B) E = 1, 2 ; 2, 3 ; 3, 4; 4, 5

$$n(E) = 4$$

$$n(S) = {}^5C_2 = 10$$

$$P(E) = \frac{n(E)}{n(S)} = \frac{4}{10} = \frac{2}{5}$$

11. (A) E = {(1,2), (2,1), (2,3), (3,2), (3,4), (4,3), (4,5), (5, 4), (5,6), (6,5)}

$$n(E) = 10$$

$$n(S) = 6 \times 6 = 36$$

$$P(E) = \frac{n(E)}{n(S)} = \frac{10}{36} = \frac{5}{18}$$

12. (B) $n(E) = 5$

$$n(S) = 3+5 = 8$$

$$P(E) = \frac{n(E)}{n(S)} = \frac{5}{8}$$

13. (C) E = {2, 4, 6}

$$n(E) = 3$$

S = {1, 2, 3, 4, 5, 6}

$$n(S) = 6$$

$$P(E) = \frac{n(E)}{n(S)} = \frac{3}{6} = \frac{1}{2}$$

14. (A) E = {1, 4, 9, 16, 25, 36, 49, 64, 81, 100}

$$n(E) = 10$$

S = {1, 2, 3, ..., 100}

$$n(S) = 100$$

$$P(E) = \frac{n(E)}{n(S)} = \frac{10}{100} = \frac{1}{10}$$

15. (D) E = {2, 3, 5, 7 11, 13 17, 19, 23}

$$n(E) = 9$$

S = {1, 2, 3, 4, ..., 25}

$$n(S) = 25$$

$$P(E) = \frac{9}{25}$$

16. (A) E = {11, 22, 33, 44, 55, 66, 77, 88, 99}

$$n(E) = 9$$

S = {1, 2, 3, ..., 100}

$$n(S) = 100$$

$$P(E) = \frac{9}{100}$$

17. (C) S = {HH, HT, TH, TT}

$$n(S) = 4$$

E = {HT, TH, HH}

$$n(E) = 3$$

$$P(E) = \frac{n(E)}{n(S)} = \frac{3}{4}$$

18. (C) E $= \{2, 3, 4, 5, 6\}$

n(E) = 5

S $= \{1, 2, 3, 4, 5, 6\}$

n(S) = 6

$P(E) = \dfrac{n(E)}{n(S)} = \dfrac{5}{6}$

19. (A) S $= \{BBB, BBG, BGB, BGG, GBB, GBG, GGB, GGG\}$

n(S) = 8

E $= \{BBB, BBG, BGB, BGG, GBB, GBG, GGB\}$

n(E) = 7

$\therefore$ $P(E) = \dfrac{n(E)}{n(S)} = \dfrac{7}{8}$

20. (B) A non-leap year contains 365 days, i.e., 52 weeks + 1 day.

S $= \{S, M, T, W, Th, F, Sa\}$

n(S) = 7

E $= \{Sa\}$

n(E) = 1

$\therefore$ $P(E) = \dfrac{n(E)}{n(S)} = \dfrac{1}{7}$

◆ ◆ ◆

 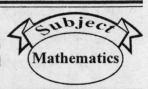
1. The two irrational numbers between $\sqrt{2}$ and $\sqrt{3}$ are

   (A) $2^{\frac{1}{2}}$, $6^{\frac{1}{4}}$ (B) $3^{\frac{1}{4}}$, $3^{\frac{1}{6}}$

   (C) $6^{\frac{1}{8}}$, $3^{\frac{1}{4}}$ (D) none

2. The greatest among $\sqrt[3]{4}$, $\sqrt[4]{5}$, $\sqrt[4]{3}$ is

   (A) $\sqrt[3]{4}$

   (B) $\sqrt[4]{5}$

   (C) $\sqrt[4]{3}$

   (D) none of these

3. If $x = \dfrac{\sqrt{a}+\sqrt{b}}{\sqrt{a}-\sqrt{b}}$, $y = \dfrac{\sqrt{a}-\sqrt{b}}{\sqrt{a}+\sqrt{b}}$ then the value of $x^2 + xy + y^2$ is

   (A) $\dfrac{4(a-b)}{(a+b)}$

   (B) $\dfrac{4(a+b)}{(a-b)}$

   (C) $\dfrac{2(a+b)}{a-b}$

   (D) $\dfrac{2(a-b)}{a+b}$

4. If A : Rational numbers are always closed under division and

   R : Division by Zero is not defined, then which of the following statement is correct?

   (A) A is True and R is the correct explanation of A

   (B) A is False and R is the correct explanation of A

   (C) A is True and R is False

   (D) None of these

5. The greatest among the following is

   I. $\sqrt[3]{1.728}$ II. $\dfrac{\sqrt{3}-1}{\sqrt{3}+1}$

   III. $\left(\dfrac{1}{2}\right)^{-2}$ IV. $\dfrac{17}{8}$

   (A) I   (B) IV

   (C) II   (D) III

6. Which of the following expressions is a polynomial?

   (A) $3x^{\frac{1}{2}} - 4x + 3$

   (B) $4x^2 - 3\sqrt{x} + 5$

   (C) $3x^2y - 2xy + 5x^4$

   (D) $2x^4 + \dfrac{3}{x^2} - 1$

7. The remainder obtained when $t^6 + 3t^2 + 10$ is divided by $t^3 + 1$ is

(A) $t^2 - 11$ (B) $t^3 - 1$

(C) $3t^2 + 11$ (D) none

8. One of the factors of

$$x^2 + \frac{1}{x^2} + 2 - 2x - \frac{2}{x} \text{ is}$$

(A) $x - \dfrac{1}{x}$ (B) $x + \dfrac{1}{x} - 1$

(C) $x + \dfrac{1}{x}$ (D) $x^2 + \dfrac{1}{x^2}$

9. The remainder when

$P(x) = 4x^4 - 3x^3 - 2x^2 + x - 7$ is divided by $x - 1$ is

(A) -7   (B) -6

(C) 7   (D) 6

10. If $5^{2n} - 2^{3n}$ is divisible by 17 then the remainder is

(A) 0   (B) 1

(C) -1   (D) 2

11. The point (3, 2) is at a distance of _____ units from Y-axis.

(A) 2 units   (B) 3 units
(C) 5 units   (D) none

12. The point (-2, -3) belongs to Quadrant

(A) Q_1 (B) Q_2

(C) Q_3 (D) Q_4

13. From the adjoining figure the value of x^0 is

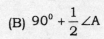

(A) 15°

(B) 60°

(C) 30°

(D) none of these

14. The difference of two complementary angles is 40°. Then the angles are

(A) 50°, 40°   (B) 65°, 25°

(C) 70°, 30°   (D) 40°, 50°

15. In the adjoining figure BO, CO are angle bisectors of external angles of $\triangle ABC$. Then $\angle BOC$ is

(A) $90^0 - \dfrac{1}{2}\angle A$

(B) $90^0 + \dfrac{1}{2}\angle A$

(C) $180^0 - \dfrac{1}{2}\angle A$

(D) $180^0 + \dfrac{1}{2}\angle A$

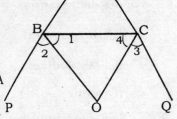

16. In the given figure PQ||RS

$\angle PAB = 70^0$, $\angle ACS = 110^0$ then

$\angle BAC$ is

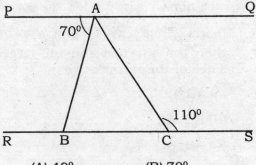

(A) 40°   (B) 70°

(C) 110°   (D) 30°

17. Supplementary angle of 108.5° is

(A) 70.5°   (B) 71.5°

(C) 71°   (D) 72.5°

18. At 6 o'clock the angle formed between the hands of a clock is

(A) straight angle

(B) right angle

(C) acute angle

(D) obtuse angle

19. If two lines are parallel then the perpendicular distance between them remains

(A) decreasing

(B) increasing

(C) constant

(D) none

20. Instruments used to draw a pair of parallel lines are

(A) protractor and scale

(B) compass and scale

(C) set square and scale

(D) none

21. In a $\triangle ABC$ if $\angle A = 45^0$ and $\angle B = 70^0$ then the shortest and the largest sides of the triangle are

(A) AB, BC

(B) BC, AC

(C) AB, AC

(D) none

22. In $\triangle ABC$, AB = AC and AD is perpendicular to BC. State the property by which $\triangle ADB \cong \triangle ADC$.

(A) SAS property   (B) SSS property

(C) RHS property   (D) ASA property

23. Which of the following statement(s) is/are false?

(A) Two $\triangle$les having same area are congruent

(B) If two sides and one angle of a $\triangle$le are equal to the corresponding two sides and the angle of another $\triangle$le, then the two $\triangle$les are congruent

(C) If the hypotenuse of one right triangle is equal to the hypotenuse of another triangle, then the triangles are congruent

(D) All the above

24. ABCD is a quadrilateral. AB = BC = CD = DA and $\angle A = \angle B = \angle C = \angle D = 90^0$. Then ABCD can be called

(A) rhombus

(B) square

(C) parallelogram

(D) all of the foregoing

25. One of the diagonals of a rhombus is equal to a side of the rhombus. The angles of the rhombus are

(A) 60^0 and 80^0

(B) 60^0 and 120^0

(C) 120^0 and 240^0

(D) 100^0 and 120^0

26. If a quadrilateal has two adjacent sides equal and the other two sides equal it is called

(A) parallelogram   (B) square

(C) rectangle   (D) kite

27. Which of the following statements is true?

(A) The diagonals of a rectangle are perpendicular

(B) The diagonals of a rhombus are equal

(C) Every square is a rhombus

(D) None of these

28. A quadrilateral is a rhombus but not a square if

(A) its diagonals do not bisect each other

(B) its diagonals are not perpendicular

(C) opposite angles are not equal

(D) the length of diagonals are not equal

29. A chord of a circle is 12 cm in length and its distance from the centre is 8 cm. Find the length of the chord of the same circle which is at a distance of 6 cm from the centre.

(A) 30 cm   (B) 24 cm

(C) 16 cm   (D) 18 cm

30. Which of the following statement(s) is/are true?

(A) Sum of the opposite angles of a cyclic quadrilateral is 180°

(B) If one side of a cyclic quadrilateral is produced, the exterior angle soformed is equal to the interior opposite angle

(C) A cyclic parallelogram is a rectangle

(D) All the above

31. An equilateral triangle XYZ is inscribed in a circle with centre O. The measure of XOY is

(A) 60^0

(B) 120^0

(C) 45^0

(D) 75^0

32. The number of tangents that can be drawn to a circle at a given point on it is

(A) two

(B) one

(C) zero

(D) three

33. A triangle ABC is inscribed in a circle, and the bisectors of the angles meet the circumference at X, Y, Z. The angles of the triangle X, Y, Z are respectively

(A) $90^0 - \dfrac{A}{2}, 90^0 - \dfrac{B}{2}, 90^0 - \dfrac{C}{2}$

(B) $90^0, 60^0, 30^0$

(C) $\dfrac{A}{2}, \dfrac{B}{2}, \dfrac{C}{2}$

(D) $\dfrac{B}{2}, \dfrac{A}{2}, \dfrac{A}{2} - \dfrac{B}{2}$

34. The diameter is

(A) smallest chord of a circle

(B) greatest chord of a circle

(C) three times radius of circle

(D) none of the foregoing

35. ABCD is a quadrilateral. If $\angle ACB = \angle ADB$ then

(A) ABCD is a cyclic quadrilateral

(B) ABCD is a parallelogram

(C) ABCD is a square

(D) ABCD is not a cyclic quadrilateral

36. The $\triangle$le formed by BC = AC = 7.2 cm and $\angle C = 90°$ is

(A) a right angled $\triangle$le

(B) an isosceles $\triangle$le

(C) a right angled isosceles $\triangle$le

(D) no $\triangle$le is formed

37. If a, b and c are the sides of a $\triangle$le, then

(A) a - b > c   (B) c > a + b

(C) c = a + b   (D) b < c + a

38. The number of independent measurements required to construct a $\triangle$le is

(A) 3   (B) 4

(C) 2   (D) 5

39. Which of the following statement is correct?

(A) The difference of any two sides is less than the third side

(B) A $\triangle$le cannot have two obtuse angles

(C) A $\triangle$le cannot have an obtuse angle and a right angle

(D) All the above

40. The top of a broken tree touches the ground at a distance of 15 m from its base. If the tree is broken at a height of 8 m from the ground, then the actual height of the tree is

(A) 20 m   (B) 25 m

(C) 30 m   (D) 17 m

41. The total surface area of a cylinder is 220 sq cm with height 6.5 cm. Then its volume is _____

(A) 25.025 cm³   (B) 2.5025 cm³

(C) 2502.5 cm³   (D) 250.25 cm³

42. A cylindrical vessel of diameter 9 cm has some water in it. A cylindrical iron piece of diameter 6 cm and height 4.5 cm is dropped in it. After it was completely immersed, the raise in the level of water is _____

(A) 0.8 cm   (B) 0.5 cm

(C) 0.1 cm   (D) none

43. A cone of radius 10 cm is divided into two parts by drawing a plane through the midpoint of its axis, parallel to its base. The ratio of volumes of the two parts formed is _____

(A) 1 : 7   (B) 2 : 7

(C) 3 : 7   (D) none

44. The largest sphere is cut off from a cube of side 5 cm. The volume of the sphere will be :

(A) 27π cm³

(B) 30π cm³

(C) 108π cm²

(D) $\dfrac{125\pi}{6}$ cm³

45. Two cylinders of same volume have their heights in the ratio 1 : 3. Find the ratio of their radii.

(A) $\sqrt{3}:1$ (B) $\sqrt{2}:1$

(C) $\sqrt{5}:2$ (D) $2:\sqrt{5}$

46. If the arithmetic mean of 6, 8, 5, 7, x and 4 is 7, then x is

(A) 12 (B) 6

(C) 8 (D) 4

47. The median of the following data

46, 64, 87, 41, 58, 77, 35, 90, 55, 33, 92 is

(A) 87 (B) 77

(C) 58 (D) 60.2

48. The mean of 20 observations is 12.5. By error, one observation was noted as –15 instead of 15. Then the correct mean is

(A) 11.75 (B) 11

(C) 14 (D) none

49. When two dice are thrown, the probability of getting a number always greater than 4 on the second dice is

(A) $\dfrac{1}{6}$ (B) $\dfrac{1}{3}$

(C) $\dfrac{1}{36}$ (D) none

50. The chance that a non-leap year contains 53 saturdays is

(A) $\dfrac{2}{7}$ (B) $\dfrac{1}{7}$

(C) $\dfrac{2}{365}$ (D) $\dfrac{1}{365}$

Answers

1. C	2. A	3. B	4. B	5. D	6. C	7. C	8. C	9. A	10. A
11. B	12. C	13. C	14. B	15. A	16. A	17. B	18. A	19. C	20. C
21. B	22. C	23. D	24. D	25. B	26. D	27. C	28. D	29. C	30. D
31. B	32. B	33. A	34. B	35. A	36. C	37. D	38. A	39. D	40. B
41. D	42. B	43. A	44 D	45. A	46. A	47. C	48. C	49. B	50. B

❖ ❖ ❖

PHYSICS

Chapter 1

Motion

Rest and motion

If the object's position does not change with respect to time and surroundings, it is said to be at rest. If the position of an object changes with time and surroundings, it is said to be in motion.

Describing motion

The position of a particle is described in a graph by representing :

(a) its distance from a fixed point called the origin and

(b) its direction as seen from the origin.

(c) The position of a particle moving along a straight line with its sign indicating whether the particle is in the positive or in the negative direction as seen from the origin.

Displacement

The change in the position of a particle during a time interval is called its displacement in that time interval. The displacement tells us about :

a) how far the final position is from the initial position and

b) the direction in which the final position is as seen from the initial position.

Scalar quantity

A quantity that has only magnitude is called scalar quantity.

e.g. distance, speed, etc.

Vector quantity

A quantity that has both magnitude and direction is called a vector quantity.

e.g. displacement, velocity, etc.

w/direction   w/direction

Speed

The speed of an object is equal to the distance traversed by it in a very short interval divided by the time interval.

Average speed

The average speed of a body for the complete journey is given by :

$$\text{Average speed} = \frac{\text{total distance}}{\text{total time taken}}$$

Uniform speed

If an object covers equal distances in equal time intervals (however small the interval be), it is said to be moving with a uniform or constant speed.

Velocity

The velocity of an object is a quantity that gives the speed of the object as well as the direction of its motion. Velocity changes if either speed or the direction of motion changes.

Acceleration

(a) The acceleration of an object is equal to the change in its velocity per unit time.

(b) If the velocity of an object changes by equal amounts in equal intervals the object is said to have uniform acceleration.

Distance-time graph

(a) The distance–time graph of an object moving with <u>uniform speed</u> is a straight line. Conversely, if the distance–time graph of an object is a straight line, the object is said to be moving with a uniform speed.

(b) The slope of the distance–time graph of an object equals its speed.

(c) If an object moves with nonuniform speed, its distance–time graph is not a straight line. The slope of the tangent at any point in the graph gives the speed at the corresponding time.

Displacement–time graph

(a) The displacement--time graph of an object moving with a uniform velocity is a straight line.
→ both direction + speed are equal

(b) The slope of the displacement–time graph of an object equals its velocity.

(c) The displacement–time graph for a uniformly accelerated object has a parabolic shape.

Speed–time graph

(a) If an object moves with a constant speed, its speed–time graph is a straight line parallel to the time axis.

(b) The area under the speed–time graph gives the distance traversed by the object in the corresponding time interval.

Velocity–time graph

(a) If an object moves with a constant acceleration in a straight line, its velocity–time graph is a straight line.

(b) The slope of the velocity–time graph gives the acceleration of the object.

(c) The area under the velocity–time graph gives the displacement of the object.

Circular motion

A particle moving in a circular path changes its direction continuously and hence is in acceleration.

Mathematical equations

$s = vt$

(s is the distance, v is the speed, t is the time)

$v = u + at$

u is the initial velocity, v is the final velocity, a is the acceleration (assumed constant).

$$s = ut + \frac{1}{2}at^2$$

[s is the displacement during time 0 to t, u is the initial velocity, a is the acceleration (assumed constant)]

$v^2 = u^2 + 2as$

where 'v', 'u', 's' and 'a' have their usual meaning.

Devices used to analyse motion

(a) *Motion Sensors* : The ultrasonic echo technique is used to determine the distance of an object from a sensor connecting a data logger and a computer enabling a distance-time graph to be plotted directly. Further analysis by the computer allows a velocity-time graph to be obtained.

(b) *Ticker-tape Timer* : This enables us to measure speed and distance. From this data, we can estimate acceleration. It has a marker which vibrates at a certain frequency (50 per second) and makes dots at 1/50th of every second on the paper tape, which is pulled through it. The distance between successive dots can be measured along with the time and hence velocity can be estimated. Tape charts can be made by sticking successive strips of tape.

(c) Photographic Timer : This is used to record the time taken for a trolley to pass through a gate.

Circular Motion

When a body describes a circular path while moving it is said to be having circular motion. If it moves with a uniform speed it has uniform circular motion.

The speed of a body in circular motion may be constant but never the velocity because of a constant change in direction.

e.g. planets revolving around the sun, an athlete running on a circular path, satellites, etc.

Other kinds of motion are rotatory motion, projectile motion and free-fall.

Multiple Choice Questions

1. A particle is travelling with a constant speed. This means that :

(A) its position remains constant as time passes

(B) it covers equal distances in equal time intervals

(C) its acceleration is zero

(D) it does not change its direction of motion

2. m/s^2 is the unit of :

(A) speed

(B) acceleration

(C) displacement

(D) time

3. A particle has a value of 46.0 ms^{-1}. It may be the :

(A) force of the particle

(B) velocity of the particle

(C) acceleration of the particle

(D) momentum of the particle

4. The position of a particle going along a straight line is x_1 = 50 m at 10.30 a.m. and x_2 = 55 m at 10.35 a.m. The displacement between 10.30 a.m. and 10.35 a.m. is :

(A) 2 m   (B) 5 m

(C) 7 m   (D) 9 m

5. A car covers 30 km at a uniform speed of 60 km/hr. and the next 30 km at a uniform speed of 40 km/hr. The total time taken is :

(A) 30 min   (B) 45 min

(C) 75 min   (D) 120 min

6. The velocity of a car at 10.50 a.m. is 60 km/hr and at 10.52 a.m. it is 80 km/hr. Assuming constant acceleration in the given period, its value is :

(A) 600 kmhr^{-2} (B) 500 kmhr^{-2}

(C) 400 kmhr^{-2} (D) 300 kmhr^{-2}

7. An object is sliding down an inclined plane. The velocity changes at a constant rate from 10 cm/s to 15 cm/s in 2 seconds. Its acceleration is :

(A) 5 cm/s^2 (B) 3 cm/s^2

(C) 2.5 cm/s^2 (D) 4.5 cm/s^2

8. A particle moving with an initial velocity of 5 m/s is subjected to a uniform acceleration of – 2.5 ms^{-2}. The displacement in the next 4 seconds is :

(A) 40 m (B) 0

(C) 20 m (D) 60 m

9. An insect moves along a circular path of radius 10 cm with a constant speed. If it takes 1 minute to move from a point on the path to the diametrically opposite point, then the distance covered, speed, displacement and average velocity respectively are :

(A) 3.14 cm, 3.14 cm/min, 10 cm, 10 cm/min

(B) 31.4 cm, 31.4 cm/min, 20 cm, 0.33 cm/s.

(C) 0.314 cm, 0.314 cm/min, 1 cm, 1 cm/min

(D) 314 cm, 314 cm/min, 0.1 cm, 0.1 cm/min

10. A particle is pushed along a horizontal surface in such a way that it starts with a velocity of 12 m/s. and decreases at the rate of 0.5 m/s^2. The time it will take to come to rest is :

(A) 42 s (B) 48 s

(C) 24 s (D) 84 s

11. A train accelerates from 20 km/h to 80 km/h in 4 minutes. The distance it covers in this period is (assuming that the tracks are straight) :

(A) $\dfrac{20}{3}$ km (B) 30 km

(C) $\dfrac{10}{3}$ km (D) $\dfrac{40}{3}$ km

12. A stone is thrown vertically upwards with an initial velocity of 14 ms^{-1}. The acceleration due to gravity is 9.8 ms^{-2}. The time that the stone takes to strike the ground is :

(A) 2.86 s (B) 3.46 s

(C) 4.86 s (D) 3.86 s

13. The speed-time graph of an object moving in a fixed direction is a straight line. The object :

(A) is at rest

(B) moves with fluctuating speed

(C) moves with constant velocity

(D) moves with a non-zero acceleration

14. A car covers the first half of the distance between two places at a speed of 40 km/hr and second half at 60 km/hr. The average speed of the car is :

(A) 100 km/hr (B) 50 km/hr

(C) 48 km/hr (D) 52 km/hr

15. A particle is moving along a circular track of radius 1 m with a uniform speed. The ratio of the distance covered and the displacement in half revolution is :

(A) 1 (B) 0

(C) π (D) $\dfrac{\pi}{2}$

16. A body travels 200 cm in the first two seconds and 220 cm in the next four seconds. The velocity at the end of seventh second from start is :

(A) 5 cm/s

(B) 10 cm/s

(C) 15 cm/s

(D) 20 cm/s

17. An iron ball and a wooden ball of same radius are released from a height 'h' in vacuum. Which of the two balls would take more time to reach the ground?

(A) Iron ball

(B) Both would take same time

(C) Wooden ball

(D) None of these

18. The distances travelled by a body falling freely from rest in the first, second and third seconds respectively are in the ratio

(A) 1 : 4 : 9

(B) 1 : 2 : 3

(C) 1 : 9 : 25

(D) 1 : 3 : 5

19. A stone is thrown upwards with a speed 'u' from the top of a tower. It reaches the ground with a velocity '3u'. The height of the tower is :

(A) $\dfrac{u^2}{g}$

(B) $\dfrac{2u^2}{g}$

(C) $\dfrac{3u^2}{g}$

(D) $\dfrac{4u^2}{g}$

20. The distance- time graph of an object moving in a fixed direction is shown in figure. The object :

(A) is at rest

(B) is moving with constant velocity

(C) is moving with variable velocity

(D) is moving with constant acceleration

21. The figure below shows a speed-time graph. What can be inferred from the graph?

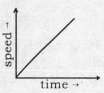

(A) Speed is constant

(B) Speed is decreasing

(C) Speed is increasing

(D) Speed increases to a maximum and then decreases

22. Two scooters starting from rest accelerate uniformly at the same rate. The second travels for twice the time of the first. Then the relation between the distance covered by the first scooter (s_1) to that of the second scooter (s_2) is :

(A) $s_1 = s_2$

(B) $s_1 = 2s_2$

(C) $s_2 = 3s_1$

(D) $s_2 = 4s_1$

23. From the top of a building of height 40 m , a boy projects a stone vertically upwards with an initial velocity of 10 ms⁻¹ such that it eventually falls to the ground. At what time will the stone reach the ground? (g = 10 m/s²)

(A) 4 s

(B) 3 s

(C) 2 s

(D) 1 s

24. When the brakes are applied on a moving cycle, the directions of velocity and acceleration are :

(A) opposite

(B) same

(C) perpendicular

(D) not related

25. What is the acceleration of a particle moving with uniform velocity?

(A) 1 ms⁻²   (B) 2 ms⁻²

(C) 0   (D) ∞

26. Points P, Q and R are in a vertical line such that PQ = QR. A ball at the top most point 'P' is allowed to fall freely. What is the ratio of the times of descent through PQ and QR?

(A) $\dfrac{3}{2}$ (B) $\dfrac{3}{\sqrt{2}+1}$

(C) $\dfrac{1}{\sqrt{2}-1}$ (D) $\dfrac{5}{2}$

27. If it is safe to jump from a height of 2 m on the earth, then what would be the same height on a planet where the value of 'g' is 1.96 ms⁻²?

(A) 2 m   (B) 4 m

(C) 6 m   (D) 10 m

28. A wooden block of mass 10 g is dropped from the top of a cliff 100 m high. Simultaneously, a bullet of mass 10 g is fired from the foot of the cliff upward with a velocity of 100 ms⁻¹. At what time will the bullet and the block meet?

(A) 4 s   (B) 3 s

(C) 2 s   (D) 1 s

29. A body is projected vertically upwards with a velocity of 96 ft/s. What is the total time for which the body will remain in the air?

(A) 3 s

(B) 6 s

(C) 9 s

(D) 12 s

30. A body falling freely from rest covers $\dfrac{7}{16}$ of the total height in the last second of its fall. The height from which it falls is :

(A) 24.2 m   (B) 38.4 m

(C) 78.4 m   (D) 46.8 m

31. A ball projected vertically upwards from 'A', the top of a tower, reaches the ground in 't_1' seconds. If it is projected vertically downwards from 'A' with the same velocity, it reaches the ground in 't_2' seconds. If it falls freely from 'A', the time taken to reach the ground is :

(A) $\dfrac{t_1 + t_2}{2}$

(B) $\sqrt{t_1 + t_2}$

(C) $\sqrt{t_1 t_2}$

(D) $\sqrt{t_1 - t_2}$

32. A particle in uniform acceleration in a straight line has a speed of 'v' ms⁻¹ at position 'x' metres is given by $v = \sqrt{25 - 16x}$. The acceleration of the particle is :

(A) – 8 ms⁻²   (B) –3 ms⁻²

(C) 3 ms⁻²   (D) 8 ms⁻²

33. Two bodies of different masses m_a and m_b are dropped from two different heights 'a' and 'b' respectively. The ratio of the times taken by the two to drop through these distances is :

(A) a : b   (B) b : a

(C) $\sqrt{a} : \sqrt{b}$ (D) a² : b²

34. A particle starts from rest with a uniform acceleration. It travels a distance 'x' in the first 2 seconds and a distance 'y' in the next 2 seconds. Then :

(A) y = x   (B) y = 2x

(C) y = 3x   (D) y = 4x

35. If a freely falling body travels in the last second, a distance equal to the distance travelled by it in the first 3 seconds, the time of its travel is :

(A) 3 s   (B) 4 s

(C) 5 s   (D) 6 s

36. For motion on a straight line path with constant acceleration, the ratio of magnitude of displacement and the distance covered is :

(A) = 1   (B) > 1

(C) < 1   (D) ≤ 1

37. For motion on a curved path with constant acceleration, the ratio of magnitude of distance and displacement covered is

(A) = 1   (B) < 1

(C) ≥ 1   (D) > 1

38. The slope of velocity–time graph for motion with uniform velocity is equal to :

(A) initial velocity

(B) final velocity

(C) zero

(D) average velocity

39. Which of the following can decrease in motion in a straight line with constant acceleration?

(A) Speed

(B) Acceleration

(C) Displacement

(D) Force

40. The slope of velocity–time graph for retarded motion is :

(A) positive

(B) negative

(C) zero

(D) both positive and negative

41. Which of the following can be zero when the particle is in motion for some time?

(A) Displacement

(B) Distance covered

(C) Speed

(D) None of these

42. The figure given here shows the velocity-time graph of a one-dimensional motion. Which of the following characteristics of the particle is represented by the shaded area?

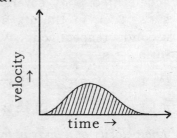

(A) Momentum

(B) Acceleration

(C) Distance covered

(D) Speed

43. A simple pendulum hangs from the roof of train. The string is inclined towards the rear of the train. What is the nature of motion of the train?

(A) Uniform

(B) Accelerated

(C) Retarded

(D) At rest

44. A ball dropped from a height 'h' reaches the ground in time 'T'.

What is the height at time $\frac{T}{2}$?

(A) $\frac{h}{28}$ (B) $\frac{h}{4}$

(C) $\frac{h}{2}$ (D) $\frac{3h}{4}$

45. A passenger travelling in a train moving with a constant velocity drops a stone from the window. To the passenger, the path will appear to be :

(A) straight line   (B) parabola

(C) arc of a circle   (D) elliptical

46. Starting from rest, a uniformly accelerated body covers distances s_1, s_2 & s_3 in the 1st, 2nd and 3rd seconds respectively. What is the ratio $s_1 : s_2 : s_3$?

(A) 1 : 4 : 9   (B) 1: 3 : 5

(C) 1 : 1 : 1   (D) 1 : 2 : 3

The velocity of a body in four different situations is shown below. Based on these answer the questions from 47 to 51.

(1)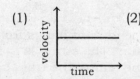

(2)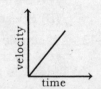

(3)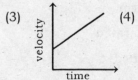

(4)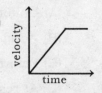

47. Uniform velocity is represented by :

(A) 1   (B) 2

(C) 3   (D) 4

48. Uniform acceleration of the body from rest is represented by:

(A) 1   (B) 2

(C) 3   (D) 4

49. Uniform acceleration of the body (initially not at rest) is represented by :

(A) 1   (B) 2

(C) 3   (D) 4

50. Body starting with uniform acceleration that becomes zero is represented by :

(A) 1   (B) 2

(C) 3   (D) 4

51. Which graph represents the motion of rockets (cracker) used in fireworks?

(A) 1   (B) 2

(C) 3   (D) 4

52. An object, dropped from a height, falls freely under the influence of gravity. The variation of velocity 'v' of the body with its vertical fall 's' is shown graphically. Which of the following graphs is the correct representation?

(A)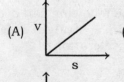

(B)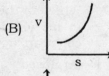

(C)

(D)

53. A body is left free on a frctionless inclined plane as shown in the figure. It takes 4 seconds to reach the bottom of the plank. What time would it take to slide from point 'A' to point 'B'?

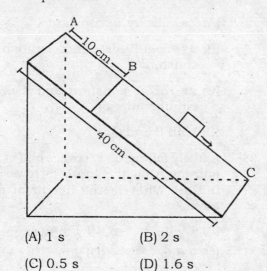

(A) 1 s   (B) 2 s

(C) 0.5 s   (D) 1.6 s

54. Two stones are thrown from the top of a building with the same speed u, one in the upward direction and the other in the downward direction. When they reach the ground they acquire certain velocities v_1 and v_2 respectively v_1 and v_2 will in the ratio of :

(A) 1 : 1   (B) 1 : 2

(C) 2 : 1   (D) 2 : 3

55. A car moving on a road with uniform acceleration covers 20m in the first second and 30m in the next second. What is its acceleration?

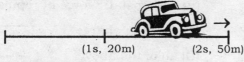

(1s, 20m)   (2s, 50m)

(A) 20ms^{-2} (B) 10ms^{-2}

(C) 30ms^{-2} (D) 5ms^{-2}

56. A body is dropped from the top of a building. Sensors are fixed in the building at different distances. The distance recorded by the sensors in the 1st, 2nd and 3rd second would be in the ratio of :

(A) 1 : 1 : 1   (B) 1 : 2 : 3

(C) 1 : 2 : 4   (D) 1 : 4 : 9

57. A photographer arranges to expose photographs of a ball describing motion under free fall such that it is photographed on a vertical scale starting from zero. He photographed it when the ball was at 76.05 m and the next exposure was when the ball was at 80 m. The time of exposure is :   (g = 10 ms^{-2})

(A) 0.5 s   (B) 2 s

(C) 3 s   (D) 0.1 s

58. A car moves towards north with a speed of 20ms^{-1}. It changes its direction to east and moves with a speed of 20ms^{-1}. What is its velocity now?

(A) 20ms^{-1}NE

(B) 40 ms^{-1} NS

(C) 10 ms^{-1} NE

(D) $20\sqrt{2}$ ms^{-1}NE

59. The depth of a well till its water surface is 125 m. A boy drops a stone into it and hears the sound of the splash after 5.35 s. What is the speed of sound? [Assume g = 10ms^{-2}]

(A) 300 ms^{-1}

(B) 357 ms^{-1}

(C) 320 ms^{-1}

(D) 386 ms^{-1}

60. What does the area of an 'acceleration-displacement' graph represent?

(A) Distance

(B) Velocity

(C) $\dfrac{v^2 - u^2}{2}$

(D) None of these

61. A stone is dropped from a tower. It is found that it describes 45 m during its last second of fall. Can you estimate the time of fall and the height of the tower? (g = 10 ms⁻²)

(A) 5 s, 45 m

(B) 10 s, 90 m

(C) 5 s, 125 m

(D) 10 s, 100 m

62. A and B start their journey towards their homes 'P' and 'Q' from different points. Which of the following statements is not represented by the graph given here?

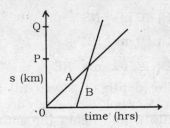

(A) A starts his journey earlier

(B) B is faster than A

(C) A and B meet during their journey

(D) A and B reach their homes at the same time

63. A particle is acted upon by a constant force, the magnitude of which is always perpendicular to the velocity of the particle. The motion of the particle takes place in a plane. It follows that :

(A) its velocity is constant

(B) its magnitude of acceleration is constant

(C) its K.E is constant and it is in circular motion

(D) both B and C

64. A freely falling body covers half of its journey from the top of a tower in 0.5 s. What is the height of the tower?

(A) 4.9 m   (B) 2.4 m

(C) 9.8 m   (D) 9 m

65. A man shot a bullet with a speed of 10ms⁻¹ which just penetrates a plank of wood. With what speed should he shoot a bullet to pass through 10 similar planks?

(A) 100 ms⁻¹

(B) 10⁴ ms⁻¹

(C) $10\sqrt{10}\,\text{ms}^{-1}$

(D) $5\sqrt{10}\,\text{ms}^{-1}$

66. For an electron revolving around the atomic nucleus the necessary centripetal force is provided by the :

(A) electrostatic force of attraction

(B) electrostatic force of repulsion

(C) nuclear charge

(D) all of the above

Study the distance-time graph for a girl on a cycle ride as shown in the graph and answer the questions from 67 to 69.

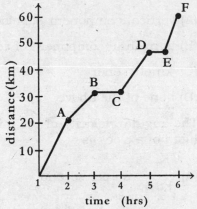

67. What was the total distance covered by her?

(A) 40km   (B) 60 Km

(C) 50 Km   (D) 20 Km

68. How long did she take to complete her journey?

(A) 6 hr   (B) 5 hr

(C) 3.5 hr   (D) 3 hr

69. How may stops did she make ?

(A) 1   (B) 2

(C) 3   (D) 4

Study the graph given below showing the movement of a car and answer the questions from 70 to 72 :

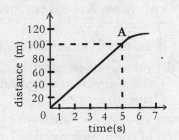

70. How far has the car travelled at the end of 5 seconds ?

(A) 40 m   (B) 60 m

(C) 100 m   (D) 50 m

71. What is the speed of the car during the first 5 seconds ?

(A) 40 ms^{-1} (B) 20 ms^{-1}

(C) 25 ms^{-1} (D) 100 ms^{-1}

72. What happens to the car after the 5th second ?

(A) Continues with the same speed

(B) Slows down

(C) Speeds up

(D) None of these

The given figure shows a velocity-time graph for a boy running a distance of 100 m. Based on the graph answer the questions from 73 to 77.

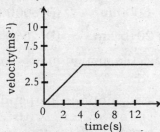

73. What is his acceleration during the first 4 seconds ?

(A) 5/4 ms^{-2} (B) 4/5 ms^{-2}

(C) 5 ms^{-2} (D) 4 ms^{-2}

74. How far does the boy travel during the first 4 seconds ?

(A) 10m   (B) 20m

(C) 5m   (D) 8m

75. How far did he travel during next 9 seconds?

(A) 10m   (B) 20m

(C) 45m   (D) 50m

76. Assuming that the speed is constant, what time would he have taken to cover another 120 m?

(A) 20 s   (B) 24 s

(C) 30 s   (D) 22 s

77. What time would he have taken to cover 100 m from beginning ?

(A) 20 s   (B) 24 s

(C) 30 s   (D) 22 s

78. A space shuttle is launched into space. During the first 8 minutes of its launch the average acceleration of the shuttle is 17.5 m/s^2. What is its speed after 8 minutes?

(A) 8000 ms^{-1} (B) 8400 ms^{-1}

(C) 1200 ms^{-1} (D) 1500 ms^{-1}

79. In the above question how far does it travel in the first 8 minutes ?

(A) 8000 m   (B) 80000 m

(C) 2016 km   (D) 2600 km

80. Projectile motion may be considered as :

(A) two motions perpendicular to each other with velocity remaining constant in both the directions.

(B) two motions perpendicular to each other with velocity remaining constant in one plane and uniform acceleration in another plane.

(C) two motions perpendicular to each other with uniform acceleration is both the planes.

(D) None of these

81. Trajectory of a projectile is :

(A) a straight line   (B) a circle

(C) a parabola   (D) a ellipse

82. One of the components that remains constant when a projectile is thrown upwards at an angle with the horizontal is the :

(A) vertical component of velocity

(B) horizontal component of velocity

(C) kinetic energy

(D) none of the above

83. The angular velocity of the minutes hand of a clock is :

(A) $\dfrac{\pi}{180}$ rad per second

(B) $\dfrac{\pi}{1800}$ rad per second

(C) $\dfrac{\pi}{60}$ rad per second

(D) $\dfrac{\pi}{360}$ rad per second

84. The motion of the earth around the sun once every year requires some force of attraction between them. The centripetal force acting between them is provided by the :

(A) gravitational force between them

(B) weight of the sun

(C) weight of the earth

(D) none of these

85. Centrifugal force is an inertial force experienced by :

(A) an observer outside the system

(B) an observer moving along with the particle that is subjected to the force

(C) an observer sitting at the centre of the trajectory

(D) all of the above

1. B	2. B	3. B	4. B	5. C	6. A	7. C	8. B	9. B	10. C
11. C	12. A	13. C	14. C	15. D	16. B	17. B	18. D	19. D	20. B
21. C	22. D	23. A	24. A	25. C	26. C	27. D	28. D	29. B	30. C
31. C	32. A	33. C	34. C	35. C	36. A	37. D	38. C	39. A	40. B
41. A	42. C	43. B	44 D	45. A	46. A	47. A	48. B	49. C	50. D
51. D	52. C	53. B	54. A	55. B	56. D	57. D	58. D	59. B	60. C
61. C	62. D	63. D	64. B	65. C	66. A	67. B.	68. B	69. B	70. C
71. B	72. B	73. A	74. A	75. C	76. B	77. D	78. B	79. C	80. B
81. C	82. B	83. B	84. A	85. B					

Explanatory Answers

4. (B) $x_1 = 50$ m, $x_2 = 55$ m.

   The displacement is

   $d = x_2 - x_1 = 55 - 50 = 5$ m.

5. (C) Case 1 = 30 km

   $= (60 \text{ kmhr}^{-1}) \times t_1$

   $\Rightarrow t_1 = \dfrac{30}{60} = \dfrac{1}{2}$ hr = 30 min.

   Case 2 = 30 km

   $= (40 \text{ kmhr}^{-1}) \times t_2$

   $\Rightarrow t_2 = \dfrac{30}{40} = \dfrac{3}{4}$ hr = 45 min.

   $t = t_1 + t_2 = 30 + 45 = 75$ min

6. (A) $u = 60 \text{ kmhr}^{-1}$, $v = 80 \text{ kmhr}^{-1}$,

   $t_1 = 10.50$ cm, $t_2 = 10.52$ cm.

   $\Delta t = t_2 - t_1 = 2 \text{ min} = \dfrac{1}{30}$ hr

   $a = \dfrac{v - u}{\Delta t}$

   $= \dfrac{80 - 60}{\dfrac{1}{30}} = 20 \times 30$

   $= 600 \text{ kmhr}^{-2}$

7. (C) $u = 10 \text{ cms}^{-1}$, $v = 15 \text{ cms}^{-1}$, $\Delta t = 2$ sec.

   $a = \dfrac{v - u}{\Delta t}$

   $= \dfrac{15 - 10}{2} = \dfrac{5}{2} = 2.5 \text{ cm/sec}^2$

8. (B) $u = 5 \text{ ms}^{-1}$; $a = -2.5 \text{ ms}^{-2}$; $5 = 4$ sec.

   $s = 5 \times 4 + \dfrac{1}{2} \times (-2.5) \times 16$

   $= 20 - 8 \times 2.5 = 20 - 20 = 0$ m.

9. (B) The distance covered

   $= \pi r = 3.14 \times 10$

   $= 3.14 \times 10 = 31.4$ cm.

   $\text{Speed} = \dfrac{dis\tan ce}{time} = \dfrac{31.4}{60 \sec .}$

$$= \frac{31.4}{60}$$

$$= 0.52 \text{ cm/s}$$

Displacement $= 2r = 2 \times 10$

$$= 20 \text{ cm.}$$

Average velocity

$$= \frac{\text{displacement}}{\text{time}}$$

$$\frac{20}{60} = \frac{20 \text{cm}}{60 \text{sec}} = 0.33 \text{ cm/s}$$

10. (C) Formula : $v = u + at$

We have

$u = 12 \text{ m/s}; v = 0$;
$a = -0.5 \text{ m/s}^2$.

So,

$$0 = 12 - 0.5 \times t$$

$$\Rightarrow 0.5t = 12$$

$$\Rightarrow t = \frac{12}{0.5} = 24 \text{ s.}$$

11. (C) We have,

$u = 20 \text{ km/h}; v = 80 \text{ km/h}.$

$$t = 4 \text{ min} = \frac{4}{60} \text{ hour} = \frac{1}{15} \text{ h.}$$

$$a = \frac{v-u}{t} = \frac{80-20}{\left[\dfrac{1}{15}\right]} = 900 \text{ km/h.}$$

Now, $s = ut + \dfrac{1}{2}at^2$

$$s = 20 \times \frac{1}{15} + \frac{1}{2} \times 900 \times \frac{1}{15} \times \frac{1}{15}$$

$$= \frac{10}{3} \text{ km.}$$

12. (A) $u = 14 \text{ m/s}; g = 9.8 \text{ m/s}^2.$

$$t = \frac{2u}{g} = \frac{2 \times 14}{9.8} = 2.86 \text{ s.}$$

14. (C) $u = 40 \text{ km/hr}, \ v = 60 \text{ km/hr}.$

$$V_{avg} = \frac{2uv}{u+v} = \frac{2 \times 40 \times 60}{(40+60)}$$

$$= 48 \text{ km/hr.}$$

15. (D) In a circular track,

(i) the distance covered in one complete revolution = $2\pi r$.

(ii) the displacement in one complete revolution = 0.

(iii) the displacement in half revolution = 2r.

We have, r = 1 m.

So, distance covered in half revolution

$$\frac{2\pi r}{2} = \pi r = \pi \times 1 = \pi \text{ m.}$$

Displacement $= 2r = 2 \times 1$

$$= 2 \text{ m.}$$

Ratio $= \dfrac{\pi}{2}$.

16. (B) We have, $s_1 = 200$ cm; $s_2 = 420$ cm;

$t_1 = 2s$ and $t_2 = 6s$.

Case 1:

$$s_1 = ut_1 + \frac{1}{2}at_1^2$$

$$\Rightarrow 200 = 2u + \frac{1}{2}a \times 4$$

$$\Rightarrow 200 = 2u + 2a$$

$$\Rightarrow u + a = 100 --- (1)$$

Case 2:

$$s_2 = ut_2 + \frac{1}{2}at_2^2$$

$$\Rightarrow 420 = u \times 6 + \frac{1}{2}a \times 6^2$$

$$\Rightarrow 420 = 6u + 18a$$

$$\Rightarrow u + 3a = 420 --- (2)$$

Solving (1) and (2), we get

$a = -15 \text{ m/s}^2$

and $u = 115$ cm/s.

Since, $v = u + at$

$v = 115 - 15 \times 7 = 10$ cm/s.

18. (D) $s_n = u + a\left[n - \dfrac{1}{2}\right]$

For a freely falling body,

$u = 0$ and $a = +g$.

$\therefore s_1 : s_2 : s_3 = g\left[1 - \dfrac{1}{2}\right]$

$: g\left[2 - \dfrac{1}{2}\right] : g\left[3 - \right]$

$= \dfrac{1}{2} : \dfrac{3}{2} : \dfrac{5}{2} = 1 : 3 : 5$

19. (D) $v^2 - u^2 = 2as$

$v = 3u, a = -g, s = -h$

$\therefore (3u)^2 - u^2 = 2(-g)(-h)$

$\Rightarrow 8u^2 = 2gh$

$\Rightarrow h = \dfrac{4u^2}{g}$.

22. (D) $s = ut + \dfrac{1}{2}at^2$

$u = 0$.

$\Rightarrow s = \dfrac{1}{2}at^2$

Since, 'a' is constant, $s \propto t^2$

$$\Rightarrow \frac{s_1}{s_2} = \frac{t_1^2}{t_2^2} \Rightarrow \frac{s_1}{s_2} = \frac{t_1^2}{\left(2t_2^2\right)} = \frac{t_1^2}{4t_1^2}$$

$\Rightarrow s_2 = 4s_1$.

23. (A) $h = -ut + \dfrac{1}{2}gt^2$

$h = 40$ m; $u = 10$ m/s;

$g = 10 \text{ m/s}^2$.

$40 = -10t + \dfrac{1}{2} \times 10 \times t^2$

$\Rightarrow 5t^2 - 10t - 40 = 0$

body moving with u...... n velocity, change in velocity is zero. So, acceleration is nil.

26. (C) For motion from P to Q

$$y = \frac{1}{2}gt_1^2 \; - - - (1)$$

For motion from P to R:

$$2y = \frac{1}{2}g(t_1 + t_2)^2 \; - - - (2)$$

From (1) and (2),

$2t_1^2 = (t_1 + t_2)^2$

$\Rightarrow t_1 + t_2 = \sqrt{2}\, t_1$

$\Rightarrow t_1\left(\sqrt{2} - 1\right) = t_2$

$$\Rightarrow \frac{t_1}{t_2} = \frac{1}{\sqrt{2}-1}.$$

27. (D) $h_1 = 2$ m, $g_1 = 9.8$ m/s^2, $g_2 = 1.96$ m/s^2.

$h_1 g_1 = h_2 g_2$

$$h_2 = \frac{h_1 g_1}{g_2} = \frac{2 \times 9.8}{1.96} = 10\,\text{m}.$$

28. (D) Height of the tower = $s_1 + s_2 = 100$ m.

For the block:

$$s_1 = \frac{1}{2}gt^2 = \frac{1}{2} \times 9.8 \times t^2 = 4.9t^2$$

For the bullet:

$$s_2 = ut - \frac{1}{2}gt^2$$

$$= 100t - \frac{1}{2} \times 9.8 \times t^2$$

$$= 100t - 4.9t^2$$

Since, $s_1 + s_2 = 100$ m,

$4.9t^2 + 100t - 4.9t^2 = 100$

$\Rightarrow 100t = 100$

$\Rightarrow t = 1$s.

29. (B) $u = 96$ ft/s; $g = 32$ ft/s^2.

$$t = \frac{2u}{g} = \frac{2 \times 96}{32} = 6\,\text{s}$$

30. (C) Total height $\Rightarrow h = \frac{1}{2}gn^2$

In the last second, the body covers $\frac{7}{16}$th of total height.

So, $S_n = \frac{7}{16}h$.

We have $S_n = u + a\left[n - \frac{1}{2}\right]$

Here, $u = 0$ and $a = g$.

So, $S_n = g\left[n - \frac{1}{2}\right]$

$$\Rightarrow \frac{7}{16}\left[\frac{1}{2}gn^2\right] = g\left[n - \frac{1}{2}\right]$$

$$\Rightarrow 7n^2 = 16(2n - 1)$$

$$\Rightarrow 7n^2 - 32n + 16 = 0$$

$$\Rightarrow n = 4s.$$

so, $h = \dfrac{1}{2} \times 9.8 \times 4^2 = 78.4 m$

31. **(C)** $h = -ut_1 + \dfrac{1}{2} gt_1{}^2 \ldots\ldots\ldots(1)$

$h = ut_2 + \dfrac{1}{2} gt_2{}^2 \ldots\ldots\ldots(2)$

$h = \dfrac{1}{2} gt^2 \ldots\ldots\ldots(3)$

Solving (1) and (2),

$u(t_1 + t_2) = \dfrac{1}{2} g(t_1{}^2 - t_2{}^2)$

$\Rightarrow u = \dfrac{1}{2} g(t_1 - t_2) \ldots\ldots\ldots\ldots(4)$

Substituting (4) in (2)

$h = \dfrac{1}{2} g(t_1 - t_2)t_2 + \dfrac{1}{2} gt_2{}^2$

$= \dfrac{1}{2} g\, t_1 t_2 \ldots\ldots\ldots(5)$

Comparing (5) and (3)

$t^2 = t_1 t_2$

$\Rightarrow t = \sqrt{t_1 t_2}$.

32. **(A)** Given $v = \sqrt{25 - 16x}$

$\Rightarrow v^2 = 25 - 16x$

Comparing with $v^2 - u^2 = 2as.$

$2a = -16$

$\Rightarrow a = -8 \text{ m/s}^2.$

33. **(C)** Time taken to drop through is independent of mass.

$$t = \sqrt{\dfrac{2h}{g}} \Rightarrow t \,\alpha\, \sqrt{h}$$

$$\Rightarrow \dfrac{t_1}{t_2} = \sqrt{\dfrac{a}{b}}$$

$$\Rightarrow t_1 : t_2 = \sqrt{a} : \sqrt{b}.$$

34. **(C)** $s = ut + \dfrac{1}{2} at^2$

$u = 0, \ s_1 = x, \ t_1 = 2s.$

$\therefore \ x = \dfrac{1}{2} at_1{}^2 = \dfrac{1}{2} a \times 4 = 2a$.

$s_2 = x + y = 2a + y, t_2 = 2 + 2 = 4s.$

$\therefore \ x + y = \dfrac{1}{2} at_2{}^2 = \dfrac{1}{2} a \times 16 = 8a$.

$\Rightarrow 2a + y = 8a$

$\Rightarrow y = 6a = 3(2a)$

$\Rightarrow y = 3x.$

35. **(C)** We have, the distance travelled by the body in the nth second equal to the distance travelled by it in 't' seconds.

Given, $t = 3s.$

So, $s_n = s$

$\Rightarrow g\left[n - \dfrac{1}{2}\right] = \dfrac{1}{2} gt^2$

$\Rightarrow n - \dfrac{1}{2} = \dfrac{1}{2} \times 3^2 = \dfrac{9}{2}$

$\Rightarrow n = 5 \text{ seconds}.$

36. (A) Since, in a straight line motion, distance is equal to displacement their ratio will be equal to one.

37. (D) For a curved path, distance is greater than displacement. So, ratio is greater than one.

41. (A) When a particle is projected upwards, it will return to its starting point. So, the displacement will be zero.

42. (C) Area covered will be the product of quantities taken on x and y axes.

Velocity $\times$ time = distance

43. (B) Train is accelerating horizontally. So, the resultant of horizontal acceleration and vertical acceleration is inclined to the vertical.

44. (D) We know $h = \dfrac{1}{2}gT^2$

Vertically downward distance covered in time $\dfrac{T}{2}$ is

$$x = \dfrac{1}{2}g\left(\dfrac{T}{2}\right)^2 = \dfrac{1}{4}\left[\dfrac{1}{2}gT^2\right] = \dfrac{h}{4}.$$

Hence, the height at time $\dfrac{T}{2}$ is

$$h - x = h - \dfrac{h}{4} = \dfrac{3h}{4}.$$

52. (D) For free fall,

$$v^2 - u^2 = 2gs$$

but $u = 0$

$\therefore v^2 = 2gs$

This is the equation of a parabola $\left(y \alpha x^2\right)$

53. (B) Since $s = ut + \dfrac{1}{2}gt^2$ and $u = 0$

$$s = \dfrac{1}{2}gt^2$$

$\therefore s \alpha \ t^2$

$$\dfrac{s_1}{s_2} = \dfrac{t_1^2}{t_2^2}$$

$$\dfrac{40}{10} = \dfrac{4^2}{t_2^2}$$

$$t_2^2 = 4^2 \times \dfrac{10}{40}$$

$$= \dfrac{4^2}{4}$$

$t_2^2 = 4$; $t = \sqrt{4} = 2s$

54. (A) The first stone and second stone will possess same velocity 'u' during their downward journey at the roof of the building. They are acted on by the same acceleration. Therefore they will strike the ground with the same velocity.

55. (B) $s_n = u + \dfrac{a}{2}(2n - 1)$

$$20 = u + \frac{a}{2}(2-1) \quad (\because n = 1\,s)$$

$$20 = u + \frac{a}{2} \quad \text{....... (1)}$$

For the second case :

$$30 = u + \frac{a}{2}(2 \times 2 - 1) \quad (\because n = 2\,s)$$

$$30 = u + \frac{3a}{2} \quad \text{...... (2)}$$

solving (1) and (2) for 'a'

$$30 = u + \frac{3a}{2}$$

$$20 = u + \frac{a}{2}$$

$$\overline{}$$

$$10 = a$$

$$\overline{}$$

$$\therefore a = 10\,ms^{-2}$$

Alternately, $a = \dfrac{s_2 - s_1}{\Delta t^2}$

$$\frac{30 - 20}{1^2} = \frac{10}{1}\,ms^{-2}$$

57. (D) For the first time :

$$76.05 = \frac{1}{2} \times 10 \times t^2$$

$$t^2 = \frac{76.06}{5} = 15.35$$

$$\therefore t = 3.9\,s$$

For the second time :

$$80 = \frac{1}{2} \times 10 \times t^2$$

$$\therefore t = 4\,s$$

$\therefore$ Time of exposure is 4 3.9 = 0.1s

58. (D)

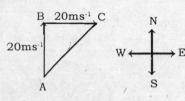

$\overrightarrow{AC}$?

$$AC^2 = AB^2 + BC^2$$

$$AC = \sqrt{AB^2 + BC^2}$$

$$= \sqrt{20^2 + 20^2}$$

$$= 20\sqrt{2}$$

$$\overrightarrow{AC} = 20\sqrt{2}\ m/s^{-1}\ NE$$

60. (C) $v^2 - u^2 = 2as$

$$\therefore a \times s = \frac{v^2 - u^2}{2} \quad (a \times s \text{ is the}$$
area of the graph).

61. (C) During the last second it fell through 45 m

$$s_n = \frac{g}{2}\,(2n - 1)$$

$$45 = \frac{10}{2}\,(2n - 1)$$

$$45 = 5\,(2n - 1)$$

$45 = 10n - 5$

$50 = 10n$

$\therefore n = 5 \text{ s}$

Time of flight is 5 s.
Therefore the height of the tower:

$$s = \frac{1}{2} \times g \times t^2$$

$$= \frac{1}{2} \times 10 \times 25$$

$$= 125 \text{ m}$$

64   (B) $s = ut + \frac{1}{2}gt^2$

It is a free fall, so $y = 0$

$$\frac{1}{2}s = 0\left(\frac{1}{2}\right) + \frac{1}{2} \times 9.8\left(\frac{1}{2}\right)^2$$

$$\frac{1}{2}s = 4.9 \times \frac{1}{4}$$

$$\therefore s = 4.9 \times \frac{1}{4} \times \frac{2}{1}$$

$$= 2.45 \text{ m}$$

65.   (C) $v^2 - 0 = 2as$

$\therefore v^2 \alpha s$

$$\therefore \frac{v_1^2}{v_2^2} = \frac{s_1}{s_2}$$

$$\frac{(10)^2}{v_2^2} = \frac{1}{10}$$

$$\therefore v_2^2 = [10 \times 10] \times 10$$

$$v_2 = 10\sqrt{10} / ms^{-1}$$

78.   (B) $v = u + at$

$v = 0 + 17.5 \times (8 \times 60)$

$= 8400 \text{ m/s}$

79.   (C) $s = ut + \frac{1}{2}at^2$

$$= 0 + \frac{1}{2}(17.5)(480)^2$$

$$= 2016000 \text{ m.}$$

$$= 2016 \text{ km.}$$

83.   (B) $\omega = \dfrac{\theta}{t} = \dfrac{2\pi}{3600} = \dfrac{\pi}{1800}$

❖ ❖ ❖

Chapter 2

Force & Laws of Motion

Synopsis

Force

Force is that cause which produces acceleration in the body on which it acts.

A force or a set of forces can :

(a) change the speed of body,

(b) change the direction of motion of the body and

(c) change the shape of the body.

The S.I. unit of force is newton, denoted by the symbol N.

Balanced and unbalanced forces

If a set of forces acting on a body produces no acceleration in it, the forces are called balanced. If the set of forces produces an acceleration, they are said to be unbalanced.

Types of forces

A string that pulls an object tied at its end. The magnitude of the force of the pull is called the *tension* in the string.

The force by which the earth attracts a body is called the *weight* of the body. It is equal to the product of mass of the body and the acceleration due to gravity.

Friction between two surfaces in contact is generated due to the area of contact between the surfaces.

The effect of friction is to oppose the movement of the two surfaces against each other.

Friction exerted by the surfaces, which are in contact with each other, when there is no relative motion between them is called *static friction*. When two surfaces slip against each other the friction exerted by them is called *kinetic* or *sliding* friction.

Newton's laws of motion

First law

A body at rest will remain at rest and a body in motion will remain in motion unless a (set of unbalanced forces) force acts on it.

Second law

The resultant force acting on a body is proportional to the product of the mass of the body and its acceleration.

Third law

In any interaction between two bodies, the force applied by the first body on the second is equal and opposite to the force applied by the second body on the first.

Definition of newton

If a force acting on 1 kg of mass produces an acceleration of 1 m/s^2 in it, the amount of force acting on it is one newton (1N).

Linear momentum

The product of the mass and velocity of a body is called the linear momentum of the body.

(The resultant force on a body is equal to the change in its momentum per unit time.)

Conservation of linear momentum

If the total external force acting on a system of particles (or bodies) is zero, then the total linear momentum of the system remains constant.

Impulse and impulsive force

The product of the force and time is defined as the impulse of that particular force in that particular time. It is equal to the change in momentum by the force. If a force has large magnitude but acts for a short time, it is called an impulsive force.

Properties of force

The most simple forces are pulls and pushes. If we push or pull an object, it moves. Sometimes forces may change the shape of objects.

(a) A force can make an object to move.

A force can also slow down or speed up a moving object.

(b) A force may change the shape of an object.

(c) Sometimes a force seems to be doing nothing (balanced forces). This might be because it would be cancelling the effect of other forces.

(d) There are many types of forces like elastic, magnetic, electrostatic, compressive, tensile, gravitational, twisting & stretching.

Force is a vector quantity.

The straight line along which force is applied is the called line of action of force.

A force is needed to accelerate a particle.

Many forces acting on a body at one point are called concurrent forces.

Forces acting on the same line are called collinear forces.

Forces acting in a single plane are called co-planar forces.

Forces not confined to a single plane are called general forces.

Accelerated motion of a body is always due to either a change in position or due to a change in the direction.

Impulse is not something that the object possesses, but what an object provides when it interacts with other objects.

Multiple Choice Questions

1. An unbalanced force acts on a body. Then the body :

   (A) must remain at rest

   (B) must move with uniform velocity

   (C) must be accelerated

   (D) must move along a circle

2. If no force acts on a body, it will :

   (A) change its shape

   (B) move with an increased speed

   (C) either remain at rest or move in a straight line

   (D) break up

3. By applying a force of 1 N, one can hold a body of approximate mass :

(A) 100 mg   (B) 100 g

(C) 1 kg   (D) 10 kg

4. The force of friction between two bodies is :

(A) parallel to the contact surface

(B) perpendicular to the contact surface

(C) inclined at 30^0 to the contact surface

(D) inclined at 60^0 to the contact surface

5. The speed of a falling body increases continuously. This is because :

(A) no force acts on it

(B) it is very light

(C) the air exerts a frictional force on it

(D) the earth attracts it

6. When a bus starts, the passengers are pushed back. This is an example of :

(A) Newton's first law

(B) Newton's second law

(C) Newton's third law .

(D) None of Newton's laws

7. A force of a given magnitude acts on a body. The acceleration of the body depends on the :

(A) mass of the body

(B) volume of the body

(C) density of the body

(D) shape of the body

8. If a constant force acts on a body at rest, the distance moved by the body in time 't' will be proportional to :

(A) t   (B) t^2

(C) t^3 (D) t^4

9. The momentum of a body of given mass is proportional to its :

(A) volume

(B) shape

(C) speed

(D) colour

10. The principle of conservation of linear momentum states that the linear momentum of a system :

(A) cannot be changed

(B) cannot remain constant

(C) can be changed only if internal forces act

(D) can be changed only if external forces act

11. Action–reaction forces :

(A) act on the same body

(B) act on different bodies

(C) act along different lines

(D) act in the same direction

12. Consider a porter standing on a platform with a suitcase which presses his head with a force of 200 N. If this force is taken to be action, then the reaction force is exerted by :

(A) the head on the suitcase

(B) the earth on the suitcase

(C) the earth on the porter

(D) the suitcase on the earth

13. A force produces an acceleration of 0.5 m/s² in a body of mass 3.0 kg. If the same force acts on a body of mass 1.5 kg the acceleration produced in it is :

(A) 3.0 m/s²

(B) 1.0 m/s²

(C) 5.0 m/s²

(D) 7 m/s²

14. A force produces an acceleration of 5.0 cm/s² when it acts on a body of mass 20 g. The force in newton is :

(A) 2×10^{-3} N

(B) 4×10^{-3} N

(C) 1.0×10^{-3} N

(D) 5×10^{-3} N

15. A force produces an acceleration of 2.0 m/s² in a body 'A' and 5.0 m/s² in another body 'B'. The ratio of the mass of 'A' to the mass of 'B' is :

(A) 2.5   (B) 3.5

(C) 5.5   (D) 4.5

16. A force acts on a particle of mass 200 g. The velocity of the particle changes from 15 m/s to 25 m/s in 2.5 s. Assuming the force to be constant, it magnitude is :

(A) 0.4 N   (B) 0.6 N

(C) 0.8 N   (D) 0.5 N

17. A force of 1.0 N acts on a body of mass 10 kg. The body covers 100 cm in 4 seconds moving along a straight line. The initial velocity is :

(A) 2 cm/s   (B) 4 cm/s

(C) 6 cm/s   (D) 5 cm/s

18. A force of 0.6 N acting on a particle increases its velocity from 5.0 m/s to 6.0 m/s in 2 sec. The mass of the particle is :

(A) 1.2 kg   (B) 2.2 kg

(C) 4.2 kg   (D) 6.2 kg

19. A force acting on a particle of mass 200 g displaces it through 400 cm in 2 seconds. The magnitude of the force if the initial velocity of the particle is zero is :

(A) 0.1 N   (B) 0.3 N

(C) 0.4 N   (D) 0.5 N

20. A body of mass 300 g kept at rest breaks into two parts due to internal forces. One part of mass 200 g is found to move at a velocity of 12 m/s towards east. The velocity of the other part is :

(A) 24 m/s towards west

(B) 14 m/s towards east

(C) 24 m/s towards north

(D) 54 m/s towards south

21. A force of 16 N is distributed uniformly on one surface of a cube of edge 8 cm. The pressure on this surface is :

(A) 3500 Pa

(B) 2500 Pa

(C) 4500 Pa

(D) 5500 Pa

22. Friction exerted by surfaces on each other when they are at rest is called:

(A) static friction

(B) kinetic friction

(C) sliding friction

(D) none of the above

23. A body (without airspaces) of mass 150 gm and volume 250 cm³ is put in water. The body will :

(A) float   (B) sink

(C) partially sink (D) none of these

24. A mass of 2 kg at rest travels for 4 seconds with an acceleration of 1.5 m/s². The gain of momentum of the body is :

(A) 5 kgm/s   (B) 10 kgm/s

(C) 12 kgm/s   (D) 14 kgm/s

25. Two forces of 5 N and 3 N act on a body in opposite directions in a straight line as shown here. The resultant force is :

(A) 3 N in the direction of AB

(B) 2 N in the direction of AB

(C) 4 N in the direction of AC

(D) 5 N in the direction of AC

26. A 6 kg mass 'A' moving with a velocity of 2 m/s collides with a 4 kg mass 'B' moving with a velocity of 1.5 m/s in the opposite direction in a straight line. If the two masses get stuck, then the velocity of the combination is :

(A) 0.4 m/s   (B) 0.2 m/s

(C) 0.1 m/s   (D) 0.6 m/s

27. Two bodies collide at the same temperature. Which of the following is conserved?

(A) Velocity

(B) Momentum

(C) Kinetic energy

(D) All of the above

28. Impulse is equal to :

(A) the change of momentum

(B) the change of velocity

(C) the change of force

(D) the change of position

29. In the S.I. system, momentum is expressed as :

(A) kgs

(B) $kgms^{-1}$

(C) $kgm^{-1}s^{-1}$

(D) $kgms^{-2}$

30. The property by which a body tends to retain its original state of rest or uniform motion in a straight line is called :

(A) impulse

(B) inertia

(C) instantaneous velocity

(D) momentum

31. 'Rate of change of momentum is proportional to the exerted force and takes place in the direction in which the force acts' is a statement of Newton's :

(A) first law of motion

(B) second law of motion

(C) third law of motion

(D) all the three laws of motion

32. Which of the following are vector quantities?

(A) Force

(B) Velocity

(C) Momentum

(D) All of the above

33. Due to an impulse, the change in momentum of a body is 1.8 kgms^{-1}. If the duration of the impulse is 0.2 sec, the force produced in it is :

(A) 9 N   (B) 8 N

(C) 7 N   (D) 6 N

34. Action and reaction take place on :

(A) one body

(B) two bodies

(C) three bodies

(D) four bodies

35. Vehicles are provided with shock absorbers, which obey Newton's :

(A) first law of motion

(B) second law of motion

(C) third law of motion

(D) all of the above

36. A jet engine works on the principle of :

(A) conservation   of   linear momentum

(B) conservation of kinetic energy

(C) conservation   of   angular momentum

(D) conservation of inertia

37. A ball of mass 100 gm is moving with a velocity of 10 ms^{-1}. The force of the blow by the bat acts for 0.01 seconds. The average force exerted on the ball by the bat is :

(A) 100 N

(B) 200 N

(C) 300 N

(D) 400 N

38. Passengers standing in a bus are thrown outward when the bus takes a sudden turn. This happens due to :

(A) outwards pull on them

(B) inertia

(C) change in momentum

(D) change in acceleration

39. Ratio of force and acceleration measures :

(A) velocity   (B) impulse

(C) momentum   (D) mass

40. When we kick a stone, we get hurt. Due to which of the following properties of the stone does it happen?

(A) Inertia

(B) Velocity

(C) Reaction

(D) Momentum

41. A body is at rest on the surface of earth. Which of the following statements is correct?

(A) Only weight of the body acts on it

(B) Only upward force acts on the body

(C) Frictional force acts on the body

(D) Net upward force is equal to the net downward force

42. A book is lying on a table. What is the angle between the action of the book on the table and the weight of the book?

(A) 0°   (B) 45°

(C) 90°   (D) 180°

43. In which of the following cases is the net force not equal to zero?

(A) A kite skillfully held stationary in the sky

(B) A ball falling freely from a height

(C) An aeroplane rising upwards at an angle of 45^0 with the horizontal with a constant speed

(D) A cork floating on the surface of water

44. An electric fan is placed on a stationary boat and air is blown with it on the sail of the boat. Which of the following statements is correct?

(A) The boat will start moving with uniform speed

(B) The boat will be uniformly accelerated in the direction of the flow of air

(C) The boat will be uniformly accelerated opposite to the direction of flow of air

(D) The boat will remain stationary as before

45. When the total force acting on the system of particles is zero the linear momentum of the system of the particles is :

(A) positive

(B) negative

(C) either positive or negative

(D) zero

46. Let E, G and N represent the magnitudes of electromagnetic, gravitational and nuclear forces between two electrons at a given separation, then :

(A) N > E > G   (B) E > N > G

(C) G > N > E   (D) E > G > N

47. A 60 kg man pushes a 40 kg man by a force of 60 N. Then the 40 kg man has pushed the other man with a force of :

(A) 40 N

(B) 0

(C) 60 N

(D) 20 N

48. A body of weight W_1 is suspended from the ceiling of a room through a chain of weight W_2. The ceiling pulls the chain by a force of :

(A) W_1 (B) W_2

(C) $W_1 + W_2$ (D) $\dfrac{W_1 + W_2}{2}$

49. When a horse pulls a cart, the force that helps the cart to move forward is the force exerted by :

(A) the cart on the horse

(B) the ground on the horse

(C) the ground on the cart

(D) the horse on the ground

50. A car accelerates on a horizontal road due to the force exerted by :

(A) the engine of the car

(B) the driver of the car

(C) the earth

(D) the road

51. While walking on ice, one should take small steps to avoid slipping. This is because smaller steps ensure :

(A) larger friction

(B) smaller friction

(C) larger normal force

(D) smaller normal force

52. Newton's first law of motion gives the concept of :

(A) energy

(B) work

(C) momentum

(D) inertia

53. Inertia of motion depends on:

(A) mass

(B) velocity

(C) acceleration

(D) displacement

54. A man drawing a bucket of water falls back when the rope snaps. This is because of :

(A) law of gravitation

(B) Ist law of motion

(C) Newton's II law of motion

(D) Newton's III law of motion

55. Impulse has the same unit as that of :

(A) momentum   (B) force

(C) torque   (D) couple

56. Match the following and select the correct answer.

a. Displacement	1. ms^{-1}
b. Speed	2. newton
c. Acceleration	3. metre
d. Force	4. Ns
e. Momentum	5. ms^{-2}

(A) a-1, b-2, c-3, d-4, e-5

(B) a-3, b-1, c-5, d-2, e-4

(C) a-2, b-3, c-4, d-5, e-1

(D) a-3, b-2, c-1, d-5, e-4

57. A rider on the horse falls forward when the horse stops suddenly. This is due to :

(A) inertia of rest

(B) inertia of the horse

(C) inertia of the rider

(D) loss of balance

58. Three blocks A, B and C of masses 10kg, 2kg & 3kg respectively are connected by a light inextensible string and they are moved on a smooth horizontal plane. If a force of 36N is applied to the string connected to C

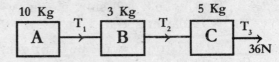

The ratio of T_1 & T_2, the tensions in the string is :

(A) 10 : 13

(B) 10 : 2

(C) 13 : 10

(D) 5 : 1

59. A cricket ball weighing 100 g and moving with a speed of $20ms^{-1}$ strikes a bat and remains is contact with it for 0.1s. The average force exerted by the ball on the bat is :

(A) 100 N   (B) 10 N

(C) 40 N   (D) 1 N

60. Two bodies of equal masses move with uniform velocities 'v' and '4v' respectively. Find the ratio of their K.E ?

(A) 1 : 4   (B) 1 : 16

(C) 1 : 9   (D) 1 : 1

61. Match the following and choose the correct answer :

a. Force	1. Nm^{-2}
b. Weight	2. Kg
c. Pressure	3. N
d. Impulse	4. NS^{1}
	5. $Kgwt.$

(A) a-3, b-2, c-4, d-1,

(B) a-5, b-4, c-3, d-1

(C) a-3, b-5, c-1, d-4

(D) a-4, b-2, c-1, d-3

62. A boy is standing in a lift. The force on the floor of the lift due to the weight of the boy becomes zero :

(A) when the lift moves up with an acceleration of 9.8 ms^{-2}

(B) when the lift moves down with an acceleration 9.8 ms^{-2}

(C) when the lift is not moving

(D) none of these

63. A body weighs less at the equator than at the poles because :

(A) earth rotates around an axis passing through the poles

(B) equatorial diameter is less than the polar diameter

(C) both A & B

(D) polar caps are formed at the poles

64. The moment of a force is a measure of the :

(A) capacity to turn a body

(B) stability of a body

(C) change in the momentum of a body

(D) force acting on a body

65. A bullet of mass 'm' moving with a speed 'v' strikes a wooden block of mass M and gets embedded in it. The speed of this embedded block will be:

(A) $\left(\sqrt{\dfrac{M}{M+m}}\right)v$ (B) $\left(\sqrt{\dfrac{m}{M+m}}\right)v$

(C) $\left(\dfrac{m}{M+m}\right)v$ (D) $\left(\dfrac{m+M}{Mm}\right)v$

66. If we know the magnitude and direction of force exerted on a body of given mass, Newtons' II law of motion permits us to calculate its :

(A) speed

(B) momentum

(C) position

(D) acceleration

67. A body whose momentum is constant must always :

(A) be accelerated

(B) decelerated

(C) be moving in a circle

(D) be having constant velocity

68. If a bomb at rest explodes and splits into two equal fragments. These fragments will move in

(A) one direction and with the same velocity

(B) opposite directions with different velocities

(C) opposite directions with unequal speeds

(D) opposite directions with equal speeds.

69. A lift is descending with a constant velocity 'v'. A man in the lift drops a coin. The coin experiences an acceleration towards the floor equal to :

(A) g + v   (B) g – v

(C) g   (D) zero

70. If a book is pressed against a wall using a horizontal force you can avoid its falling down. The frictional force along the wall in the upward direction acts, if the book moves down. Suppose a block of weight 'W' is held against a vertical wall by applying a horizontal force 'F', the minimum value of 'F' needed to hold the block would be :

(A) less than W

(B) equal to W

(C) greater than W

(D) can not be determined

71. A body of mass 20 g moving horizontally with a velocity 100 cms⁻¹ strikes a pendulum bob of mass 20 g and both of them move together. Estimate the height to which the system moves up.
(Assume g = 10m/s²)

(A) 1.25 cm

(B) 12.5 cm

(C) 0.125 cm

(D) 125 cm

72. The linear momentum 'P' of a moving body in one dimensional frame varies with time as $P = x + yt^2$, where x and y are position constants. The rate of change of momentum is the force that acts on the body.

In such a case the force is :

(A) proportional to t^2

(B) proportional to t

(C) inversely proportional to t^2

(D) inversely proportional to t

73. If there is an option for the soldiers to use rifles of different weights but with bullets of a fixed weight, they would prefer :

(A) light guns, because handling them is easy

(B) heavy guns so that they can be held firmly

(C) heavy guns because they have less recoil.

(D) light guns so that they can be carried easily

The following table shows the data recorded for a cyclist. Study it carefully and answer the questions from 74 to 76.

Time in (hrs)	Distance (km)
0	0
1	0.5
2	2
3	4.5
4	8
5	12.5
6	18
7	24.5
8	32.0

74. The cyclist's speed is :

(A) uniform

(B) non uniform

(C) can be both

(D) cannot be determined

75. The cyclist moves with :

(A) uniform speed

(B) non-uniform speed

(C) constant acceleration

(D) variable acceleration

76. The graph between 't' and 'v' should be a :

(A) straight line parallel to X-axis

(B) straight line inclined to X-axis & originating from origin

(C) straight line originating from Y-axis and inclined to X-axis

(D) straight line parallel to Y-axis

Following is the data recorded for a car in a race. Study it carefully and answer the questions from 77 to 78.

Time (hrs)	Distance (km)
0	0
1	1
2	8
3	27
4	64
5	125
6	216
7	343

77. The motion is:

(A) uniform   (B) non-uniform

(C) both   (D) none

78. The acceleration is:

(A) uniform

(B) non-uniform

(C) both

(D) none

79. A freely falling body strikes a surface and rebounds. The velocity of the body with respect to time during its fall and rebound is best represented by :

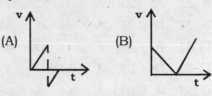
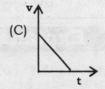
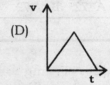

80. The acceleration of a body against time is shown in the figure given here :

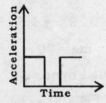

Which of the following figures shows the velocity-time graph for the same body?

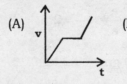

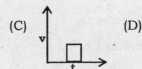

1.	C	2.	C	3.	B	4.	A	5.	D	6.	A	7.	A	8.	B	9.	C	10.	A
11.	A	12.	C	13.	B	14.	C	15.	A	16.	C	17.	D	18.	A	19.	C	20.	A
21.	B	22.	A	23.	A	24.	C	25.	B	26.	D	27.	B	28.	A	29.	B	30.	B
31.	B	32.	D	33.	A	34.	B	35.	C	36.	A	37.	B	38.	B	39.	D	40.	C
41.	D	42.	A	43.	B	44	D	45.	D	46.	D	47.	C	48.	C	49.	B	50.	D
51.	D	52.	D	53.	A	54.	D	55.	A	56.	B	57.	C	58.	A	59.	C	60.	B
61.	C	62.	B	63.	A	64.	A	65.	C	66.	D	67.	D	68.	D	69.	C	70.	A
71.	A	72.	B	73.	C	74.	B	75.	C	76.	B	77.	B	78.	B	79.	A	80.	A

Explanatory Answers

2. (C) $F = mg \Rightarrow 1 N = m \times 9.8 \approx 100g$

13. (B) Force is constant.

But $F = ma$ = constant.

$\Rightarrow m_1 a_2 = m_2 a_2$

$\Rightarrow 3 \times 0.5 = 1.5 a_2 \Rightarrow a_2 = 1 ms^{-2}$.

14. (C) $F = ma = 20 \times 5 = 100$ dynes.

But 1 dyne $= 10^{-5}$ N

$\therefore F = 100 \times 10^{-5}$ N

$= 1 \times 10^{-3}$ N.

15. (A) F = constant $\Rightarrow ma$ = const.

$\Rightarrow \dfrac{m_A}{m_B} = \dfrac{a_B}{a_A} = \dfrac{5}{2} = 2.5$

16. (C) $m = 200$ gm $= 0.2$ kg;

$u = 15 ms^{-1}$; $v = 25 ms^{-1}$;

$t = 2.5$ seconds.

F = constant = ?

$F = ma = m\left(\dfrac{v-u}{t}\right) = 0.2\left(\dfrac{25-15}{2.5}\right)$

$= 0.2 \times \dfrac{10}{2.5} = \dfrac{20}{25} = \dfrac{4}{5} = 0.8N$.

17. (D) $F = 1$ N; $m = 10$ kg; $s = 100$ cm;

$t = 4$ seconds; $u = ?$

$a = \dfrac{F}{m} = \dfrac{1}{10} = 0.1 ms^{-2}$

$s = ut + \dfrac{1}{2}at^2 \Rightarrow 1 = u \times 4 + \dfrac{1}{2} \times 0.1 \times 16$

$\Rightarrow 1 = 4u + 0.8$

$\Rightarrow 4u = 0.2$

$\Rightarrow u = 0.05$ ms^{-1} = 5 cms^{-1}.

18. (A) $F = ma = m\left(\dfrac{v-u}{t}\right)$

$\Rightarrow 0.6 = m\left(\dfrac{6-5}{2}\right) \Rightarrow \dfrac{0.6 \times 2}{1}$

$\Rightarrow m = 1.2$ kg.

19. (C) $u = 0$; $m = 200$ gm $= 0.2$ kg;

$s = 400$ cm $= 4$ m;

$t = 2$ seconds.

$F = ?$

$s = ut + \dfrac{1}{2}at^2 = 0 + \dfrac{1}{2}a \times 4 = 2a$

$\Rightarrow 4 = 2a \Rightarrow a = 2 \text{ ms}^{-2}.$

$F = ma = 0.2 \times 2 = 0.4 \text{ N}.$

20. (A) According to the law of conservation of linear momentum,

$$m_1u_1 + m_2u_2 = m_1v_1 + m_2v_2$$

$$\Rightarrow 0 = m_1v_1 + m_2v_2$$

$$\Rightarrow 0 = 0.2 \times 12 + 0.1 \times v_2$$

$$\Rightarrow v_2 = \dfrac{-0.2 \times 12}{0.1} = -24 \,\text{ms}^{-1}.$$

The negative sign indicates that it is moving in the opposite direction (west) with a velocity of 24 ms^{-1}.

21. (B) Pressure, $P = \dfrac{F}{A}$ where

$F \rightarrow$ force

$A \rightarrow$ area of each surface

$A = s^2 = 0.08 \times 0.08$

$= 0 \times 0.0064 \text{ m}^2;$

$F = 16 \text{ N}.$

$P = \dfrac{F}{A} \Rightarrow P = \dfrac{16}{0.64 \times 10^{-4}} = \dfrac{10}{4}$

$= \dfrac{10000}{4} = 2500 \text{ Pa}.$

23. (A) $m = 150 \text{ gm}; v = 250 \text{ cm}^3.$

Density $d = \dfrac{m}{v} = \dfrac{150}{250} = \dfrac{3}{5}$

$= 0.6 \text{ gm/cm}^3.$

But density of water, 1 gm/cm^3, is greater than density of body which is equal to 0.6 gm/cm^3. Hence the body floats.

24. (C) $m = 2 \text{ kg}; u = 0; t = 4 \text{ seconds};$
$a = 1.5 \text{ ms}^{-2}.$

$v = u + at = 0 + 1.5 \times 4 = 6 \text{ ms}^{-1}.$

Gain in momentum = $mv - mu$

$= m(v-u) = 2(6-0) = 12 \text{ kg/ms}^{-1}.$

25. (B) The net force is

$F_{net} = F_1 - F_2 = 5 - 3 = 2 \text{ N}$ in the direction of AB.

26. (D) $m_1u_1 - m_2u_2 = (m_1 + m_2)v$

$\Rightarrow v = \dfrac{m_1u_1 - m_2u_2}{m_1 + m_2}$

$= \dfrac{6 \times 2 - 4 \times 1.5}{6 + 4} = 0.6 \text{ m}$

33. (A) Impulse = change in momentum of a body

$\Rightarrow F \times t = m(v-u)$

$\Rightarrow F \times 0.2 = 1.8 \Rightarrow F = 9 \text{ N}.$

37. (B) Impulse = change in momentum of the ball

i.e., $F \times t = m(v-u)$

$\Rightarrow \dfrac{F}{2} \times 0.01 = 0.1 \times 10$ (Average force)

$\Rightarrow F = \dfrac{2}{0.01} = 200 \text{ N}.$

42. (A) If the compression of the book on the table in downward direction is considered as action, then the force exerted

by the table on the book will be reaction. Weight of the book is also in the downward direction. The angle between the action of the book (in the downward direction) and the weight of the book (also in the downward direction) is 0.

44. (D) The air blown at the sail will apply forward force. But equal and opposite force will be experienced by the fan. Hence net force on the boat will be zero.

53. (A) Greater the mass more is inertia of the body for any change

54. (D) Action and reaction act on two different bodies on the bucket and the man in opposite direction.

58. (A) Acceleration on of the system

$$a = \frac{F}{m} = \frac{36}{10+3+5} = 2ms^{-2}$$

T_1 pulls only A

$$\therefore T_1 = 2 \times 10 = 20N$$

$$T_2 = 13 \times 2 = 26N$$

59. (D) Momentum before impact

m x u

$$= 0.1 \times 20 = 2\,kgms^{-1}$$

momentum after impact

$$= -2\,kgms^{-1}$$

$\therefore$ change in momentum

$$= 2 - (-2) = 4\,Kgms^{-1}$$

$$\therefore Force = \frac{dp}{dt} = \frac{4}{0.1} = 40N$$

60. (B) $K.E_1 = m_1 v_1^2$

$K.E_2 = m_2 v_2^2$

as $m_1 = m_2$

& $v_2 = 4v_1$

$\therefore KE_1 = mv_1^2$

$KE_2 = m(4v_1)^2$

$= 16mv_1^2$

$\therefore KE_1 : KE_2 = 1 : 16$

61. (D) Impulse has the dimension of momentum. Its unit can be Ns^{-1} or $Kgms^{-1}$

62. (B) When the lift moves down the reaction will be in the upward direction. Therefore tension *mg* acts down and reaction *mg* acts in the opposite direction. The net force acting will be zero

64. (C) Momentum of a force brings out change in momentum. Moment of force brigs change in its state of motion and hence change in momentum.

65. (C) Total momentum before impact = mV

Total momentum after impact $= (M + m)v$

$mV = (M + m)v$

$$\therefore v_2 \left(\frac{m}{M+m} \right) v$$

$$\therefore v = \left(\frac{mn}{M+m}\right)v$$

66. (D) Force = m x a

If we know F and m, a can always be found at.

68. (D) $mv = \left(\dfrac{M}{2} - \dfrac{M}{2}\right)V$

So that mv = 0 initially and

$\dfrac{M}{2}V - \dfrac{M}{2}V$ is also equal to zero

$\therefore$ momentum before explosion = momentum after explosion

69. (C) Since the lift in moving down with constant velocity, it encounters no acceleration in the downward direction. So the coin experiences only acceleration due to gravity.

70. (A) The friction between the box and the wall reduces the reaction to support the weight of the box.

72. (B) $P = x + yt^2$

$$F = \frac{dP}{dt}$$

$$\frac{dP}{dt} = 2yt$$

as '2y' is constant.

$F \alpha t$

✦ ✦ ✦

Chapter 3

Gravitation and Pressure

1. Gravitation

All bodies that have mass, attract each other with a force called the 'gravitational force'.

(i) Universal law of gravitation

The gravitational force of attraction between any two bodies is directly proportional to the product of the masses of the bodies and inversely proportional to the square of the distance between them and acts along the line joining the bodies.

(ii) Force of gravitation between spherical bodies

Two non-overlapping spherical bodies with the same density in all directions attract each other with a force, which is given by :

$$F = \frac{Gm_1 m_2}{r^2}$$

where, m_1 & m_2 are their masses and 'r' is the distance between their centres.

(The man of the earth is gR_e^2 / G and it is estimated to be 5.98×10^{24} kg.)

(iii) Universal constant of gravitation

The constant 'G' appearing in Newton's law of gravitation is called the "Universal constant of Gravitation". Its value in the S.I. unit is :

$$G = 6.67 \times 10^{-11} \frac{Nm^2}{kg^2}$$

(iv) Projectile motion

When a body is thrown near the earth's surface in a direction other than the vertical, its motion is called projectile motion. Its path is parabolic for small speeds.

Variation of 'g' with height.

As one goes above the earth's surface, the value of acceleration due to gravity (g) decreases. At a height H above the surface of earth, the value of 'g' is

$$g^i = g \left(\frac{R_e}{R_e + H} \right)^2$$

When the 'H' is of a considerable value.

$$g^i = g \left(1 - \frac{2H}{R_e} \right)$$

The value of 'g' also decreases with an increase in depth as we go inside the earth.

(v) Orbital Velocity

The orbital velocity of a satellite is equal to :

$$v_0 = \sqrt{g R_e} \text{ or } v_0 = \sqrt{\frac{GM_e}{R_e}},$$

when revolving near the surface of the earth and :

when orbiting at a height 'h' from the surface of the earth it is given by :

$$v_0 = \sqrt{\frac{g R_e^2}{R_e + h}} \text{ or } v_0 = \sqrt{\frac{GM_e}{R_e + h}}$$

A satellite that remains fixed at a particular point above the earth is known as a *geostationary* or *communication* or *synchronous* satellite. For such a satellite the period is same as that of the earth around its own axis. The minimum height where the geostationary satellite can be placed is 36,000 km.

(vi) Gravitational Potential

The potential energy U at a point that is at a distance 'r' from the centre of the earth is given by :

$$U = \frac{-GMm}{r}$$

The negative sign indicates that gravitational force is attractive.

The gravitational potential 'V' at a point is the gravitational energy of a unit mass placed at that point.

For a point at a distance 'r' from the centre of the earth, the gravitational potential is given by :

$$V = -\frac{GM}{r}$$

Gravitational potential is a scalar quantity. Its unit is J/kg.

(vii) Escape velocity

The minimum speed with which a body should be projected so that it goes out of the gravitational field of the earth is known as escape velocity.

It is given by :

$$V_e = \sqrt{\frac{2GM}{R}},$$

where 'M' and 'R' represent the mass and radius of the earth.

Because of low escape velocity on moon, it does not have any atmosphere.

(viii) Gravity

The gravitational force that is experienced by an object due to a heavenly body such as the earth is called *gravity*.

(*Centre of gravity* of a body is a point where all the mass of the body may be assumed to be concentrated for the calculation of the force of gravity.)

All bodies near the earth's surface fall towards it with the same acceleration called "acceleration due to gravity (g)", unless other forces act them.

(ix) Acceleration due to gravity

The acceleration due to gravity near the earth's surface is given by :

$$g = \frac{GM_e}{R_e^2} = 9.8 \, ms^{-2}$$

The direction of this acceleration is vertically downwards, that is, towards the centre of the earth.

Under the influence of 'gravity', the acceleration of a body moving near the earth's surface is same regardless of whether it moves up or falls down or is moving with an angle to the vertical.

If the upward direction is taken as the positive direction, the acceleration of a particle moving near the earth's surface is : $a = -g$. If the downward direction is taken as the positive direction, the acceleration is : $a = +g$.

(x) Weight and mass

The force by which the earth attracts a body is called the weight of the body on earth. Weight of a body changes with the height above the earth's surface, but mass remains the same everywhere.

The weight of a body on the moon is about $\frac{1}{6}$ th of its weight on the earth.

(xi) Geotropism

Growth of plants also gets affected by gravity. Roots always tend to grow in the downward direction and stems, in the upward direction. This phenomenon is called "geotropism".

2. Pressure

Pressure is the force (thrust) acting on a unit area.

$$Pressure = \frac{Force}{Area}$$

The unit of 'pressure' is Nm^{-2}.

The greater the area over which a force acts, the less is the pressure.

Pressure in liquids

(i) The pressure of a liquid of density 'd', is given by $P = hdg$, where, 'h' is the depth and 'g' is the acceleration due to gravity.

(ii) Pressure in a liquid increases with depth because the further down we go, greater is the weight of the liquid above.

(iii) Pressure at a point acts equally in all directions.

(iv) A liquid finds its own level. This level depends on the density of liquid and the atmospheric pressure.

(v) Pressure depends on the density of the liquid. The denser the liquid, the greater is the pressure at any given depth as force exerted by the liquid is greater ($P = hdg$).

3. Upthrust

An object in a liquid, whether floating or submerged, is acted upon by an upward force called upthrust. This makes it seem to be of less weight than its original one.

4. Archimedes Principle

When a body is wholly or partially submerged in a fluid the upthrust equals the weight of the fluid displaced.

Multiple Choice Questions

1. The value of the acceleration due to gravity at a height of 12,800 km from the surface of the earth

   ($R_e = 6400$ km) $g_1 = g^0 \left(\dfrac{R}{R + h} \right)^2$ is :

   (A) 3.09 m/s²
   (B) 1.09 m/s²
   (C) 4.08 m/s²
   (D) 5.07 m/s²

2. The weight of a body of mass 5 kg is

   (A) 69.0 N   (B) 79.0 N
   (C) 49.0 N   (D) 39.0 N

3. The weight of the body at the surface of the earth is 20 N and the radius of the earth is 6400 km. The weight of a body at a height 6400 km above is :

(A) 7 N   (B) 5 N

(C) 4 N   (D) 6 N

4. Consider a heavenly body which has a mass twice that of the earth and a radius thrice that of the earth. The weight of a book on this heavenly body, if its weight on the earth is 900 N will be :

(A) 400 N   (B) 600 N

(C) 500 N   (D) 200 N

5. Two protons are kept at a separation of 1 femtometre (1 femtometre = 10^{-15} m). The mass of a proton is 1.67×10^{-27} kg. The gravitational force between them is :

(A) 1.86×10^{-34} N

(B) 5.86×10^{-34} N

(C) 2.8×10^{-34} N

(D) 4.86×10^{-34} N

6. The mass of the sun is 2.0×10^{36} kg and that of the earth is 6.0×10^{24} kg. The distance between the sun and the earth is 1.5×10^{11} m. The gravitational force between the sun and earth is :

(A) 3.56×10^{28} N   (B) 4.56×10^{28} N

(C) 6.56×10^{28} N   (D) 5.56×10^{28} N

7. A particle is taken to a height of $2R_e$ above the earth's surface, where R_e is the radius of the earth. If it is dropped from this height, its acceleration is will be :

(A) 3.1 m/s^2 (B) 5.1 m/s^2

(C) 1.1 m/s^2 (D) 2.1 m/s^2

8. Consider a heavenly body whose mass is 3×10^{24} kg (half of that of the earth) and radius is 3,200 km (half of that of the earth). The acceleration due to gravity at the surface of this heavenly body will be:

(A) 39.6 m/s^2 (B) 19.6 m/s^2

(C) 29.6 m/s^2 (D) 49.6 m/s^2

9. Two bodies 'A' and 'B' having masses 'm' and '2m' respectively are kept at a distance 'd' apart. A small particle is to be placed so that the net gravitational force on it, due to the bodies A and B, is zero. Its distance from the mass A should be :

(A) $x = \dfrac{d}{1 + \sqrt{2}}$ (B) $x = \dfrac{d}{1 + \sqrt{4}}$

(C) $x = \dfrac{d}{1 + \sqrt{3}}$ (D) $x = \dfrac{d}{1 + \sqrt{6}}$

10. Two bodies of masses 1 kg and 2 kg respectively are placed at a separation of 1 m. Find the accelerations of the bodies assuming that only gravitational force acts between them.

(A) 1.33×10^{-10} & 6.67×10^{-11} m/s^2

(B) 1.33×10^{-11} & 6.25×10^{-11} m/s^2

(C) 5.36×10^{-11} & 5.26×10^{-11} m/s^2

(D) 3.11×10^{-11} & 5.26×10^{-11} m/s^2

11. Communication satellites move in the orbits of radius 44,400 km around the earth. The acceleration of such a satellite assuming that the only force acting on it is that due to the earth is :   ($M_e = 6 \times 10^{24}$ kg)

(A) 0.4 ms^{-2} (B) 0.6 ms^{-2}

(C) 0.2 ms^{-2} (D) 0.1 ms^{-2}

12. Two persons weighing 50 kg and 60 kg are seated across a table. If they are one metre apart, the gravitational force between them is:

   (A) 5×10^{-7} N   (B) 2×10^{-7} N

   (C) 4×10^{-7} N   (D) 3×10^{-7} N

13. The mass of a planet is twice and its radius is 3 times that of the earth. The weight of a body, which has a mass of 5 kg on the surface of the earth, on that planet is :

   (A) 11.95 N   (B) 20.9 N

   (C) 10.85 N   (D) 9.9 N

14. The height at which a body has one fourth of its weight when it is on the surface of the earth is :

   (A) at a height r where r is the radius of the earth

   (B) at a height 2r where r is the radius of the earth

   (C) at a height $\frac{r}{2}$ where r is the radius of the earth

   (D) at a height $\frac{r}{4}$ where r is the radius of the earth

15. A space vehicle is moving vertically upward with a constant acceleration 'a'. An astronaut of weight 'mg' feels heavier. When will the astronants weight becomes '2mg'?

   (A) a = 2g

   (B) a = g/2

   (C) a = g

   (D) a = 3g

16. Two particles are kept at a separation of distance 'r'. The gravitational force between them is proportional to :

   (A) r   (B) r^2

   (C) $\frac{1}{r}$ (D) $\frac{1}{r^2}$

17. The universal constant of gravitation G has the units :

   (A) N   (B) m/s^2

   (C) Nm^2kg^{-2} (D) J

18. The equation $F = \dfrac{Gm_1 m_2}{r^2}$ is valid for :

   (A) rectangular bodies

   (B) circular bodies

   (C) elliptical bodies

   (D) spherical bodies

19. The force acting on a ball due to the earth has a magnitude F_b and that acting on the earth due to the ball has a magnitude F_e. Then :

   (A) $F_b = F_e$ (B) $F_b > F_e$

   (C) $F_b < F_e$ (D) $F_e = 0$

20. The value of gravitational force between two friends sitting across a table is closest to :

   (A) 10^{-8} N   (B) 1 N

   (C) 10^4 N   (D) 10^8 N

21. The force of gravitation between two bodies of mass 1 kg each kept at a distance of 1 m is :

   (A) 6.67 N

   (B) 6.67×10^{-9} N

   (C) 6.67×10^{-7} N

   (D) 6.67×10^{-11} N

22. The earth attracts a body of mass 1 kg on its surface with a force of :

(A) 1 N

(B) 6.67×10^{-11} N

(C) 9.8 N

(D) $\dfrac{1}{9.8}$ N

23. A coin and a feather are dropped together in a vacuum. Then :

(A) the coin will reach the ground first

(B) the feather will reach the ground first

(C) both will reach the ground at the same time

(D) the feather will not fall down

24. Two bodies A and B of masses 100 g and 200 g respectively are dropped near the earth's surface. Let the accelerations of A and B be 'a_1' and 'a_2' respectively. Then :

(A) $a_1 = a_2$ (B) $a_1 < a_2$

(C) $a_1 > a_2$ (D) $a_1 \neq a_2$

25. Newton's law of gravitation is valid

(A) on the earth only

(B) on the moon only

(C) in the laboratory only

(D) everywhere

26. The acceleration due to gravity is 9.8 ms^{-2} at :

(A) a height much above the earth's surface

(B) near the earth's surface

(C) deep inside earth

(D) at the centre of the earth

27. The acceleration due to gravity near the moon's surface is :

(A) approximately equal to that near the earth's surface

(B) approximately six times that near the earth's surface

(C) approximately one-sixth of that near the earth's surface

(D) slightly greater than that near the earth's surface

28. A particle is taken to a height R above the earth's surface, where R is equal to the radius of the earth. The acceleration due to gravity there is

(A) 2.45 ms^{-2}

(B) 4.9 ms^{-2}

(C) 9.8 ms^{-2}

(D) 19.6 ms^{-2}

29. Consider a heavenly body that has mass $2M_e$ and radius $2R_e$, where M_e and R_e are the mass and the radius of earth respectively. The acceleration due to gravity at the surface of this heavenly body is :

(A) 2.45 ms^{-2}

(B) 4.9 ms^{-2}

(C) 9.8 ms^{-2}

(D) 19.6 ms^{-2}

30. The value of 'g' is :

(A) constant everywhere in space

(B) constant everywhere on the surface of the earth

(C) greater at the poles than at the equator

(D) greater at the equator than at the poles

31. When a body is thrown up, the force of gravity is :

(A) in the upward direction

(B) in the downward direction

(C) zero

(D) in the horizontal direction

32. The mass of a body is measured to be 12 kg on the earth. If it is taken to the moon, its mass will be :

(A) 12 kg   (B) 6 kg

(C) 2 kg   (D) 72 kg

33. The weight of a body is measured to be 120 N on the earth. If it is taken to the moon, its weight will be about:

(A) 120 N

(B) 60 N

(C) 20 N

(D) 720 N

34. Consider two solid uniform spherical objects of the same density ρ. One has a radius R and the other, 2R. They are in outer space where the gravitational force due to other objects is negligible. If they are at rest with their surfaces touching, what is the force between the objects due to their gravitational attraction?

(A) $\dfrac{158}{81} G\pi^2 R^4 \rho^2$

(B) $\dfrac{128}{81} G\pi^2 R^4 \rho^2$

(C) $\dfrac{168}{81} G\pi^2 R^4 \rho^2$

(D) $\dfrac{148}{81} G\pi^2 R^4 \rho^2$

35. If the radius of the earth were to be increased by a factor of 3, by what factor would its density have to be changed to keep 'g' the same?

(A) 3   (B) $\dfrac{1}{3}$

(C) 6   (D) $\dfrac{1}{6}$

36. An astronaut on the moon measures the acceleration due to gravity to be 1.7 ms^{-2}. He knows that the radius of the moon is about 0.27 times that of the earth. What is his estimate of the ratio of the mass of the earth to that of the moon? (The acceleration due to gravity on the earth's surface is 9.8 ms^{-2}).

(A) 67   (B) 58

(C) 46   (D) 79

37. A body weighs 90kgwt on the surface of the earth. How much will it weigh on the surface of Mars whose mass is $\dfrac{1}{9}$th and the radius half of those earth?

(A) 50 kg wt   (B) 40 kg wt

(C) 30 kg wt   (D) 35 kg wt

38. What will be the acceleration due to gravity on the surface of the moon if its radius is $\dfrac{1}{4}$th the radius of the earth and its mass is 1/80th the mass of the earth?

(Assume : g = 10 ms^{-2})

(A) 2 ms^{-2} (B) 4 ms^{-2}

(C) 6 ms^{-2} (D) 8 ms^{-2}

39. If the diameter of the earth becomes two times its present value and its mass remains unchanged, then how would the weight of an object on the surface of the earth be affected?

   (A) Weight would become one–third

   (B) Weight would become one–fourth

   (C) Weight would become one–fifth

   (D) Weight would become one–sixth

40. The Mount Everest is 8,848 m above the sea level. Estimate acceleration due to gravity at this height, given that the mean 'g' on the surface of earth is 9.8 ms^{-2} and mean radius of earth is 6.37×10^6 m. (Ignore the variation in 'g' due to the earth's rotation and small departure from the spherical shape.)

   (A) 6.77 ms^{-2}

   (B) 5.67 ms^{-2}

   (C) 9.77 ms^{-2}

   (D) 6.67 ms^{-2}

41. A body weighs 63 N on the surface of the earth. What is the gravitational force on it due to the earth at a height equal to half the radius of the earth?

   (A) 39 N   (B) 58 N

   (C) 43 N   (D) 28 N

42. At what height from the surface of the earth will the value of 'g' be reduced by 40% from its value at the surface? (Radius of the earth is equal to 6400 km)

   (A) 1.47×10^3 km

   (B) 3.86×10^3 km

   (C) 5.76×10^3 km

   (D) 1.56×10^3 km

43. At what height will a man's weight be half his weight on the surface of earth?   (R is the radius of earth)

   (A) 0.214 R

   (B) 0.514 R

   (C) 0.414 R

   (D) 0.516 R

44. A meteor is falling. How much gravitational acceleration would it experience when its height from the surface of the earth is equal to three times the radius of the earth? (Given that the acceleration due to gravity on the surface of the earth is g)

   (A) g/16   (B) g/14

   (C) g/10   (D) g/15

45. At what height from the surface of the earth will the value of acceleration due to gravity be reduced by 36% from the value at the surface?   (Radius of earth = 6400 km)

   (A) 1500 km   (B) 1200 km

   (C) 1000 km   (D) 1600 km

46. The weight of a body on the moon is one-sixth of its weight on the earth. How will the mass of the body vary?

   (A) Becomes $\frac{1}{6}$ th

   (B) Remains the same

   (C) Becomes 6 times

   (D) Becomes $\frac{1}{8}$

47. When you put an object on a spring balance, do you get mass of an object or its weight?

   (A) Weight   (B) Force

   (C) Mass   (D) Acceleration

48. Where is the value of 'g' greater, at the poles or at the equator?

(A) Equator

(B) At the centre

(C) Poles

(D) None of these

49. An apple falls towards the earth because the earth attracts it. The apple also attracts the earth by the same force. Why do we not see the earth rising towards the apple?

(A) Acceleration of the earth is very large when compared to that of apple

(B) Acceleration of the earth is equal to that of apple

(C) Acceleration of the earth is neither high nor too low

(D) Acceleration of the earth is very small when compared to that of apple

50. How would the value of 'g' change if the earth were to shrink slightly without any change of mass?

(A) Increases

(B) Decreases

(C) Remains constant

(D) None of these

51. A rock is brought from the surface of the moon. Then :

(A) its mass will change

(B) its weight will change but not mass

(C) both mass and weight change

(D) both mass and weight remain the same

52. Suppose we have taken a stone to the centre of the earth :

(A) its weight becomes zero

(B) its weight increases as R decreases

(C) its weight is unaffected

(D) its mass increases

53. The force of gravitation between two bodies does not depend on :

(A) their separation

(B) the gravitational constant

(C) their masses

(D) sum of their masses

54. The type of force that exists between two charged bodies is :

(A) only gravitational

(B) only electrostatic

(C) neither A nor B

(D) both A and B

55. Gravitational force is a :

(A) repulsive force

(B) action at a distance force

(C) neither A nor B

(D) both A and B

56. Which of the forces is responsible for the flow of water in rivers ?

(A) Frictional forces

(B) Gravitational forces

(C) Electrical forces

(D) Magnetic forces

57. Atmosphere is held to the earth due to :

(A) frictional force

(B) gravitational force

(C) electrical force

(D) magnetic force

58. A body submerged in the sea was brought up slowly from the sea bed to the sea surface. Variation of pressure on the body with decrease in the depth of sea is shown in the figures below. Which of these is correct ?

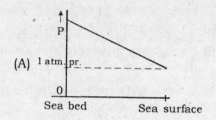

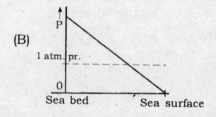

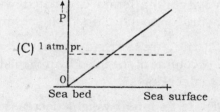

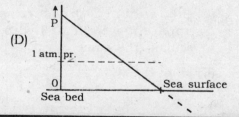

59. The gravitational pull exerted by the earth on a body is called :

(A) true weight

(B) gravitational mass

(C) apparent weight

(D) inertial mass.

60. A steel needle can be made to float on water due to :

(A) cohesion

(B) Archimedes principle

(C) adhesion

(D) surface tension

61. Variation of 'g' w.r.t. height or depth is correctly represented by :

(A)

(B)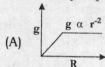

(C)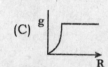

(D)

62. A balloon of mass 'm' is rising with an acceleration 'a'. A fraction of its mass is detached from the balloon. Its acceleration will :

(A) decrease

(B) increase

(C) remain the same

(D) none of these

63. A geostationary satellite :

(A) can move about any axis

(B) must move about the polar axis

(C) must move on an axis in the equatorial plane

(D) both B & C

64. If the radius of the earth shrinks by 4% and there is no change in its mass, the acceleration due to gravity, which depends on mass and radius, will change. By how much does the value of 'g' change ?

(A) 2%   (B) 4%

(C) 16%   (D) 8%

65. The escape velocity from the earth is about 11.2 kms^{-1}. The escape velocity from the planet having thrice the radius and the same mean density will be :

(A) 33.6 km s^{-1} (B) 11 km s^{-1}

(C) 11.2 km s^{-1} (D) 22.4 km s^{-1}

66. Sun is about 330 times heavier and about 100 times bigger in size than the earth. But mean density of earth is more that of sun. The ratio of their mean densities ($d_s : d_e$) will be :

(A) $3.3 \times 10^{-4} : 1$ (B) $1 : 3.3 \times 10^{-4}$

(C) 330 : 1   (D) 1 : 330

67. At what height over earth's pole, the acceleration due to gravity decreases by 2%? (The radius of the earth may be taken as 6400 km).

(A) 32 km   (B) 64 km

(C) 12 km   (D) 16 km

68. An artificial satellite is moving in a circular orbit with a speed equal to half the magnitude of escape velocity from the earth. The height of the satellite from the surface of the earth is :

(A) 640 km   (B) 6400 km

(C) 64 km   (D) 6.4 km

69. The mean density of the earth is :

(A) $3g/4\pi RG$ (B) $3G/4\pi Rg$

(C) $3gG/4\pi R$ (D) $3\pi/4GR$

70. The weight of a body will increase significantly, if it is taken to :

(A) the centre of the earth

(B) the highest place on the earth

(C) the pole

(D) the equator

71. A liquid is taken in different shaped vessels as shown in the figure.

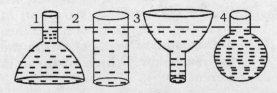

The vessels are filled with the liquid up to same level. We know that :

(i) Pressure is inversely proportion to the area on which force acts.

(ii) Pressure depends on the depth of liquid column.

Which vessel will have the highest pressure at the bottom?

(A) 1

(B) 2

(C) 3

(D) 4

72. Voyager balloons are filled with hydrogen to move up. As it goes up :

(A) the pressure decreases and volume of the filled hydrogen also decreases

(B) its apparent weight decreases

(C) the volume, pressure and apparent weight of hydrogen remain the same.

(D) all of these

73. Archimedes principle tells about buoyancy that is noticed is :
   (A) solids   (B) liquids
   (C) gases   (D) fluids

74. Which of the following is not matched correctly?
   (A) Force – kg ms^{-1}
   (B) Pressure – Nm^{-2}
   (C) Buoyancy – N
   (D) Density – kgm^{-3}

75. A ship floats with $\dfrac{1}{3}$ of its volume outside water and $\dfrac{2}{3}$ of its volume in a liquid. What is the relative density of the liquid ?

   (A) $\dfrac{2}{3}$ (B) 2/3

   (C) 2   (D) 3

76. Which of the following statements is wrong ?
   (A) Buoyancy is an upward force and acts in the vertically upward direction
   (B) Upthrust depends on the volume of liquid displaced but not on the weight of the floating body.
   (C) Upthrust balances only a partial weight of the floating body
   (D) None of these

77. An astronaut in the orbit in a space-craft feels weightlessness :
   (A) due to the absence of gravity inside
   (B) due to the fact that space craft has no energy
   (C) because acceleration in the orbit is equal to acceleration of gravity outside
   (D) there is no gravity outside

78. A ball is floating on water. It is in :
   (A) stable equilibrium
   (B) unstable equilibrium
   (C) neutral equilibrium
   (D) Both B and C

79. When a body is wholly or partly immersed in a liquid, it experiences
   (A) a net downward thrust
   (B) a net upthrust
   (C) A or B depending on the density of the liquid
   (D) A or B depending on the density of the body

80. The resultant upthrust in a liquid acts at a point called :
   (A) centre of gravity
   (B) geometric centre
   (C) centre of buoyancy
   (D) all of these

81. It is easy to lift a stone inside water than out of it, because :
   (A) acceleration due to gravity in water is less
   (B) there is apparent loss of mass of the stone in water
   (C) the stone experiences a net upthrust
   (D) Both A & B

82. *Study the given statements and select the correct answer.*
   P. *Helium gas is filled in balloons*
   Q. *Helium is less denser than air*
   (A) Both P and Q are correct and Q is the correct explanation of P
   (B) Both P and Q are true but Q is not the correct explanation of P
   (C) P is true but not Q
   (D) P is false but Q is true

1. $g^1 = g\left(\dfrac{R}{R+h}\right)^2$

2. Weight = mg

3. $g^1 = g\left(\dfrac{R}{R+h}\right)^2 \Rightarrow mg^1 = mg\left(\dfrac{R}{R+h}\right)^2$

4. $w_e = \dfrac{GM_e m}{R^2_e}$; $W = \dfrac{GMm}{R^2}$

5. $F = \dfrac{Gm_1m_2}{r^2}$

6. $F = \dfrac{Gm_1m_2}{r^2}$

7. $g^1 = g\left(\dfrac{R}{R+h}\right)^2$

8. $g = \dfrac{GM}{R^2}$; $g^1 = \dfrac{G \times \dfrac{M}{2}}{\left(\dfrac{R}{2}\right)^2} = 2\left(\dfrac{GM}{R^2}\right) = 2g$

9. $F_1 = F_2$

11. $F = \dfrac{Gm_1m_2}{r^2}$

12. $F = \dfrac{Gm_1m_2}{r^2}$

13. $g = \dfrac{GM}{R^2}$; $g^1 = \dfrac{G(2M)}{(3R)^2}$

16. $F = \dfrac{Gm_1m_2}{r^2}$

17. $F = \dfrac{Gm_1m_2}{r^2} \Rightarrow G = \dfrac{Fr^2}{m_1m_2}$

20. & 21. $F = \dfrac{Gm_1m_2}{r^2}$

22. $F = mg$

30. $g = \dfrac{GM}{R^2} \Rightarrow g \propto \dfrac{1}{R^2}$

34. $m = V\rho = \dfrac{4}{3}\pi R^3 \rho$

    V = volume of the sphere, ρ = density

35. $g = \dfrac{GM}{R^2} = \dfrac{4}{3}G\pi\rho$

    (since $M = V\rho = \dfrac{4}{3}\pi R^3 \rho$)

36. $g_e = \dfrac{GM_e}{R^2_e}$; $g_m = \dfrac{GM_m}{R_m^2}$

    $\Rightarrow \dfrac{M_e}{M_m} = \dfrac{g_e}{g_m} \cdot \dfrac{R_e^2}{R_m^2}$

37. $g_e = \dfrac{GM}{R^2}$; $g_m = \dfrac{G\left(\dfrac{M}{9}\right)}{\left(\dfrac{R}{2}\right)^2} = \dfrac{4}{9}g_e$

38. $g_e = \dfrac{GM}{R^2}$; $g_m = G\left(\dfrac{M}{80}\right)\left(\dfrac{4}{R}\right)^2 = \dfrac{1}{5}g_e$

39. $g_e = \dfrac{GM}{R^2}$; $g^1_e = \dfrac{GM}{4R^2} = \dfrac{1}{4}g_e$

40. $g = \dfrac{GM}{R^2}$; $g^1_e = \dfrac{GM}{(R+h)^2}$

41. $\dfrac{g^1}{g} = \left(\dfrac{R}{R+h}\right)^2$

42. $g^1 = \dfrac{60}{100}g = \dfrac{3}{5}g$; $\dfrac{g^1}{g} = \left(\dfrac{R}{R+h}\right)^2$

43. $\dfrac{g^1}{g} = \left(\dfrac{R}{R+h}\right)^2 \Rightarrow \dfrac{mg^1}{mg} = \left(\dfrac{R}{R+h}\right)^2$

44. $\dfrac{g^1}{g} = \left(\dfrac{R}{R+h}\right)^2$

45. $\dfrac{g^1}{g} = \dfrac{64}{100}$; $\dfrac{g^1}{g} = \left(\dfrac{R}{R+h}\right)^2$

Answers

1. B	2. C	3. B	4. D	5. A	6. A	7. C	8. B	9. A	10. A
11. C	12. B	13. C	14. A	15. C	16. D	17. C	18. D	19. A	20. A
21. D	22. C	23. C	24. A	25. D	26. B	27. C	28. A	29. B	30. C
31. B	32. A	33. C	34. B	35. B	36. D	37. B	38. A	39. B	40. C
41. D	42. A	43. C	44. A	45. D	46. B	47. A	48. C	49. D	50. A
51. B	52. A	53. D	54. D	55. B	56. B	57. B	58. A	59. A	60. D
61. B	62. B	63. C&B	64. D	65. A	66. A	67. B	68. B	69. A	70. C
71. D	72. A	73. D	74. A	75. C	76. C	77. C	78. C	79. B	80. C
81. D	82. A								

Explanatory Answers

1. (B) $g^1 = 9.8\left(\dfrac{6400\times10^3}{(6400+12,800)\times10^3}\right)^2$

$= 9.8\left(\dfrac{6400}{3\times6400}\right)^2 = \dfrac{9.8}{9}$

$= 1.09 \text{ ms}^{-2}$.

2. (C) Weight $= mg = 5 \times 9.8 = 49$ N.

3. (B) $W^1 = W\left(\dfrac{R}{R+h}\right)^2$

$= 20\left(\dfrac{6400}{2\times6400}\right)^2$

$\dfrac{20}{4} = 5$N.

4. (D) $\dfrac{W^1}{W_e} = \dfrac{M^1}{M_e} \times \left(\dfrac{R_e}{R^1}\right)^2 =$

$\dfrac{2M_e}{M_e} \times \left(\dfrac{R_e}{3R_e}\right)^2 = \dfrac{2}{9}$

$\Rightarrow W^1 = \dfrac{2}{9}W_e = \dfrac{2}{9} \times 900 = 200$N.

5. (A)

$F = \dfrac{6.67\times10^{-11}\times\left(1.67\times10^{-27}\right)^2}{10^{-15}}$

$= 1.86\times10^{-34}$

6. (A) $F = \dfrac{6.67 \times 10^{-11} \times 2 \times 10^{36} \times 6 \times 10^{24}}{\left(1.5 \times 10^{11}\right)^2}$

$= 3.56 \times 10^{28}$ N

7. (C) $g^1 = g\left(\dfrac{R}{R + 2R}\right)^2$

$= g\left(\dfrac{1}{3}\right)^2 = \dfrac{g}{9} = \dfrac{9.8}{9} = 1.1$ ms^{-2}.

8. (B) $g^1 = 2g = 2 \times 9.8 = 19.6$ ms^{-2}.

9. (A) Let m^1 be the mass of particle, which is place of a distance 'x' from A.

$F_1 = \dfrac{Gmm^1}{x^2}$ towards A

$F_2 = \dfrac{G(2m)m^1}{(d - x)^2}$ towards B

The net force = 0 if

$F_1 = F_2$

$\Rightarrow \dfrac{Gmm^1}{x^2} = \dfrac{G(2m)m^1}{(d - x)^2}$

$\Rightarrow x = \dfrac{d}{1 + \sqrt{2}}$

10. (A)

$F = \dfrac{Gm_1m_2}{r^2} = \dfrac{6.67 \times 10^{-11} \times 1 \times 2}{(1)^2}$

$= 1.33 \times 10^{-10}$N

(i) Acceleration of 1 kg body :

$a = \dfrac{F}{m} = \dfrac{0.33 \times 10^{-10}}{1}$

$= 1.33 \times 10^{-10}$ ms^{-2}.

(ii) Acceleration of 2 kg body :

$a = \dfrac{F}{m} = \dfrac{1.33 \times 10^{-10}}{2}$

$= 6.67 \times 10^{-11}$ ms^{-2}.

11. (C) $F = \dfrac{GM_e m_{sat}}{r^2}$

$a = \dfrac{F}{m_{sat}} = \dfrac{GM_e}{r^2}$

$= \dfrac{6.67 \times 10^{-11} \times 6 \times 10^{24}}{\left(44,400 \times 10^3\right)^2}$

$= 0.2$ ms^{-2}.

12. (B) $F = \dfrac{6.67 \times 10^{-11} \times 50 \times 60}{(1)^2}$

$= 6.67 \times 3 \times 10^{-8}$

$= 20.01 \times 10^{-8}$ N

$= 2.001 \times 10^{-7}$ N.

13. (C) $g^1 = \dfrac{2}{9}g = \dfrac{2}{9} \times 9.8 = \dfrac{19.6}{9}$

$= 2.17$ ms^{-2}.

Weight of the body on a planet.
$W^1 = mg^1 = 5 \times 2.17 = 10.85$ N.

14. (A) $W = \dfrac{GMm}{r^2}$; $W^1 = \dfrac{GMm}{(r + h)^2}$

But $W^1 = \dfrac{1}{4}W \Rightarrow \dfrac{GMm}{(r + h)^2} = \dfrac{1}{4}\dfrac{GMm}{r^2}$

$$\Rightarrow (r+h)^2 = 4r^2 \Rightarrow r+h = 2r$$

$$\Rightarrow h = r.$$

15. (C) $W = mg$

$W^1 = m(g+a)$

$$\Rightarrow 2mg = m(g+a) \Rightarrow ma = mg$$

$$\Rightarrow a = g.$$

19. (A) According to Newton's third Law of motion, for every action (force), there is an equal and opposite reaction (force).

21. (D) $$F = \frac{6.67 \times 10^{-11} \times 1 \times 1}{(1)^2}$$

$$= 6.67 \times 10^{-11} \text{ N.}$$

22. (C) $F = mg = 1 \times 9.8 = 9.8$ N.

28. (A) $$g = \frac{GM}{R^2}, g^1 = \frac{GM}{(R+h)^2} = \frac{GM}{4R^2}$$

as $$\frac{GM}{4R^2} = \frac{g}{4} \cdot g^1 = \frac{g}{4} = \frac{9.8}{4}.$$

29. (B) $$g = \frac{GM}{R^2}; g^1 = \frac{G(2M)}{(2R)^2}$$

$$= \frac{GM}{2R^2} = \frac{g}{2} = \frac{9.8}{2} = 4.9 \text{ms}^{-2}.$$

30. (C) Radius at the poles is less than that at the equator. Another reason is the centrifugal force that is experienced at the equator.

32. (A) Mass of a body always remains constant.

34. (B) $$m_1 = \frac{4}{3}\pi R^3 \rho \; ; \; m_2 = \frac{4}{3}\pi (2R)^3 \rho$$

$$F = \frac{Gm_1 m_2}{r^2}, \text{ But } r = 3R$$

$$F = \frac{G \times \frac{4}{3}\pi R^3 \rho \times \frac{4}{3}\pi (2R)^3 \rho}{9r^2}$$

$$= \frac{128}{81} G\pi^2 R^4 \rho^2.$$

35. (B) $\frac{4}{3}$, G & π are constants and in order to keep 'g' as constant, R & ρ should be constant.

$$\Rightarrow R \propto \frac{1}{\rho}.$$

If R is made 3R, ρ becomes $\frac{\rho}{3}$.

36. (D) $$\frac{M_a}{M_m} = \frac{9.8}{1.7} \times \frac{R_e^2}{(0.27R_e)^2}$$

$$= \frac{9.8}{1.7 \times 0.27 \times 0.27} = 79.$$

37. (B) $$mg_m = \frac{4}{9} mg_e = \frac{4}{9} \times 90$$

$$= 40 \text{ kgwt.}$$

38. (A) $$\therefore g_m = \frac{1}{5} g_e = \frac{1}{5} \times 10 = 2 \text{ ms}^{-2}$$

39. (B) $$F^1 = \frac{GMm}{4R^2} = \frac{1}{4} F$$

one –fourth of weight.

40. (C) $\dfrac{g^{1}}{g} = \left(\dfrac{R}{R+h}\right)^{2}$

$\Rightarrow g^{1} = \left(\dfrac{R}{R+h}\right)^{2} g$

$g = \left(\dfrac{6.37 \times 10^{6}}{6.37 \times 10^{6} + 8848}\right)^{2} \times 9.8$

$= 9.77 \ ms^{-2}.$

41. (D) $\dfrac{g^{1}}{g} = \left(\dfrac{R}{R+h}\right)^{2} = \dfrac{4}{9}$

$\Rightarrow \dfrac{g^{1}}{g} = \left(\dfrac{R}{R+\dfrac{R}{2}}\right)^{2} = \dfrac{4}{9}$

$\therefore \ \dfrac{w^{1}}{w} = \dfrac{mg^{1}}{mg} = \dfrac{4}{9}$

$\Rightarrow w^{1} = \dfrac{4}{9} w = \dfrac{4}{9} \times 63 = 28 \ N.$

42. (A) $\dfrac{g^{1}}{g} = \left(\dfrac{R}{R+h}\right)^{2} = \dfrac{3}{5}$

$\Rightarrow h = 1.47 \times 10^{3} \ km$

43. (C) $\dfrac{mg^{1}}{mg} = \left(\dfrac{R}{R+h}\right)^{2} = \dfrac{1}{2}$

$\Rightarrow h = 0.414 \ R.$

44. (A) $g^{1} = g\left(\dfrac{R}{R+h}\right)^{2}$

$g^{1} = \left(\dfrac{R}{R+3R}\right)^{2}$

$g^{1} = \dfrac{g}{16}.$

45. (D) $\dfrac{g^{1}}{g} = \left(\dfrac{R}{R+h}\right)^{2} = \dfrac{64}{100}$

$\Rightarrow \dfrac{R}{R+h} = \dfrac{8}{10} \Rightarrow h = \dfrac{R}{4}$

46. (B) The mass of the body remains same, both on the earth and the moon. But the weight of the body on the moon is $\dfrac{1}{6}$ th that of the weight of earth due to the variation of 'g'.

47. (A) We can measure weight of an object by spring balance and mass of an object by physical balance.

48. (C) 'g' value is greater at poles than at the equator as earth is not a perfect sphere. The radius at the poles is less than the radius at the equator and 'g' and 'R' are inversely related as

$$g = \dfrac{GM}{R^{2}}$$

49. (D) The mass of earth is extremely large as compared to that of apple. So, acceleration of earth is very small than the acceleration of the apple.

50. (A) Since $g \propto \dfrac{1}{R^{2}}$, 'g' would increase when 'R' is decreases.

58. (A) At sea bed upthrust is =
1 atmospheric pressure + hdg.

As the body moves up in the sea, upthrust decreases as pressure in the liquid is *hdg*.

62. (B) Suppose upthrust
= Reaction = R

$R = m(g + a)$

If mass m_1 is detached

$R = (m - m_1)g + (m - m_1)2a$

$m(g + a) = (m - m_1)g + $

$(m - m_1)2a$

$= (m - m_1)(g + 2a)$

$\therefore m_1 = \dfrac{m(g + a)}{g + 2a}$

64. (D) M_e and R are the mass and radius of the earth, g_1 is the acceleration due to gravity.

Taking :

$g_1 = \dfrac{GM_e}{R_1^2}$

& $g_2 = \dfrac{GM_e}{R_2^2}$

Given $R_2 = \left(\dfrac{96}{100}R\right)$

$\therefore \dfrac{g_2}{g_1} = \dfrac{GM}{0.96^2\,R^2} \times \dfrac{R^2}{GM}$

$= \dfrac{1}{0.96 \times 0.96} = 1.08$

$\therefore g_1$ increases by 8%.

65. (A) $V_e = \sqrt{\dfrac{GM}{R}} \qquad M = \dfrac{4}{3}\pi R^3 d$

$\therefore V_e = \sqrt{\dfrac{2G}{R}\dfrac{4}{3}\pi R^3 d}$

$\therefore V_e \,\alpha\, R$

$\dfrac{V_{e1}}{V_{e2}} = \dfrac{R_1}{R_2}$

$V_{e\,planet} = (V_e\,earth) \times 3$

$= 11.2 \times 3 = 33.6\ kms^{-1}$

66. (A) $d_s = \dfrac{M_s}{\frac{4}{3}\pi R_s^3}$

$d_e = \dfrac{M_e}{\frac{4}{3}\pi R_e^3}$

$\therefore \dfrac{d_s}{d_e} = \dfrac{density\ of\ sun}{density\ of\ earth}$

$\dfrac{M_s}{M_e} \cdot \dfrac{R_e^3}{R_s^3} = 330 \times \left(\dfrac{1}{100}\right)^3$

$= 3.3 \times 10^{-4}$

67. (B) $g^1 = g\left(1 - \dfrac{2h}{R}\right)$

$\dfrac{98}{100}g = g\left(1 - \dfrac{2h}{R}\right)$

$\dfrac{98}{100} = 1 - \dfrac{2h}{R}$

$$\therefore \frac{2h}{R} = 1 - \frac{98}{100}$$

$$\frac{2h}{R} = \frac{100 - 98}{100}$$

$$2h = \frac{2}{100} \times R$$

$$h = \frac{2}{100} \times \frac{6400}{2}$$

$$= 64 \text{ km}$$

68. (B)   Orbital velocity

$$V_0 = \sqrt{\frac{GM}{r}} \text{ and escape velocity}$$

$$V_e = \sqrt{\frac{2GM}{R}}$$

Given :

$$V_0 = \frac{1}{2} V_e$$

$$\therefore \sqrt{\frac{GM}{r}} = \left(\sqrt{\frac{GM}{R}} \right) \frac{1}{2}$$

Here R is the radius of the earth and r is the new radius.

$$r = 2R$$

So the satellite will be at a height of 6400 km from the surface of the earth.

69. (A)

$$\text{Density} = \frac{\text{Mass}}{\text{Volume}} = \frac{M}{\frac{4}{3} \pi R^3} \quad \dots\dots (1)$$

$$g = \frac{GM}{R^2}$$

$$\therefore M = \frac{gR^2}{G}$$

substituting this is (1)

$$\text{Density} = \frac{gR^2}{G} \Big/ \frac{4}{3} \pi R^3 = 3g/4\pi RG$$

75. (C)   (i) Water displaced × density of water

= weight of ship (floating body)

(ii) Liquid displaced × density of liquid

= weight of ship (floating body)

$$\therefore \frac{2}{3} \times d_w = \frac{1}{3} \times d_l \qquad \text{i.e. } \frac{2}{3} = \frac{1}{3} d_l$$

$$\therefore d_l = 2$$

✦ ✦ ✦

Chapter 4

Work, Energy & Power

Synopsis

1. Work

Work is said to be done only when a force displaces an object.

(a) The work done W by a force F on an object is given by :

$$W = Fs \cos \theta$$

where 's' is the displacement of the object and θ is the angle between the force and displacement.

(b) If the displacement is along the force then $\theta = 0$ & $\cos \theta = 1$, so

$$W = Fs$$

If the displacement is opposite to the force then $\theta = 180^0$ & $\cos \theta = -1$, so

$$W = -Fs$$

(c) If the displacement is perpendicular to the force, then the work done is zero ($\theta = 90^0$, $\cos \theta = 0$).

2. Energy

The capacity to do work is called energy.

The energy possessed by an object by virtue of its motion is called *kinetic energy.*

The energy possessed by an object by virtue of its position or shape is called *potential energy.*

The sum of kinetic energy and potential energy of an object is called *mechanical energy.*

If a light body and a heavy body have the same momentum, the lighter body will have more K.E. since

$$K.E. \propto \frac{1}{m}.$$

A body can have energy without momentum.

For example vector momenta of all particles in a gas or liquid may be zero, but they have average K.E.

A body cannot have momentum without energy.

If a rocket explodes in its mid journey, its momentum remains unaffected, but its total K.E. increases.

Exchange of energy is maximum during elastic collisions when the masses are same.

3. Gravitational potential energy

The potential energy of an object due to its height above the earth's surface is called its gravitational potential energy.

4. Elastic potential energy

A stretched or compressed object such as a spring or a rubber band has elastic potential energy.

5. Relation between work and energy

Work done by external forces on a system is equal to the increase in the energy of the system.

6. Principle of conservation of energy

Energy can neither be produced nor destroyed. It can only be changed from one form to another.

7. Power

Work done per unit time is called power. Watt is the unit of power.

1 Horse Power = 746 W

8. Mathematical equations

Work	$W = Fs \cos\theta$	'F' Force, 's' is displacement and 'θ' is the angle between them.
Gravitational Potential Energy (P.E.)	$U = mgh$	'm' is the mass of the body, 'g' is the acceleration due to gravity, 'h' is the height above the earth's surface.
Kinetic Energy (K.E)	$K.E. = \dfrac{1}{2}mv^2$ or $E_K = \dfrac{p^2}{2m}$	'm' is the mass of the body and 'v' is the velocity. 'p' is the momentum, E_K is the kinetic energy.
Power	$P = W/t$	'W' is the work done and 't' is the time taken by the body.

9. Thermal energy of the sea

The sea has not only P.E. in its tidal waters. It also has heat energy in its water molecules. The sun's energy is trapped by the water of the ocean.

Multiple Choice Questions

1. Find the work done by a force of 5N to displace a book through 20 cm along the direction of the push.

    (A) 3.0 J   (B) 5.0 J

    (C) 1.0 J   (D) 4.0 J

2. A ball of mass 1 kg thrown upwards reaches a maximum height of 5.0 m. Calculate the work done by the force of gravity during this vertical displacement.

    (A) – 59 J   (B) –49 J

    (C) – 30 J   (D) –48 J

3. A person pulls a body on a horizontal surface by applying a force of 5.0 N at an angle of 30^0 with the horizontal. Find the work done by this force in displacing the body through 2.0 m.

    (A) $5\sqrt{3}$ J   (B) $6\sqrt{2}$ J

    (C) $7\sqrt{3}$ J   (D) $4\sqrt{3}$ J

4. An object of mass 1 kg is raised through a height 'h'. Its potential energy is increased by 1 J. Find the height 'h'.

    (A) 0.102 m   (B) 0.105 m

    (C) 0.130 m   (D) 0.110 m

5. The kinetic energy of a ball of mass 200 g moving at a speed of 20 cm/s is:

    (A) 0.005 J   (B) 0.004 J

    (C) 0.001 J   (D) 0.007 J

6. The work done by a student in lifting a 0.5 kg book from the ground and keeping it on a shelf of height 1.5 m is :

    (A) 8.30 J   (B) 7.35 J

    (C) 5.40 J   (D) 6.45 J

7. A block of mass 1 kg slides down on an inclined plane of inclination 30^0. Find the work done by the weight of the block as it slides through 50 cm.

(A) 3.45 J   (B) 5.30 J

(C) 2.45 J   (D) 3.50 J

8. A force of 10 N displaces an object through 20 cm and does work of 1 J in the process. Find the angle between the force and displacement.

(A) $\theta = 60^0$ (B) $\theta = 30^0$

(C) $\theta = 35^0$ (D) $\theta = 45^0$

9. A body of mass 0.5 kg is taken to a height R_e above the earth's surface, where R_e is the radius of the earth. If the body is now raised through a height of 2 m, what is the increase in its potential energy?

(A) 2.45 J   (B) 5.45 J

(C) 6.35 J   (D) 8.30 J

10. A ball is dropped from a height 'h'. When it reaches the ground, its velocity is 40 m/s. Find the height?

(A) 71.6 m

(B) 32.5 m

(C) 81.6 m

(D) 51.6 m

11. How much time will it take to perform 440 J of work at a rate of 11 W?

(A) 50 s   (B) 40 s

(C) 30 s   (D) 20 s

12. When a stone tied to a string is whirled in a circle, the work done on it by the string is :

(A) positive   (B) negative

(C) zero   (D) undefined

13. A man with a box on his head is climbing up a ladder. The work done by the man on the box is :

(A) positive

(B) negative

(C) zero

(D) undefined

14. When a body rolls down on an inclined plane, it has :

(A) only kinetic energy

(B) only potential energy

(C) both kinetic and potential energy

(D) neither kinetic nor potential energy

15. The kinetic energy of a body depends

(A) on its mass only

(B) on its speed only

(C) on its mass as well as the speed

(D) neither on its mass nor the speed

16. A ball is thrown upwards from a point A. It reaches up to a highest point B and returns. Here :

(A) Kinetic energy at A = kinetic energy at B

(B) Potential energy at A = potential energy at B

(C) Potential energy at B = kinetic energy at B

(D) Potential energy at B = kinetic energy at A

17. Two bodies of unequal masses are dropped from a cliff. At any instant, they have equal :

   (A) momentum

   (B) acceleration

   (C) potential energy

   (D) kinetic energy

18. When the speed of a particle is doubled, its kinetic energy :

   (A) remains the same

   (B) gets doubled

   (C) becomes half

   (D) becomes four times

19. When the speed of a particle is doubled, the ratio of its kinetic energy to its momentum :

   (A) remains the same

   (B) gets doubled

   (C) becomes half

   (D) becomes four times

20. A person A does 500 J work in 10 minutes and another person B does 600 J of work in 20 minutes. Let the power delivered by A and B be P_1 and P_2 respectively, then :

   (A) $P_1 = P_2$

   (B) $P_1 > P_2$

   (C) $P_1 < P_2$

   (D) P_1 and P_2 are undefined

21. By what factor does the kinetic energy of a particle increase if the velocity is increased by a factor of three ?

   (A) 6   (B) 7

   (C) 8   (D) 9

22. The mass of a ball A is twice the mass of another ball B. The ball A moves at half the speed of the ball B. The ratio of the kinetic energy of A to that of B is :

   (A) $\frac{3}{2}$ (B) $\frac{1}{2}$

   (C) $\frac{5}{2}$ (D) $\frac{4}{2}$

23. A block is thrown upwards with a kinetic energy 1 J. If it goes up to a maximum height of 1 m, then the mass of the block is :

   (A) 110 g   (B) 100 g

   (C) 105 g   (D) 104 g

24. Two persons do the same amount of work, one in 10 s and the other in 20 s. Find the ratio of the power used by the first person to that by the second person.

   (A) 6   (B) 2

   (C) 5   (D) 4

25. Calculate the work done in raising a stone of mass 5 kg and specific gravity 3 lying at the bed of a lake through a height of 5 metre.

   (A) 133.3 J   (B) 173.3 J

   (C) 163.3 J   (D) 143.3 J

26. Calculate the velocity of the bob of a simple pendulum at its mean position if it is able to rise to a vertical height of 10 cm.

   (Given : g = 980 cms^{-2})

   (A) 1.40 ms^{-1} (B) 2.54 ms^{-1}

   (C) 3.43 ms^{-1} (D) 5.35 ms^{-1}

27. A one kilowatt motor pumps out water from a well 10 metres deep. Calculate the quantity of water pumped out per second.

(A) 10.204 g   (B) 15.302 g

(C) 11.201 g   (D) 16.204 g

28. The heart of a man pumps 4 litres of blood per minute at a pressure of 130 mm of mercury. If the density of mercury is 13.6 gcm^{-3}, then calculate the power of the heart.

(A) 1.144 W   (B) 2.145 W

(C) 1.155 W   (D) 3.155 W

29. Which of the following equations show the correct relationship between mass, momentum and kinetic energy?

(A) $P = \sqrt{2mE_k}$

(B) $P = \sqrt{5mE_k}$

(C) $P = \sqrt{4mE_k}$

(D) $P = \sqrt{6mE_k}$

30. A light body and a heavy body have the same kinetic energy. Which one will have a greater momentum?

(A) Lighter body

(B) Heavier body

(C) Both bodies have same momentum

(D) None of the above

31. The momentum of a body is doubled. What is the percentage increase in kinetic energy?

(A) 500%   (B) 300%

(C) 200%   (D) 600%

32. Two bodies of masses M and 4 M are moving with equal kinetic energies. What is the ratio of their linear momenta ?

(A) $\dfrac{2}{1}$ (B) $\dfrac{1}{4}$

(C) $\dfrac{1}{2}$ (D) $\dfrac{1}{6}$

33. A body falling from a height of 10 m rebounds from a hard floor. It loses 20% of energy in the impact. What is the height to which it would rise after the impact ?

(A) 7 m   (B) 5 m

(C) 8 m   (D) 6 m

34. Two masses, one 'n' times as heavy as the other, have equal kinetic energy. What is the ratio of their momenta ?

(A) $1 : \sqrt{n}$ (B) $\sqrt{n} : 1$

(C) $1 : n$ (D) $n : 1$

35. The momentum of a body is numerically equal to the kinetic energy of the body. What is the velocity of the body?

(A) $\dfrac{1}{\sqrt{2}}$ units   (B) 2 units

(C) $\dfrac{1}{\sqrt{3}}$ units   (D) $\sqrt{3}$ units

36. A force of 5 N acts on an object. The displacement is perpendicular to the direction of the force. Calculate the work done.

(A) 5 J   (B) 1 J

(C) 100 J   (D) 0

37. The kinetic energy of a body is increased by 21%. What is the percentage increase in the linear momentum of the body?

(A) 20%   (B) 10%

(C) 30%   (D) 5%

38. A lorry and a car with the same kinetic energy are brought to rest by the application of brakes which provide equal retarding forces. Which of them will come to rest in a shorter distance ?

(A) Lorry

(B) Car

(C) Both will stop at the same distance

(D) None of these

39. What should be the angle between the force and displacement for maximum work ?

(A) 0^0 (B) 30^0

(C) 60^0 (D) 90^0

40. A car is accelerated from 10 ms^{-1} to 15 ms^{-1}. The increase in kinetic energy is E_{k1}. Again, the car is accelerated from 15 ms^{-1} to 20 ms^{-1}. The increase in kinetic energy is now E_{k2}. What is the ratio of $\dfrac{E_{k1}}{E_{k2}}$?

(A) 0.5

(B) 0.7

(C) 0.1

(D) 0.4

41. A body A is 'n' times heavier than an another body B. They are dropped from same height. What is the ratio of their momenta just before they hit the ground?

(A) $\dfrac{\sqrt{n}}{1}$ (B) $\dfrac{1}{\sqrt{n}}$

(C) $\dfrac{1}{n}$ (D) $\dfrac{n}{1}$

42. The work done upon a body is :

(A) a vector quantity

(B) a scalar quantity

(C) always positive

(D) always negative

43. Match the following and select the correct answer :

a. Force	1. kgm^2s^{-2}
b. Work	2. $kgms^{-1}$
c. Momentum	3. kgm^2s^{-3}
d. Power	4. $kgms^{-2}$

(A) a-1, b-2, c-3, d-4

(B) a-2, b-3, c-4, d-1

(C) a-4, b-1, c-2, d-3

(D) a-4, b-2, c-3, d-1

44. Study the given statements P & Q and select the correct answer.

P. *Gas must be cooled considerably irrespective of pressure on it so that it can be liquified.*

Q. *Gas can be liquified under a temperature less than its critical temperature and under pressure more than its critical pressure*

(A) Both P and Q are true and Q explains P

(B) Both P and Q are true but Q does not explain P

(C) Only P is true

(D) P is false but Q is true

45. A block of mass 20 kg is pulled over a smooth inclined plane through 3 m as shown in the figure.

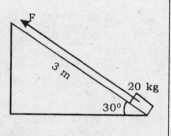

The plane makes an angle of 30° with the base. Force applied is parallel to the base. Assuming that no energy is lost otherwise, what is the gain in the P.E. of the block ? (g = 10 ms⁻²)

(A) 30 J   (B) 20 J

(C) 300 J   (D) 600 J

46. If a graph between P.E. of the body in relation to the height through which it falls freely is plotted, it may be noted that the total energy remains the same. Which of the following graphs shows this relation correctly?

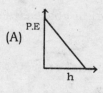

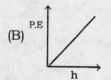

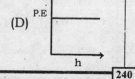

47. A graph of the total energy, (P.E + K.E.) of a freely falling body from a height is plotted. Which of the following is the best approximation?

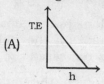

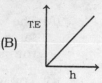

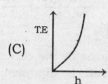

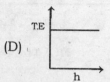

48. When a person is climbing a hill, he has :

(A) only P.E   (B) only K.E

(C) both A and B   (D) none of these

49. A stone is thrown up vertically. What happens to its P.E. during its motion during its upward journey ?

(A) Decreases

(B) Increases till it becomes maximum

(C) First decreases and then increases

(D) First increases and then decreases

50. A particle is projected vertically upwards. Variation of the magnitude of K.E. with time 't' is given by :

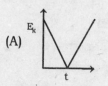

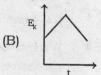

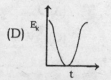

51. Which of the following statements is correct regarding the relation between centripetal force and radius of the circular path ?

(A) The work done by the centripetal force increases if the radius of the path is increased

(B) The work done by the centripetal force decreases by decreasing the radius

(C) The work done by the centripetal force increases by decreasing the radius

(D) The work done is always zero

52. Rectangular components of force is applied to move a body. One of the components is 30N. What should be the other component to obtain a resultant force of 50N ?

(A) 30 N

(B) 40 N

(C) 50 N

(D) 90 N

53. A photocell converts light energy into :

(A) photon energy

(B) electrical energy

(C) magnetic energy

(D) heat energy

54. Which of the following is not a measure cf energy?

(A) Js   (B) Ws

(C) kWh   (D) erg

55. A bird flying in the sky has :

(A) only K.E.

(B) only P.E.

(C) both A and B

(D) none of these

56. When the momentum of a body is increased by 100%, its K.E. increases by :

(A) 100%   (B) 200%

(C) 300%   (D) 400%

57. A girl of mass 40 kg climbs 50 stairs of average height 20 cm each in 50 s. The power of the girl is :
$(g = 10ms^{-2})$

(A) 50 W

(B) 50 × 20 W

(C) 80 W

(D) 50 × 20 × 2W

58. A body is allowed to roll down a hill, it will have :

(A) only K.E

(B) only P.E.

(C) both A and B

(D) data is insufficient

59. A stretched spring possesses :

(A) K.E.

(B) elastic potential energy

(C) electrical energy

(D) magnetic energy

60. A body at rest can have :

(A) speed

(B) velocity

(C) momentum

(D) energy

61. Ns can be identified with :

(A) J   (B) kg ms^{-1}

(C) kg ms^{-2} (D) Nms

62. In which of the following cases, is the work done maximum ?

(A)

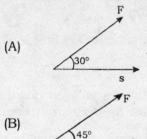

(B)

(C)

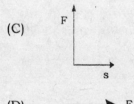

(D)   → F

     s

63. A boy lifts a book of known weight from the surface of a table and then keeps it back. To calculate the work done, he needs to know :

(A) the mass of the book

(B) the height

(C) the cost of the book

(D) the time taken by him

64. Two bodies of unequal masses possess the same momentum. The K.E. of the heavier mass will be _____ the K.E. of the lighter mass.

(A) same as

(B) greater than

(C) less than

(D) much greater than

65. Two bodies of unequal masses possess the same K.E. Then the heavier mass will have :

(A) greater momentum

(B) less momentum

(C) the same momentum

(D) greater speed

66. In a factory due to a sudden strike the work usually done in a day took a longer time. Then :

(A) power increases

(B) power decreases

(C) energy increases

(D) energy decreases

67. A boy has four options to move a body through 3m as indicated. In which case is maximum work done ?

(A) Push over an inclined plane

(B) Lift vertically upwards

(C) Push over smooth rollers

(D) Push on a plane horizontal surface

68. No work is done when an object moves :

(A) at an angle 90° to the direction of force

(B) at an angle opposite to the direction of force

(C) at any angle to the direction of force

(D) along the direction of force

69. Based on the given figure study the following statements and select the correct answer :

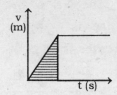

P. The shaded portion represents the distance covered in the given time.

Q. The slope at any given point gives inverse of displacement.

(A) Both P & Q are correct

(B) P is correct but Q is not the correct explanation of P.

(C) P is correct but Q is wrong.

(D) P is wrong but Q is correct

70. Study the following statements and select the correct answer :

P. Suppose we drill a hole along the diameter of the earth and drop an object. As it reaches the centre of the earth, it has only mass but no weight

Q. 'g' decreases with depth and vanishes at the centre of the earth

(A) Both P and Q are correct

(B) P is correct and Q is wrong

(C) P is wrong but Q is correct

(D) Both P and Q are wrong

71. Water is falling at the rate of 1000 kg per second. The height of the fall is about 100 m. The potential energy of water when it falls on the blades will be conveyed to them and P.E. is converted into K.E of blades. Take the value of 'g' as 10 ms^{-2}. Estimate the power that could be generated, if energy is not lost otherwise.

(A) 10 W   (B) 100 W

(C) 10^6 W   (D) 10^5 W

72. Study the following statements and select the correct answer.

P. A body can have energy without momentum

Q. Momentum of a body has nothing to contribute to energy

(A) P and Q are true and Q explains P

(B) P and Q are true but Q does not explain P

(C) P is true but Q is false

(D) P is false but Q is true

73. Study the statements given below and select the correct answer.

P. A body can have momentum without energy.

Q. Body must be in motion to contribute to energy and momentum

(A) P and Q are correct and R explains P

(B) P and Q are correct but Q does not support P

(C) P is true and Q false

(D) P is false and Q is true

74. Study the statements given below and select the correct answer.

P. If a rocket explodes in mid air, its K.E increases

Q. Chemical energy of the fuel provides additional K.E to the fragments

(A) P and Q are true and Q explains P

(B) P and Q are true but Q does not explain P

(C) P is true but Q is false

(D) P is false but Q is true

75. In the given graph the work done during the first 5 seconds is :

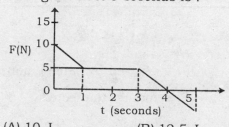

(A) 10 J   (B) 12.5 J

(C) 15 J   (D) 17.5 J

76. An object is taken from one point to another point on a rough table in different directions.
Study the statements given below and select the correct answer :

P. *Work done in moving a body from one point to the other does not depend on the direction in which the body is moved and so the amount of work done remains the same, irrespective of the nature of path.*

Q. *The net work done against the frictional force in moving a body around depends on the distance.*

(A) Both P and Q are correct and Q is the correct explanation of P

(B) Both P and Q are correct but Q is not the correct explanation of P

(C) P is true and but Q is false

(D) P is false but Q is true

77. A block of wood of mass 250 g is moving at a speed of 4m/s. Its K.E in J is :

(A) 4 J

(B) 2 J

(C) 1 J

(D) 10 J

78. A steam engine has an efficiency of 20%. It is given an energy of 1000 cal. per minute. What is the actual work done by it in joules and in calories ?

(A) 100 cal, 800 J

(B) 200cal, 873 J

(C) 10 cal, 80 J

(D) 100 cal, 100 J

79. Before the discovery of Einstein's mass-energy relationship, mass and energy were considered separate physical quantities. But Einstein proved that mass and energy are inter-convertible.
Study the following statements and select the correct answer.

P. *Mass - energy relationship is given by : $E = mc^2$*

Q. *Mass itself is a measure of energy at higher speeds especially mass contributes to energy a lot*

(A) P and Q are correct and Q is a satisfactory explanation of P

(B) P and Q are correct but Q is not a satisfactory explanation of P

(C) P is correct and Q is false

(D) P is false and Q is correct

80. A body of mass 'm' is taken up an inclined plane and is allowed to slide down to the bottom as shown in the figure.

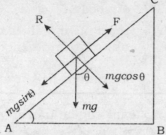

Study the following statements and select the correct answer.

P. *The work done by the gravitational force for the up journey and down journey put together is zero*

Q. *Gravitational force is a non-conservative force*

(A) P and Q are true and Q is a correct explanation of P

(B) P and Q are true and Q is not a correct explanation of P

(C) P is true and Q is false

(D) P is false and Q is true

81. If momentum of a body is increased by 10%, its K.E. :

(A) decreases

(B) increased by same amount

(C) remains unaffected

(D) increases by 1.21 times

Answers

1. C	2. B	3. A	4. A	5. B	6. B	7. C	8. A	9. A	10. C
11. B	12. C	13. A	14. C	15. C	16. D	17. B	18. D	19. B	20. B
21. D	22. B	23. B	24. B	25. C	26. A	27. A	28. C	29. A	30. B
31. B	32. C	33. C	34. B	35. B	36. D	37. B	38. C	39. A	40. B
41. D	42. B	43. C	44. D	45. C	46. A	47. D	48. C	49. B	50. A
51. D	52. B	53. B	54. A	55. C	56. C	57. C	58. C	59. B	60. D
61. B	62. D	63. B	64. C	65. A	66. B	67. B	68. A	69. C	70. A
71. C	72. C	73. D	74. A	75. D	76. D	77. B	78. B	79. A	80. C
81. D									

Explanatory Answers

1. (C) $W = 5 \times 0.2 \times \cos 0^0 = 1$ J

($\theta = 0^0$ since 'F' and 's' are in the same direction)

2. (B) $W = Fs \cos\theta = mgd \cos\theta$

$= 1 \times 9.8 \times 5 \times \cos 180^0$

$= -49$ J.

($\theta = 180^0$ since F and 's' are in the opposite direction)

3. (A) $W = 5 \times 2 \times \cos 30^0 = 10 \times \dfrac{\sqrt{3}}{2}$

$= 5\sqrt{3}$ J.

4. (A) $mgh = 1$ J $\Rightarrow 1 \times 9.8 \times h = 1$

$\Rightarrow h = \dfrac{1}{9.8} = 0.102$ m.

5. (B) $K.E. = \dfrac{1}{2} \times 0.2 \times 0.2 \times 0.2$

$= 0.004$ J.

6. (B) $W = P.E. = 0.5 \times 9.8 \times 1.5$

$= 4.9 \times 1.5 = 7.35$ J.

7. (C) $W = 1 \times 9.8 \times \sin 30^0 \times 0.5$

$= \dfrac{9.8}{4} = 2.45$ J.

8. (A) $W = Fs \cos \theta$

$\Rightarrow 1 = 10 \times 0.2 \times \cos \theta$

$\Rightarrow \cos \theta = \dfrac{1}{2}, (\theta = 60^0)$

9. (A) $g^l = g\left(\dfrac{R_e}{R_e + R_e}\right)^2 = \dfrac{g}{4}$

$= 2.45$ ms^{-2}

$\therefore$ Increase in P.E. $= mg^l h$

$= 0.5 \times 2.45 \times 2 = 2.45$ J.

10. (C) $mgH = \dfrac{1}{2} mv^2 \Rightarrow H = \dfrac{v^2}{2g}$

$= \dfrac{40 \times 40}{2 \times 9.8} = 81.6$

11. (B) $11 = \dfrac{440}{t} \Rightarrow t = \dfrac{440}{11} = 40$ sec.

12. (C) Work done by the centripetal force is zero.

13. (A) Since the force and the displacement are in the same direction angle between them is 0^0. $W = Fs \cos \theta = Fs \cos 0^0$

$= Fs$ (since $\cos 0^0 = 1$)

14. (C) As the body rolls down on an inclined plane from a certain height, it acquires both PE and K.E.

15. (C) $KE = \dfrac{1}{2} mv^2$ and hence KE depends on both mass and speed of a body.

16. (D) From point A, the body is thrown upwards and hence it acquires K.E. and when it reaches the maximum height at point B, it acquires P.E.

17. (B) Both the bodies of different masses fall due to the same amount of acceleration due to gravity.

18. (D) $KE = \dfrac{1}{2} mv^2$

$\Rightarrow E \propto v^2 \Rightarrow \dfrac{E_1}{E_2} = \left(\dfrac{v^1}{v}\right)^2$

$\left(\dfrac{2v}{v}\right)^2 = 4$

$\therefore E^1 = 4E$.

19. (B) $KE = \dfrac{1}{2} mv^2$

$\Rightarrow E^1 = \dfrac{1}{2} m \times (2v)^2 = 4 \times \dfrac{1}{2} mv^2$

$= 4E$.

$p = mv \Rightarrow p^1 = m \times 2v$

$\Rightarrow p^1 = 2mv = 2p$

$\therefore \dfrac{E^1}{p^1} = \dfrac{4E}{2p} = 2\left(\dfrac{E}{p}\right) \Rightarrow$ ratio of

K.E. to momentum becomes doubled.

20. (B) $P_1 = \dfrac{W_1}{t_1} = \dfrac{500}{10 \times 60} = \dfrac{5}{6}$ watt

= 0.83 watt

$$P_2 = \frac{W_2}{t_2} = \frac{600}{20 \times 60} = \frac{1}{2} \text{ watt}$$

= 0.5 watt.

21. (D) K.E., $E = \frac{1}{2}mv^2$

$$E^1 = \frac{1}{2}m \times (mv)^2 = 9\left(\frac{1}{2}mv^2\right)$$

= 9 E.

∴ kinetic energy increases by a factor of 9 if the speed increases by a factor of three.

22. (B) $\dfrac{E_A}{E_B} = \dfrac{\frac{1}{2}m_A v_A^2}{\frac{1}{2}m_B v_B^2} = \left(\dfrac{m_A}{m_B}\right)\left(\dfrac{v_A}{v_B}\right)^2$

$$= \frac{1}{2}$$

$$\left(\text{since } m_A = 2m_B \ \& \ V_A = \frac{1}{2}V_B\right)$$

23. (B) $1 = mgh \Rightarrow m = \dfrac{1}{gh}$

$$\Rightarrow m = \frac{1}{9.8 \times 1} = \frac{1}{9.8} \text{ kg}$$

$$\frac{1000}{9.8} = 102 \text{ gm}.$$

24. (B) $\dfrac{P_1}{P_2} = \dfrac{t_2}{t_1} = \dfrac{20}{10} = 2$

25. (C) $3 = \dfrac{5}{5 - w_2}$

$$\Rightarrow 5 - w_2 = \frac{5}{3} \Rightarrow w_2 = \frac{10}{3} \text{ kg wt.}$$

∴ force $= \dfrac{10}{3}$ kgwt

$$= \frac{10}{3} \times 9.8 = \frac{98}{3} N$$

$$W = F \times d = \frac{98}{3} \times 5 = 163.3 \text{ J}.$$

26. (A) $mgh = \dfrac{1}{2}mv^2 \Rightarrow v = \sqrt{2gh}$

$$= \sqrt{2 \times 980 \times 10} = \sqrt{19600}$$

$$= 140 \text{ cms}^{-1} = 1.4 \text{ ms}^{-1}.$$

27. (A) $\dfrac{m}{t} = \dfrac{P}{gh} = \dfrac{1000}{9.8 \times 10}$

$$= \frac{1000}{98} = 10.204 \text{ gm}.$$

28. (C)

$$P = \frac{130 \times 10^{-3} \times 13.6 \times 10^{+3} \times 9.8 \times 4 \times 10^{-3}}{60}$$

$$= 1.155 \text{ W}$$

29. (A) $E_k = \dfrac{1}{2}mv^2 = \dfrac{m^2 v^2}{2m} = \dfrac{p^2}{2m}$

$$\Rightarrow p = \sqrt{2mE_k}$$

$$p = \sqrt{2mE_k} \Rightarrow mE_k = \text{constant}$$

(since P is constant)

$$\Rightarrow E_k \propto \frac{1}{m}$$

∴ Light body has greater KE.

30. (B) $p = \sqrt{2mE_k} \Rightarrow p \propto \sqrt{m}$

(Since E_k = const.)

So, the heavy body will have greater momentum.

31. (B)

$\dfrac{E_2 - E_1}{E_1} \times 100\% = \dfrac{P_2^2 - P_1^2}{P_1^2} \times 100\%$

$= \dfrac{3P^2}{P^2} \times 100\% = 300\%$

32. (C) $\dfrac{p_1}{p_2} = \sqrt{\dfrac{m_1}{m_2}} \Rightarrow \dfrac{p_1}{p_2} = \sqrt{\dfrac{m}{4m}} = \dfrac{1}{2}$

33. (C) 80% of mgh = mgh^1

$\Rightarrow \dfrac{80}{100} \times mgh = mgh^1$

$\Rightarrow h^1 = \dfrac{8}{10} \times 10 = 8\,m.$

34. (B) $\dfrac{p_1}{p_2} = \dfrac{\sqrt{nm}}{\sqrt{m}} = \dfrac{\sqrt{n}}{1}$

35. (B) $mv = \dfrac{1}{2}mv^2 \Rightarrow v = 2$ units

36. (D) Since the displacement is in the perpendicular direction, the work done by the force will be zero.

37. (B) $\dfrac{p_2 - p_1}{p_1} \times 100\%$

$= \dfrac{\sqrt{121} - \sqrt{100}}{\sqrt{100}} \times 100\%$

$\dfrac{p_2 - p_1}{p_1} \times 100\% = \dfrac{1}{10} \times 100 = 10\%$

38. (C) Loss of K.E. = work done = Fs

Both the retarding force F and KE are the same. So, both the lorry and car would come to rest in the same distance.

39. (A) When $\theta = 0^0$,

$\cos\theta$ is maximum.

So, W is maximum at $\theta = 0^0$

40. (B) $\dfrac{E_{k1}}{E_{k2}} = \dfrac{125}{175} = \dfrac{5}{7} = 0.7$

41. (D) $\dfrac{p_A}{p_B} = \dfrac{m_A v_A}{m_B v_B} = \dfrac{nm_B v_A}{m_B v_A} = \dfrac{n}{1}$

(since $m_A = 2m_B$ & $v_A = v_B$)

42. (B) Work is a scalar quantity

W = F.s

45. (C) $W = F\sin\theta \times s$

$= mg\sin\theta \times s$

$= 20\,kg \times 10\,ms^{-2} \times 3\sin 30^0$

$= 20 \times 10 \times 3 \times \dfrac{1}{2}$

$= 300\,J$

46. (A) As the body falls down P.E goes on decreasing.

47. (D) Total energy remains the same

51. (D) Force is perpendicular to displacement

$W = F \times \cos 90 = 0$

52. (B) Let the unknown component be 'x'.

$\therefore 50^2 = 30^2 + x^2$

$x^2 = 2500 - 900$

$$x^2 = 1600$$

$$x = \sqrt{1600}$$

$$\therefore x = 40N$$

56. (C) $K.E. = \dfrac{p^2}{2m}$

p increase by 100%

i.e. 2p

$$K.E. = \dfrac{(2p)^2}{2m}$$

$$K.E. = \dfrac{p^2}{2m} \times 4$$

∴ K.E. increases by 300%.

57. (C) W = mgh

$= 40 \text{ kg} \times 10 \text{ ms}^{-2} \times .2 \times 50 J$

$$P = \dfrac{W}{t} = \dfrac{40 \times 10 \times 0.2 \times 50}{50}$$

= 80 W

60. (D) By virtue of its height it mg have energy

61. (B) Ns is F × time

Thus momentum

units of momentum = kg ms^{-1}

62. (D) Work will be maximum if angle between F and s is zero.

63. (B) P.E. is involved, mass is known. So he requires height.

64. (C) Momentum of heavy body MV

Momentum of height body mv

The momenta are equal

MV = mv

$$\therefore \dfrac{M}{m} = \dfrac{v}{V}$$

Masses are in the inverse ratio of velocities.

So heavier mass will possesses less K.E.

66. (B) $P = \dfrac{w}{t}$

greater t less is P

68. (A) $W = F.S = F \cos\theta .S$

$= F \cos 90 \; S = 0$

71. (C) P.E = mgh = 1000 × 10 × 10

$$\text{Power} = \dfrac{10^6}{1} = 10^6 \text{ W}$$

75. (D) Hint : find area of the graph.
Work done during last second is negative.

77. (B) $K = \dfrac{1}{2} mv^2$

$= \dfrac{1}{2} \times 0.25 \times 16$

= 2 J

78. (B) $\dfrac{20}{100} = \dfrac{W}{1000} = 200$ cal

$200 \times 4.18 = 873$ J

❖ ❖ ❖

Chapter 5

Sound

Synopsis

1. Sound is a form of energy.

2. Waves may be mechanical or electromagnetic.

3. Mechanical waves are produced by a disturbance in the material medium.

4. Electromagnetic waves consist of disturbances in the form of electric and magnetic forces.

5. Sound is a wave motion produced by a vibrating source. A medium is necessary for its propagation as it is a mechanical wave.

6. Sound cannot travel in vacuum.

7. The vibration source produces compression and rarefaction pulses, which travel one after the other in the medium. *Sound waves are longitudinal waves.*

Compression pulses correspond to the regions of high density and pressure, where as rarefaction pulses correspond to the regions of low density and pressure in the medium.

The minimum distance at which the density of the medium repeats its value regularly is called the wavelength (λ) of the wave.

The time needed to complete one oscillation is called the time period (T). The number of oscillations per unit time is called frequency. Frequency is denoted by 'υ', the Greek letter 'Nu'. It is also denoted by 'f' or 'n'.

$$f = \frac{1}{T}$$

The speed (υ), frequency and wavelength of a sound wave are related by the equation :

$$\upsilon = f\lambda$$

8. In a wave motion, particles of the medium move up and down from their mean position for a while, but they suffer no permanent displacement.

9. *Wave Motion* : When a disturbance produced in one part of a medium travels to another part without involving the transfer of any material with it, the motion of the disturbance is called wave motion. The disturbance itself is called a wave.

A wave does not transfer material from one place to the other, but it transfers energy wherever it goes.

10. Progressive waves are of two types *transverse waves* and *longitudinal waves.*

11. *Longitudinal and transverse waves* : If the particles of a medium move along the direction of motion of the wave, the wave is called a

longitudinal wave. On the other hand, if the particles of the medium move perpendicular to the direction of the motion of the wave, the wave is called a *transverse wave*.

12. *Mechanical waves* : Waves which need a material medium to propagate are called mechanical waves.

Non-mechanical waves do not need a medium to propagate. A mechanical wave generally has a velocity smaller than that of non-mechanical waves. Water waves, waves on slinky, etc., are mechanical waves. Electromagnetic radiation like light, radio, etc., are non-mechanical waves.

13. *Wave pulse* : A disturbance is called a wave pulse if it is confined to a small part of the medium at any given time.

14. *Periodic wave* : A wave is called a periodic wave, if the particles of the medium carrying the wave repeat their motion after fixed intervals of time.

At any given time, the state of each particle in a periodic wave is the same as that of another at a fixed separation.

15. *Wave quantity* : In each wave, a particular quantity, such as the displacement of a particle, has different values at different positions at a given time. Also, at a given position, this quantity changes its value as time passes. Such a quantity is called the wave quantity.

16. *Crests and troughs* : A portion of the medium, where the wave quantity has a value larger than its normal value is called a crest. A portion where it has a value smaller than the normal value is called a trough.

17. *Mathematical equations involving wavelength, time period, frequency and amplitude.*

$$\text{(i)} \quad f = \frac{1}{T}$$

$$\text{(ii)} \quad \lambda = vT$$

$$\text{(iii)} \quad v = f\lambda$$

Where f is the frequency, T is the time period, λ is the wavelength and v is the velocity of the wave.

18. *Reflection of sound* : When sound is reflected, the direction in which the sound is incident and reflected make equal angles with the normal to the reflecting surface and all the three lie in the same plane.

Hard surfaces reflect sound better than the soft ones. Reflection of sound has many applications such as stethoscope, horns, megaphones, sonar ultrasonography, etc.

If the sound and its reflection from a surface arrive at an interval of $1/15^{th}$ of a second or more, we hear an echo.

19. *Refraction of sound* : During night, distant sounds such as that of traffic are often louder than during the day due to refraction of sound.

20. *Diffraction and Interference* : The wavelengths of audible range varies from 1.5 cm to 15 m. If obstacles of similar dimensions are in the path of sound, diffraction of sound takes place.

21. *Resonance* : Resonance is a particular case of forced vibrations. When a

body 'A' is vibrating near another body 'B' of the same natural frequency, 'B', starts vibrating on its own. 'B' is said to vibrate in resonance (is in tune) with 'A'.

22. *Doppler's effect* : The apparent frequency of a source depends on the relative velocity between the source and the observer.

23. *Characteristics of sound* :

Pitch - Depends on frequency. Higher the frequency, higher is the pitch.

Loudness - Depends on amplitude. More the amplitude, more is the loudness.

Quality - Quality depends on the combination of harmonics produced by different instruments.

24. *Beats* - When two notes, slightly different in their pitch, are sounded together, the loudness rises and falls at regular intervals. These are known as beats.

Application of beats : Determination of frequency, tuning of musical instruments, determination of the direction of motion of stars with respect to earth, determination of the speed of a submarine, Radar, thief alarms, etc.

25. *Musical instruments* : The sound produced by a musical instrument depends on many factors like material, size, shape, the way it is played, etc.

26. *Ultrasound* : Two properties of ultrasound make it useful to us – its high power and the fact that it does not bend appreciably around obstacles.

27. *Properties of Ultrasonic waves* :
   (a) They travel in straight lines with high frequencies greater than 20 kHz.
   (b) They travel with the velocity of sound.
   (c) Because of their low wavelengths, they can be produced as a sharp penetrating beam.
   (d) They have high kinetic energy.
   (e) They can bring about chemical reactions.

   Industrial applications : Cutting and drilling holes in fragile materials, cleaning parts or areas which are small and hard to reach, fault detection in metallic components and structures, etc.

28. *Sonic boom* : An object travelling faster than the speed of sound is said to be travelling at supersonic speed. A source of sound travelling at supersonic speed causes the formation of shock waves. When a shock wave reaches a person, he hears a sharp and loud sound called the sonic boom.

29. *Audible range of frequencies* : An average person can hear sounds in the frequency range of 20 Hz - 20 kHz.

30. *Time period of a simple pendulum* :

$$T = 2\pi \sqrt{\frac{g}{L}}$$

where 'T' is the time period of simple pendulum, 'L' is the effective length of the pendulum and 'g' is the acceleration due to gravity.

Frequency (f) of a simple pendulum is given by :

$$f = \frac{1}{T} = \frac{1}{2p} \sqrt{\frac{g}{L}}$$

31. **Velocity of longitudinal waves in solids, liquids and gases** : Newton, on the basis of theoretical considerations, deduced the velocity of longitudinal waves in an elastic medium.

$$v = \sqrt{\frac{E}{\rho}}$$

Where 'E' is the elasticity of the medium and 'ρ' is the density of the undisturbed medium. In the case of solids, 'E' represents the Young's modulus of elasticity. In the case of liquids and gases, 'E' represents the bulk modulus of elasticity.

Multiple Choice Questions

1. A mechanical wave travels in a medium. The quantity that is transferred from one place to the other with the wave is :

   (A) mass   (B) speed

   (C) density   (D) energy

2. On a slinky, one can produce :

   (A) a longitudinal wave but not a transverse wave

   (B) a transverse wave but not a longitudinal wave

   (C) a longitudinal as well as a transverse wave

   (D) neither a longitudinal nor a transverse wave

3. Non–mechanical waves can travel :

   (A) in vacuum as well as in a medium

   (B) in vacuum but not in a medium

   (C) in a medium but not in vacuum

   (D) neither in a medium nor in vacuum

4. The distance between a crest and the next trough in a periodic wave is :

   (A) λ (B) $\frac{\lambda}{2}$

   (C) $\frac{\lambda}{4}$ (D) 2λ

5. The minimum distance between two crests is called :

   (A) wavelength   (B) amplitude

   (C) displacement   (D) wave pulse

6. The time period of a periodic wave is 0.02 seconds. At a particular position there is a crest at t = 0. A trough will appear at this position when 't' is equal to :

   (A) 0.005 s   (B) 0.010 s

   (C) 0.015 s   (D) 0.025 s

7. A longitudinal wave travels from east to west in air. In which direction do the particles of air move?

   (A) East to west   (B) West to east

   (C) North to south   (D) South to north

8. A sitar player plucks the wire of a sitar. After a short time each part of the wire starts vibrating in a direction perpendicular to the wire. Is the propagation of this disturbance a longitudinal or a transverse wave?

   (A) Longitudinal

   (B) Transverse

   (C) Stationary

   (D) Both longitudinal and transverse

9. A long spring is fixed at one end. A person holding the other end compresses the spring with a jerk. The compression travels along the length of the spring. Is it an example of a longitudinal or transverse wave?

(A) Stationary

(B) Transverse

(C) Longitudinal

(D) Both longitudinal and transverse

10. Find the time period of a wave whose frequency is 400 MHz?

(A) 0.0012 s   (B) 0.0025 s

(C) 0.0015 s   (D) 0.0010 s

11. Calculate the wavelength of radio waves of frequency 10^9 Hz. The speed of radio waves is 3×10^8 m/s .

(A) 60 cm   (B) 40 cm

(C) 30 cm   (D) 10 cm

12. A wave pulse moving through air causes change in the density of the air. The variation of density at two different instants are shown in the figures given below. The figure (a) corresponds to t =10 s and figure (b) to t = 10.5 s.

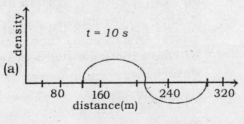

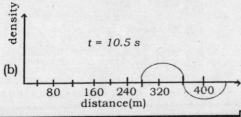

The speed of the wave pulse is :

(A) 520 m/s   (B) 320 m/s

(C) 300 m/s   (D) 220 m/s

13. A wave source produces 20 crests and 20 troughs in 0.2 sec. Find the frequency of the wave.

(A) 200 Hz   (B) 500 Hz

(C) 100 Hz   (D) 300 Hz

14. A stone dropped from the top of a tower of height 300 m splashes into a pond of water at its base. When will the sound of the splash be heard at the top?

(Velocity of sound = 340 ms^{-1} and g = 9.8 ms^{-2})

(A) 5.6 s   (B) 8.7 s

(C) 5.4 s   (D) 6.7 s

15. A sound wave consists of :

(A) a number of compression pulses one after the other

(B) a number of rarefaction pulses one after the other

(C) compression and rarefaction pulses one after the other

(D) a compression and a rarefaction pulse separated by a distance equal to one wavelength

16. The time period of a sound wave travelling in a mcdium is T. At a given instance (t = 0) a particular region in the medium has minimum density. The density of this region will be minimum again at :

(A) t = T

(B) t = T/2

(C) t = T/3

(D) t = T/4

17. If the density of air at a point through which a sound wave is passing is maximum at an instant, the pressure at that point will be :

(A) minimum

(B) same as the density of air

(C) equal to the atmospheric pressure

(D) maximum

18. An object moving at a speed greater than that of sound is said to be moving at :

(A) ultrasonic speed

(B) sonic speed

(C) infrasonic speed

(D) supersonic speed

19. Ultrasonic waves are used for detecting objects under water. What technique/device is used for this?

(A) Ultrasonography

(B) Echocardiography

(C) Phakoemulsification

(D) Sonar

20. In which of the three media; air, water and steel, does sound travel the fastest ?

(A) Air   (B) Water

(C) Steel   (D) None of these

21. A sound wave has a frequency of 1000 Hz and a wave length of 34 cm. How long will it take to travel 1 km?

(A) 3.20 s   (B) 2.94 s

(C) 5.94 s   (D) 3.10 s

22. An object is 11 km below sea level. A research vessel sends down a sonar signal to confirm this depth. After how long can it expect to get the echo? (Take the speed of sound in sea water as 1,520 m/s.)

(A) 15.30 s   (B) 14.47 s

(C) 12.20 s   (D) 11.13 s

23. An oil-tanker explodes in the sea. At that instant an aircraft and a submarine were present vertically above and below the oil–tanker respectively at equal distances from it. Find the ratio of the time taken by sound waves to reach them. (Speed of sound in air = 340 m/s. Speed of sound in sea water = 1520 m/s.)

(A) 5.40   (B) 4.47

(C) 5.57   (D) 6.40

24. A construction worker's helmet slips and falls down when he is 78.4 m above the ground. He hears the sound of the helmet hitting the ground 4.23 seconds after it has slipped. Find the speed of sound in air.

(A) 512 m/s   (B) 215 m/s

(C) 341 m/s   (D) 651 m/s

25. Which of the following is an elastic wave?

(A) Sound waves

(B) Light waves

(C) X – rays

(D) Radio waves

26. Which one of the following properties of sound is affected by change in the air temperature?

(A) Frequency

(B) Amplitude

(C) Intensity

(D) Wavelength

27. In a stationary wave, the particle velocity at the nodal points is :

(A) zero

(B) maximum

(C) minimum but non zero

(D) none of the above

28. The distance between any two consecutive nodes or antinodes in a stationary wave of wavelength λ is:

(A) λ (B) $\lambda/2$

(C) $\lambda/4$ (D) $\lambda/8$

29. If you go on increasing the stretching force on a wire in a guitar, its frequency :

(A) increases

(B) decreases

(C) remains unchanged

(D) none of the above

30. Two sources of sound are said to be in resonance when :

(A) they are similar

(B) they produce sounds of same frequency

(C) they are situated at a particular distance from each other

(D) they are excited by the same agency

31. The velocity of sound is greatest in :

(A) air

(B) steel

(C) ammonia

(D) water

32. A simple pendulum has a metal bob which is negatively charged. If it is allowed to oscillate above a positively charged metallic plate then its time period will :

(A) increase

(B) decrease

(C) remain the same

(D) become zero

33. The velocity of sound in vacuum is :

(A) 332 ms^{-1} (B) 330 ms^{-1}

(C) 288 ms^{-1} (D) 0

34. Longitudinal waves cannot travel through :

(A) vacuum   (B) solids

(C) liquids   (D) gases

35. A bomb explodes on the moon. How long will it take for the sound to reach the earth?

(A) 10 seconds

(B) 1000 seconds

(C) 1 day

(D) None of these

36. The sound waves of frequency more than 20 kHz are called :

(A) supersonics   (B) audible

(C) infrasonics   (D) ultrasonics

37. A pendulum vibrates with a time period of 1 second. The sound produced by it is :

(A) supersonic   (B) audible

(C) infrasonic   (D) ultrasonic

38. Resonance is a special case of :

(A) forced vibrations

(B) natural vibrations

(C) damped vibrations

(D) none of these

39. Waves used in sonography are :

(A) infrared waves

(B) micro waves

(C) sound waves

(D) ultrasonic waves

40. Flash and thunder are produced simultaneously. But thunder is heard a few seconds after the flash is seen. This is because :

(A) speed of sound is greater than speed of light

(B) speed of sound is equal to the speed of light

(C) speed of light is much greater than the speed of sound

(D) none of these

41. A simple pendulum is transferred from the earth to the moon. It will :

(A) slow down

(B) become faster

(C) remain the same

(D) none of these

42. The bob of a pendulum moves from the mean position to an extreme position in 0.28 seconds. Then the time period of the pendulum is :

(A) 2.24 seconds

(B) 1.12 seconds

(C) 0.84 seconds

(D) 3.84 seconds

43. The length of the pendulum for which the time period is 1 second is :   (take $g = \pi^2$ ms^{-2})

(A) 50 cm   (B) 75 cm

(C) 25 cm   (D) 100 cm

44. The time period of a pendulum whose length is 9.8 m is :

(A) 3.14 seconds

(B) 6.28 seconds

(C) 9.42 seconds

(D) 1.57 seconds

45. The time period of a simple pendulum is 1.2 second. If the length of the pendulum is doubled, the new time period will be :

(A) 1.1 seconds   (B) 1.3 seconds

(C) 1.5 seconds   (D) 1.7 seconds

46. The acceleration due to gravity on the surface of the moon is $\dfrac{1}{6}$ th of the value on earth. The time period of a simple pendulum of length 30 cm at the surface of the moon will be :

(A) 2.69   (B) 1.42

(C) 0.84   (D) 7.62

47. A simple pendulum has a time period of 2 seconds on the earth's surface. It is taken to a height R_e above the earth's surface, where R_e is the radius of earth. Now the time period will be :

(A) 4 s   (B) 6 s

(C) 8 s   (D) 10 s

48. The speed of the bob of an oscillating pendulum is zero :

(A) at the mean position

(B) at an extreme position

(C) between the mean position and the left extreme

(D) between the mean position and the right extreme

49. If the length of the pendulum is doubled, its time period :

(A) increases   (B) decreases

(C) is doubled   (D) is halved

50. Let A be the mean position and, B and C be the extreme positions in the oscillation of a simple pendulum. Which of the following represents a complete oscillation?

(A) ABA   (B) ACA

(C) BAC   (D) BCB

51. Because of the air friction, the amplitude of a simple pendulum gradually :

(A) increases

(B) decreases

(C) remains same

(D) none of these

52. Match the following and choose the correct answer.

a. Microphone	1. Wind energy into mechanical energy
b. Speaker	2. Mechanical energy into sound energy
c. Reeds of a harmonium	3. Electrical energy into sound energy
d. Sails of a ship	4. Sound energy into electrical energy

(A) a-4, b-3, c-1, d-2

(B) a-1, b-2, c-3, d-4

(C) a-4, b-2, c-3, d-1

(D) a-4, b-3, c-2, d-1

53. Bats can fly in the pitch dark because :

(A) they only produce ultrasonic waves

(B) they only hear ultrasonic waves

(C) they use ultrasonic waves transmitted by them in a three dimensional space

(D) none of these

Displacement of a progressive wave at different intervals of time is shown in the graph given here. Study it carefully and answer the questions from 54 to 56.

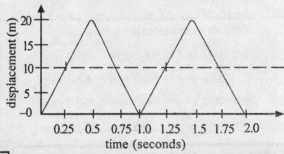

54. Amplitude of the wave is :

    (A) 1 m   (B) 10 m

    (C) 0.5 m   (D) 20 m

55. Period of its vibration is :

    (A) 0.1 s   (B) 1 s

    (C) 1.25 s   (D) 1.2 s

56. Frequency of the wave is :

    (A) 1 Hz

    (B) 1.5 Hz

    (C) 1.25 Hz

    (D) 0.5 Hz

57. When sound waves travel from one medium to the other the physical quantity that does not alter is :

    (A) amplitude

    (B) velocity

    (C) frequency

    (D) intensity

In an experiment with different tuning forks in different media, (data is recorded) as follows :

Medium	Frequency	Wavelength
1	512 Hz	0.6 m
2	480 Hz	1.0 m
3	256 Hz	2.5 m

Based on the data answer the questions 58 & 59.

58. Velocities of sound in the media 1, 2 & 3 respectively are :

    (A) 307 ms⁻¹, 480 ms⁻¹, 640 ms⁻¹

    (B) 256 ms⁻¹, 512 ms⁻¹, 480 ms⁻¹

    (C) 300 ms⁻¹, 400 ms⁻¹, 500 ms⁻¹

    (D) 480 ms⁻¹, 256 ms⁻¹, 512 ms⁻¹

59. Density of the medium in decreasing order is :

    (A) 3, 2, 1

    (B) 2, 3, 1

    (C) 1, 2, 3

    (D) 3, 1, 2

60. During night, distant sounds such as that of the traffic and the loudspeakers become louder than during day. This is due to :

    (A) reflection of sound waves

    (B) refraction of sound waves

    (C) absence of other sounds

    (D) clear perception of hearing

61. Sesmic waves are :

    (A) Non-mechanical waves

    (B) Elastic waves

    (C) Mechanical waves

    (D) None of these

62. Waves produced in a string are :

    (A) One dimensional

    (B) Two dimensional

    (C) Three dimensional

    (D) Multi dimensional

63. Waves produced on the water surface are :

    (A) One-dimensional

    (B) Two-dimensional

    (C) Three-dimensional

    (D) Multi-dimensional

64. Arrange the following media in ascending order of speed of sound in them :

   I – Water

   II – Steel

   III – Nitrogen

   (A) III, II, I   (B) I, III, II

   (C) III, I, II   (D) II, I, III

65. The most commonly used unit for relative intensity of sound is :

   (A) Candela   (B) Watt

   (C) H.P   (D) Decibel

66. Bells and drums are examples of :

   (A) percussion instruments

   (B) wind instruments

   (C) string instruments

   (D) wind instruments

67. Who among the following is associated with SONAR ?

   (A) Doctors   (B) Engineers

   (C) Astronauts   (D) Navigators

68. Timbre is called the quality of sound. One can recognise the voice of a familiar human being or instrument without actually seeing them. This quality is associated with :

   (A) material of the body

   (B) overtones present in the sound

   (C) shape of the body

   (D) all of the above

69. Stationary waves are formed by the superposition of two waves having the same frequency and amplitude and :

   (A) different wavelengths travelling in opposite directions

   (B) the same wavelength travelling in the same direction

   (C) the same wavelength travelling in opposite directions

   (D) all of these

70. In a stationary wave, the portion that stays stationary is :

   (A) the wave as a whole

   (B) only the nodes

   (C) only the antinodes

   (D) all of these

71. Nodes and antinodes are places of :

   (A) maximum and minimum displacements respectively

   (B) minimum and maximum displacements respectively

   (C) minimum and maximum pressure changes respectively

   (D) none of these

72. Which of the following statements is correct ?

   (A) Alternate nodes are in the same phase and differ from the next antinode by a path difference of $\lambda/4$.

   (B) All antinodes are in the same phase and differ from the immediate node by a distance of $\lambda/4$.

   (C) Consecutive nodes and antinodes are separated by a distance of $\lambda/2$.

   (D) All of these

73. Which of the following statements is correct ?

(A) Alternate nodes transport energy

(B) Alternate antinodes transport every and not nodes

(C) Neither of them transport energy

(D) Both of them transport energy

74. Intensity of sound depends on :

(A) amplitude of vibrations

(B) surface area of the vibrating source

(C) density of the medium

(D) all of the above

75. Ultrasonic waves can be produced using :

(A) Galton whistle

(B) Piezo-electric oscillator

(C) Magnetostriction

(D) All of these

76. Ultrasonic waves have higher frequency than audible waves. They travel with the velocity of :

(A) light

(B) electromagnetic waves

(C) sound

(D) none of these

77. A pipe closed at one end and open at the other will give :

(A) even harmonics

(B) odd harmonics

(C) mixed harmonics

(D) none of these

78. A pipe open at both the ends has a fundamental frequency 'n'. If one of its ends is closed, its fundamental frequency alters to :

(A) $n/3$ (B) $n/4$

(C) $n/2$ (D) 2n

79. Two tuning forks are taken. One is loaded with wax at its arms. When they are struck, two beats are heard every second. The number of beats is also :

(A) equal to the sum of their frequencies

(B) equal to the difference of their frequencies

(C) the ratio of their frequencies

(D) the product of their frequencies

80. During refraction of sound waves, which of the following properties change ?

(A) Frequency & wavelength

(B) Frequency & speed

(C) Speed & wavelength

(D) None of these

81. The sound from an open pipe is more pleasant than the sound from a closed pipe. This is because :

(A) sound is heard from both the sides of an open pipe

(B) there are more overtone combinations in an open pipe than in a closed one

(C) it is very easy to operate an open pipe

(D) the length of the open pipe is shorter

82. Loudness of sound depends on :

(A) amplitude of the vibrations of the source

(B) surface area of the vibrating source

(C) density of the medium in which sound is travelling

(D) all of these

83. Which of the following is not correct ?

(A) The characteristic of sound that distinguishes a shrill noise from a grave one is called pitch

(B) Pitch is not frequency, but it changes with frequency

(C) Voice of a girl is shriller than that of a boy

(D) The roaring of a lion is shriller than the buzz of an insect

84. Unit of intensity of sound is :

(A) Watt m^{-2}

(B) Watt kHz^{-1}

(C) Watt

(D) J s^{-1}

85. For a frequency of 1 kHz, the threshold of hearing is :

(A) 10 Watt m^{-2}

(B) 10 Wm^{-2}

(C) 10^{-12} Wm

(D) 10^{-12} Wm^{-2}

86. Two waves produced by different sources are represented by :

$$y_1 = A \sin 200\pi t$$

and $y_2 = A \sin 208\pi t$

where, y_1 and y_2 are displacements and 'A' is the amplitude of the two waves.

The usual equation of a wave is given by :

$$y = A \sin 2\pi ft.$$

If these two waves are sounded and heard simultaneously, we would observe :

(A) 8 beats in every second

(B) 4 beats in every second

(C) resonance

(D) destructive interference

87. A progressive sound wave travelling in a direction gets reflected from a surface in the same direction as that of the incident wave. The pattern forms a standing wave as shown here.

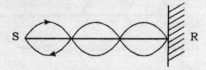

What is the minimum distance required from the source 'S' and the reflecting medium 'R' to observe atleast one loop ?

(A) $\lambda/4$ (B) 2λ

(C) $\lambda/2$ (D) $\frac{3}{2}\lambda$

1. D	2. C	3. A	4. B	5. A	6. B	7. A	8. B	9. C	10. B
11. C	12. B	13. C	14. B	15. C	16. A	17. D	18. D	19. D	20. C
21. B	22. B	23. B	24. C	25. A	26. D	27. A	28. B	29. A	30. B
31. B	32. B	33. D	34. A	35. D	36. D	37. C	38. A	39. D	40. C
41. A	42. B	43. C	44. B	45. D	46. A	47. A	48. B	49. A	50. D
51. B	52. D	53. C	54. B	55. B	56. A	57. C	58. A	59. A	60. B
61. C	62. A	63. B	64. C	65. D	66. A	67. D	68. D	69. C	70. A
71. B	72. D	73. C	74. D	75. D	76. C	77. B	78. C	79. B	80. C
81. B	82. D	83. D	84. A	85. C	86. B	87. C			

Explanatory Answers

2. (C) On a slinky, longitudinal waves as well as transverse waves can be produced.

3. (A) Non-mechanical waves can travel in vacuum as well as in a medium.

4. (B) The distance between a crest and the next trough in a periodic wave is $\dfrac{\lambda}{2}$.

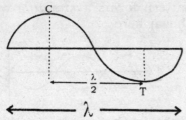

5. (A)

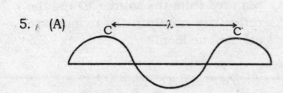

6. (B)

The time period of a periodic wave i.e., the distance between two consecutive crests is 0.02 sec. The distance between the crest and the next trough is 0.01 sec.

7. (A) The particles of air move in the same direction (parallel) to the direction of wave.

8. (B) If the particles of air vibrate perpendicular to the direction of the propagation of wave, then such a wave is called transverse wave.

9. (C) If the compression travels along the length of the spring, then the wave is a longitudinal wave.

10. (B) $T = \dfrac{1}{n} = \dfrac{1}{400} = 0.0025$ seconds.

11. (C) $v = n\lambda \Rightarrow \lambda = \dfrac{v}{n}$

$$= \dfrac{3 \times 10^8}{10^9} = 0.3 \text{ m} = 30 \text{ cm.}$$

12. (B) The density is maximum at x = 160 m at time t = 10 sec. At t = 10.5 sec, the maximum. density occurs at x = 320 m. So,

the pattern has shifted through a distance 320 − 160 = 160 m. This shift has taken place in 10.5 − 10 = 0.5 sec.

The speed of the wave pulse is

$$v = \frac{x}{t} = 320 \text{ ms}^{-1}.$$

13. (C) A crest is the maximum value of the wave quantity. So at the source, the wave quantity attains maximum value for 20 times in 0.2 sec. The number of times it becomes maximum in 1 second is $\frac{20}{0.2} = 100$.

So the frequency is 100 Hz.

14. (B) Time after which the splash is heard at the top is equal to the sum of the time t_1 taken by the stone to fall down and the time t_2 taken by the sound to travel from bottom to top.

Using $s = ut + \frac{1}{2}at^2$.

We get $s = \frac{1}{2}gt_1^2$

$$t_1 = \sqrt{\frac{2s}{g}} = \sqrt{\frac{2 \times 300}{9.8}}$$

$$s = 7.82 \text{ s}.$$

Again $t_2 = \frac{\text{height of tower}}{\text{velocity of sound}}$

$$t_2 = \frac{300}{340 \text{ ms}^{-1}} = 0.885 \text{ s}.$$

Total time $= t_1 + t_2$

$$= (7.82 + 0.88) \text{ s} = 8.7 \text{ s}.$$

16. (A) The density will be minimum again at t = T

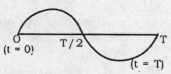

17. (D) As pressure of a gas is directly proportional to its density, density will also be maximum.

18. (D) Supersonic speed is the speed that is greater than the speed of sound.

19. (D) SONAR means Sound Navigation and Ranging.

20. (C) Sound travels the fastest in solids, then in liquids and the least in gases.

Hence the sound travels fastest in steel.

21. (B) We have $f = 1000$ Hz and

$$\lambda = 34 \text{ cm} = \frac{34}{100} \text{ m}.$$

The wave speed is

$$v = f\lambda = (1000 \text{ s}^{-1}) \left[\frac{34}{100} \text{ m} \right]$$

$= 340$ m/s.

The time taken by the wave to travel 1 km is :

$$t = \frac{s}{v} = \frac{1 \text{km}}{340 \text{ m/s}} = \frac{1000 \text{ m}}{340 \text{ m/s}}$$

$= 2.94$ s.

22. (B) The total distance travelled by the sonar signal from the ship to the sea bed and back :

$s = 2 \times 11 \text{ km} = 22{,}000 \text{ m}$

Time taken by the sound to travel this distance is :

$t = \dfrac{s}{v} = \dfrac{22000 \text{ m}}{1520 \text{ m/s}} = 14.147$ s.

∴ the echo will reach the ship 14.47 seconds after the signal is sent.

23. (B) Let the aircraft and the submarine be 'x' m above and below the tanker respectively. Time taken by sound to reach the aircraft is

$$t_{air} = \dfrac{x}{340} = \dfrac{x}{340} \text{ s}$$

Time taken by sound to reach the submarine

$$t_{water} = \dfrac{x}{1520} = \dfrac{x}{1520} \text{ s}$$

Ratio of the time taken

$$= \dfrac{t_{air}}{t_{water}} = \dfrac{(x/340)}{(x/1520)} = \dfrac{1520}{340}$$

$$= 4.47$$

24. (C) Let t be the time taken by the helmet to reach the ground. Here u = 0, h = 78.4 m and g = 9.8 m/s².

$$h = \dfrac{1}{2} gt^2$$

$$\Rightarrow 78.4 = \dfrac{1}{2} \times \left(9.8 \text{ m/s}^2\right) \times t^2$$

or $t^2 = \dfrac{2 \times 78.4}{9.8}$ or t = 4 sec.

∴ the time taken by the helmet to drop to the ground = 4 s.
The time taken by sound to travel 78.4 m = (4.23 − 4) s
                    = 0.23 s
∴ The speed of sound in air

$= \dfrac{78.4 \text{ m}}{0.23 \text{ s}} = 340.87$ m/s

≈ 341 m/s.

25. (A) Elastic waves require a medium for their propagation.

26. (D) $v \alpha \sqrt{T}$

But, $v = f\lambda$ As f does not change $\lambda \alpha \sqrt{T}$.

27. (A) At the nodal points, velocity of the particle is zero.

28. (B) Successive nodes or antinodes are separated by $\lambda/2$.

29. (A) $f \alpha \sqrt{tension}$

31. (B) Elasticity of steel is greatest and $v \alpha \sqrt{E}$. Hence the velocity of sound is greatest in solids.

32. (B) Frequency of oscillation will increase due to interaction. Hence time period will decrease.

33. (D) Sound does not travel through vacuum. Hence the velocity of sound is zero.

34. (A) Sound waves are longitudinal and hence they cannot travel through vacuum. They require a material medium for propagation.

35. (D) As there is no atmosphere on the moon, sound does not travel through vacuum.

37. (C) T = 1 sec $\Rightarrow$ n = $\dfrac{1}{T}$ = 1 Hz

The sound waves of frequency less than 20 Hz are called infrasonic waves.

40. (C) This is because the speed of light (flash) is much greater than the speed of sound.

41. (A) As $T \alpha \dfrac{1}{\sqrt{g}}$, and the value of 'g' decreases from the earth to the moon, the time period T increases. Hence the clock shall slow down.

42. (B) The distance from mean position to one extreme position is equal to $\dfrac{1}{4}$th of a complete oscillation.

But time period is the time taken by the bob to complete one oscillation.

$\therefore$ for $\dfrac{1}{4}$th of a complete oscillation, time is 0.28 s.

For 1 complete oscillation, time period = 4 × 0.28 = 1.12 s.

43. (C) $T = 2\pi\sqrt{\dfrac{L}{g}}$

$\Rightarrow L = \dfrac{gT^2}{4\pi^2} = \dfrac{g \times 1 \times 1}{4 \times g} = \dfrac{1}{4}$ m.

= 0.25 m = 25 cm.

44. (B) $T = 2\pi\sqrt{\dfrac{L}{g}} = 2\pi\sqrt{\dfrac{9.8}{9.8}} = 2\pi$

seconds

= 2 × 3.14 = 6.28 s.

45. (D) $T = 2\pi\sqrt{\dfrac{L}{g}}$

π & g are constants.

$\therefore T \alpha \sqrt{L} \Rightarrow \dfrac{T_1}{T_2} = \sqrt{\dfrac{L_1}{L_2}}$

$\Rightarrow \dfrac{1.2}{T_2} = \sqrt{\dfrac{t_1}{2t_1}} \Rightarrow T_2 = 1.2\sqrt{2}$

= 1.2 × 1.414

= 1.7 s.

46. (A) $T = 2\pi\sqrt{\dfrac{L}{g}}$

Here L = 30 cm = 0.3 m;

$g_m = \dfrac{g}{6}$ ms^2

$T_m = 2\pi\sqrt{\dfrac{1}{g_m}} = 2 \times 3.14\sqrt{\dfrac{0.3}{g/6}}$

$= 2 \times 3.14\sqrt{\dfrac{0.3}{g}}$

$= 2 \times 3.14\sqrt{\dfrac{1.2}{9.8}} = 2.69$ s.

47. (A) $g = \dfrac{GM}{R_e^2}; \; g' = \dfrac{GM}{(R_e + h)^2}$

But $h = R_e$

$\therefore g = \dfrac{GM}{(2R_e)^2} = \dfrac{GM}{4R_e^2} = \dfrac{g}{4}$

Let T → time period of a simple pendulum on the earth's surface and T^1 → time period of a simple pendulum at a height 'h'.

$\therefore T = 2\pi\sqrt{\dfrac{T}{g}}$ & $T' = 2\pi\sqrt{\dfrac{L}{g'}}$

$\Rightarrow \dfrac{T'}{T} = \sqrt{\dfrac{g}{g'}} = \sqrt{\dfrac{g}{g/4}} = \sqrt{4} = 2$ s.

$\Rightarrow \dfrac{T}{T} = 2 \Rightarrow T' = 4$ s

48. (B) Speed of the bob will be minimum (zero) at each of the extreme positions and maximum at the mean position.

49. (A) $T \alpha \sqrt{L}$ where

T – time period

L – length of pendulum

Hence, the time period increases with the increase of the length.

50. (D)

51. (B) Because of air friction, the pendulum gets damped and hence its amplitude decreases.

60. (B) After sunset the surface near the earth cools down more than air in succeeding layers above.

The waves undergo a special kind of refraction called total internal reflection and reaches us back.

62. (A) Standing waves form in one plane

79. (B) Beat frequency is $f_1 - f_2$

86. (B) $y_1 = \sin 2\pi\,100\,t$

$y_1 = A\,\sin 2\pi\,104\,t$

The difference $f_1 - f_2 = 4$

So we hear 4 beats in a second.

✦ ✦ ✦

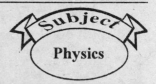
1. For an electron revolving around the atomic nucleus the necessary centripetal force is provided by the :

   (A) electrostatic force of attraction

   (B) electrostatic force of repulsion

   (C) nuclear charge

   D) all of the above

2. A stone is dropped from a tower. It is given no extra push and is left free to fall. It is found that it describes 45 m during its last second of fall. Can you estimate the time of the fall and the height of the tower ?

   $(g = 10 \ ms^{-2})$

   (A) 5 s, 45 m

   (B) 10 s, 90 m

   (C) 5 s, 125 m

   (D) 10 s, 100 m

3. What does the area of an 'acceleration-displacement' graph represents ?

   (A) Distance

   (B) Velocity

   (C) $\dfrac{v^2 - u^2}{2}$

   (D) None of these

4. A photographer arranges to expose photographs of a ball describing motion under free fall such that it is photographed on a vertical scale starting from zero. He photo-graphed it when the ball was at 76.05 m and the next exposure was when the ball was at 80 m. The time of exposure is : $(g = 10 \ ms^{-2})$

   (A) 0.5 s   (B) 2 s

   (C) 3 s   (D) 0.1 s

5. A block of mass 20 kg is pulled over a smooth inclined plane through 3 m as shown in the figure. The plane makes an angle of 30° with the base. Force applied is parallel to the base. The block, by this action is taken upto a higher position w.r.t. the ground. Assuming that no energy is lost otherwise. What is the gain in its P.E. ? $(g = 10 \ ms^{-2})$

   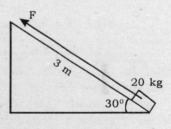

   (A) 30 J   (B) 20 J

   (C) 300 J   (D) 600 J

6. The velocity of a car at 10.50 a.m. is 60 km/hr and at 10.52 a.m., it is 80 km/hr. Assuming constant acceleration in the given interval, its value is :

(A) 600 km/hr^2

(B) 500 km/hr^2

(C) 400 km/hr^2

(D) 300 km/hr^2

7. A particle is moving along a circular track of radius 1 m with uniform speed. The ratio of the distance covered and the displacement in half revolution is :

    (A) 1

    (B) 0

    (C) π

    (D) $\dfrac{\pi}{2}$

8. The distances travelled by a body freely falling from rest in the first, second and the third seconds are in the ratio :

    (A) 1 : 4 : 9

    (B) 1 : 2 : 3

    (C) 1 : 9 : 25

    (D) 1 : 3 : 5

9. A stone is thrown upwards with a speed 'u' from the top of a tower. It reaches the ground with a velocity 3u. The height of the tower is

    (A) $\dfrac{4u^2}{g}$

    (B) $\dfrac{2u^2}{g}$

    (C) $\dfrac{3u^2}{g}$

    (D) $\dfrac{u^2}{g}$

10. When the brakes are applied on a moving cycle, the directions of velocity and acceleration are :

    (A) opposite

    (B) same

    (C) perpendicular

    (D) not related

11. A body projected vertically upwards from A, the top of a tower, reaches the ground in t_1 seconds. If it is projected vertically downwards from A with the same velocity, it reaches the ground in t_2 seconds. If it falls freely from A, the time taken by the ball to reach the ground will be :

    (A) $\dfrac{t_1 + t_2}{2}$

    (B) $\sqrt{t_1 + t_2}$

    (C) $\sqrt{t_1 t_2}$

    (D) $\sqrt{t_1 - t_2}$

12. Points P, Q and R are in a vertical line such that PQ = QR. A ball at point P is allowed to fall freely. What is the ratio of the times of descent through PQ and QR ?

    (A) $\dfrac{3}{2}$

    (B) $\dfrac{3}{\sqrt{2} + 1}$

    (C) $\dfrac{1}{\sqrt{2} - 1}$

    (D) $\dfrac{5}{2}$

13. A passenger travelling in a train with constant velocity drops a stone from the window. To the passenger, the path will appear to be :

    (A) straight line

    (B) parabola

    (C) arc of a circle

    (D) elliptical

14. A force of a certain magnitude acts on a body. The acceleration of the body depends on its :

    (A) mass   (B) density

    (C) volume   (D) shape

15. Pascal is a unit of :

    (A) pressure

    (B) force

    (C) linear momentum

    (D) energy

16. A force produces an acceleration of 0.5 m/s^2 in a body of mass 3.0 kg. If the same force acts on a body of mass 1.5 kg, the acceleration produced in it will be :

    (A) 3.0 m/s^2

    (B) 1.0 m/s^2

    (C) 5.0 m/s^2

    (D) 7.0 m/s^2

17. When two bodies collide with each other, the quantity that is conserved is :

    (A) velocity

    (B) momentum

    (C) kinetic energy

    (D) all of the above

18. A jet engine works on the principle of :

    (A) conservation of linear momentum

    (B) conservation of kinetic energy

    (C) conservation of angular momentum

    (D) conservation of inertia

19. The mass of the sun is 2.0×10^{36} kg and that of the earth is 6.0×10^{24} kg. The distance between the sun and the earth is 1.5×10^{11} m. The gravitational force between them is :

    (A) 3.56×10^{22} N

    (B) 4.56×10^{22} N

    (C) 6.56×10^{22} N

    (D) 5.56×10^{22} N

20. Two bodies A and B having masses 'm' and '2m' are separated by a distance 'd' between them. A small body is to be placed between them such that the net gravitational pull on it by the masses A and B is zero. Its distance from the mass A is :

    (A) $\dfrac{d}{1+\sqrt{3}}$ (B) $\dfrac{d}{1+\sqrt{4}}$

    (C) $\dfrac{d}{1+\sqrt{2}}$ (D) $\dfrac{d}{1+\sqrt{6}}$

21. The units of universal gravitation constant G are :

    (A) N   (B) N m/s^2

    (C) N m/kg^2 (D) N m^2/kg^2

22. The acceleration due to gravity on a heavenly body which has twice the mass and twice the radius of the earth is :

    (A) 2.45 m/s^2 (B) 4.9 m/s^2

    (C) 9.8 m/s^2 (D) 19.6 m/s^2

23. The value of 'g' is :

(A) constant everywhere in the universe

(B) constant everywhere on the surface of the earth

(C) greater at the poles than at the equator

(D) greater at the equator than at the poles

24. If the radius of the earth is increased by a factor of 3, by what factor would its density has to be changed, so that the value of 'g' remains the same ?

(A) 3
(B) $\dfrac{1}{3}$

(C) 9
(D) $\dfrac{1}{6}$

25. The mass of the moon is one–sixth that of the mass of the earth. The mass of a body on the earth is 60 kg. What will be its mass on the moon ?

(A) 10 kg

(B) 60 kg

(C) 360 kg

(D) 30 kg

26. A man with a box on his head is climbing up a ladder. The work done by the man on the box is :

(A) positive

(B) negative

(C) zero

(D) undefined

27. Two bodies of unequal masses are dropped from a cliff. At any instant, they have equal :

(A) momentum

(B) acceleration

(C) potential energy

(D) kinetic energy

28. If the radius of the earth shrinks by 4% and there is no change in its mass, the acceleration due to gravity which depends on mass and radius will change. By how much does the value of 'g' change ?

(A) 2%   (B) 4%

(C) 16%   (D) 8%

29. The heart of a man pumps 4 litres of blood per minute at a pressure of 130 mm of mercury. If the density of mercury is 13.6 g/cm³, then the power of the heart is :

(A) 1.144 W

(B) 2. 145 W

(C) 1.155 W

(D) 3.155 W

30. The angle between the force and the acceleration for maximum work is :

(A) 0⁰   (B) 60⁰

(C) 90⁰   (D) 180⁰

31. A body submerged in the sea was brought up slowly from the sea bed to the sea surface. Variation of pressure on the body with decrease in the depth of sea is shown in the figures below. Which of these is correct ?

(A)

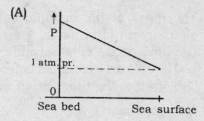

(B)

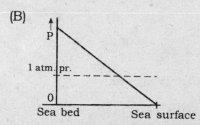

(C)

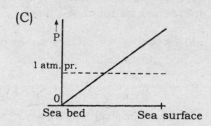

(D)

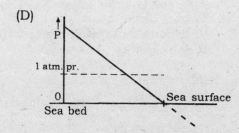

32. Study the given statements P & Q and select the correct answer.

P. *Gas must be cooled considerably irrespective of pressure on it so that it can be liquified.*

Q. *Gas can be liquified under a temperature less than its critical temperature and under pressure more than its critical pressure*

(A) Both P and Q are true and Q explains P

(B) Both P and Q are true but Q does not explain P

(C) Only P is true

(D) P is false but Q is true

33. A force produces an acceleration of 0.5 m/s^2 in a body of mass 3.0 kg. If the same force acts on a body of mass 1.5 kg the acceleration produced in it is :

(A) 3.0 m/s^2 (B) 1.0 m/s^2

(C) 5.0 m/s^2 (D) 7 m/s^2

34. A 6 kg mass 'A' moving with a velocity of 2 m/s collides with a 4 kg mass 'B' moving with a velocity of 1.5 m/s in the opposite direction in a straight line. If the two masses get stuck, then the velocity of the combination is :

(A) $\dot{0}.4$ m/s   (B) 0.2 m/s

(C) 0.1 m/s   (D) 0.3 m/s

35. Two waves produced by different sources are represented by :

$$y_1 = A \sin 200\pi t$$

and $y_2 = A \sin 208\pi t$

where y_1 and y_2 are displacements and 'A' is the amplitude of the two waves.

The usual equation of a wave is given by :

$$y = A \sin 2\pi f t.$$

If these two waves are sounded and heard simultaneously, we would observe :

(A) 8 beats in every second

(B) 4 beats in every second

(C) resonance

(D) destructive interference

36. Sound waves in air cannot be polarised because :

(A) sound waves have very low frequency

(B) sound waves are longitudinal in air

(C) sound waves require material medium,

(D) sound waves are transverse in air

37. A progressive sound wave travelling in a direction gets reflected from a surface in the same direction as that of the incident wave. The pattern forms a standing wave as shown here.

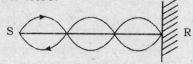

What is the minimum distance required from the source(S) and the reflecting medium(R) to observe atleast one loop ?

(A) $\lambda/4$ (B) 2λ

(C) $\lambda/2$ (D) $\frac{3}{2}\lambda$

38. The time period of a seconds pendulum is :

(A) 0 s   (B) 1 s

(C) 2 s   (D) 0.5 s

39. The mass of the metallic bob of a simple pendulum is 'm' grams and the time period is 'x' seconds. If the bob is replaced by another bob of mass '2m' grams, the time period will be :

(A) x seconds

(B) $\frac{x}{2}$ seconds

(C) 2x seconds

(D) x^2 seconds

40. The potential energy of the bob increases as it moves from :

(A) extreme position to extreme position

(B) extreme position to mean position

(C) mean position to mean position

(D) mean position to extreme position

41. If the length of the simple pendulum is doubled, its time period :

(A) increases

(B) decreases

(C) remains same

(D) none of the above

42. Kinetic energy of the bob of a simple pendulum is zero at :

(A) mean position

(B) left extreme position

(C) right extreme position

(D) both the extreme positions

43. Bats can fly in the pitch dark because :

(A) they only produce ultrasonic waves

(B) they only hear ultrasonic waves

(C) they use ultrasonic waves transmitted by them in a three dimensional space

(D) none of these

44. The distance between a crest and the next trough in a periodic wave is :

(A) λ (B) $\dfrac{\lambda}{2}$

(C) $\dfrac{\lambda}{3}$ (D) 2λ

45. If a longitudinal wave travels from east to west in the air, the direction in which the particles of air move is :

(A) east to west

(B) west to east

(C) north to south

(D) south to north

46. Which of the following are elastic waves ?

(A) Light waves (B) Sound waves

(C) X – rays (D) Radio waves

47. Assuming the distance between the sun and the earth to be 150 million kilometres, how long will it take for an explosion on the sun to be heard by an observer on the earth ?

(A) 454,545 seconds

(B) 545,454 seconds

(C) 330 seconds

(D) None of these

48. The distance between any two consecutive nodes and antinodes in a stationary wave of wavelength λ is :

(A) λ (B) $\dfrac{\lambda}{2}$

(C) $\dfrac{\lambda}{4}$ (D) $\dfrac{\lambda}{8}$

49. A simple pendulum is transferred from the earth to the moon without any disturbance. It will :

(A) become faster

(B) remain the same

(C) slow down

(D) none of the above

50. The time period of a pendulum of length 9.8 m is :

(A) 3. 14 s (B) 6.28 s

(C) 9. 42 s (D) 1.57 s

Answers

1. D	2. C	3. C	4. D	5. C	6. A	7. D	8. D	9. A	10. A
11. C	12. C	13. A	14. A	15. A	16. B	17. B	18. A	19. A	20. C
21. D	22. B	23. C	24. B	25. B	26. A	27. B	28. D	29. C	30. A
31. A	32. D	33. B	34. D	35. B	36. B	37. C	38. C	39. A	40. D
41. A	42. D	43. C	44 B	45. A	46. B	47. D	48. B	49. C	50. B

CHEMISTRY

Chapter 1

Matter

1

1. All substances – from a pin-head to a star are made of atoms. Atoms constitute matter.

2. Matter is any physical substance that exists in three dimensions of space. Whatever its size may be, matter exists in one of the three main forms-solid, liquid or gas.

3. The same matter can change states from solid to liquid or from liquid to gas and so on.

4. *Three states of matter*

   (i) *Solid* : The molecules in a solid move, but very little. They are held in a rigid frame-work or pattern by bonds between them. So solids stay in the same shape unless subjected to powerful forces like twisting or crushing.

   (ii) *Liquid* : In a liquid, the molecules can move about easily. Liquids flow and take the shape of the container. Nevertheless, molecules in a liquid cannot be brought nearer nor pulled apart. So, we cannot compress or expand liquids by mechanical force.

   (iii) *Gas* : In a gas, molecules move about very easily. Gases flow and take the shape of the container. The molecules in a gas can be brought together or moved farther apart. So a gas can be compressed or subjected to expansion.

5. In 1920, plasma-the fourth state of matter was discovered. Plasma exists only at incredibly high temperatures as in nuclear power experiments or inside stars. Small amounts of plasma form during lightening. Plasma is like gas made up of ions.

6. When some substances dissolve, they change slightly. Their atoms are no longer neutral, one group of atoms lose electrons and become positively charged while the other group of atoms gain electrons and become negatively charged. eg. NaCl dissolved in water splits into Na^+ ions and Cl^- ions. Ionic compounds.

7. The spreading of a substance on its own is called diffusion and it takes place because of molecular motion.

   The speed of diffusion of a gas depends on the speed of its molecules. It is greater for light molecules.

8. The states of matter are inter convertible by bringing out changes in temperature or pressure.

9. Normally there is a transition phase between solid to liquid or liquid to gas conversions. But certain substances

change directly from gaseous state to solid and vice versa without undergoing the liquid state.

e.g. Naphthalene & Iodine.

10. When a liquid that is being heated reaches a particular temperature, bubbles form within the liquid containing vapours of that particular liquid. This temperature is called its boiling point and the process is called *boiling*. It is a bulk pheno-mena.

11. When a liquid is heated, the surface molecules gain sufficient K.E. and escape. This process is called *evaporation*. This happens at different temperatures.

Evaporation depends on :

(a) Temperature - higher the tempe-rature, more is the evaporation.

(b) Surface area - larger the area, more is the evaporation

(c) Wind also increases the rate of evaporation.

12. *Vapourisation* : Liquid molecules need a lot of energy to overcome the forces of attraction holding them together and gain freedom to move independently. The molecules receive this energy as *latent heat of vapourisation*, which increases the potential energy of the molecules, but not the kinetic energy. It also gives the molecules the energy required to push back the surrounding atmosphere.

13. *Latent heat of fusion* : Heat that is absorbed by a solid during melting or given out by a liquid during solidification is called latent heat of fusion.

14. 'Latent heat of fusion' of a substance is the quantity of heat required to change a unit mass of solid to liquid, without any change in temperature. It is denoted by l_f.

$$l_f = Q/m$$

The Kinetic theory explains 'latent heat of fusion', as the energy that enables the molecules of a solid to overcome the intermolecular forces that hold them together. When it exceeds a certain value, they break free. Their vibratory motion about their fixed position changes to a greater range. Because there is no change in temperature, their P.E. increases but not the K.E.

Units - The units of 'latent heat of fusion' are J/kg or cal/gm.

15. *Evaporation* : Evaporation occurs when fast moving molecules escape the surface of the liquid. The average speed and the average K.E. of molecules left behind decreases. So, the temperature of the remaining liquid falls.

16. *Liquification of gases and vapour* : Vapours can be liquified when compressed. However, a gas must be cooled below a certain temperature called 'Critical Tempe-rature' to change it into a liquid.

Liquid hydrogen and oxygen are used as the fuel and oxidant respectively in space-crafts. Liquid nitrogen is used in industry as a coolant.

17. *Physical properties of solids*

Density, specific gravity, hardness, odour, colour, melting point, freezing point, viscosity, solubility and heat conduction are some of the physical properties of solids.

18. *Properties of Liquids* : Surface tension, adhesion, cohesion, viscosity, buoyancy and vapourisation are some important properties of liquids.

19. *Properties of Gases* : Pressure, volume, temperature, kinetic energy and speed are some important properties of gases.

Multiple Choice Questions

1. In the Kinetic theory of gases, it is assumed that molecular collisions are :

   (A) inelastic

   (B) short in duration

   (C) one-dimensional

   (D) not able to exert mutual forces

2. K.E. of molecular motion appears as :

   (A) pressure

   (B) P.E.

   (C) temperature

   (D) all of the above

3. Triple point of water is :   C

   (A) 373.16 K

   (B) 273.16° F

   (C) 273.16 K

   (D) 273.16° F

4. Based on the statements given here choose the correct answer.

   P. Some sugar can be added to a full glass of water without causing overflow.

   Q. A liquid is continuous even-though space is present between the molecules.   A

   (A) P and Q are true and Q explains P

   (B) P and Q are true but Q does not explain P

   (C) Only P is true

   (D) Only Q is true

5. Vanderwaal's forces are also known as :

   (A) intermolecular forces

   (B) intramolecular forces

   (C) atomic forces

   (D) molecular forces

6. Based on the statements given here choose the correct answer.

   P. If we increase the temperature of a gas inside a container, its pressure also increases.

   Q. Upon heating, the rate of collisions of the gas molecules increase and increases the impact of force on the walls of the container.

   (A) Both P and Q are true and Q explains P

   (B) Both P and Q are true but Q does not explain P

   (C) Only P is true

   (D) Only Q is true

7. Match the following and choose the correct answer.

a. Solid	i. Super energetic particles
b. Liquid	ii. No shape nor fixed volume at a given pressure.
c. Gas	iii. Has definite shape
d. Plasma	iv. Definite shape with less molecular forces than that in solids.

(A) a-i, b-ii, c-iii, d-iv

(B) a-iii, b-iv, c-ii, d-i

(C) a-iii, b-iv, c-i, d-ii

(D) a-i, b-iv, c-ii, d-iii

8. According to Kinetic theory of gases, molecules are :

(A) perfectly inelastic particles in random motion

(B) perfectly elastic particles in random motion

(C) perfectly inelastic particles at rest

(D) perfectly elastic particles at rest

9. Match the following and choose the correct answer.

a. Evaporation	i. Liquid to gas at a fixed temperature
b. Vaporisation	ii. Solid to gas
c. Sublimation	iii. Gas to solid
d. Hoar frost	iv. Liquid into gas at any temperature

(A) a-iv, b-i, c-ii, d-iii

(B) a-i, b-ii, c-iii, d-iv

(C) a-ii, b-iii, c-iv, d-i

(D) a-iv, b-i, c-iii, d-ii

10. Which of the following has a regular repeated molecular pattern in three dimensional space ?

(A) Solids and liquids

(B) Liquids and gases

(C) Solids

(D) Gases

11. Fog may also be called as :

(A) foam

(B) solid

(C) liquid

(D) anaerosol

12. When water particles condenses on air on dust, it forms :

(A) mist

(B) fog

(C) frost

(D) vapour

13. Based on the statements given here choose the correct answer. A

P. Gas can be cooled and converted into liquid below its Critical temperature by increasing the pressure on it.

Q. Above the Critical temperature, a gas (vapour) can not be liquefied however great the pressure it is subjected to

(A) Both P and Q are true and Q explains P

(B) Both P and Q are true but Q cannot explains P

(C) Only P is true

(D) Q is true only if P is false

14. At a given temperature, 'Kinetic theory of gas' predicts that : B

(A) all the molecules have the same average speed

(B) all the molecules have the same average K.E.

(C) lighter molecules have higher average K.E.

(D) lighter molecules have lower average K.E.

15. At a temperature less than Critical temperature, to liquefy a gas : B

(A) lower the temperature, higher is the pressure required

(B) lower the temperature, lower is the pressure required

(C) higher the temperature, lower is the pressure required

(D) none of these

16. During a hail storm, it was observed that ice pieces turned into water when they reached the ground. At what height could the rain drops have formed into ice pieces?

(assume g = 10 m/s²)

(A) 334 km

(B) 33 km

(C) 300 km

(D) 30 km

17. Heat needed to melt 1kg of ice is :

(A) 40 J

(B) 3.35×10^5 J

(C) 80 J

(D) 800 J

18. Which is more effective in cooling ? C

(A) Water at 0°C

(B) Water at 100°C

(C) Ice at 0°C

(D) All of these

19. 5kg of steam at 100°C is changed into water at 100°C. How much heat is taken out of the system ?

(A) 5 J   (B) 50 J

(C) $5 \times 22.5 \times 10^5$ J (D) 22.5×10^5 J

20. The temperature at which Celsius and Fahrenheit scales shows the same reading is :

(A) 40° K   (B) 100° F

(C) -40° C   (D) -100° C

21. Latent heat of fusion for ice is :

(A) 80 gm cal⁻¹   (B) 80 cal/gm

(C) 19 J cal⁻¹   (D) None of these

22. Based on the statements given here choose the correct answer.

P. In polar regions aquatic life is safe in water under frozen ice

Q. Water has a high latent heat of fusion and the upper portion of ice does not allow the heat of the water to escape to the surroundings.

(A) Both P and Q are correct and Q is the satisfactory explanation of P.

(B) Both P and Q are correct but Q is not the satisfactory explanation of P

(C) Only P is correct

(D) Only Q is correct

23. Gas and vapour :

    (A) obey the same gas laws

    (B) do not obey gas laws

    (C) gas obeys gas laws while vapour does not

    (D) vapour obeys gas laws but not gas

24. 1KWh $(3.6 \times 10^6 J)$ of heat is supplied to 10kg of water. The rise in temperature will be :

    (A) 100^0C

    (B) 86^0C

    (C) 1000^0C

    (D) 10^0C

25. Based on the statements given here choose the correct answer.   A

    P. Boiling point of a liquid increases with increase in temperature

    Q. The volume of liquids increases on boiling and the vaporisation curve shows the variation of the boiling point of a liquid with pressure and expands the equilibrium state between liquid and vapour phase.

    (A) Both P and Q are true and Q explains P

    (B) Both P and Q are true but Q does not explain Q

    (C) Only P is true

    (D) Only Q is true

26. Find the rise in temperature of 1kg of water if 1000 J of heat is supplied to it.

    (A) $\left(\dfrac{1000}{4186}\right)^0 C$ (B) $\left(\dfrac{4186}{1000}\right)^0 C$

    (C) $(1000 \times 4186)^0 C$ (D) $(4186 - 1000)^0 C$

27. Based on the statements given here choose the correct answer.

    P. Aquatic animals breathe oxygen inside water

    Q. Gases can diffuse into water.

    (A) Both P and Q are true and Q explains P

    (B) Both P and Q are true but Q does not explain P

    (C) Only P is true

    (D) Only Q is true

28. In an experiment of conversion of ice into water and water into vapour, observations were recorded and a graph plotted for temperature against time as shown below. From the graph it can be concluded that :

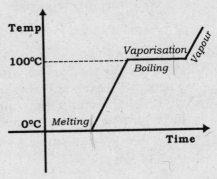

    (A) ice takes time to heat up to 0^0C

    (B) during melting and boiling temperature does not rise

    (C) process of boiling takes longer time than the process of melting

    (D) all of the above

29. The SI unit of temperature is :

    (A) ^0C (B) ^0F

    (C) K   (D) all of the above

30. Study the graph given below and select the correct statement.

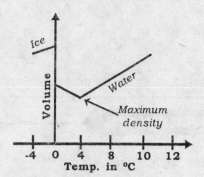

(A) When water is cooled to 4°C it contracts

(B) At 0°C water freezes

(C) The volume of ice is more than that of water

(D) All of these

31. The solid state of CO_2 is called : C

(A) Tear gas

(B) Cooking gas

(C) Dry ice

(D) Laughing gas

32. Mathematical value of 1 atmospheric pressure is :

(A) $1.01 \times 10^5 \, Nm^{-2}$

(B) $1.01 \times 10^6 \, Nm^{-2}$

(C) $1.01 \times 10^4 \, Nm^{-2}$

(D) $1.01 \times 10^3 \, Nm^{-2}$

33. Corresponding temperature in the Kelvin scale for 104° F is :

(A) 313 K   (B) 203 K

(C) 308 K   (D) 377 K

34. Normal temperature of the human body is :

(A) 40°F

(B) 40°C

(C) 37°C

(D) 37°F

35. When the vapour pressure of a liquid is equal to its atmospheric pressure, then it : C

(A) freezes

(B) evaporates

(C) boils

(D) does not undergo any change A

36. When ice is converted into water :

(A) heat is absorbed

(B) heat is released

(C) temperature increases

(D) temperature decreases

37. The thermal energy of a body is the same as the :

(A) K.E. of the body

(B) P.E. of the body

(C) mechanical energy of the body

(D) K.E. of its molecules

38. Rise in temperature of a body means :

(A) its K.E. has increased

(B) its P.E. has increased

(C) its mechanical energy has increased

(D) its thermal energy has increased

Answers

1. B	2. C	3. C	4. A	5. A	6. A	7. B	8. B	9. A	10. C
11. D	12. A	13. A	14. B	15. B	16. B	17. B	18. C	19. C	20. C
21. B	22. A	23. A	24. B	25. A	26. A	27. A	28. D	29. C	30. D
31. C	32. A	33. A	34. C	35. C	36. A	37. D	38. D		

Explanatory Answers

16. (A) $mgh = mL$

$gh = L$

$h = \dfrac{8 \times 10^4 \times 4.18}{10}$

$= 8 \times 4.18 \times 10^3$

$= 33.44 \times 10^3 \, m$

$= 33.44 \, km$

17. (B) Heat needed to melt 1kg of ice is

$mL = 1 \times 8 \times 10^4 \, cal$

as $4.18 \, J = 1 \, cal$

$mL = 8 \times 10^4 \times 4.18 \, J = 33.44 \times 10^4$

$= 3.35 \times 10^5 \, J$

18. (C) Heat that can be removed by ice is 80 kcal for every kg.

19. (C) $Q = mL$

$= 5 \times 22.5 \times 10^5$

$= 11.25 \times 10^6 \, J$

24. (B) $Q = mc\Delta T$

$3.6 \times 10^6 \, J = (10kg)(4186)\Delta T$

$\Delta T = \dfrac{3.6 \times 10^6}{4186 \times 10} = 86^0 C$

26. (A) 4186 J of heat raises the temperature of 1kg of water by $1^0 C$

$\therefore$ 1000 J of heat rises 1kg of water by

$= \left(\dfrac{1}{4186} \times 1000 \right)^0 C$

33. (A) Hint : $\dfrac{F - 32}{180} = \dfrac{C}{100}$

$K = C + 273$

✦ ✦ ✦

Chapter 2

The Nature of Matter

2

Synopsis

1. Any substance which possesses definite mass, occupies definite volume and offers resistance to external force is called matter.

2. An elementary substance contains only one kind of atoms.

3. A chemical substance which can be split into or built up from two or more dissimilar substances is called a compound.

4. All elements and compounds are homogeneous.

5. If the components mix up thoroughly in all proportions then it is called a homogeneous mixture.

6. If the components do not mix up thoroughly and can be demarcated by boundaries, then it is called a heterogeneous mixture.

Differences between compounds and mixtures

7. Compound formation is a chemical change.

   Formation of a mixture is a physical change.

8. Compounds are formed by the combination of two or more elements which combine in a fixed ratio by weight.

   In the formation of a mixture, no fixed ratio is maintained.

9. The constituent elements lose their individual properties.

   The components retain their individual properties.

10. All compounds are homogeneous.

    Mixtures may be homogeneous or heterogeneous.

11. Compounds have definite values for density, melting point and boiling point.

    Mixtures do not have definite values for density, melting point and boiling point.

12. The proportion of the constituent elements is same.

    The proportion of the components can be varied.

13. Compound formation is accompanied by heat energy changes.

    Heat energy changes rarely occur in the preparation of mixtures.

14. The constituents are not easily separable.

    The components are easily separable.

15. Compounds have definite molecular weights.

    Mixtures do not have molecular weights.

Multiple Choice Questions

1. Milk is a ____ solution while vinegar is a ____ solution.
   - (A) suspension, colloidal
   - (B) colloidal, suspension
   - (C) true, colloidal
   - (D) colloidal, true

2. A liquid and a solid together consisting a single phase is known as :
   - (A) solution
   - (B) solute
   - (C) solvent
   - (D) emulsion

3. Which of the following is a homogeneous system?
   - (A) Muddy water
   - (B) Bread
   - (C) Concrete
   - (D) A solution of sugar in water

4. The zig-zag movement of dispersed phase particle in a colloidal system is known as :
   - (A) transitional motion
   - (B) circular motion
   - (C) linear motion
   - (D) brownian motion

5. An emulsion is a colloidal system of :
   - (A) solid dispersed in solid
   - (B) liquid dispersed in liquid
   - (C) gas dispersed in liquid
   - (D) liquid dispersed in solid

6. Milk is :
   - (A) fat dispersed in water
   - (B) fat dispersed in milk
   - (C) fat dispersed in fat
   - (D) water dispersed in milk

7. Scattering of light takes place in :
   - (A) electrolytic solutions
   - (B) colloidal solutions
   - (C) electrodialysis
   - (D) electroplating

8. Foam is a colloidal solution of :
   - (A) gaseous particles dispersed in gas
   - (B) gaseous particles dispersed in liquid
   - (C) solid particles dispersed in liquid
   - (D) solid particles dispersed in gas

9. Which of the following forms a colloidal solution in water ?
   - (A) Salt
   - (B) Glucose
   - (C) Starch
   - (D) Barium nitrate

10. Movement of colloidal particles under the influence of electrical field is called :
    - (A) electrophoresis
    - (B) dialysis
    - (C) ionisation
    - (D) electrodialysis

11. Gelatin is also called as :
    - (A) protective colloid
    - (B) hydrophilic colloid
    - (C) emulsion
    - (D) none of these

12. The sky looks blue due to :
    - (A) dispersion effect
    - (B) reflection
    - (C) scattering
    - (D) transmission

13. In colloidal state, particle size ranges from :
    - (A) 1 to 10 A^0
    - (B) 20 to 50 A^0
    - (C) 10 to 100 A^0
    - (D) 1 to 280 A^0

14. Tyndall effect is observed in :

(A) solution   (B) precipitate

(C) sol   (D) vapour

15. Brownian movement is due to :

(A) temperature fluctuations within the liquid phase

(B) attraction and repulsion between the charges on the colloidal particles

(C) impact of molecules of the dispersion medium on the colloidal particles

(D) convention currents

16. Difference between a crystalloid and a colloid is in :

(A) particle size

(B) the nature of solute

(C) diffusion through a membrane

(D) all of the above

17. Blood is _____ charged sol.

(A) negatively   (B) positively

(C) neutral   (D) none of these

18. Ice cream is an example of :

(A) true solution (B) emulsion

(C) colloid   (D) suspension

19. Water loving colloids are called :

(A) hydrophobic colloids

(B) reversible colloids

(C) irreversible colloids

(D) hydrophilic colloids

20. The technique used in ultra-microscope is :

(A) adsorption

(B) coagulation

(C) Tyndall effect

(D) electrophoresis

21. Coagulation occurs due to :

(A) the scattering of light

(B) the presence of charges

(C) the neutralization of charges

(D) unequal bombardment by solvent molecules

22. Sol is :

(A) solid dispersed in liquid

(B) liquid dispersed in gas

(C) gas dispersed in liquid

(D) gas dispersed in solid

23. In both dialysis and osmosis which particles do not pass through the semi-permeable membrane?

(A) Water

(B) Small molecules

(C) Colloids

(D) All of these

24. The separation of colloidal particles from those of molecular dimensions is called :

(A) dialysis   (B) pyrolysis

(C) peptization (D) photolysis

25. Electrophoresis is due to :

(A) the neutralization of charge

(B) the presence of charge

(C) the scattering light

(D) all of the above

26. Adsorption property is applied in :

(A) sewage disposal

(B) ultramicroscope

(C) smoke precipitator

(D) medicine

27. Liquid dispersed in gas is called :

(A) aerosol   (B) solid sol

(C) sol   (D) solid foam

28. Drinking soda is an example of a solution of :

(A) gas in liquid (B) liquid in gas

(C) gas in gas   (D) solid in liquid

29. Amalgam is a solution of :

(A) solid in solid

(B) solid in liquid

(C) liquid in solid

(D) liquid in liquid

30. Which of the following is a true solution?

(A) NaCl in sulphur dioxide

(B) Copper in silver

(C) Salt in petrol

(D) Mud in water

31. Which of the following statements is correct ?

(A) Compounds can be separated into constituents by physical processes

(B) The boiling points and melting points of compounds are not fixed

(C) The composition of compounds are not fixed

(D) The properties of compounds are entirely different from those of its constituents

32. Water is :

(A) a compound (B) a mixture

(C) true solution (D) all of these

33. The material which contains at least two pure substances and shows the properties of their constituents is called :

(A) a compound

(B) an element

(C) a mixture

(D) a solution

34. Select the odd one.

(A) Hydrogen   (B) Oxygen

(C) Steam   (D) Chlorine

35. Milk of Magnesia is an example of :

(A) emulsion

(B) true solution

(C) colloid

(D) suspension

36. A solution of iodine in carbon tetra-chloride is known as :

(A) aqueous solution

(B) alcoholic solution

(C) nonaqueous solution

(D) tincture of iodine

37. Solid foam is :

(A) solid dispersed in solid

(B) liquid dispersed in solid

(C) gas dispersed in solid

(D) solid dispersed in liquid

38. What is the property used in sewage disposal ?

(A) Coagulation

(B) Adsorption

(C) Electrophoresis

(D) Tyndall effect

39. Which of the following is a characteristic of both mixtures and compounds ?

(A) They contain components in fixed proportions

(B) Their properties are the same as those of their components

(C) Their weight equals the sum of the weights of their components

(D) Energy is given out when they are being prepared

40. When salt is dissolved in water, there is :

(A) an increase of boiling point

(B) no change in boiling point

(C) a decrease of boiling point

(D) none of the above

41. How many grams of hydrochloric acid are formed when 2 grams of hydrogen combine with excess of chlorine?

(A) 35.5 gm

(B) 36.5 gm

(C) 73 gm

(D) 37.7 gm

42. The size of a colloidal particle is :

(A) 10^{-1} to 10^{-3} cm

(B) 10^{-5} to 10^{-7} cm

(C) 10^{-8} to 10^{-5} cm

(D) 10^{-6} to 10^{-8} cm

43. Which of the following is not a compound?

(A) Sugar

(B) Common salt

(C) Diamond

(D) Plaster of Paris

44. Which of the following is an example of a mixture?

(A) Sugar

(B) Brass

(C) CO_2

(D) NO_2

45. Which of the following properties is different for solids, liquids and gases?

(A) Movement of molecules

(B) Particle size of the substance

(C) Mass of the substance

(D) Energy exchanges

46. Sublimation of iodine, camphor and naphthalene is an example of :

(A) chemical change

(B) energy change

(C) physical change

(D) irreversible change

47. Which of the following obey the law of constant proportions in their formation?

(A) Mixtures

(B) Compounds

(C) Elements

(D) Colloids

48. Which of the following is not a chemical change?

(A) Rusting of iron

(B) Converting water into steam

(C) Preparing curd from milk

(D) Burning of coal

49. Burning of a candle is a/an :

(A) chemical change

(B) physical change

(C) energy change

(D) reversible change

50. 'A chemical compound always consists of the same elements which combine in the same fixed ratio by weight', is the statement of :

(A) Law of definite proportions

(B) Gay–Lussac's law

(C) Law of multiple proportions

(D) None of these

51. The most abundant metal in the earth's crust is :

(A) Fe   (B) Cu

(C) Al   (D) Au

52. The number of nonmetallic elements which are liquids at room temperature is :

(A) 2   (B) 1

(C) 4   (D) 3

53. The most abundant element in the earth's crust is :

(A) Si

(B) C

(C) O

(D) Ca

54. Which of the following is expected to conduct electricity?

(A) Diamond

(B) Molten sulphur

(C) Molten KCl

(D) Crystalline NaCl

55. Diamond is the strongest naturally occurring substance. Its hardness is due to :

(A) high solubility in water

(B) covalent bonds

(C) high electrical conductance

(D) high boiling point

56. Which of the following is an insulator?

(A) Aluminium

(B) Diamond

(C) Graphite

(D) Silicon

57. Paramagnetic substances are :

(A) strongly magnetic

(B) weakly magnetic

(C) nonmagnetic

(D) none of these

Answers

1.	D	2.	A	3.	D	4.	D	5.	B	6.	A	7.	B	8.	B	9.	C	10.	A
11.	A	12.	C	13.	C	14.	C	15.	C	16.	D	17.	A	18.	B	19.	D	20.	C
21.	C	22.	A	23.	C	24.	A	25.	B	26.	D	27.	A	28.	A	29.	C	30.	B
31.	D	32.	A	33.	C	34.	C	35.	D	36.	C	37.	C	38.	A	39.	C	40.	A
41.	C	42.	B	43.	C	44	B	45.	A	46.	C	47.	B	48.	B	49.	A	50.	A
51.	C	52.	A	53.	C	54.	C	55.	B	56.	B	57.	B								

Explanatory Answers

34. **(C)** Steam does not belong to this set because all others are elements whereas steam is a compound.

41. **(C)** $H_2 + Cl_2 \rightarrow 2HCl$

$2 \times 1 + (35.5)_2 \rightarrow 2[1 + 35.5]$

$= 2 \times 36.5 = 73.$

Hence 73 grams of HCl is formed.

Chapter 3

Atoms and Molecules

Synopsis

1. The simplest form of matter which can neither be split into nor built up from two or more dissimilar substances is called an element.

2. An atom of an element is denoted by the symbol of the element.

3. An atom of an element also denotes the atomic weight possessed by that element.

4. Each atom of an element is characterised by its atomic number and mass number.

5. An aggregation of two or more atoms of the same or different elements is called a molecule.

6. All molecules have stability.

7. Molecules are characterised by their molecular weights.

8. The smallest part of a substance that exists independently is called a molecule.

9. *Law of definite proportions:* A chemical compound always consists of the same elements which combine in the same fixed ratio by weight.

10. Law of multiple proportions was stated by John Dalton.

11. *Law of multiple proportions:* When two elements combine to form two or more compounds, the different weights of one element which combine with a fixed weight of the other bear a simple integral ratio.

12. Atomic weight of an element in grams is called *gram atomic weight* or *gram atom.*

13. Molecular weight of a compound expressed in grams is called *gram molecular weight* or *gram molecule.*

14. Mole is the unit for quantity of substance. It contains the same number of particles as are present in 12 g of carbon (or) mole is the collection of Avogadro number of particles.

15. Avogadro's number is 6.023×10^{23}. It is denoted by N.

16. Number of moles

$$= \frac{weight\ of\ a\ substance\ in\ grams}{gram\ molecular\ weight}$$

$$= \frac{number\ of\ molecules}{Avogadro\ number}$$

Number of moles of a gaseous substance

$$= \frac{volume\ of\ the\ gas\ at\ STP}{gram\ molar\ volume}$$

17. Weight of single molecule

$$= \frac{gram\ molecular\ weight}{Avogadro\ number}$$

18. Atomic weight of gaseous element

$$= \frac{molecular\ weight}{atomicity}$$

19. Stoichiometry is the mass relationship that exists in a balanced chemical equation.

20. Empirical formula is the ratio of atoms of various elements in a compound.

21. Molecular formula represents the actual number of atoms of each element in a compound.

22. Empirical formula is derived from percentage composition.

23. Molecular formula

=(empirical formula) × n

where 'n' is a small whole number.

24. One gram atomic weight of any element contains 6.023×10^{23} atoms which is called Avogadro number.

25. The weight of 6.023×10^{23} atoms of any element is equal to its gram atomic weight.

26. The absolute weight of an atom of any element is

$$= \frac{gram\ atomic\ weight}{Avogadro\ number}$$

27. Atomic weight of gaseous element

$$= \frac{molecular\ weight}{atomicity}$$

28. Weight of the substance

= Number of moles × gram molecular weight

29. Number of molecules

= Number of moles × Avogadro number

(or)

$$\frac{weight\ of\ the\ substance}{gram\ molecular\ weight} \times Avogadro\ number$$

30. **Atomic properties** : Ionisation potential and electron affinity are the properties of isolated atoms.

31. Electronegativity is the property of a bonded atom.

32. The minimum amount of energy required to remove an electron from a neutral gaseous atom is called its first ionisation potential.

33. The successive ionisation potentials are in the order $I_1 < I_2 < I_3 < I_4 \ldots$

34. Metals have low ionisation potentials and nonmetals have high ionisation potentials.

35. Inert gases have the highest ionisation potentials.

36. The capacity of an atom, in a molecule, to attract an electron is called its electronegativity.

37. Halogens have high electronegativities.

38. Ionic radius is the distance from the nucleus of the ion to the point where its influence on its electron cloud ceases.

39. Cation is smaller in size than the parent atom.

40. Anion is larger than the parent atom.

Multiple Choice Questions

1. The law of multiple proportions was proposed by :

   (A) Lavoisier   (B) Dalton

   (C) Preistley   (D) Ritcher

2. The weights of two elements which combine with each other are in the ratio of their :

   (A) atomic heights

   (B) atomic volumes

   (C) equivalent weights

   (D) molecular weights

3. 180 grams of water contains _____ moles.

(A) 100   (B) 10

(C) 180   (D) 0.01

4. What is the weight of 3 gram atoms of sulphur?

(A) 96 gm   (B) 99 gm

(C) 100 gm   (D) 3 gm

5. How many gram atoms are present in 144 g of magnesium?

(A) 12   (B) 6

(C) 100   (D) 144

6. How many moles of oxygen atoms are present in one mole of acetic acid?

(A) 1 mole   (B) 3 moles

(C) 2 moles   (D) 6 moles

7. What is the number of particles in one mole of a substance?

(A) 6.023×10^{23} (B) 6.023×10^{-23}

(C) 6.023   (D) 3×10^{8}

8. How many atoms and how many gram atoms are there in 10 grams of calcium?

(A) 0.25 gram atoms, 6.023×10^{-23} atoms

(B) 0.25 gram atoms, 1.50×10^{23} atoms

(C) 0.1 gram atoms, 6.023×10^{23} atoms

(D) 0.1 gram atoms, 1.50×10^{23} atoms

9. Calculate the weight of 0.1 mole of sodium carbonate.

(A) 1.06 g   (B) 11.06 g

(C) 10.6 g   (D) 1.106 g

10. How many molecules of glucose are present in 5.23 g of glucose (molecular weight of glucose is 180 a.m.u.)?

(A) 1.75×10^{22} molecules

(B) 17.5×10^{-22} molecules

(C) 17.5×10^{22} molecules

(D) 1.75×10^{-22} molecules

11. How many number of moles are present in 540 g of glucose?

(A) 2 moles   (B) 3 moles

(C) 4 moles   (D) 1 mole

12. How much of lime can be obtained by burning 400 g of lime stone?

(A) 224 g   (B) 220 g

(C) 400 g   (D) 320 g

13. The approximate production of sodium carbonate per month is 424×10^{6} g while that of methyl alcohol is 320×10^{6} g. Which is produced more in terms of number of moles?

(A) Sodium carbonate

(B) Methyl alcohol

(C) Both A & B

(D) None of these

14. Chemical analysis of a carbon compound gave the following percentage composition by weight of the elements present in it. Carbon = 10.06%, hydrogen = 0.84%, chlorine = 89.10%. Calculate the empirical formula of the compound.

(A) $C_2H_2Cl_2$

(B) $CHCl_2$

(C) $CHCl_3$

(D) $C_4H_4Cl_4$

15. 0.202 g of a carbon compound, on combustion, gave 0.361 g of carbon dioxide and 0.47 g of water. Calculate the percentage composition of carbon.

(A) 48.76%   (B) 8.07%

(C) 43.17%   (D) 42.17%

16. Calculate the empirical formula of a compound having percentage composition : Potassium (K) 26.57,

Chromium (Cr) = 35.36,

Oxygen (O) = 38.07.

(A) K_2CrO_4

(B) $K_2Cr_2O_7$

(C) $K_3Cr_2O_3$

(D) $K_3Cr_2O_7$

17. Calculate the number molecules present in 31.6 g of $KMnO_4$.

(A) 1.204×10^{23}

(B) 12.04×10^{23}

(C) 120.4×10^{23}

(D) 12.04×10^{-23}

18. One mole of CO_2 contains :

(A) 1 gram atom of carbon

(B) 2 gram atoms of oxygen

(C) 3 gram atoms of carbon and oxygen

(D) all of the above

19. The percentage of nitrogen in ammonia is given by the expression :

(A) $\dfrac{14 \times 100}{17}$ (B) $\dfrac{3}{17} \times 100$

(C) $\dfrac{14 \times 100}{34}$ (D) $\dfrac{3}{34} \times 100$

20. The empirical formula of a compound is CH_2O. Its molecular weight is 90. Calculate the molecular formula of the compound. (Atomic weight C = 12, H = 1, O = 16)

(A) $C_3H_7O_3$

(B) $C_4H_6O_3$

(C) $C_3H_6O_3$

(D) $C_4H_2O_3$

21. The percentage of oxygen in NaOH is :

(A) 40   (B) 16

(C) 20   (D) 32

22. 3.6 grams of a sample, on combustion, gave 3.3 grams of CO_2. The percentage of carbon in the sample is :

(A) 10   (B) 20

(C) 25   (D) 40

23. A compound contains 38.8% C, 16% H and 45.2% N. The empirical formula of the compound is :

(A) CH_3NH_2

(B) CH_3CN

(C) C_2H_5CN

(D) $CH_2(NH_2)_2$

24. Calculate the weight of 2.5 mole of $CaCO_3$.

(A) 200 g   (B) 230 g

(C) 240 g   (D) 250 g

25. Calculate the number of moles present in 12 g of ozone and 32 g of sulphur dioxide in a gas mixture.

(A) 0.5 and 0.25

(B) 0.25 and 0.5

(C) 0.5 and 0.5

(D) 0.25 and 0.25

26. What is the mass of one molecule of oxygen?

(A) 5.33×10^{-23} g (B) 5.33×10^{23} g

(C) 5.25×10^{23} g (D) 5.02×10^{-23} g

27. Calculate the number of atoms present in 6.4 g of sulphur.

(A) 2.4×10^{23} atoms

(B) 2.4×10^{-23} atoms

(C) 1.2×10^{23} atoms

(D) 1.2×10^{-23} atoms

28. How many gram atoms are present in 256 g of O_2?

(A) 16   (B) 32

(C) 14   (D) 36

29. Calculate the number of atoms present in 71 g of Cl_2.

(A) 1.205×10^{-24}

(B) 1.205×10^{23}

(C) 1.205×10^{24}

(D) 1.205×10^{-23}

30. How many gram atoms are present in 60 g of carbon?

(A) 6   (B) 10

(C) 16   (D) 5

31. The number of moles present in 20 grams of $CaCO_3$ is :

(A) 0.1   (B) 0.2

(C) 0.3   (D) 0.25

32. A hydrocarbon contains 90% of carbon and 10% hydrogen. The empirical formula of the compound is :

(A) C_2H_5 (B) C_3H_2

(C) C_3H_4 (D) CH_3

33. The empirical formula of acetic acid is CH_2O. Its molecular weight is 60. Find its molecular formula.

(A) CH_2O (B) CH_3O_2

(C) $C_2H_4O_2$ (D) $C_3H_6O_2$

34. An element has only one type of :

(A) molecules   (B) atoms

(C) mixtures   (D) solutes

35. Calculate the number of moles of helium present in 6.46 g. (Atomic weight of helium is 4 amu).

(A) 16.15   (B) 1.615

(C) 161.5   (D) 0.1615

36. Calculate the weight of 0.885 moles of $Mg(NO_3)_2$.

(A) 13.1 g   (B) 131 g

(C) 130 g   (D) 88.5 g

37. How many grams of Na_2CO_3 are to be weighed to get 0.1 mole Na_2CO_3?

(A) 10 g   (B) 5 g

(C) 10.6 g   (D) 12.6 g

38. 64 g of an organic compound contains 24 g of carbon, 8 g of hydrogen and the rest oxygen. The empirical formula of the compound is :

(A) CH_2O

(B) C_2H_4O

(C) CH_4O

(D) $C_2H_4O_2$

39. The simplest formula of a compound having 50% of X (atomic weight 10) and 50% of Y (atomic weight 20) is :

(A) XY   (B) X_2Y

(C) XY_3 (D) X_2Y_2

3. Atoms and Molecules   Class IX –Chemistry

40. Percentage of carbon is highest in :

(A) CH_4 (B) C_3H_4

(C) C_6H_6 (D) C_3H_8

41. Find out the percentage of carbon in aluminium carbonate $Al_2(CO_3)_3$ [Al = 27, C = 12, O = 16].

(A) 15.38%   (B) 14.38%

(C) 27.2%   (D) 12.16%

42. Calculate the number of molecules of the substance present in 0.5 moles of magnesium oxide (MgO). [Atomic weights: Mg = 24, O = 16]

(A) 14.09×10^{23}

(B) 3.0115×10^{23}

(C) 30.12×10^{23}

(D) 14.09×10^{-23}

43. Calculate the percentage of oxygen in $Al_2(SO_4)_3$.

(A) 55.14%   (B) 34.2%

(C) 56.14%   (D) 14.56%

44. Calculate the number of iron atoms in a piece of iron weighing 2.8 g. (Atomic mass of iron = 56)

(A) 30.11×10^{23} atoms

(B) 3.11×10^{23} atoms

(C) 3.011×10^{22} atoms

(D) 301.1×10^{23} atoms

45. Calculate the total number of atoms present in 0.05 moles of glucose.

(A) 6.224×10^{23}

(B) 7.224×10^{22}

(C) 7.224×10^{23}

(D) 8.024×10^{23}

46. Calculate the number of atoms of each element present in 0.5 moles of $MgSO_4$.

(A) 3.01×10^{23} atoms of Mg, 3.01×10^{23} atoms of S and 12.05×10^{23} atoms of O

(B) 3×10^{23} atoms of Mg, 3×10^{23} atoms of S and 1.2×10^{23} atoms of O

(C) 3.01×10^{23} atoms of Mg, 2.05×10^{23} atoms of S and 12.05×10^{23} atoms of O

(D) 3×10^{23} atoms of Mg, 12.05×10^{23} atoms of S and 12.05×10^{23} atoms of O

47. Sulphur molecule exists as S_8. How many moles of sulphur are present in 25.6 grams of sulphur?

(A) 0.01   (B) 0.1

(C) 0.02   (D) 0.2

48. Calculate the number of molecules present in 0.75 moles of CO_2.

(A) 4.515×10^{-23} (B) 45.15×10^{23}

(C) 451.5×10^{-23} (D) 4.515×10^{23}

49. Calculate the number of moles of zinc in 23.3 g.

(A) 0.37 moles   (B) 0.35 moles

(C) 0.5 moles   (D) 0.53 moles

50. How many grams of sodium oxalate are to be weighed to get 0.1 mole of sodium oxalate ($Na_2C_2O_4$)?

(A) 13.4 g   (B) 1.34 g

(C) 134 g   (D) 0.134 g

51. Calculate the number of atoms of sulphur present in 0.5 moles of $Na_2S_2O_3$.

(A) 62.02×10^{23} (B) 622×10^{23}

(C) 6.02×10^{23} (D) 6.02×10^{-23}

52. How many moles of glucose ($C_6H_{12}O_6$) are present in 5.4 g?

(A) 0.03   (B) 0.02

(C) 0.01   (D) 0.1

53. Calculate the number of gram atoms present in 8 g of helium.

(A) 3   (B) 4

(C) 2   (D) 1

54. Calculate the number of gram atoms and gram moles present in 12.4 g of phosphorus.

(A) 0.1 gram atoms, 0.1 gram moles

(B) 0.2 gram atoms, 0.1 gram moles

(C) 0.1 gram atoms, 0.4 gram moles

(D) 0.4 gram atoms, 0.1 gram moles

55. How many moles are present in 5.3 g of anhydrous sodium carbonate?

(A) 0.03   (B) 0.04

(C) 0.05   (D) 0.01

56. How many molecules are there in 1.8 g of glucose?

(A) 60.23×10^{22} (B) 6.023×10^{23}

(C) 62.03×10^{22} (D) 6.023×10^{22}

57. Calculate the number of moles present in 14.2 grams of chlorine.

(A) 0.1   (B) 0.2

(C) 0.02   (D) 0.01

58. Calculate the number of grams present in 0.25 moles of Na_2CO_3.

(A) 26.5 g   (B) 23.5 g

(C) 20.2 g   (D) 21.3 g

59. Calculate the number of moles present in 4.9 g of H_2SO_4.

(A) 0.01   (B) 0.02

(C) 0.05   (D) 0.03

60. Calculate the number of moles present in 60 g of NaOH.

(A) 1.2   (B) 1.5

(C) 2.5   (D) 0.15

61. How many molecules and atoms of phosphorous are present in 0.1 moles white phosphorous?

(A) 6.023×10^{22} molecules, 2.409×10^{23} atoms

(B) 2.409×10^{23} molecules, 60.23×10^{22} atoms

(C) 24.09×10^{23} molecules, 60.23×10^{22} atoms

(D) 60.23×10^{23} molecules, 2.409×10^{23} atoms

62. Calculate the number of atoms present in 10 g of $CaCO_3$.

(A) 31.5×10^{23} (B) 3.015×10^{22}

(C) 3.015×10^{23} (D) 31.5×10^{23}

63. How many molecules are present in 1.25 moles of $KMnO_4$?

(A) 7.525×10^{23} (B) 75.25×10^{23}

(C) 7.52×10^{22} (D) 7.52×10^{-23}

64. How many atoms and gram atoms are present in 20 g of calcium?

(A) 3.1×10^{23} and 0.05

(B) 3.01×10^{23} and 0.5

(C) 0.5 and 3.1×10^{23}

(D) 0.2 and 3.1×10^{23}

65. Calculate the weight of nitrogen present in 0.5 moles of NH_3.

(A) 8 g   (B) 9 g

(C) 1 g   (D) 7 g

66. Calculate the weight of **sulphur** present in 1.5 moles of hydrogen sulphide.

   (A) 48 g   (B) 50 g

   (C) 60 g   (D) 70 g

67. Calculate the weight of carbon and oxygen present in 3 moles of carbon dioxide.

   (A) 35 g, 95 g   (B) 36 g, 96 g

   (C) 96 g, 35 g   (D) 40 g, 58 g

68. Calculate the number of molecules present in 7.1 grams of chlorine.

   (A) 6.02×10^{22} (B) 60.2×10^{23}

   (C) 6.023×10^{23} (D) 6.02×10^{-23}

69. Calculate the mass of one molecule of H_2O.

   (A) 29.88×10^{23} (B) 2.988×10^{23}

   (C) 0.2988×10^{23} (D) 2.988×10^{-23}

70. Calculate the number of atoms and molecules present in 124 g of white phosphorus.

   (A) 24.08×10^{23} atoms,

   6.02×10^{23} molecules

   (B) 2.408×10^{23} atoms,

   6.02×10^{22} molecules

   (C) 2.08×10^{22} atoms,

   6.02×10^{-23} molecules

   (D) 6.02×10^{-23} atoms,

   2.408×10^{-22} molecules

71. Calculate the weight of carbon which contains the same number of atoms as those present in 15 grams of oxygen.

   (A) 13 g   (B) 12 g

   (C) 10 g   (D) 14 g

72. Calculate the weight of 2.5 gram moles of oxygen.

   (A) 70 g   (B) 90 g

   (C) 80 g   (D) 50 g

73. What weight of calcium contains the same number of atoms as those in a 3 g of carbon?

   (A) 10 g   (B) 20 g

   (C) 30 g   (D) 40 g

74. Calculate the weight of 2.0 moles of glucose.

   (A) 365 g   (B) 350 g

   (C) 355 g   (D) 360 g

75. Calculate the number of carbon atoms present in 24 grams of methane.

   (A) 6.023×10^{23}

   (B) 6.02×10^{23}

   (C) 9.03×10^{23}

   (D) 9.02×10^{-22}

76. What weight of sodium contains the same number of atoms as those in 8 grams of oxygen?

   (A) 10.5 g

   (B) 13.5 g

   (C) 11.5 g

   (D) 14.2 g

77. Calculate the number of moles present in 17grams of $AgNO_3$.

   (A) 0.2   (B) 0.1

   (C) 2   (D) 1

78. What will be the weight in grams of 0.1 mole of $CaCO_3$?

   (A) 11 g   (B) 12 g

   (C) 3 g   (D) 10 g

79. Calculate the number of moles present in 7.3 g of HCl.

    (A) 0.2   (B) 0.1

    (C) 1   (D) 0.02

80. Calculate the weight in grams of 0.9 gram atoms of zinc.

    (A) 50.5 g   (B) 58.5 g

    (C) 56.3 g   (D) 53.2 g

81. How many atoms are present in 0.25 mole of SO_3?

    (A) 1.505×10^{23} atoms of sulphur and 4.515×10^{23} atoms of oxygen

    (B) 4.15×10^{23} atoms of oxygen and 2.505×10^{22} atoms of sulphur

    (C) 2.505×10^{23} atoms of sulphur and 3.505×10^{22} atoms of oxygen

    (D) 3.05×10^{22} atoms of sulphur and 2.515×10^{23} atoms of oxygen

82. How many molecules are present in 0.50 moles of KCl?

    (A) 4.01×10^{23}

    (B) 3.01×10^{22}

    (C) 3.01

    (D) 3.01×10^{23}

83. Calculate the weight of 0.4 gram atoms of carbon.

    (A) 2.8 g

    (B) 4.8 g

    (C) 3.2 g

    (D) 4.0 g

84. Calculate the number of gram atoms present in 103 g of barium.

    (A) 103   (B) 0.4

    (C) 0.5   (D) 0.3

85. Calculate the number of moles and molecules present in 40 g of oxygen.

    (A) $1.25, 7.525 \times 10^{23}$

    (B) $1.25, 6.4 \times 10^{22}$

    (C) $7.25, 1.2 \times 10^{-22}$

    (D) $1.25, 6.4 \times 10^{23}$

86. Calculate the weight of 0.4 gram atoms of phosphorous.

    (A) 11.3 g   (B) 12.4 g

    (C) 13.4 g   (D) 10.4 g

87. Calculate the number of gram atoms and atoms present in 80 g of sulphur.

    (A) $2.5, 15.05 \times 10^{23}$

    (B) $3.5, 16.05 \times 10^{23}$

    (C) $0.5, 13.3 \times 10^{22}$

    (D) $2.3, 15.05 \times 10^{23}$

88. Calculate the weight in grams present in 0.7 moles of sodium.

    (A) 16.1 grams

    (B) 16.2 grams

    (C) 16.3 grams

    (D) 0.161 grams

89. Calculate the number of grams present in 0.5 moles of acetylene.

    (A) 13 grams   (B) 14 grams

    (C) 16 grams   (D) 13.5 grams

90. Calculate the weight of 0.8 moles of magnesium.

    (A) 20 g   (B) 19.2 g

    (C) 30 g   (D) 31.2 g

91. Calculate the weight of 10^{24} molecules of nitric oxide.

    (A) 49.8 g   (B) 50 g

    (C) 50.1 g   (D) 39.4 g

92. Calculate the weight in grams of 0.75 gram moles of $NaHCO_3$.

   (A) 64 g   (B) 63 g

   (C) 65 g   (D) 66 g

93. Calculate the number of moles present in 400 grams of $CaCO_3$.

   (A) 2   (B) 3

   (C) 1   (D) 4

94. Calculate the weight of 2.0 moles of $KClO_3$.

   (A) 245 g   (B) 249 g

   (C) 2 g   (D) 24.5 g

95. Calculate the total number of atoms present in 0.8 moles of H_2S.

   (A) 14.4

   (B) 14.4×10^{22}

   (C) 14.428×10^{23}

   (D) 14.4×10^{-23}

96. Calculate the number of oxygen atoms present in 0.75 moles of SO_2.

   (A) 9.03×10^{23}

   (B) 9.03×10^{22}

   (C) 9.03

   (D) 9.03×10^{-23}

97. What is the weight of 3 gram atoms of sulphur?

   (A) 98 g   (B) 99 g

   (C) 95 g   (D) 96 g

98. If a mole of oxygen contains 1.00×10^{24} particles calculate the mass of a single oxygen particle.

   (A) 32×10^{-24} g   (B) 32×10^{-23} g

   (C) 32 g   (D) 32×10^{24} g

99. Calculate the number of moles and molecules present in 4 grams of methane.

   (A) 0.25 moles, 1.505×10^{23} molecules

   (B) 0.3 moles, 1.505 molecules

   (C) 0.25 moles, 1.505×10^{-23} molecules

   (D) 0.3 moles, 2.0 molecules

100. Calculate the weight of the mixture which contains 3.0×10^{22} atoms of helium and 6.0×10^{23} molecules of oxygen.

   (A) 32.2 g   (B) 40.3 g

   (C) 31.4 g   (D) 30.3 g

101. The empirical formula of a compound is CH_2O. Its vapour density is 45. Find its molecular formula.

   (A) $C_2H_4O_6$ (B) $C_3H_6O_3$

   (C) CH_2O (D) $C_4H_6O_6$

102. 16 grams of oxygen is equal to:

   (A) 1 gram atom

   (B) 0.5 gram mole

   (C) 2 gram equivalents

   (D) all of these

103. The mass of oxygen which contains the same number of atoms as those present in 64 grams of sulphur is:

   (A) 16 g

   (B) 32 g

   (C) 48 g

   (D) 64 g

104. If nitrogen and ethylene are in the ratio 1 : 2 by weight then their molecules are in the ratio of:

   (A) 1 : 2   (B) 2 : 1

   (C) 1 : 4   (D) 4 : 1

105. The weight of 10^{22} molecules of $CuSO_4.5H_2O$ is :

(A) 4.16 g

(B) 41.6 g

(C) 25 g

(D) 0.416 g

106. The atomic radius of potassium is _____ than that of sodium.

(A) less   (B) greater

(C) equal   (D) none of these

107. Which of the following is chemical name of the substance whose formula is Ag_3AsO_3?

(A) Argento arsenide

(B) Aagento arsenous oxide

(C) Silver arsenite

(D) Argento arsenite

108. Which element with the following atomic number may be bigger than aluminium atom?

(A) 12   (B) 14

(C) 16   (D) 17

109. Size of Ca^{+2} is smaller than K^+. This is due to :

(A) low effective nuclear charge

(B) high effective nuclear charge

(C) more number of electrons in Ca^{+2}

(D) high IP value

110. When a neutral atom is converted into anion its :

(A) size increases

(B) size decreases

(C) atomic number increases

(D) atomic number decreases

111. The correct order of atomic size of Na, Be, Mg is :

(A) Be > Mg > Na

(B) Na > Mg > Be

(C) Mg > Na > Be

(D) Mg > Be > Na

112. The covalent compound HCl has the polar character because :

(A) the electronegativity of hydrogen is greater than that of chlorine

(B) the electronegativity of chlorine is greater than that of hydrogen

(C) the electronegativity of hydrogen is equal to that of chlorine

(D) hydrogen and chlorine are gases

113. Which set has the strongest tendency to form anions?

(A) Ga, In and Te (B) Na, Mg and Al

(C) N, O and F   (D) V, Cr and Mn

114. Which of the following statements is incorrect?

(A) The size of cation is less than that of the parent atom

(B) The size of anion is greater than that of the parent atom

(C) The size of the cation increases in a group

(D) The size of the anion decreases in a period

115. Which of the following is an ionic compound?

(A) HCl

(B) Na_2O

(C) CO_2

(D) SO_2

116. Which of the following is likely to have the highest melting point?

(A) He (B) CsF

(C) NH_3 (D) $CHCl_3$

117. Many ionic crystals dissolve in water because :

(A) water is amphoteric solvent

(B) water is a high boiling liquid

(C) the process is accompanied by a positive heat of solution

(D) water decreases the interionic attraction in the crystal lattices due to solvation

118. When elements form compounds they do so by :

(A) decreasing the energy content

(B) increasing the energy content

(C) mutual repulsion

(D) becoming inert

119. An electrovalent compound is made of :

(A) electrically charged particles

(B) neutral molecules

(C) neutral atoms

(D) electrically charged atoms or group of atoms

120. Chemical bond formation takes place when :

(A) energy is absorbed

(B) forces of attraction overcome forces of repulsion

(C) forces of repulsion overcome forces of attraction

(D) forces of attraction are equal to forces of repulsion

121. The linkage between two or more atoms is known as :

(A) a chain

(B) a bond

(C) an atomic link

(D) ionic bond

122. Atoms or group of atoms which are electrically charged are known as :

(A) anions (B) cations

(C) ions (D) atoms

123. The charge on cation M is +2 and anion A is –3. The compound has the formula :

(A) MA_2 (B) M_3A_2

(C) M_2A_3 (D) M_2A

124. All chemical bonds are the result of :

(A) interaction of nuclei

(B) interaction of electrons

(C) difference in electronegativity

(D) interaction of the electrons and nuclei

125. The bond formed between two atoms of an electronegative element is :

(A) electrovalent

(B) covalent

(C) coordinate

(D) none

126. An atom becomes ion when there is :

(A) gain of electrons

(B) loss of electrons

(C) gain or loss of electrons

(D) neither gain nor loss

127. Chemical reactions involve participation of :

(A) electrons

(B) protons

(C) neutrons

(D) mesons

128. Ionic compounds :

(A) have bonds which are directional

(B) conduct electricity in solid state

(C) do not conduct electricity in molten state

(D) are generally more soluble in polar solvents than in nonpolar solvents

129. During the formation of an ionic bond the atom that receives electrons is the atom with :

(A) higher electronegativity

(B) lower oxidation number

(C) higher ionisation energy

(D) lower electronegativity

130. In covalency :

(A) the transfer of electrons takes place

(B) sharing of electrons takes place

(C) the electrons are shared by only one atom

(D) none of these

131. CCl_4 is insoluble in water because :

(A) CCl_4 is nonpolar and water is polar

(B) water is nonpolar and CCl_4 is polar

(C) water and CCl_4 both are polar

(D) none of these

132. Covalent compounds commonly exhibit :

(A) high solubilities in water

(B) low melting points

(C) high electrical conductivity

(D) high boiling points

133. The compound which contains both ionic and covalent bonds is :

(A) CH_3–CH_3 (B) CS_2

(C) HCN   (D) KCl

134. The molecule/ion having a pyramidal shape is :

(A) PCl_3 (B) SO_3

(C) CO_3^{2-} (D) NH_4^+

135. Methanol and ethanol are miscible in water due to :

(A) covalent character

(B) hydrogen bonding character

(C) ionic bonding character

(D) tendency to form coordinate bonds

136. The weakest bond among the following is :

(A) metallic

(B) ionic

(C) covalent

(D) hydrogen bond

137. Linear molecule among the following is :

(A) CO_2 (B) NO_2

(C) SO_2 (D) SiO_2

138. An excellent solvent for both ionic and covalent compounds is :

(A) water   (B) liquid NH_3

(C) CH_3COOH (D) CCl_4

139. 'V' shaped molecule is :

(A) $BeCl_2$ (B) NH_3

(C) H_2O (D) CO_2

140. Which of the following is an example of nonpolar covalent molecule?

(A) H_2S

(B) NaCl

(C) H_2SO_4

(D) Cl_2

141. More the energy is decreased during bond formation in a molecule, the _____ is the bond between the atoms.

(A) weaker

(B) stronger

(C) more polar

(D) none of these

142. The abbreviation used for the lengthy name of an element is termed as :

(A) formulae

(B) symbol

(C) equation

(D) none of these

143. Co stands for _____ while CO stands for _____ .

(A) the atoms of the element cobalt; carbon monoxide

(B) the atoms of the element carbon monoxide

(C) the atom of the element cobalt; the molecules of the compound carbon monoxide

(D) the molecules and atoms of element carbon

144. Combining capacity of an atom or a radical is called its _____ . It is equal to the number of _____ atoms or double the number of _____ atoms which combine with it.

(A) oxidation state, chlorine, oxygen

(B) oxidation state, oxygen, chlorine

(C) valency, oxygen, hydrogen

(D) valency, hydrogen, oxygen

145. Which of the following is the formula of the compound nickel bisulphate?

(A) $Ni\ HSO_4$ (B) Ni_2HSO_4

(C) Ni_2SO_4 (D) $Ni(HSO_4)_2$

146. What is the chemical name of the substance whose formulae is $Na(NH_4)HPO_4$?

(A) Sodium hydrogen phosphate

(B) Ammonium hydrogen phosphate

(C) Sodium ammonium hydrogen phosphate

(D) None of these

147. Which of the following is the formula of the compound zinc ferricyanide?

(A) $ZN_3\left[Fe(CN)_6\right]$

(B) $ZN_4\left[Fe(CN)_4\right]$

(C) $ZN_2\left[Fe(CN)_2\right]$

(D) $ZN_2\left[Fe(CN)_6\right]$

148. Which of the following is the formula of the compound stannic phosphate?

(A) $Sn_3(PO_4)_4$ (B) $Sn_2(PO_3)_2$

(C) $Sn_3(PO_3)_2$ (D) $Sn_2(PO_3)_4$

149. Which of the following is the formula of the compound magnesium phosphite?

(A) Mg_2PO_3

(B) $Mg_2(PO_3)_4$

(C) $MgHPO_3$

(D) None of these

150. Which of the following is the formula of the compound calcium borate?

(A) $Ca_3(BO_3)_4$ (B) $Ca_2(BO_2)_3$

(C) $Ca_2(BO_2)_3$ (D) $Ca_2(BO_2)_3$

151. Which of the following is the formula of the compound nickel nitrate?

(A) $Ni_2(NO_3)_3$ (B) $Ni(NO_3)_2$

(C) Ni_2NO_3 (D) $NiNO_3$

152. Which of the following is the chemical name of $Ba(ClO_3)_2$?

(A) Barium chloride

(B) Barium chlorate

(C) Barium chlorite

(D) Barium hypochlorite

153. Which of the following is the formula of barium peroxide?

(A) Ba_2O (B) Ba_2O_2

(C) BaO_2 (D) BaO_3

Answers

1. B	2. C	3. B	4. A	5. B	6. C	7. A	8. B	9. C	10. A
11. B	12. A	13. B	14. C	15. A	16. B	17. A	18. D	19. A	20. C
21. A	22. C	23. A	24. D	25. B	26. A	27. C	28. A	29. C	30. D
31. B	32. C	33. C	34. B	35. B	36. B	37. C	38. C	39. B	40. C
41. A	42. B	43. C	44. C	45. C	46. A	47. B	48. D	49. B	50. A
51. C	52. A	53. C	54. D	55. C	56. D	57. B	58. A	59. C	60. B
61. A	62. C	63. A	64. B	65. D	66. A	67. B	68. A	69. D	70. A
71. B	72. C	73. A	74. D	75. C	76. C	77. B	78. D	79. A	80. B
81. A	82. D	83. B	84. C	85. A	86.B	87. A	88. A	89. A	90. B
91. A	92. B	93. D	94. A	95. C	96. A	97. D	98. A	99. A	100. A
101. B	102. D	103. B	104. A	105. A	106. B	107. C	108. A	109. B	110. A
111. B	112. B	113. C	114. D	115. B	116. B	117. D	118. A	119. D	120. D
121. B	122. C	123. B	124. D	125. D	126. B	127. C	128. A	129. D	130. A
131. B	132. A	133. B	134. C	135. A	136. D	137. A	138. A	139. C	140. D
141. A	142. B	143. C	144. D	145. D	146. C	147. A	148. A	149. C	150. D
151. B	152. C	153. B							

4. (A) The atomic mass of sulphur is 32.

1 gram atom of S weighs = 32 g.

3 gram atoms of S weighs

$$= 3 \times 32 = 96 \text{ g.}$$

5. (B) 1 gram atom of magnesium weighs = 24 g.

1 g of magnesium accounts for

$\dfrac{1}{24}$ gram atoms of magnesium.

144 g magnesium accounts for

$\dfrac{1}{24}$ 44 = 6 gram atoms.

6. (C) One molecule of CH_3COOH contains 2 oxygen atoms.

∴ one mole of CH_3COOH contains 2 moles of Oxygen atoms.

8. (B) 40 g of calcium constitutes one gram atom.

10 g of calcium accounts for

gram atom = $\dfrac{1}{40} \times 10$

= 0.25 gram atoms

According to Avogadro's number the number of atoms in 1 g of calcium = 6.02×10^{23}

The number of atoms in 0.25 gram atom

$= 0.25 \times 6.02 \times 1023$

$$= 1.50 \times 10^{23} \text{ atoms.}$$

9. (C) Formula of sodium carbonate

$= Na_2CO_3$

Gram molecular weight of

$Na_2CO_3 = 106$ g.

1 mole of Na_2CO_3 weighs

$$= 106 \text{ g.}$$

0.1 mole of Na_2CO_3 weighs

$\dfrac{106}{1} \times 0.1 = 10.6$ g.

10. (A) Number of moles

$$= \dfrac{\text{weight}}{\text{gram molecular weight}}$$

Number of molecules = number of moles

$= \dfrac{5.23}{180} \times 6.02 \times 10^{23}$

$= 1.75 \times 10^{22}$ molecules.

11. (B) Formula of glucose = $C_6H_{12}O_6$

Molecular weight = 180 amu

One mole gram glucose = 180 g.

180 g of glucose contains

= 1 mole of glucose.

540 g of glucose contains

$= \dfrac{1}{180 \text{ g}} \times 540 \text{ g} = 3$ moles.

12. (A) $CaCO_3 \xrightarrow{\text{heat}} Cao + CO_2 (g)$

Lime stone   Lime

(40 + 12 + 48)   (40 + 16)

= 100 g   = 50 g.

400 g   ?

100 g of $CaCO_3$ on burning gives 56 g CaO.

400 g of $CaCO_3$ on burning gives

$$\frac{56\,g}{100\,g} \times 400\,g = 224\,g.$$

13. (B) Gram formula weight or weight of 1 mole of Na_2CO_3 = 106 g.

Gram formula weight of methyl alcohol or weight of one mole of CH_3OH = 32 g.

Number of moles of Na_2CO_3

produced per month = $\dfrac{424 \times 10^6}{106}$

$= 4 \times 10^6$ moles.

Number of moles of CH_3OH produced per month

$= \dfrac{320 \times 10^6}{32}$

$= 10 \times 10^6$ moles.

Hence methyl alcohol is produced more than the sodium carbonate in terms of number of moles.

14. (C) Percentage of the elements present:

Carbon	Hydrogen	Chlorine
10.06	0.84	89.10

Dividing the percentage compositions by the respective atomic weights of the elements:

$$\frac{10.06}{12} \quad : \quad \frac{0.84}{1} \quad : \quad \frac{89.10}{35.5}$$

0.84	0.84	2.51

Dividing by the smallest number to get simple atomic ratio:

$$\frac{0.84}{0.84} \quad : \quad \frac{0.84}{0.84} \quad : \quad \frac{2.51}{0.84}$$

Ratio of the atoms present in the molecule is

| 1 | : | 1 | : | 3 |

The empirical formula of the compound is $CHCl_3$.

15. (A) 44 g of CO_2 contains 12 g of carbon.

0.361 g CO_2 contains

$$\frac{12\,g}{44\,g} \times 0.361\,g = 0.0985\,g$$

of carbon.

The percentage composition of carbon present in the compound: 0.202 g of the carbon compound contains 0.0985 g of carbon.

100 g of the carbon comound

contains $\dfrac{0.0985\,g}{0.202\,g} \times 100\,g$

$= 48.76\%$

16. (B) Percentage composition of the elements present in the compound:

K	Cr	O
26.57	35.36	38.07

Dividing by respective atomic weights of the elements:

$\dfrac{26.57}{39}$	$\dfrac{35.36}{52}$	$\dfrac{38.07}{16}$
0.67	0.67	2.38

Dividing by the smallest number:

$\dfrac{0.67}{0.67}$	$\dfrac{0.67}{0.67}$	$\dfrac{2.38}{0.67}$
1	1	3.5

Multiplication by a suitable integer to get whole number ratio:

$1 \times 2 = 2 \qquad 1 \times 2 = 2 \qquad 3.5 \times 2 = 7$

∴ The empirical formula of the compound is $K_2Cr_2O_7$.

20. (C) Empirical formula = CH_2O

Empirical formula weight

$$= 12 + 12 + 16 = 30$$

$$n = \frac{\text{molecular weight}}{\text{empirical formula weight}}$$

$$\therefore n = \frac{90}{30} = 3$$

The molecular formula

$(CH_2O)_3 = C_3H_6O_3$.

24. (D) Formula weight of $CaCO_3$

$= 40 + 12 + 3 \times 16 = 100$ amu.

1 mole of $CaCO_3$ = 100 g.

Hence 2.56 moles of $CaCO_3$

$= 2.5 \times 100 = 250$ g.

25. (B) Molecular weight of ozone (O_3) = 48 amu.

1 mole of O_3 = 1 GMW = 48 g.

Number of moles of ozone

$$= \frac{\text{weight given}}{\text{GMW}} = \frac{12g}{48g} = 0.25$$

Molecular weight of

$SO_2 = (32 + 2 \times 16)$ amu = 64 amu.

1 mole of SO_2 = 64 g.

Number of moles of SO_2 =

$$\frac{32g}{64g} = 0.5$$

26. (A) Weight of 1 molecule

$$\frac{\text{GMW}}{\text{Avagadro's Number}} = \frac{32g}{6.023 \times 10^{23}}$$

$= 5.33 \times 10^{-23}$ g.

27. (C) Atomic weight of S = 32.06 amu.

1 gram atomic weight of S

= 32.06 g = 6.023×10^{23} atoms.

Number of atoms in 6.4 g of S

$$= \frac{6.4}{32.06} \times 6.023 \times 10^{23}$$

$= 1.2 \times 10^{23}$

28. (A) Atomic weight of an element expressed in grams is called gram atomic weight or gram atom (or) Quantity of an element that contains 6.023×10^{23} atoms is gram atom.

Number of gram atoms of oxygen

$$= \frac{\text{weight of element}}{\text{gram atomic weight}}$$

$$= \frac{256\,g}{16\,g} = 16.$$

29. (C) Number of atoms

= Number of gram atoms × Avogadro Number.

Atomic weight of Cl = 35.50

Number of atoms of Cl =

$$= \frac{71.00}{35.50} \times 6.023 \times 10^{23}$$

$$= 2 \times 6.023 \times 10^{23}$$

$$= 1.205 \times 10^{24}$$

30. (D) Number of gram atoms of carbon

$$= \frac{\text{weight of element}}{\text{gram atomic weight}} = \frac{60\,g}{12\,g}$$

$$= 5.$$

33. (C) Formula weight of CH_2O

$$= 12 + 2 + 16 = 30$$

Empirical formula weight $\times n = 60$

$$30 \times n = 60$$

$$n = 2$$

So the molecular formula is

$C_2H_4O_2$.

35. (B) Gram atomic weight of He = 4 g.
Number of moles

$$= \frac{\text{given weight of element}}{\text{gram atomic weight}} = \frac{6.46}{4}$$

$$= 1.615.$$

36. (B) Gram molecular weight of magnesium nitrate

$$= 24 + 2(14 + 3 \times 16) = 148\,g.$$

Weight of $Mg(NO_3)_2$

= number of moles $\times$ gram molecular weight

$$= 0.885 \times 148 = 131\,g.$$

37. (C) 1 mole of Na_2CO_3 = 106 g (GMW)

Weight of 0.1 mole of Na_2CO_3

$$= 0.1 \times 106 = 10.6\,g.$$

42. (B) Number of molecules of MgO

$$= 0.5 \times 6.023 \times 10^{23}$$

$$= 3.0115 \times 10^{23}.$$

43. (C) $Al_2(SO_4)_3$ contains 12 atoms of oxygen.

Mass of oxygen in $Al_2(SO_4)_3$

= mass of 12 O atoms

$$= 12 \times 16 = 192$$

Molecular mass of $Al_2(SO_4)_3$

$$= 27 \times 2 + 32 \times 3 + 16 \times 12$$

$$= 54 + 96 + 192 = 342.$$

So the percentage of oxygen

$$= \frac{\text{mass of oxygen in } Al_2(SO_4)_3}{\text{molecular mass of } Al_2(SO_4)_3} \times 100$$

$$= \frac{192}{342} \times 100 = 56.14\%$$

44. (C) 1 mole of iron

= gram atomic mass of iron

= 56 grams.

We know that 1 mole of iron element contains 6.023×10^{23} atoms of iron.

56 g of iron contains

$$= 6.023 \times 10^{23} \text{ atoms}$$

2.8 g of iron contains

$$= \frac{6.023 \times 10^{23}}{56} \times 2.8$$

$$= \frac{6.023 \times 10^{22}}{2}$$

$$= 3.011 \times 10^{22} \text{ atoms.}$$

49. (B) Atomic weight of zinc = 65.38 g.
Number of moles

$$= \frac{\text{given weight of element}}{\text{gram atomic weight}}$$

$$= \frac{23.3}{65.38} = 0.35 \text{ moles.}$$

50. (A) 1 mole of sodium oxalate =134 g.

Weight of 0.1 mole of $Na_2C_2O_4$
= 0.1 × 134 = 13.4 g.

55. (C) Gram molecular weight of

Na_2CO_3 = 2 × 23 + 12 + 3 × 16
= 106 g.

$$n = \frac{5.3}{106} = 0.05.$$

56. (D) Number of molecules

$$= \frac{1.8}{180 \,(\text{i.e., GMW of glucose})} \times 6.023 \times 10^{23}$$

$= 6.023 \times 10^{22}$.

61. (A) In white phosphorous, molecules exist as P_4 units.

1 mole of P_4 molecules

= 6.023 × 10²³ molecules.

∴ 0.1 mole of P_4 molecules

= 6.023 × 10²² molecules

= 6.023 × 10²³ × 0.1 atoms.

Each P_4 molecule contains 4 phosphorous atoms.

6.023 × 10²² molecules contain

4 × 6.023 × 10²²

= 2.409 × 10²³ atoms.

69. (D) Weight of 1 molecule of H_2O

$$= \frac{\text{gram molecular weight of } H_2O}{\text{Avagadro number}}$$

$$= \frac{18}{6.023 \times 10^{23}} = 2.988 \times 10^{-23} \text{ g.}$$

100. (A) 1 mole of He = 6.0 × 10²³ atoms of He = 4.0026 g.

Weight of 3.0 × 10²² atoms of

$$He = \frac{3.0 \times 10^{22}}{6.0 \times 10^{23}} \times 4 = 0.2 \text{ g.}$$

1 mole of O_2 = 6.0 × 10²³ molecules

of O_2 = 32.0 g.

Weight of O_2 = 32 g.

Total weight of the mixture

= 0.2 + 32 = 32.2 g.

101. (B) Empirical formula weight

= 12 + 2 + 16 = 30.

Molecular weight

= 2 × VD = 2 × 45 = 90.

Molecular formula

= Empirical formula × n

$$n = \frac{M.Wt}{EFW} = \frac{90}{30} = 3$$

∴ MF = (CH_2O) × 3 = $C_3H_6O_3$.

❖ ❖ ❖

Chapter 4

Structure of the Atom

Synopsis

1. Electrons, protons and neutrons are the fundamental particles of an atom.

2. *Electrons* were discovered in discharge tube experiments as cathode rays.

3. Cathode rays are streams of negatively charged particles.

4. They are deflected by electric and magnetic fields.

5. They produce fluorescence on zinc sulphide screen.

6. The mass, charge and the specific charge of the cathode rays are independent of the nature of the gas used in the tube and the material with which the cathode is made of.

7. Electrons were discovered by J.J.Thomson.

8. The specific charge of electron was determined by J.J.Thomson.

9. The charge of the electron is 1.602×10^{-19} C or 4.8×10^{-10} e.s.u.

10. The absolute mass of electron is 9.108×10^{-28} g or 9.108×10^{-31} kg.

11. The mass of electron on atomic mass unit scale is 0.0005486 a.m.u.

12. The energy of electron increases with the increase in velocity.

13. The electrons produced by the incidence of light on a metal surface are called photoelectrons and the phenomenon is called photoelectric effect.

14. Electrons produced during the decay of a radioactive element are called β –particles.

15. The radius of the electron is approximately 1.0×10^{-15} cm.

16. The charge of one mole of electrons is 96500 coulomb or one farad.

17. *Protons* are positive rays that were discovered by Goldstein in the discharge tube experiments when a perforated metal cathode was used.

18. Positive rays are also known as anode rays.

19. Positive rays are deflected by electric and magnetic fields.

20. The lightest positive ray having the highest specific charge was taken in the discharge tube.

21. Positive ray carrying unit charge and unit mass is called proton.

22. The charge of a proton is equal to that of electron in magnitude but they differ in sign.

23. The mass of a proton is almost equal to that of a hydrogen atom.

24. The magnitude of charge of a proton is 1.602×10^{-19} coulombs or 4.8×10^{-10} e.s.u.

25. The absolute mass of a proton is 1.672×10^{-24} g or 1.672×10^{-27} kg.

26. The mass of a proton on atomic mass unit scale is 1.00727 a.m.u.

27. The mass of a proton is approximately 1837 times greater than that of an electron.

28. The specific charge of a proton is 1837 times less than that of an electron.

29. The existence of a neutral particle with unit mass was predicted by Ernest Rutherford.

30. *Neutrons* were discovered by James Chadwick.

31. Neutrons were produced when atoms of low atomic weight elements were bombarded by α – particles.

$$_3Li^7 + {}_2He^4 \rightarrow {}_5B^{10} + {}_0n^1$$

$$_4Be^9 + {}_2He^4 \rightarrow {}_6C^{12} + {}_0n^1$$

$$_5B^{11} + {}_2He^4 \rightarrow {}_7N^{14} + {}_0n^1$$

32. Neutrons are unaffected by electric or magnetic field.

33. On atomic mass unit scale, its mass is 1.00866 amu.

34. The specific charge of a neutron is zero.

35. According to Rutherford's atomic model the electrons revolve around the nucleus in circular paths.

36. Electrons maintain the circular path as the inward force (or) centripetal force is balanced by the outward force or centrifugal force.

37. Rutherford's atomic model could not explain the stability of the atoms and the line spectra of atoms.

38. Max Planck proposed quantum theory to explain the black body radiation.

39. Energy in any form from any source is radiated discontinuously in the form of packets called quanta.

40. Energy associated with a quantum is directly proportional to the frequency of radiation.

41. According to Einstein light propagates in space in bundles or packets.

42. Each packet or bundle of energy is called a photon.

43. The energy associated with a photon is $E = h\upsilon$.

44. Einstein's theory is applicable to all types of radiations.

45. *Bohr's atomic model* : Bohr's atomic model is based on Max Planck's quantum theory.

46. Electrons revolve round the nucleus in certain concentric circular orbits called stationary orbits.

47. These orbits are designated as K, L, M, N.

48. As long as the electron revolves in the stationary orbit it neither radiates nor absorbs energy.

49. When an electron jumps from a lower orbit to higher orbit it absorbs energy.

50. If an electron jumps from a higher orbit to a lower orbit it radiates energy.

51. The radiated or absorbed energy is equal to the difference between the energies of the two orbits in which the electron transition takes place.

52. *Defects of Bohr's theory* : It failed to explain the spectra of multielectron species.

53. Multiplication of spectral lines in the presence of magnetic field is called Zeeman effect.

54. Splitting up of spectral lines in the presence of electric field is called Stark effect.

55. It could not explain the difference in the energies of the electrons in the same orbit.

56. According to Heisenberg's uncertainity principle the position and velocity of the electron cannot be calculated simultaneously and accurately.

57. The maximum number of electrons in any energy level is $2n^2$.

58. The maximum number of electrons in the ultimate energy level or the outermost energy level is 8.

59. The maximum number of electrons in the penultimate energy level is 18.

60. The maximum number of electrons that can be accommodated in the antipenultimate energy level is 32.

61. Half filled or completely filled orbitals give greater stability to an atom.

62. Most of the metals have less than 4 electrons in their valence shell.

63. Most nonmetals contain more than four electrons in their valence shell.

64. Elements having only one electron in their valence shell are the most electropositive metals (alkali metals).

65. Elements with two electrons in their valence shell are also more electropositive (alkaline earths).

66. Inert gases have 8 electrons in their valence shells. Helium is the exception which contains 2 electrons.

67. Halogen have 7 electrons in their valence shell.

68. The valence shell represents the periods to which the element belongs.

69. The number of electrons in the valence shell is equal to the group number (except zero group and group VIII)

70. Isotopes are the atoms of the same element with the same atomic number but different mass numbers.

71. Isotopes differ in the number of neutrons in their nuclei.

72. Isotopes have similar electronic configuration and exhibit similar chemical properties.

73. Isobars are the atoms of different elements with the same mass number but different atomic numbers.

$$Ar_{18}^{40}, K_{19}^{40}, Ca_{20}^{40}$$

74. Isobars differ in their physical and chemical properties. They differ in the number of all the three fundamental particles.

75. Atoms of the different elements with different atomic numbers and mass numbers but the same number of neutrons are called isotones. Some examples are:

1) $Na_{11}^{23}, Mg_{12}^{24}$

2) P_{15}^{31}, S_{16}^{32}

3) $Al_{13}^{27}, Si_{14}^{28}$

76. The branch of chemistry which deals with the changes that occur inside the nucleus is called nuclear chemistry.

77. Atomic nucleus with a specific atomic number and mass number is called nuclide.

78. Nuclear stability is related to the nuclear binding energy.

79. 1 a.m.u. mass is equivalent to 931.5 MeV.

80. Binding energy increases progressively with the atomic mass.

81. Radioactive elements may undergo α–decay or β–decay.

82. All nuclides having atomic number of more than 82 exhibit natural radioactivity.

83. An α–particle carries two units positive charge and four units mass.

84. They have great momentum due their large mass and velocity.

85. They have low penetrating power.

86. β–particles are the fast moving electrons.

87. β–rays have greater penetrating power than α–particles.

88. The gamma rays have no mass. They are electrically neutral.

89. Gamma rays travel with the velocity of light.

90. Radioactive decay or disintegration is a nuclear change and a chemical change.

91. The time taken to disintegrate half of the initial amount of radioactive substance is called half–life period.

Multiple Choice Questions

1. Metals and hydrogen are always:
   (A) electropositive
   (B) electronegative
   (C) both A and B
   (D) none of the above

2. Mg^{+2} and F^- ions differ in which of the following fundamental particles?
   (A) Electrons, protons and neutrons
   (B) Protons and neutrons
   (C) Only protons
   (D) Neutrons and electrons

3. The firmness with which an electron is held by an atom is a measure of its:
   (A) electronegativity
   (B) ionisation potential
   (C) ionic character
   (D) metallic character

4. Al^{+3} has a lower ionic radius than Mg^{2+} ion because:
   (A) Mg atom has less number of neutrons than Al
   (B) Al^{+3} has a higher nuclear charge than Mg^{+2}
   (C) their electronegativities are different
   (D) Al has a lower ionisation potential than an Mg atom

5. Which of the following has no units?
   (A) Ionisation potential
   (B) Electron affinity
   (C) Electronegativity
   (D) None of these

6. Which of the following is true?

(A) Halogens are metals

(B) ZnO is more basic than CO

(C) A nonmetal is more electropositive than a metal

(D) A metal is more electronegative than a nonmetal

7. Nitrogen exhibits its group valency in:

(A) ammonia

(B) hydrazine

(C) NO_2

(D) silver nitrate

8. Elements having 7 electrons in the valence shell are called:

(A) halogens

(B) chalcogens

(C) alkali metals

(D) alkaline earths

9. Cesium is the most _____ and flourine the most _____ of all elements.

(A) electropositive, electronegative

(B) electronegative, electropositive

(C) oxidising agent, reducing agent

(D) none of the above

10. The halogen with smallest electron affinity is:

(A) Fluorine   (B) Chlorine

(C) Bromine   (D) Iodine

11. Which of the following has zero electron affinity?

(A) Oxygen

(B) Fluorine

(C) Nitrogen

(D) Neon

12. When metals react with nonmetals the metal atoms tend to:

(A) lose electrons

(B) gain electrons

(C) share electrons

(D) none

13. Valency is the :

(A) combining capacity of an element

(B) atomicity of an element

(C) oxidation number of an element

(D) none

14. Bond length decreases with:

(A) increase in the size of the atom

(B) increase in the number of bonds between the atoms

(C) decrease in the number of bonds between the atoms

(D) decrease in the bond angle

15. Linus Pauling received the Nobel prize for his work on:

(A) atomic structure

(B) photosynthesis

(C) thermodynamics

(D) chemical bonds

16. If in forming a compound AB, an electron is transferred from an atom A to atom B then:

(A) A is divalent

(B) B is oxidised and A is reduced

(C) the compound AB is electrovalent

(D) A and B are covalently bonded

17. The number of valency electrons in carbon atoms (atomic number 6)is:

(A) 0   (B) 2

(C) 4   (D) 6

18. Valency of carbon in CH_4, C_2H_6, C_2H_4 and C_2H_2 is ____ , ____ , ____ and ____ respectively.

    (A) 1, 2, 3, 4   (B) 4, 3, 2, 1

    (C) 2, 3, 1, 4   (D) 4, 1, 3, 2

19. Valency of iron in $FeCl_2$ and $FeCl_3$ is ____ and ____ respectively.

    (A) 1, 2   (B) 2, 1

    (C) 2, 3   (D) 3, 2

20. Valency of tin in $SnCl_2$ and $SnCl_4$ is _____ and ____ respectively.

    (A) 2, 4   (B) 4, 2

    (C) 3, 4   (D) 2, 3

21. Valency of sulphur in SO_2 and SO_3 is ____ and ____ respectively.

    (A) 3, 6   (B) 2, 3

    (C) 2, 6   (D) 4, 6

22. The charge carried by an electron is :

    (A) 1.602×10^{19} coulombs

    (B) 1.602×10^{-19} coulombs

    (C) 1.609 coulombs

    (D) 6.02×10^{19} coulombs

23. Which of the following electronic configurations is wrong?

    (A) Be (3) = 2, 1

    (B) O (8) = 2, 6

    (C) S (16) = 2, 6, 8

    (D) P (15) = 2, 8, 5

24. The mass of a proton is :

    (A) 1.609 g

    (B) 1.6×10^{24} g

    (C) 1.6×10^{-23} g

    (D) 1.6×10^{-24} g

25. An atom has mass number 23 and atomic number 11. The atom has ____ electrons, ____ protons and ____ neutrons.

    (A) 11, 12, 13   (B) 11, 11, 12

    (C) 11, 11, 13   (D) 11, 14, 15

26. The nucleus of an atom has atomic number 17 and mass number 37. There are 17 electrons outside the nucleus. Then the number of neutrons in it is :

    (A) 20   (B) 21

    (C) 17   (D) 37

27. Which of the following electronic configurations represents a noble gas?

    (A) 2, 8, 2   (B) 2, 8, 6

    (C) 2, 8   (D) 2, 8, 8, 2

28. Which of the following statements is not true?

    (A) Most of the space in an atom is empty

    (B) The total number of neutrons and protons is always equal in a neutral atom

    (C) The total number of electrons and protons in an atom is always equal

    (D) The total number of electrons in any energy level can be calculated by the formula $2n^2$

29. $_{17}Cl^{35}$ and $_{17}Cl^{37}$ are examples of :

    (A) isobars   (B) isotopes

    (C) isotones   (D) none

30. Which of the following species are isoelectronic?

    (A) Cl^- and Br^- (B) Na^+ and Mg^{++}

    (C) Ar and Ne   (D) Mg^{++} and Ca^{++}

31. $^{55}_{25}Mn^{++}$ has :

(A) 25 protons and 25 neutrons

(B) 25 protons and 55 neutrons

(C) 55 protons and 25 neutrons

(D) 25 protons and 30 neutrons

32. An atom of an element has 10 electrons, 10 protons and 12 neutrons. The atomic mass of the element is:

(A) 10   (B) 12

(C) 22   (D) 32

33. Which of the following fundamental particles is not deflected by a magnetic field?

(A) Proton   (B) Neutron

(C) Electron   (D) Positron

34. When the speed of an electron increases, the specific charge :

(A) decreases

(B) increases

(C) remains same

(D) none of these

35. Mass number of an atom represents the number of :

(A) protons only

(B) protons and neutrons

(C) protons and electrons

(D) neutrons and electrons

36. The ratio of the masses of proton and neutron is :

(A) > 1   (B) < 1

(C) = 1   (D) > $\sqrt{1}$

37. Which of the following consist of particles of matter?

(A) Alpha rays   (B) Beta rays

(C) Cathode rays (D) All of these

38. The e/m is not constant for :

(A) cathode rays   (B) positive rays

(C) α–rays   (D) β–rays

39. Size of the nucleus is :

(A) 10^{-15} cm   (B) 10^{-13} cm

(C) 10^{-10} cm   (D) 10^{-8} cm

40. An atom has a net charge of –1. It has 18 electrons and 20 neutrons. Its mass number is :

(A) 37   (B) 35

(C) 38   (D) 20

41. Bohr's model can explain :

(A) spectrum of hydrogen atom only

(B) spectrum of any atom or ion having one electron only

(C) spectrum of hydrogen molecule

(D) solar spectrum

42. Nucleus model of the atom was proposed by :

(A) Thomson

(B) Neils Bohr

(C) Moseley

(D) Rutherford

43. Cathode rays have :

(A) only mass

(B) only charge

(C) neither mass nor charge

(D) both mass and charge

44. Positive charge in an atom is :

(A) scattered all over the atom

(B) concentrated in the nucleus

(C) revolving around the nucleus

(D) none of these

45. Mass of an electron is :

(A) 9.1×10^{-28} g (B) 9.1×10^{-25} g

(C) 9.1×10^{-10} g (D) 9.1×10^{-18} g

46. For which of the following species, Bohr's theory does not apply?

(A) H   (B) H^+

(C) He^+ (D) Li^{2+}

47. Number of neutrons in a heavy hydrogen atom is :

(A) 0   (B) 1

(C) 2   (D) 3

48. Mass of a hydrogen atom is equal to:

(A) 1.673×10^{-24} g

(B) 5.56×10^{-4} amu

(C) the sum of a proton, an electron and a neutron

(D) mass of 1836 electrons

49. Which of the following is false?

(A) Neutron has highest mass among fundamental particles

(B) The mass of an electron is negligible

(C) e/m is highest for a proton

(D) Charge of neutron is zero

50. The ratio of specific charge of a proton and α particle is

(A) 2 : 1   (B) 1 : 2

(C) 1 : 4   (D) 1 : 1

51. Which of the following particles is the heaviest?

(A) Meson

(B) Eelectron

(C) Proton

(D) Neutron

52. In Rutherford's alpha–ray scattering experiment, the alpha particles are detected using a screen coated with:

(A) carbon black

(B) platinum black

(C) zinc sulphide

(D) polytetrafluoroethylene

53. A species 'X' contains 9 protons, 10 electrons and 11 neutrons. It is :

(A) a neutral atom

(B) an isotope

(C) a cation

(D) an anion

54. In a stationary orbit of an atom the electron will be :

(A) revolving with constant energy

(B) at rest

(C) losing energy constantly

(D) losing energy discontinuously

55. An atom with atomic number 82 and mass number 208 contains :

(A) 82 protons and 82 electrons

(B) 82 protons and 126 neutrons

(C) 82 protons, 82 electrons and 126 neutrons

(D) 82 neutrons, 126 protons and 126 electrons

56. The emission of light on heating a gas is due to :

(A) excitation of electrons

(B) de–excitation of electrons

(C) initial excitation and then de-excitation

(D) none of these

57. Outer orbits have _____ energy level than inner orbits.

(A) greater

(B) smaller

(C) same

(D) none of these

58. Bohr's model of atom explains

(A) Zeeman effect

(B) Heisenberg's principle

(C) Stark effect

(D) none of these

59. Bohr's atomic theory gave the idea of :

(A) quantum numbers

(B) shape of sublevels

(C) nucleus

(D) stationary states

60. Energy of an orbit :

(A) increases as we move away from the nucleus

(B) remains same as we move away from the nucleus

(D) decreases as we move away from the nucleus

(D) none of the above

61. According to Bohr's model of hydrogen atom :

(A) the linear velocity of the electron is quantised

(B) the angular velocity is quantised

(C) the linear momentum of the electron is quantised

(D) the angular momentum of the electron is quantised

62. Which of the following is false about electrons?

(A) The negatively charged electrons in an atom are attracted by the positive nucleus by electrostatic attractive force

(B) An electron near the nucleus is strongly attracted by the nucleus and has low potential energy

(C) An electron distant from the nucleus is less firmly held and has high potential energy

(D) On heating an atom strongly, all of its electrons are ejected

63. Atoms consist of electrons, protons and neutrons. If the mass attributed to neutrons were halved and that attributed to the electrons were doubled the atomic mass of $_6C^{12}$ would approximately be :

(A) same   (B) doubled

(C) halved   (D) reduced by 25%

64. If three neutrons are added to the nuclei of $_{92}U^{235}$, the new nucleus will have an atomic number of :

(A) 89   (B) 95

(C) 90   (D) 92

65. Which of the following is not an electromagnetic radiation?

(A) Infrared rays

(B) X–rays

(C) Cathode rays

(D) γ –rays

66. The specific charge of positive rays is maximum when the gas taken in the discharge tube is :

(A) oxygen   (B) nitrogen

(C) helium   (D) hydrogen

67. In a species the number of protons, electrons and neutrons are respectively 1, 0 and 1. The species is :

(A) D^+ (B) H^+

(C) He (D) Li^+

68. When alpha particles are sent through a goldfoil most of them go straight through the foil. The reason is :

(A) alpha particles are much heavier than the electrons

(B) alpha particles are positively charged

(C) most of the atom is empty

(D) none of the above

69. Oxygen atom and oxide ion have :

(A) same size

(B) same electron number

(C) same electronic configuration

(D) same proton number

70. Which of the following ions is the smallest in size?

(A) Mg^{2+} (B) Na^+

(C) O^{2-} (D) F^-

71. Which of the following statements is true?

(A) F^- has more electrons than Na^+

(B) F^- has less electrons than Na^+

(C) Na^+ and F^- has equal electrons

(D) None of the above

72. It is impossible to determine simultaneously with certainity the position and the momentum of a particle. The above principle was given by :

(A) Zeeman (B) Bohr

(C) Heisenberg (D) Sommerfeld

73. The maximum number of electrons in a main shell of an atomic orbital is equal to :

(A) n^2 (B) $2n^2$

(C) $2n$ (D) $4n + 1$

74. The phenomenon in which there is a change in wavelength of the scattered X–rays is called :

(A) Zeeman effect

(B) Stark effect

(C) Compton effect

(D) Hypochromic effect

75. A _____ is the smallest unit of waves in the form of which a hot body emits radiant energy and it can exist independently.

(A) electron (B) proton

(C) quantum (D) neutron

76. Why do the orbitals in an atom tend to become half-filled or completely filled?

(A) For less stability

(B) For more stability

(C) For more reactivity

(C) For more electropositivity

77. The maximum number of electrons that can be accommodated in the 4th energy level is :

(A) 32 (B) 18

(C) 2 (D) 8

78. Neutrons were discovered by :

(A) Rutherford

(B) Bohr

(C) Chadwick

(D) J J Thomson

79. The existence of protons in the atoms was shown by :

(A) Neils Bohr

(B) Chadwick

(C) Madam Curie

(D) Goldstein

80. The fractional atomic masses of elements are due the existence of :

(A) isotopes having different masses

(B) diagonal relationship

(C) equal number of electrons and protons

(D) none of these

81. Give the number of electrons present in the outermost shell of atoms of each of the following elements.

(i) Helium (ii) Magnesium (iii) Sulphur

(A) i – 2, ii – 3, iii – 4

(B) i – 1, ii – 4, iii – 6

(C) i – 2, ii – 2, iii – 6

(D) i – 3, ii – 4, iii – 5

82. The atomic numbers of three elements A, B and C are 5, 9 and 13 respectively. Which two elements show similar chemical properties?

(A) A and B

(B) A and C

(C) B and C

(D) none of these

83. The p–orbitals in an atom are :

(A) spherical shaped

(B) dumbell shaped

(C) rectangular shaped

(D) double dumbbell shaped

84. The principal quantum number denotes the _____ of an electron.

(A) energy sublevel

(B) energy level

(C) magnetic field

(D) orbital

85. Size of an atom is expressed in terms of :

(A) atomic radius

(B) Vander Waals radius

(C) ionic radius

(D) either A or B

86. The metals of s–block elements combine directly with halogens (X) at appropriate temperatures to form halides of the :

(A) MX and MX_2 type

(B) MX_2 and MX_3 type

(C) MX_3 and MX_4 type

(D) MX and MX_3 type

87. If stability of the elements goes on increasing, their _____ goes on decreasing.

(A) electronegativity

(B) solubility

(C) activity

(D) none of the above

88. With the increase in the number of shells or the principal quantum number, _____ increases.

(A) atomic radius

(B) ionic radius

(C) both A and B

(D) covalent radius

89. While revolving round the nucleus in a fixed orbit, the electron neither loses nor gains energy. Under this condition the atom as a whole is said to be in a :

(A) reactive energy state

(B) neutral energy state

(C) stationary energy state

(D) none of the above

90. According to Rutherford's atomic model, if the electrons lose energy continuously, the observed atomic spectra should be _____, consisting of _____ merging one into other.

(A) continuous, sharp lines

(B) discontinuous, sharp lines

(C) continuous, broad bands

(D) discontinuous, broad bands

91. Elements having 1, 2 or 3 valence electrons in their atoms are metals except :

(A) hydrogen

(B) chlorine

(C) magnesium

(D) sodium

92. The distribution of electrons in various subshells of the outermost shell is called :

(A) inner shell configuration

(B) valence shell configuration

(C) inner shell conformation

(D) valence shell conformation

93. The valency of the elements with respect to hydrogen in each short period increases from ____ and then falls to one, while the same with respect to oxygen increases from ____.

(A) 1 to 4, 1 to 6 (B) 1 to 5, 1 to 7

(C) 1 to 6, 1 to 7 (D) 1 to 4, 1 to 7

94. $M(g) - e^- + $ energy supplied $\rightarrow M^+(g)$. The above equation defines :

(A) electropositivity

(B) first ionisation energy

(C) electronegativity

(D) electron affinity

95. The distance between the nucleus of an ion and the point where the nucleus exerts its influence on the electron cloud is called :

(A) atomic radius

(B) ionic radius

(C) crystal radius

(D) none of the above

96. What is the reason for the identical chemical properties of all the isotopes of an element?

(A) Same number of valence electrons

(B) Same number of protons

(C) Same number of neutrons

(D) Both B and C

97. The total number of electrons in a nitrogen atom and chlorine atom is 7 and 17 respectively. Find the number of valence electrons in them.

(A) 3, 1   (B) 5, 8

(C) 4, 1   (D) 5, 7

98. Name the element having two electrons in the K shell of its atom.

(A) Hydrogen

(B) He⁺

(C) Helium

(D) none of these

99. The number of neutrons in the three isotopes of hydrogen are :

(A) 1, 1, 1   (B) 1, 2, 3

(C) 2, 1, 0   (D) 0, 1, 2

100. Isotopes differ in :

(A) physical properties

(B) chemical properties

(C) number of protons

(D) none of these

101. An element has an atomic number 20. How many electrons will be present in the K, L, M and N energy shells of its atom?

(A) 2, 8, 8, 1   (B) 2, 8, 7, 3

(C) 3, 7, 7, 3   (D) 2, 8, 8, 2

102. The decrease in the attractive force exerted by the nucleus on the valence shell electrons is called :

(A) shielding effect

(B) Stark effect

(C) Zeeman effect

(D) none of these

103. The distance between the nuclei of two bonded atoms of a homonuclear or heteronuclear diatomic molecule is called :

(A) atomic radius

(B) molecular distance

(C) bond length

(D) none of these

104. What happens when an electron jumps from a lower energy level to higher energy level and when an electron comes down from a higher energy level to a lower energy level?

(A) Electron loses energy & electron gains energy respectively

(B) Electron gains energy & electron loses energy respectively

(C) Loses and gains energy simultaneously

(D) Neither loses nor gains any energy

105. The three quantum numbers used to describe position, energy and other features of electrons are :

(A) K, L, M   (B) a, b, c

(C) s, p, d   (D) n, l, m

106. The elements that have high electron affinity values are :

(A) strong oxidising agents

(B) strong reducing agents

(C) weak oxidising agents

(D) weak reducing agents

107. When the bombarding particle is captured or absorbed by the target nucleus with the emission of γ-rays, it is called :

(A) fusion reaction

(B) fission reaction

(C) spallation reaction

(D) capture reaction

108. The energy released in the formation of a nucleus from its constituent nucleons is called :

(A) bond energy of the nucleus

(B) fusion energy of the nucleus

(C) binding energy of the nucleus

(D) fission energy of the nucleus

109. The process in which an element is converted into a new radioactive isotope by artificial means is called :

(A) artificial radioactivity

(B) induced radioactivity

(C) natural radioactivity

(D) both A and B

110. The energy absorbed by the uranium nucleus to change from spherical shape to critical shape is called :

(A) nuclear energy

(B) ionic energy

(C) threshold energy

(D) binding energy

111. The 13 elements with atomic weight higher than that of uranium (atomic number 92) are called :

(A) transuranium elements

(B) isotopes of uranium

(C) isobars of uranium

(D) none of the above

112. $_5B^{10} + _2He^4 \rightarrow X + _0n^1$

'X' in the above reaction is :

(A) $_7N^{12}$ (B) $_7N^{13}$

(C) $_6B^{13}$ (D) none of these

113. On the bombardment of $_7N^{14}$ with α-particles, the nucleus of the product after the release of a proton will be :

(A) $_8O^{17}$ (B) $_8O^{18}$

(C) $_9F^{17}$ (D) $_9F^{18}$

114. The materials that have been used as moderators in the nuclear reactors include :

(A) graphite   (B) heavy water

(C) cadmium   (D) Both A and B

115. Which of the following nuclear reactions is wrong?

(A) $_5B^{10} + _2He^4 \rightarrow _7N^{13} + _0n^1$

(B) $_{12}Mg^{25} + _2He^4 \rightarrow _{13}Al^{28} + _0n^1$

(C) $_7N^{13} + _0n^1 \rightarrow _6C^{14} + _1e^0$

(D) Both A and B

116. Which of the following statements about radioactivity is wrong?

(A) It is an exothermic process

(B) It is not affected by external temperature

(C) It is a photochemical process

(D) All of the above

117. When a heavier nucleus breaks down into two or more lighter nuclei of almost equal size, a large amount of energy is also liberated. This type of reaction is called as :

(A) fission reaction

(B) fusion reaction

(C) spallation reaction

(D) capture reaction

118. Fill in the blank in the following reaction.

$_1H^2 + _1H^3 \rightarrow \underline{\quad?\quad} + _0n^1 + 17.6$ MeV

(A) $_1H^4$ (B) $_1H^1$

(C) $_2He^4$ (D) $_2He^3$

119. An atom 'Y' of a radioactive element (atomic number = 90) loses two β-particles one after the other to give a stable species 'Z'. What would be the atomic number of 'Z' ?

(A) 88

(B) 90

(C) 91

(D) 92

120. Fill in the blank in the following reaction

$$_{92}U^{235} + _0n^1 \rightarrow _{56}Ba^{141} + _{36}Kr^{92} + \underline{\quad} + enery$$

(A) $3\,_0n^1$ (B) $5\,_0n^1$

(C) $5\,_0H^1$ (D) $3\,_0H^1$

121. An atom A (mass number 238 and atomic number 92) is radioactive and becomes atom B (mass number 234 and atomic number 90) by losing a/an :

(A) beta particle

(B) gamma particle

(C) alpha particle

(D) none of these

122. Radioactivity was discovered by :

(A) Neil Bohr

(B) Henri Becquerel

(C) Madam Curie

(D) Albert Einstein

123. Geiger counter is a device that is used to find out :

(A) haemoglobin percentage in blood

(B) age of wood

(C) exact position of tumor or blood clot in the body

(D) none of these

124. The radio-isotope used to determine the activity of thyroid gland is :

(A) sodium–24

(3) arsenic–74

(C) uranium–235

(D) iodine–131

125. The method of estimating the age of old carbon containing objects like dead plants and animals by measuring the levels of carbon–14 radioactivity in them is called :

(A) radio-therapy (B) carbon dating

(C) radioactivity (D) none of these

126. Mosley used _____ of atoms to introduce the atomic number of atoms.

(A) X–ray spectra (B) β ray spectra

(C) α ray spectra (D) none of these

127. What describes the emission spectra of atomic hydrogen?

(A) A series of only four lines

(B) A discrete series of lines cf equal intensity and equally spaced with respect to wavelength

(C) Several discrete series of lines with both intensity and spacings between lines which decrease as the wave number increases within each series

(D) A continuous emission of radiation of all frequencies

128. If S_1 is the specific charge (e/m) of cathode rays and S_2 be that of positive rays then which of the following is true?

(A) $S_1 = S_2$ (B) $S_1 < S_2$

(C) $S_1 > S_2$ (D) Any of these

129. Which of the following do not possess mass and charge?

(A) Alpha particles

(B) Beta particles

(C) Protons

(D) Gamma rays

130. The Planck's constant is a unit of :

(A) work

(B) energy

(C) angular momentum

(D) linear momentum

131. Light is treated as a form of matter by assuming that it consists of :

(A) photons or bundles of energy

(B) wave like characteristics

(C) electrically neutral neutrons

(D) none of these

132. Bohr's model violates the rules of classical physics because it assumes that :

(A) all electrons have same charge

(B) the nuclei have same charge

(C) electrons can revolve around the nucleus

(D) charged particles can be accelerate without emitting radiation

133. Wave nature of matter is not experienced in our daily life because the values of wavelengths :

(A) are very large

(B) are very small

(C) lie in the UV region

(D) lie in the IR region

134. The ratio between the neutrons present in the carbon and silicon with respect to their atomic masses (atomic number of silicon is 28) is :

(A) 3 : 7   (B) 7 : 3

(C) 3 : 4   (D) 6 : 28

135. The first element in the periodic table having a p-orbital electron is:

(A) helium

(B) lithium

(C) boron

(D) fluorine

136. The nuclear model of an atom was first proposed by :

(A) Thomson

(B) Rutherford

(C) Bohr

(D) none of these

137. Which of the following configuration represents a metallic element?

(A) 2, 8, 7

(B) 2, 8, 1

(C) 2, 8, 4

(D) 2, 8, 5

138. The atomic number of an element is 17. The number of orbitals containing electron pairs in the valence shell is :

(A) three   (B) eight

(C) two   (D) six

139. The elements with which of the following atomic numbers have similar properties?

(A) 13, 12   (B) 3, 11

(C) 4, 24   (D) 2, 4

140. One atom of $_{19}K^{39}$ contains :

(A) 19 protons + 20 neutrons + 19 electrons

(B) 19 protons + 20 neutrons + 20 electrons

(C) 20 protons + 19 neutrons + 20 electrons

(D) 20 protons + 20 neutrons + 19 electrons

141. In the C^{14} isotope the number of neutrons will be :

(A) 6   (B) 14

(C) 8   (D) 10

142. If 5 g of a radioactive substance has $t_{1/2}$ (half life) of 14 hours, 20 g of the same substance will have a $t_{1/2}$ equal to :

(A) 56 hrs

(B) 3.5 hrs

(C) 14 hrs

(D) 28 hrs

143. The half life of a radioactive isotope is 1.5 hrs. The mass of it that remains undecayed after 6 hours if the initial mass of a specimen of the isotope is 32 g is :

(A) 32 g

(B) 16 g

(C) 4 g

(D) 2 g

144. $_{20}Ca^{40}$ & $_{19}K^{40}$ are examples for :

(A) isotopes

(B) isobars

(C) isotones

(D) nuclear isomers

145. In the following reaction, 'X' is :

$$_8O^{19} + _1H^2 \rightarrow _8O^{18} + X$$

(A) $_1H^3$ (B) $_2He^4$

(C) $_0n^1$ (D) none of these

146. The half-life period of a radioactive nuclide is 3 hours. In 9 hours its mass will be reduced by a factor of :

(A) $\dfrac{1}{9}$ (B) $\dfrac{7}{8}$

(C) $\dfrac{1}{27}$ (D) $\dfrac{1}{6}$

147. Gamma rays are :

(A) high energy electrons

(B) low energy electrons

(C) high energy electromagnetic waves

(D) high energy positrons

148. The isotope used for dating archaeological findings is :

(A) $_1H^3$ (B) $_6C^{14}$

(C) $_8O^{18}$ (D) $_{92}U^{235}$

149. Radioactive disintegration differs from a chemical change in being :

(A) an exothermic change

(B) a spontaneous process

(C) a nuclear process

(D) a unimolecular first order reaction

150. The liberation of energy from the sun is due to :

(A) fission reactions

(B) fusion reactions

(C) chemical reactions

(D) none of these

151. Half life of radium is 1600 years. 2 grams of radium metal will be reduced to 0.125 grams in :

(A) 1600 years   (B) 3200 years

(C) 6400 years   (D) 8000 years

152. The radio-isotope used in agriculture is :

(A) Co^{60} (B) Na^{24}

(C) P^{32} (D) C^{14}

153. Which of the following detects radiations by flashes produced on a ZnS screen?

(A) GM counter

(B) Bubble chamber

(C) Scintillation counter

(D) Wilson's cloud chamber

154. The radioactive emission having the highest penetrating power is :

(A) visible light

(B) X–rays

(C) γ –rays

(D) β –rays

155. A radioactive isotope decays at such a rate that after 96 days only 1/8 of the original amount is left behind. The half-life of the nuclide is :

(A) 32 days   (B) 24 days

(C) 48 days   (D) 96 days

156. The half-life period of a radioactive element is 140 days. After 560 days, 1 g of the element will reduce to :

(A) $\dfrac{1}{2}$ g   (B) $\dfrac{1}{4}$ g

(C) $\dfrac{1}{8}$ g   (D) $\dfrac{1}{16}$ g

157. If 7/8 of a radioactive substance disintegrates in 12 days, its half-life period is :

(A) 4 days   (B) 6 days

(C) 8 days   (D) 2 days

158. The atomic nucleus becomes unstable due to :

(A) high binding energy

(B) low packing fraction

(C) high neutron–proton ratio

(D) strong nuclear forces

159. When a radioactive element loses a β –particle. its :

(A) group number increases by one unit

(B) n/p ratio decreases

(C) atomic number increases by one unit

(D) all of these

160. Complete the following reaction.

$2_1H^3 \rightarrow {_2}He^4 + \underline{\hspace{1cm}}$.

(A) 6_0n^1 (B) $_1H^1$

(C) $_2He^4$ (D) 2_0n^1

161. Successive emission of an α –particle and two β –particles by an atom of an element results in the formation of its :

(A) isodiapher   (B) isomorph

(C) isotope   (D) isotherm

162. Atoms of different elements having identical masses are known as :

(A) isotopes   (B) isobars

(C) isotones   (D) isomers

163. The unit of radioactivity is :

(A) Einstein   (B) Becquerel

(C) Curie   (D) Rutherford

164. The atomic number of bromine is 35 and its mass is number 80. Two isotopes of bromine are present in equal amounts. Which of the following represents the correct number of neutrons in first and second isotope respectively?

(A) 34, 36   (B) 44, 46

(C) 45, 47   (D) 79, 81

165. Which of the following elements has no naturally occurring stable isotopes?

(A) F   (B) H

(C) Cl   (D) O

166. A radioactive element has half-life of 20 minutes. How much time is required before the element is reduced to 1/8 of its original value?

(A) 40 minutes   (B) 60 minutes

(C) 80 minutes   (D) 160 minutes

167. When C–14 is heated in a flame its half-life period :

(A) decreases   (B) increases

(C) remains unchanged

(D) becomes infinity

168. Neutrons do not produce ionisation while passing through gases because :

(A) they have the same mass as protons

(B) they are not deflected by electric or magnetic field

(C) they exhibit wave nature

(D) they have no charge

169. β–decay of $_{11}Na^{24}$ produces an isotope of :

(A) Ne   (B) Na

(C) Mg   (D) Al

170. Nuclear energy is the result of conversion of :

(A) neutrons to protons

(B) protons to neutrons

(C) mass into energy

(D) none of these

171. Nuclear fusion occurs in :

(A) atom bombs

(B) hydrogen bombs

(C) neutron bombs

(D) none of these

172. The particle that experiences minimum repulsion on approaching a particular nucleus is :

(A) α -particle   (B) neutron

(C) electron   (D) β –particle

173. The radio-isotope used in the treatment of cancer is :

(A) C^{12} (B) Co^{60}

(C) I^{131} (D) P^{31}

174. Carbon–14 dating method is based on the fact that :

(A) C–14 fraction is same in all objects

(B) C–14 is highly insoluble

(C) ratio of C–14 and C–12 is constant in living species

(D) all of the above

175. In agriculture, radioactive P^{32} is used

(A) to increase the crop production

(B) in insecticides and pesticides

(C) to study how phosphorous is absorbed and distributed to various parts of plants

(D) to increase the chlorophyll content

176. Living things contain C^{12} and C^{14}. C^{12} is stable but C^{14} decays and declines in proportional quantity. The technique that uses this principle to determine the age of fossils, skeletons, old trees and dinosaurs is called :

(A) C–12 dating

(B) radio carbon dating

(C) carbon age   (D) fossil carbon

177. The atomic mass of an element is expressed in terms of :

(A) grams   (B) joules

(C) ergs   (D) a.m.u.

178. If the half life of a radioactive substance is higher, then its stability is

(A) low   (B) high

(C) both   (D) none of these

179. The radioactive element that is obtained from pitchblende is :

(A) uranium   (B) thorium

(C) radium   (D) plutonium

Answers

1. A	2. A	3. B	4. B	5. C	6. B	7. D	8. A	9. A	10. D
11. D	12. A	13. A	14. B	15. D	16. C	17. C	18. B	19. C	20. A
21. D	22. B	23. C	24. D	25. B	26. A	27. C	28. B	29. B	30. B
31. D	32. C	33. B	34. A	35. B	36. B	37. D	38. B	39. B	40. A
41. B	42. D	43. D	44. B	45. A	46. B	47. B	48. D	49. C	50. A
51. D	52. C	53. D	54. A	55. C	56. C	57. A	58. D	59. D	60. A
61. D	62. D	63. D	64. D	65. C	66. D	67. A	68. C	69. D	70. A
71. C	72. C	73. B	74. C	75. C	76. B	77. A	78. C	79. D	80. A
81. C	82. B	83. B	84. B	85. A	86. A	87. C	88. C	89. C	90. C
91. A	92. B	93. D	94. B	95. B	96. A	97. D	98. C	99. D	100. A
101. D	102. A	103. C	104. B	105. D	106. A	107. D	108. C	109. D	110. C
111. A	112. B	113. A	114. D	115. B	116. C	117. A	118. C	119. D	120. A
121. C	122. B	123. C	124. D	125. B	126. A	127. C	128. C	129. D	130. C
131. A	132. D	133. B	134. A	135. C	136. B	137. B	138. A	139. B	140. A
141. C	142. C	143. D	144. B	145. A	146. B	147. C	148. B	149. C	150. B
151. C	152. C	153. C	154. C	155. A	156. D	157. A	158. C	159. D	160. D
161. C	162. B	163. B	164. B	165. A	166. B	167. C	168. D	169. C	170. C
171. B	172. B	173. B	174. C	175. C	176. B	177. D	178. B	179. A	

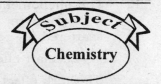
1. Foam is a colloidal solution of :
   (A) gaseous particles dispersed in gas
   (B) gaseous particles dispersed in liquid
   (C) solid particles dispersed in liquid
   (D) solid particles dispersed in gas

2. Burning of candle is a :
   (A) chemical change
   (B) physical change
   (C) reversible change
   (D) endothermic change

3. The e/m is not constant for :
   (A) cathode rays
   (B) positive rays
   (C) α–rays
   (D) β–rays

4. Bohr's model of atom explains :
   (A) Zeeman effect
   (B) Heisenberg's principle
   (C) Stark effect
   (D) none of these

5. β–decay of $_{11}Na^{24}$ produces an isotope of :
   (A) Ne   (B) Na
   (C) Mg   (D) Al

6. An atom has a net charge of −1. It has 18 electrons and 20 neutrons. Its mass number is :
   (A) 37   (B) 35
   (C) 38   (D) 20

7. In agriculture radioactive P^{32} is used :
   (A) to increase the crop production
   (B) is insecticides and pesticides
   (C) to study how phosphorous is absorbed and distributed to various parts of plants
   (D) to increase the chlorophyll content

8. When salt is dissolved in water :
   (A) boiling point increases
   (B) boiling point does not change
   (C) boiling point decreases
   (D) none of the above

9. The particle which does not deflect in the presence of magnetic field is:
   (A) proton   (B) neutron
   (C) positron   (D) electron

10. Mass number of an atom represents the number of :
    (A) only protons
    (B) protons and neutrons
    (C) protons and electrons
    (D) neutrons and electrons

11. In a stationary orbit of an atom, an electron :
    (A) is at rest
    (B) gains energy constantly
    (C) revolves with constant energy
    (D) loses energy discontinuously

12. The phenomenon in which there is a change in the wavelength of scattered X – rays is called :

(A) Zeeman effect

(B) Stark effect

(C) Compton effect

(D) Hypochromic effect

13. Metals have ____ valence electrons.

(A) 1 or 2 or 3   (B) 4 or 4 to 6

(C) 6 or 7 or 8   (D) 5 or 6 or 7

14. The reason for the identical chemical properties of all the isotopes of an element is :

(A) same number of electrons

(B) same number of protons

(C) same number of neutrons

(D) different number of neutrons

15. The energy absorbed by the uranium nucleus to change from spherical shape to critical shape is called :

(A) nuclear energy

(B) conversion energy

(C) binding energy

(D) threshold energy

16. The pair of elements with atomic numbers which have similar properties is :

(A) 13, 12

(B) 3, 11

(C) 4, 24

(D) 2, 4

17. The number of neutrons in C–14 isotope is :

(A) 6   (B) 14

(C) 8   (D) 10

18. Give the number of electrons present in the outermost shell of atoms of each of the following elements.

(i) Helium   *(ii) Magnesium*
(iii) Sulphur

(A) (i) – 2, (ii) – 3, (iii) – 4

(B) (i) – 1, (ii) – 4, (iii) – 6

(C) (i) – 2, (ii) – 2, (iii) – 6

(D) (i) – 3, (ii) – 4, (iii) – 5

19. When the vapour pressure of a liquid is equal to its atmospheric pressure, then it :

(A) freezes

(B) evaporates

(C) boils

(D) does not undergo any change

20. Alkali metals are powerful reducing agents because :

(A) they are monovalent

(B) their atomic radii are large

(C) their ionisation potentials are low

(D) they are metals

21. The total number of electrons in a nitrogen atom and chlorine atom is 7 and 17 respectively. Find the number of valence electrons in them.

(A) 3, 1   (B) 5, 8

(C) 4, 1   (D) 5, 7

22. Based on the statements given here choose the correct answer.

    P. *Aquatic animals breathe oxygen inside water*

    Q. *Gases can diffuse into water.*

    (A) Both P and Q are true and Q explains P

    (B) Both P and Q are true but Q does not explain P

    (C) Only P is true

    (D) Only Q is true

23. On bombardment of $_7N^{14}$ with α-particles, the nucleus of the product after the release of a proton will be :

    (A) $_8O^{17}$ (B) $_8O^{18}$

    (C) $_9F^{17}$ (D) $_9F^{18}$

24. The element having atomic number 11 forms :

    (A) a weak acidic oxide

    (B) a strong basic oxide

    (C) an amphoteric oxide

    (D) a neutral oxide

25. Fill in the blank in the following reaction.

    $_{92}U^{235} + _0n^1 \rightarrow _{56}Ba^{141} + _{36}Kr^{92} + \_\_ + energy$

    (A) 3_0n^1 (B) 5_0n^1

    (C) 5_0H^1 (D) 3_0H^1

26. When metals react with nonmetals, metals tend to :

    (A) lose electrons

    (B) gain electrons

    (C) share electrons

    (D) produce electrons

27. The compound possessing strongest ionic nature is

    (A) $SrCl_2$ (B) $BaCl_2$

    (C) $CaCl_2$ (D) $CsCl$

28. During a hail storm, it was observed that ice pieces turned into water when they reached the ground. At what height could the rain drops have formed into ice pieces?

    (assume g = 10 m/s^2)

    (A) 334 km   (B) 33 km

    (C) 300 km   (D) 30 km

29. The Planck's constant is a unit of :

    (A) work

    (B) energy

    (C) angular momentum

    (D) linear momentum

30. According to Kinetic theory of gases, molecules are :

    (A) perfectly inelastic particles in random motion

    (B) perfectly elastic particles in random motion

    (C) perfectly inelastic particles at rest

    (D) perfectly elastic particles at rest

31. Which of the following configuration represents metallic elements?

    (A) 2, 8, 7

    (B) 2, 8, 1

    (C) 2, 8, 4

    (D) 2, 8, 5

32. Half life of radium is 1600 years. 2 grams of radium metal will be reduced to 0.125 grams in :

    (A) 1600 years   (B) 3200 years

    (C) 6400 years   (D) 8000 years

33. The removal of an electron from gaseous sodium atom is :

(A) an exothermic reaction

(B) an endothermic reaction

(C) a substitution reaction

(D) an addition reaction

34. Ionic compounds conduct electricity when they are in :

(A) solid state

(B) gaseous state

(C) fused state

(D) none of the above

35. Valency of sulphur in sulphur dioxide and sulphur trioxide is____ and _____ respectively.

(A) 3 and 6

(B) 2 and 3

(C) 2 and 6

(D) 4 and 6

36. The substance that is reduced in the following reaction is :

$MnO_2 + 4HCl \rightarrow MnC_2 + 2H_2O + Cl_2$

(A) MnO_2 (B) HCl

(C) H_2O (D) Cl_2

37. The formula of barium peroxide is :

(A) Ba_2O (B) Ba_2O_3

(C) BaO_2 (D) BaO_3

38. In the reaction

$CuO + NH_3 \rightarrow Cu + N_2 + H_2O$,

the oxidation number of copper changes from :

(A) +2 to 0   (B) 0 to +2

(C) +1 to −1   (D) −2 to +2

39. Write the ionic form of the reaction:

$NaOH + HCl \rightarrow NaCl + H_2O$

(A) $OH^- + Na^+ + Cl^- \rightarrow NaCl + H_2O$

(B) $OH^- + Na^+ + H^+ \rightarrow H_2O + Na^+$

(C) $OH^- + H^+ \rightarrow H_2O$

(D) $H^+ + Cl^- \rightarrow HCl$

40. When chlorine reacts with slaked lime :

(A) bleaching powder is formed

(B) calcium carbonate is formed

(C) calcium bicarbonate is formed

(D) no reaction

41. In a redox reaction, the oxidation state of the atom in the oxidising agent :

(A) decreases

(B) increases

(C) remains constant

(D) changes but depends on the reaction

42. Name the oxidising and reducing agents in the following reaction.

(A) $PbS (S) + 4H_2O_2 (aq) \rightarrow PbSO_4(s) +$

$$4H_2O (l)$$

(A) PbS – oxidising agent,

    H_2O_2 – reducing agent

(B) H_2O_2 – oxidising agent,

    PbS – reducing agent

(C) Both PbS and H_2O_2 are oxidising agents

(D) Both PbS and H_2O_2 are reducing agents

43. The gas used in the manufacture of ammonia is :

(A) coal gas   (B) producer gas

(C) fuel gas   (D) water gas

44. Mixture of butane, ethane and propane is called :

(A) coal gas

(B) oil gas

(C) petroleum gas

(D) producer gas

45. The isomerism which arises due to the difference in the nature of carbon chain is called :

(A) chain isomerism

(B) positional isomerism

(C) functional isomerism

(D) geometrical isomerism

46. When acetylene gas is passed into ammoniacal solution of cuprous chloride :

(A) white precipitate of cuprous acetylide is formed

(B) colourless precipitate of sodium acetylide is formed

(C) red precipitate of cuprous acetylide is formed

(D) no reaction takes place

47. Which of the following alkane cannot be prepared by Wurtz reaction?

(A) C_2H_6 (B) C_3H_8

(C) CH_4 (D) C_4H_{10}

48. The method of converting high boiling point hydrocarbons into low boiling point hydrocarbons is called

(A) polymerisation

(B) isomerism

(C) condensation

(D) cracking

49. The reagent used in dehalogenation process is :

(A) alcoholic KOH or $NaNH_2$

(B) metallic zinc

(C) Na

(D) aqueous KOH

50. Electrophiles are :

(A) Lewis bases

(B) Lewis acids

(C) amphoteric

(D) none of these

Answers

1. B	2. A	3. B	4. D	5. C	6. A	7. C	8. A	9. B	10. B
11. C	12. C	13. A	14. A	15. D	16. B	17. C	18. C	19. C	20. C
21. D	22. A	23. A	24. B	25. A	26. A	27. D	28. B	29. C	30. B
31. B	32. C	33. B	34. C	35. D	36. A	37. C	38. A	39. C	40. A
41. A	42. B	43. B	44 C	45. A	46. C	47. C	48. D	49. B	50. B

BIOLOGY

Chapter 1

Fundamental Unit of Life

Synopsis

1. Cell is the basic unit of life. Cells were first discovered by Robert Hooke in 1665 by the observation of a cork slice.

2. Cell theory was proposed by Schleiden & Schwann.

3. Rudolf Virchow proposed that all cells originate from pre-existing cells.

4. Organisms that consist of a single cell are called *unicellular organisms*. Amoeba and Paramoecium are unicellular. Organisms that consist of many cells are called *multicellular organisms*. Some fungi, plants and animals are multicellular.

5. The outermost covering that separates the content of the cell from its external environment is called the *plasma membrane*, which is selectively permeable and is made of lipids and proteins.

6. Movement of substances in and out of the cell takes place by the process of *diffusion* (gaseous exchange) and *osmosis* (exchange of water molecules).

7. Plant cells have a rigid outer covering in addition to the plasma membrane called the cell wall that is composed of cellulose.

8. *Plasmolysis* is the phenomenon of contraction of the content of the cell when a plant loses water through osmosis.

9. Nucleus is covered by a double-layered nuclear membrane. It consists of chromosomes. They are composed of DNA and proteins.

10. Organisms which lack a nuclear membrane and 'cell membrane bound' organelles are called *Prokaryotes* and those having a nuclear membrane are called *Eukaryotes*.

11. *Cytoplasm* is the fluid content inside the plasma membrane of a cell.

12. *Endoplasmic reticulum(ER)* is a large network of membrane bound tubes and sheets . There are two types of ER – RER (site of protein synthesis) and SER (site of synthesis of fats, detoxification of poisons and drugs).

13. *Lysosomes* keep the cell clean by digesting the foreign materials entering the cell. They are otherwise known as *suicidal bags* of the cell.

14. *Golgi complex* is a stack of flattened sacs meant for secretion.

15. *Mitochondria*, the powerhouses of the cell generate ATP that is required for various chemical activities in a cell.

16. *Ribosomes* are responsible for protein synthesis in a cell. A chain of ribosomes is termed as a *polyribosome* or *polysome*.

17. *Plastids* are present only in plant cells. There are two types of plastids – *chromoplasts* (coloured) and *leucoplasts* (white or colourless).

18. *Vacuoles* are storage structures for solid or liquid content which are filled with cell sap.

Multiple Choice Questions

1. Which of the following structures is usually present only in animal cells?

   (A) Vacuoles

   (B) Cell wall

   (C) Nucleus

   (D) Centrioles

2. Normally, in the process of osmosis, the net flow of water molecules in or out of the cell depends upon differences in the :

   (A) concentration of water molecules inside and outside the cell

   (B) concentration of enzymes on either side of the cell membrane

   (C) rate of molecular motion on either side of the cell membrane

   (D) rate of movement of insoluble molecules inside the cell

3. The term 'nuclear envelope' is more appropriate than the term 'nuclear membrane', because :

   (A) the enclosure has pores which membranes do not

   (B) the enclosure is made up of two membranes

   (C) the chemical composition is inconsistent with cellular membranes

   (D) both the terms are the same.

4. Which of the following is not a characteristic of prokaryotes?

   (A) DNA

   (B) Cell membrane

   (C) Cell wall

   (D) Endoplasmic reticulum

5. Ribosomes are mades up of ——— subunits.

   (A) 0 (they are whole)

   (B) 2

   (C) 4

   (D) 3

6. Proteins synthesized by the rough ER are :

   (A) exported from the cell

   (B) for internal regulation

   (C) for internal storage

   (D) to digest food in lysosomes

7. In bacteria, some of the functions of eukaryotic cells are performed by :

   (A) vesicles

   (B) mitochondria

   (C) the plasma membrane

   (D) nucleoli

8. The passage through pores in the nuclear envelope is restricted primarily for :

   (A) DNA and RNA

   (B) Proteins, RNA and Protein-RNA complexes

   (C) Lipids and glycolipids

   (D) RNA and protein-carbohydrate complexes

9. Plants differ from animals in that plants have :

(A) an endoplasmic reticulum

(B) a central vacuole

(C) golgi complexes

(D) vesicles

10. Within chloroplasts, light is captured by :

(A) thylakoids within grana

(B) grana within cisternae

(C) cisternae within grana

(D) grana within thylakoids

11. The rough ER is so named because it has an abundance of :

(A) mitochondria

(B) lysosomes

(C) golgi bodies

(D) ribosomes

12. With which of the following are basal bodies not associated?

(A) Plant cells   (B) Animal cells

(C) Centrioles   (D) Microtubules

13. The bacterial cell wall is composed of :

(A) a phospholipid matrix

(B) a lipoprotein

(C) chitin

(D) a polymer of sugars

14. The smooth ER is especially abundant in cells that synthesize extensive amounts of :

(A) lipids

(B) toxins

(C) proteins

(D) nucleic acids

15. Mitochondrial enzymes for oxidative metabolism are :

(A) on or within the surface of cristae

(B) located on the outer membrane

(C) floating freely in the inner membrane space

(D) in the matrix

16. The cytoplasm of a bacterium :

(A) is supported by the cytoskeleton

(B) is supported by microtubules

(C) is supported by keratin

(D) has no internal support structure.

17. Ribosomes are found :

(A) only in the nucleus

(B) in the cytoplasm

(C) only in eukaryotic cells

(D) both B and C

18. The Golgi apparatus is involved in :

(A) transporting proteins that are to be released from the cell

(B) packaging proteins into vesicles

(C) altering or modifying proteins

(D) all of the above

19. Mechanical support to the cell is provided by :

(A) Golgi bodies

(B) microfibrils

(C) endoplasmic reticulum

(D) chromatids

20. Most cells are very small. A typical eukaryotic cell (either of plant or animal) will occur in which of the following sizes?

(A) 1 mm to 100 μm

(B) 100 um to 10 μm

(C) 10 nm to 100 μm

(D) 1 um to 100 μm

21. Enzymes embedded in the membrane of the smooth ER :

(A) synthesize lipids

(B) may be used for detoxification

(C) are mostly active only when associated with a membrane

(D) all of the above

22. Which of the following organelles is found in plant cells but not in animal cells?

(A) Ribosomes

(B) Endoplasmic reticulum

(C) Mitochondria

(D) None of the above

23. Plasmodesmata :

(A) allow the movement of materials between cells.

(B) are flattened sacs for proteins storage.

(C) contain chromatin.

(D) all of the above.

24. Plastids that contain starch are called _____ whereas those that contain red and yellow pigments are called_____.

(A) amyloplasts, chromoplasts

(B) chromoplasts, leucoplasts

(C) leucoplasts, chloroplasts

(D) chlroplasts, amyloplasts

25. The principal component of the plant cell wall is :

(A) glycoproteins

(B) cellulose

(C) lignin

(D) pectin

26. Which organelle is composed of cristae and a matrix?

(A) Chloroplast

(B) Nucleolus

(C) Mitochondrion

(D) Central vacuole

27. Ribosomes :

(A) are not membrane bound

(B) are the site of protein synthesis

(C) may be floating free in the cytoplasm

(D) all of the above

28. Ribosomes contain maximum amount of :

(A) steroids

(B) lipids

(C) RNA

(D) DNA

29. The fundamental unit of life is the :

(A) cell

(B) organism

(C) tissue

(D) organ system

30. Which of the following organelles has a double membrane with pores?

(A) mitochondria

(B) nucleus

(C) lysosome

(D) golgi apparatus

31. A threadlike material called chromatin is located within the :

(A) nucleus

(B) lysosome

(C) endoplasmic reticulum

(D) golgi apparatus

32. Which orgnelle looks like a stack of hollow pancakes?

(A) Smooth ER

(B) Rough ER

(C) Mitochondria

(D) Golgi apparatus

33. Which type of organelle forms a membranous system of tubular canals that is continuous with the nuclear envelope and branches throughout the cytoplasm?

(A) Mitochondria

(B) Rough ER

(C) Golgi apparatus

(D) Smooth ER

34. What are the cells that do not have nucleus or other membrane-bound organelles called ?

(A) Prokaryotic cells

(B) Red blood cells

(C) Eukaryotic cells

(D) White blood cells

35. What is a eukaryotic cell?

(A) A cell with a nucleus

(B) An animal cell

(C) A cell with no nucleus

(D) A plant cell

36. Which of the following organelles stores waste in the cell?

(A) Ribosome   (B) Mitochondria

(C) Golgi body   (D) Vacuole

37. What is the substance that is used by the cells as an immediate source of energy for them?

(A) Adenosine triphosphate (ATP)

(B) Amino acids

(C) Chlorofluorocarbons

(D) Phenylalanine

38. Which of the following organelles is involved in protein synthesis?

(A) Lysosome

(B) Ribosome

(C) Endoplasmic reticulum

(D) None of the above

39. Which of the following is not an organelle?

(A) Lung

(B) Endoplasmic reticulum

(C) Chloroplast

(D) Mitochondria

40. All organelles are contained by the :

(A) cell membrane

(B) nuclear envelope

(C) Thylakoid membrane

(D) None of the above

41. Osmosis is a process where _____ crosses the membrane.

    (A) Fats   (B) Proteins

    (C) Water   (D) None of these

42. Which structure includes all of the other structures?

    (A) Nucleolus

    (B) Nucleus

    (C) Chromosome

    (D) Genes

43. Most cell membranes are composed principally of :

    (A) DNA and ATP

    (B) protein and starch

    (C) chitin and starch

    (D) nucleotides and amino acids

44. The first cell that was seen under a microscope was a :

    (A) cork cell   (B) blood cell

    (C) sperm cell   (D) skin cell

45. The primary structures for the packaging of cellular secretions for export from the cell are :

    (A) Golgi bodies

    (B) ribosomes

    (C) mitochondria

    (D) lysosomes

46. The part of the cell responsible for maintaining cell shape, internal organization, and cell movement is the :

    (A) vesicle

    (B) nucleus

    (C) endoplasmic reticulum

    (D) cytoskeleton

47. Which of the following is sometimes referred to as rough or smooth, depending on the structure?

    (A) Golgi bodies

    (B) mitochondria

    (C) lysosomes

    (D) endoplasmic reticulum

48. Stroma and grana are portions of :

    (A) chloroplasts

    (B) mitochondria

    (C) ribosomes

    (D) chromosomes

49. Which of the following are examples of prokaryotes?

    (A) Protozoa   (B) Bacteria

    (C) Algae   (D) Fungi

50. Cell theory was proposed by :

    (A) Robert Hooke

    (B) Beadle and Tatum

    (C) Schleiden and Schwann

    (D) Hargovind Khorana

51. The term 'cell' was coined by :

    (A) R G Harrison

    (B) Feulgen

    (C) Weismann

    (D) Robert Hooke

52. The power house of the cell is an organelle named as :

    (A) mitochondrion

    (B) Golgi complex

    (C) ribosome

    (D) centriole

53. The site for protein synthesis in the cell is :

(A) ribosome

(B) lysosome

(C) microtubules

(D) centriole

54. DNA is found in :

(A) smooth endoplasmic reticulum

(B) ribosome

(C) nucleus

(D) lysosomes

55. Protoplasm is :

(A) liquid

(B) solid

(C) colloidal

(D) crystallo-colloidal

56. Cell wall is present in :

(A) plant cell

(B) prokaryotic cell

(C) algal cell

(D) all of the above

57. Nucleoid is present in :

(A) plant cell

(B) animal cell

(C) green algal cell

(D) bacterial cell

58. A prokaryotic cell lacks :

(A) cell wall

(B) cell membrane

(C) cytoplasm

(D) nucleolus

59. Who among the following applied the cell theory to plants?

(A) Schwann

(B) Schleiden

(C) Jenseu

(D) Swanson

60. Which of the following is absent in erythrocytes?

(A) Nucleus

(B) Aerobic respiration

(C) DNA

(D) All of the above

61. Haploid cells in angiosperms can be obtained by culturing :

(A) young leaves

(B) root tips

(C) pollen grains

(D) endosperms

62. The cell membrane is made up of :

(A) glycoproteins

(B) phospholipid proteins

(C) phosphoproteins

(D) protein bilayer

63. A cell with flacid condition is termed as :

(A) plasmolysed

(B) deplasmolysed

(C) wilted

(D) turgid

64. The average thickness of plasma membrane is :

(A) $100 - 150 \overset{\circ}{A}$ (B) $75 - 100 \overset{\circ}{A}$

(C) $60 - 75 \overset{\circ}{A}$ (D) $75 - 100 \mu$

65. Middle lamella is chemically formed of :

(A) cellulose

(B) hemicellulose

(C) pectates

(D) lignin

66. Carbohydrates of plasma membrane help in :

(A) passive transport

(B) active transport

(C) cell adhesion

(D) cellular recognition

67. Vacuolar membrane of a cell is :

(A) plasmalemma

(B) tonoplast

(C) rhizoplast

(D) mesosome

68. Plant cells differ from animal cells in having :

(A) cell wall

(B) mitochondria

(C) ribosome

(D) Golgi apparatus

69. The cell wall of most fungi is made of :

(A) lignin

(B) suberin

(C) chitin

(D) pectin

70. Aerobic respiration is performed by :

(A) glyoxisomes   (B) mitochondria

(C) lysosomes   (D) chloroplasts

71. The rough ER is specially well developed in cells actively engaged in :

(A) protein synthesis

(B) nucleotide synthesis

(C) lipid synthesis

(D) secretory functions

72. The nucleus contains :

(A) mitochondria

(B) Golgi apparatus

(C) chromosomes

(D) lysosomes

73. Which of the following organelles in the cell is referred to as the suicidal bags or disposal units?

(A) Lysosomes   (B) Peroxisomes

(C) Glyoxisomes   (D) Nucleolus

74. The plastids which make flowers and fruits conspicuous to animals for pollination and dispersal are :

(A) chloroplast   (B) chromoplast

(C) leucoplast   (D) none of these

75. True nucleus is absent in :

(A) bacteria

(B) green algae

(C) fungi

(D) lichens

76. In which of the following is endoplasmic reticulum absent?

(A) Cells of pancreas, salivary glands

(B) Erythrocytes of mammals and prokaryotes

(C) Cells of brain

(D) Nephrons

77. The transportation of materials in the cell is by :

(A) Golgi complex (B) lysosomes

(C) mitochondria (D) ER

78. Which of the following is useful for the synthesis of proteins and enzymes?

(A) SER (B) Golgi complex

(C) RER (D) mitochondria

79. The transitional cell organelle between endoplasmic reticulum and plasma membrane is :

(A) lysosome (B) ribosome

(C) Golgi complex (D) mitochondria

80. The smallest cell organelle is :

(A) mitochondria (B) microfilament

(C) microtubule (D) ribosome

81. In the egg cells, yolk is formed from :

(A) lysosome (B) Golgi complex

(C) mitochondria (D) ribosomes

82. Fat storing chloroplasts are called :

(A) aleuroplasts

(B) amyloplasts

(C) elaioplasts

(D) chromoplasts

83. Rigidity of cell wall is due to :

(A) lignin (B) suberin

(C) cutin (D) pectin

84. Semi-autonomous and self replicating cell organelles are :

(A) lysosomes (B) mitochondria

(C) ribosomes (D) ER

85. Which of the following cell organelles liberate heat for the maintenance of constant body temperature in aves and mammals?

(A) Lysosomes (B) Ribosomes

(C) ER (D) Mitochondria

86. The genetic material in the cell is :

(A) m-RNA (B) r-RNA

(C) t-RNA (D) DNA

87. The supporting framework of a cell consists of :

(A) microfilaments

(B) microtubules

(C) both A and B

(D) none of these

88. The functional activities of a cell are controlled and directed by the :

(A) protoplasm

(B) nucleus

(C) mitochondrion

(D) ER

89. The cell organelle that has electron transport system is :

(A) centriole

(B) nucleus

(C) mitochondrion

(D) nucleolus

90. Besides nucleus DNA is also present in :

(A) ribosomes

(B) mitochondrion

(C) lysosomes

(D) Golgi complex

91. Lysosomes are made up of :

(A) one membrane

(B) two membranes

(C) three membranes

(D) none of these

92. Which of the following are not membrane bound?

(A) Spherosome

(B) Mitochondria

(C) Ribosome

(D) Lysosome

93. If the ribosomes of a cell are destroyed then :

(A) respiration will not take place

(B) fats will not be stored

(C) carbon assimilation will not occur

(D) proteins will not be formed

94. Store houses of the cell are :

(A) mitochondria

(B) chloroplast

(C) nucleus

(D) vacuoles

95. If a tomato is pricked with a needle, the liquid comes out is :

(A) protoplasm

(B) tonoplasm

(C) cytoplasm

(D) nucleoplasm

96. Excretory materials are not found in :

(A) nuclear sap   (B) cytoplasm

(C) vacuole   (D) hyaloplasm

97. Rudolf Virchow stated that :

(A) cells arise from pre-existing cells

(B) cells are grouped into tissues

(C) cells are the structural and functional units

(D) cellular activities are regulated by the nucleus

98. An old living cell is characterized by the :

(A) absence of vacuole

(B) presence of two nuclei

(C) absence of nucleus

(D) presence of large vacuole

99. The type of plastids commonly found in the cells that are not exposed to light are :

(A) leucoplasts

(B) chromoplasts

(C) chloroplasts

(D) all plastids

100. Coagulation and the death of protoplasm does not occur due to :

(A) heating upto 60°C

(B) electric shock

(C) addition of water

(D) strong acids

101. Which of the following is the most primitive cell organelle is :

(A) ribosome

(B) nucleus

(C) mitochondria

(D) plastid

102. A prokaryotic cell within an eukaryotic cell is :

(A) nucleus

(B) ribosome

(C) chloroplast

(D) ER

103. Cytoplasm is a part of :

(A) karyolymph

(B) protoplasm

(C) tonoplasm

(D) nucleus

Answers

1.	D	2.	A	3.	B	4.	D	5.	B	6.	A	7.	C	8.	B	9.	B	10.	A
11.	D	12.	A	13.	D	14.	A	15.	A	16.	D	17.	B	18.	D	19.	B	20.	B
21.	D	22.	D	23.	A	24.	A	25.	B	26.	C	27.	D	28.	C	29.	A	30.	B
31.	A	32.	D	33.	B	34.	A	35.	A	36.	D	37.	A	38.	C	39.	A	40.	A
41.	C	42.	B	43.	B	44.	A	45.	A	46.	D	47.	D	48.	C	49.	B	50.	C
51.	D	52.	A	53.	A	54.	C	55.	D	56.	D	57.	D	58.	D	59.	B	60.	D
61.	C	62.	B	63.	B	64.	B	65.	C	66.	D	67.	B	68.	A	69.	C	70.	B
71.	A	72.	C	73.	A	74.	B	75.	A	76.	B	77.	D	78.	C	79.	C	80.	D
81.	B	82.	C	83.	A	84.	B	85.	D	86.	D	87.	C	88.	B	89.	C	90.	B
91.	A	92.	C	93.	D	94.	D	95.	B	96.	D	97.	A	98.	D	99.	A	100.	C
101.	A	102.	C	103.	B														

Explanatory Answers

1. (D) Animal cells contain centrioles, cylindrical organelles that direct the movement of the chromosome during mitosis. Plant cells tend to have bigger vacuoles and they also have rigid cell walls. Both have nuclei to control the cell.

2. (A) Osmosis is the diffusion of water across a membrane and is a passive process. Osmosis is a movement of solvent molecules from low concentration to high concentration.

4. (D) Cell membrane bound organelles are absent in prokaryotes. Hence they lack endoplasmic reticulum.

5. (B) Ribosomes are of two types, 70s in Prokaryotes and 80s in Eukaryotes. Each ribosome has a larger sub-unit (50s) and smaller sub-unit (30s) in prokaryotes. In Eukaryotes the larger sub-unit is 60s and smaller sub-unit is 40s.

9. (B) As the plant become old small vacuole fuse to form a central large vacuole.

13. (D) Gram-positive bacterial cell wall is made up of Murein (polypeptide) where as that of Gram Negative bacteria is made

up of lipo polysaccharides.

19. (B) Microfirbrils are part of cytoskeleton, which provides mechanical support to the cell.

20. (B) 1mm=100um = 100 nm.

23. (A) Plasmodesmata connect adjacent cells.

29. (A) Cell is the basic unit of life from which all forms of life develop.

31. (A) Chromatin is the Genetic material.

34. (A) Prokaryotes do not have true nucleus or membrane bound organelles.

35. (A) Eukaryotic cells have a true nucleus.

36. (D) Vacuoles are fluid filled bag like structures. They are store houses of various metabolic products.

39. (A) Organelles are the structures present inside the cell.

41. (C) In osmosis the solvent molecules move through the semi-permeable membrane.

42. (B) The nucleus is the large dark spot in cells. Inside are the chromosomes (pieces of DNA), which contain genes, as well as nucleoli (which are the sites of ribosome synthesis).

46. (D) Cytoskeleton is network of fibrils present all over the cell.

50. (C) Scheilden & Schwann stated that all living things are made of cells hence cell is the functional and structural unit of living things.

51. (D) Cell is derived from Latin word "cellula" which means a little room.

54. (C) The nucleus contains chromatin. The chromatin is made of DNA and proteins.

55. (D) Protoplasm is a complex colloidal mass consisting of water and dispersed substances like proteins, lipids, carbohydrates, nucleic acids, etc.

60. (D) Mature erythrocytes lack nucleus and cell organelles.

61. (C) Young leaves and root tips consists of diploid cells and endosperm consists of triploid cells. The pollen grains on the other hand have haploid cells. They are obtained due to meiotic division of spore mother cells.

62. (B) Plasma membrane consists of two layers of proteins and middle bilayer of lipids.

63. (B) Loss of water due to exosmosis makes a cells flaccid.

67. (B) The membrane surrounding vacuole is called Tonoplast. It allows certain substances to pass through.

68. (A) Cell wall made of cellulose is a unique feature of plants

69. (C) Chitin is a substance present in the insects.

71. (A) Endoplasmic Reticulum studded with ribosome is called Rough Endoplasmic Reticulum (RER).

They are attached by a glycoprotein called ribophorin

72. (C) Chromosomes are made of DNA and Proteins.

73. (A) Lysosomes are mebranous vesicles containing hydrolytic enzymes.

74. (B) Chromoplasts are coloured plastids.

75. (A) Lichen is symbiotic relationship between algae and fungi.

76. (B) Organelles are absent in erythrocytes and prokaryotes. RER of nerve cell is called Nissle's granule.

77. (D) ER is a tube like structure present in the cell, which extends all over the cell.

80. (D) Largest cell organelle in animal cells is mitochondrion and in plant cell chloroplast.

82. (C) These are found in the seeds if castor, mustard, groundnut, etc.

84. (B) Mitochondria possess small amounts of DNA and ribosomes and are capable of protein synthesis and self duplication.

89. (C) ATP is synthesized in the electron transport system.

91. (A) Lysosomes are called suicidal bags of the cell. They are bound by a single membrane.

95. (B) Tonoplasm is the fluid present in the vacuole.

98. (D) A large vacuole is present in the old living plant cells.

99. (A) Leucoplasts are colored and have storage function.

❖ ❖ ❖

Chapter 2

Tissues

2

1. A group of cells that are similar in structure and work together to perform a particular function is called a tissue. They have the same origin.

2. Plant tissues are supportive and most of them are dead so as to provide mechanical strength whereas most of the animal tissues are living.

3. Tissues in plants divide throughout their life.

4. Based on the dividing capacity of tissues, plant tissues can be classified as *meristematic* and *permanent* tissues

5. Meristematic tissues are classified as *apical* (tip of stem and roots), *lateral* (girth of stem and root), *intercalary meristems* (internodes).

6. Cells formed by meristematic tissue lose the ability to divide and form a permanent tissue, which is termed as differentiation.

7. Permanent tissues, which consist of similar type of cells are called *simple permanent tissues*. Parenchyma, collenchyma and sclerenchyma are some examples.

8. Parenchymatous cells are usually loosely packed with intercellular spaces (Chlorenchyma – performs photosynthesis, Aerenchyma – provides buoyancy).

9. The flexibility in plants is due to collenchyma. The cells of the tissue have very little intercellular spaces.

10. Sclerenchymatous tissue makes the plant hard and stiff due the presence of lignin.

11. Epidermal layer of leaf consists of pores called *stomata*, which are enclosed by two kidney-shaped cells called *guard cells*. Stomata help in transpiration.

12. Older plants have a chemical called *suberin* in their walls that makes them impervious to gases and water.

13. Complex tissues are made up of more than one type of cells. Xylem and phloem are complex tissues.

14. Xylem consists of tracheids, vessels, xylem parenchyma and xylem fibres. It transports water and minerals vertically.

15. Phloem is made up of sieve tubes, companion cells, phloem fibres and phloem parenchyma. It transports food from leaves to other parts of the plant.

16. The protective tissues in animal body are epithelial tissues. Cells in skin, lining of mouth, alveoli, etc. are some examples. The cells of these tissues are tightly packed with no intercellular spaces.

17. Different epithelia show different structures with unique functions.

18. Simple squamous epithelium (flat) is present in oesophagus and lining of the mouth. Stratified squamous epithelium (many layers) is present in skin. Columnar epithelium is present in the inner lining of the intestine. Ciliated columnar epithelium (have cilia) is present in the respiratory tract. Cuboidal epithelium is present in the lining of kidney tubules, etc.

19. The cells of connective tissues are loosely spaced in a jelly like matrix. Blood and bones are connective tissues.

20. Blood has a fluid matrix called plasma, which consists of RBC, WBC and platelets.

21. Two bones are connected by ligaments that are very elastic. Tendons are fibrous tissues, which connect bones to muscles.

22. Cartilages have widely spaced cells. Structures in the nose, ear and trachea are cartilages.

23. Areolar connective tissue is found between the skin and muscles, bone marrow, etc.

24. Adipose tissue is a fat storing tissue present below the skin and between internal organs.

25. Muscular tissue consists of elongated cells called muscle fibres that are responsible for the movement in our body.

26. Muscles that are used with our knowledge and intention are called voluntary muscles.

27. Striated muscles have dark bands and its cells are long, cylindrical and multinucleate. Cells of unstriated muscles are spindle-shaped and uninucleate. Almost all unstriated muscles are involuntary.

28. Cardiac muscle is a striated involuntary muscle.

29. Nervous tissue comprises of the brain, spinal cord and nerves.

30. Nervous tissue is made up of neurons that receive and conduct impulses.

31. An individual nerve cell can be as long as one meter.

Multiple Choice Questions

1. Which of the following is produced from bones of humans?

   (A) Red blood cell

   (B) Striated cells

   (C) Bile

   (D) Urea

2. Identify this tissue. It has tight fitting, single layer, flattened cells.

   (A) simple   (B) ciliated

   (C) striated   (D) columnar

3. The tissue, which is composed of columnar, ciliated cell that line body cavities and exposed to the exterior, is :

   (A) columnar

   (B) glandular

   (C) ciliated columnar

   (D) cuboidal

4. Which of the following tissues is long and threadlike and provide body movements under conscious control?

(A) Striated muscle

(B) Unstriated muscle

(C) Cardiac muscle

(D) Smooth muscle

5. The tissue that has central nucleus, tapered at both ends and controls movement that are not under conscious control is :

(A) Striated muscle

(B) Unstriated muscle

(C) Cardiac muscle

(D) Skeletal muscle

6. Which of the following is an example of an organ that contains a smooth muscle?

(A) Iris of eye

(B) Uterus

(C) Bronchi

(D) All of the above

7. The bones are connected to each other by :

(A) tendons   (B) cartilage

(C) ligament   (D) muscle

8. Which among the following connects bones & muscles ?

(A) Tendons

(B) Ligament

(C) Collagen

(D) Cartilage

9. The cell of hyaline cartilage are called :

(A) adipocyte

(B) osteocyte

(C) mast cells

(D) chondrocyte

10. The function of adipose tissue is :

(A) storage of fats

(B) storage of water

(C) transport of fats

(D) transport of gases

11. Which of the following is a connective tissue ?

(A) Bone   (B) Cartilage

(C) Blood   (D) All of the above

12. Which of the following is always non-myelinated?

(A) axon   (B) dendrite

(C) both A and B   (D) none of these

13. The composition of bone is :

(A) calcium carbonate

(B) calcium

(C) calcium & potassium compounds

(D) none of the above

14. Nervous system consists of :

(A) brain   (B) spinal cord

(C) nerves   (D) all of these

15. Collenchyma in plants provide :

(A) flexibility   (B) buoyancy

(C) support   (D) both A & C

16. **Which type** of tissues **support**, defend, and store food in the body?

(A) Epithelial

(B) Connective

(C) Nervous

(D) Muscular

17. One function of ____ cells is to secrete fluids :

(A) epithelial

(B) cuboidal

(C) squamous

(D) muscle

18. A tissue is made of :

(A) cells with similar structures but very different functions

(B) a diverse group of cells that perform similar functions

(C) cells with similar structures and functions

(D) cells with very different structures but the same function

19. Which type of epithelial tissue lines the inner surface of the trachea?

(A) Squamous

(B) Cuboidal

(C) Hyaline cartilage

(D) Columnar

20. Which type of tissue lines body cavities and covers body surface?

(A) Nervous tissue

(B) Muscle tissue

(C) Epithelial tissue

(D) Connective tissue

21. Which type of tissue is responsible for contractions that allow movement of organs or the entire body?

(A) Muscle tissue

(B) Nervous tissue

(C) Epithelial tissue

(D) Connective tissue

22. Which of the following tissues includes the epidermis?

(A) Nervous tissue

(B) Epithelial tissue

(C) Connective tissue

(D) Muscle tissue

23. Which of the following tissues includes bone and cartilage?

(A) Muscle tissue

(B) Nervous tissue

(C) Epithelial tissue

(D) Connective tissue

24. Which type of tissue is responsible for receiving, interpreting and producing a response to stimuli?

(A) Muscle tissue

(B) Nervous tissue

(C) Epithelial tissue

(D) Connective tissue

25. Which tissue includes blood and adipose tissue?

(A) Muscle tissue

(B) Nervous tissue

(C) Epithelial tissue

(D) Connective tissue

26. Which of the following is not a function of connective tissue?

(A) Production of blood cells

(B) Bind and support body parts

(C) Line body surfaces and cavities

(D) Store energy in the form of farts

27. The meristem present at the root or shoot apices is called :

(A) primary meristem

(B) promeristem

(C) intercalary meristem

(D) secondary meristem

28. Elongation of internodes of the stems of grasses is facilitated by :

(A) apical meristem

(B) lateral meristem

(C) intercalary meristem

(D) secondary meristem

29. Which of the following is not true for a meristematic tissue?

(A) It has living , thin walled cells

(B) Cells have dense protoplasm

(C) They have no intercellular spaces

(D) They store reserve food material

30. The tissue composed of living, thin walled cells made of cellulose is :

(A) parenchyma

(B) collenchyma

(C) sclerenchyma

(D) vessels

31. Parenchyma cells containing chloroplasts are called :

(A) aerenchyma

(B) sclerenchyma

(C) chlorenchyma

(D) prosenchyma

32. Which of the following is a living mechanical tissue ?

(A) Parenchyma

(B) Collenchyma

(C) Sclerenchyma

(D) All of the above

33. Collenchyma is considered a living tissue because :

(A) it has cell walls

(B) it has cellulose in its cell walls

(C) it has protoplasm

(D) it has angular thickenings

34. Dead mechanical tissue is :

(A) parenchyma

(B) sclerenchyma

(C) aerenchyma

(D) collenchyma

35. Cell walls of sclerenchyma are rich in :

(A) cellulose

(B) pectin

(C) lignin

(D) hemicellulose

36. The cells that form a major part of walnut shells are :

(A) fibres   (B) sclereids

(C) collenchyma   (D) parenchyma

37. Succulents are capable of storing water in their stems due to the presence of :

(A) parenchyma

(B) aerenchyma

(C) collenchyma

(D) sclerenchyma

38. The meristem responsible for increase in the girth of stem is known as :

(A) apical meristem

(B) promeristem

(C) intercalary meristem

(D) lateral meristem

39. The cell with perforation at the end walls is :

(A) sclereid

(B) tracheid

(C) tracheae

(D) sclerenchyma

40. The plant cell without nucleus is :

(A) tracheid   (B) tracheae

(C) sclereid   (D) sieve tube

41. Companion cell is associated with :

(A) sclerenchyma

(B) tracheid

(C) tracheae

(D) sieve tube

42. Conduction of water occurs through :

(A) parenchyma

(B) phloem

(C) sclerenchyma

(D) xylem

43. The dividing tissue present in between xylem and phloem of the stem in the plants is :

(A) secondary cambium

(B) apical meristem

(C) intercalary meristem

(D) vascular cambium

44. Sieve tubes are present in :

(A) phloem

(B) xylem

(C) collenchyma

(D) sclerenchyma

45. Tracheae are the components of :

(A) xylem   (B) phloem

(C) collenchyma   (D) sclerenchyma

46. Presence of tracheids is a characteristic feature of :

(A) gymnosperms

(B) dicotyledons

(C) monocotyledons

(D) protozoa

47. Silica is present in the epidermal cells of :

(A) grass   (B) equisetum

(C) both A and B   (D) none of these

48. The longest cell in the plant kingdom is :

(A) collenchyma

(B) parenchyma

(C) sclereid

(D) sclerenchyma fibre

49. The only cells of epidermis with chloroplasts are :

(A) stomata

(B) guard cells

(C) epidermal cells

(D) none of these

50. A fatty substance deposited on the walls of cork cells is :

(A) cellulose   (B) lignin

(C) pectin   (D) suberin

51. The characteristic features of cork is/are :

(A) its light weight

(B) its high compressibility

(C) its resistance to catch fire easily

(D) all of the above

52. The epidermis of root lacks :

(A) cuticle   (B) stomata

(C) guard cells   (D) all of these

53. In gymnosperms sieve cells are associated with :

(A) albuminous cells

(B) companion cells

(C) guard cells

(D) sieve plates

54. Apart from the conduction of water, xylem also :

(A) conducts organic food

(B) gives mechanical strength

(C) helps in gaseous exchange

(D) helps in transpiration

55. The components of xylem which help in lateral conduction of water are :

(A) trachea

(B) tracheids

(C) xylem fibres

(D) xylem parenchyma

56. Collenchyma differs from sclerenchyma in :

(A) having suberin cell walls and protoplasm

(B) having lignin cell walls and protoplasm

(C) not having protoplasm and pectin cell walls

(D) having pectin cell walls and protoplasm

57. Fibres differ from sclereids in :

(A) having lignified cell walls

(B) having pits

(C) their origin from parenchyma cells

(D) their origin from meristematic cells

58. The tissue that commonly forms ground tissue is :

(A) epidermis   (B) parenchyma

(C) collenchyma   (D) sclerenchyma

59. Which of the following tissues is composed of dead cells?

(A) Xylem

(B) Phloem

(C) Epidermis

(D) Ground tissue

60. The inner lining of the blood vessel is :

(A) mesothelium

(B) endothelium

(C) pavement epithelium

(D) stratified epithelium

61. The epithelium that undergoes meiosis is :

(A) germinal epithelium

(B) stratified epithelium

(C) pseudostratified epithelium

(D) transitional epithelium

62. The epithelium capable of ultrafiltration is :

(A) squamous epithelium

(B) cuboidal epithelium

(C) columnar epithelium

(D) compound epithelium

63. Pseudostratified epithelium is present in :

(A) trachea

(B) urinary bladder

(C) larynx

(D) nephron

64. Muscular tissue is_____ in origin.

(A) mesodermal   (B) ectodermal

(C) endodermal   (D) none of these

65. Adipose tissue is :

(A) connective tissue

(B) supporting tissue

(C) vascular tissue

(D) epithelial tissue

66. Which of the following is a voluntary muscle?

(A) Skeletal muscle

(B) Cardiac muscle

(C) Smooth muscle

(D) All of the above

67. A striated involuntary muscle from the following is :

(A) skeletal muscle

(B) cardiac muscle

(C) visceral muscle

(D) all of the above

68. Connective tissue is derived from :

(A) mesoderm

(B) ectoderm

(C) endoderm

(D) all of these

69. Cardiac muscles are :

(A) striated

(B) unstriated

(C) both A and B

(D) none of these

70. The structural and functional unit of striated muscle fibre is :

(A) sarcolemma

(B) sarcomere

(C) sarcoplasm

(D) myofibril

71. Strain is caused by excessive pulling of :

(A) muscles

(B) ligaments

(C) tendons

(D) nerves

72. Cardiac muscles are :

(A) smooth, spindle shaped and in-voluntary

(B) striated, syncytial and involun-tary

(C) striated, syncytial and voluntary

(D) striated, cross connected and in-voluntary

73. Cartilage is produced by :

(A) osteoblasts

(B) fibroblasts

(C) epithelium

(D) chondrocytes

74. The myofibrils contain :

(A) myosin

(B) actin

(C) ATP

(D) all of these

75. The major constituent of vertebrate bone is :

(A) calcium phosphate

(B) sodium chloride

(C) potassium hydroxide

(D) calcium carbonate

76. Nails, hooves and horns are examples of :

(A) bony tissue

(B) cartilage tissue

(C) connective tissue

(D) epidermal tissue

77. Mast cells are found in :

(A) adipose tissue

(B) yellow fibrous tissue

(C) white fibrous tissue

(D) areolar tissue

78. Nerve fibres differ from muscle fibres in having :

(A) myofibrils

(B) striations

(C) sarcolemma

(D) dendrites

79. Nissl's granules are present in :

(A) nerve cells   (B) mast cells

(C) bone cells   (D) cartilage cells

80. Sheath nuclei, Schwann cells and nodes of Ranvier are found in :

(A) neurons   (B) osteoblasts

(C) chondroblasts (D) gland cells

81. Sarcolemma is the membrane that covers :

(A) nerve fibres

(B) muscle fibres

(C) visceral fibres

(D) tendons

82. The ends of bones are composed of _____ cartilage.

(A) fibrous

(B) hyaline

(C) elastic

(D) calcified

83. The muscles which have no fatigue are :

(A) striated

(B) unstriated

(C) cardiac

(D) none of these

84. A characteristic feature of cardiac muscle is its :

(A) fatigue

(B) rhythmicity

(C) spindle shape

(D) frigidity

85. Myelin sheath is present on:

(A) cell body

(B) dendrite

(C) axon

(D) all of these

86. Synapse is :

(A) junction of two axons

(B) junction of two dendrites

(C) junction of axon and dendrite

(D) junction of cell bodies

87. The epithelium capable of reception of stimulus is :

(A) germinal   (B) sensory

(C) glandular   (D) pigmented

88. Blood is :

(A) acidic   (B) alkaline

(C) neutral   (D) watery

89. The most common connective tissue is :

(A) adipose tissue

(B) reticular tissue

(C) fibrous tissue

(D) areolar tissue

90. Voraciously phagocytic and actively mobile WBCs are :

(A) neutrophils

(B) basophils

(C) lymphocytes

(D) monocytes

91. Nonmyelinated neurons are found in:

(A) invertebrates

(B) sympathetic nerves

(C) parasympathetic nerves

(D) all of the above

92. The voluntary muscles that are not attached to bones are :

(A) muscles of tongue

(B) intercostal muscles

(C) biceps and triceps

(D) calf muscles

93. The cells that cannot be cultured as they have lost their centrioles are :

(A) neurons

(B) osteocytes

(C) chondrocytes

(D) mast cells

Answers

1. A	2. A	3. C	4. A	5. B	6. D	7. C	8. A	9. D	10. A
11. D	12. D	13. B	14. D	15. D	16. B	17. B	18. C	19. D	20. C
21. A	22. B	23. D	24. B	25. D	26. A	27. A	28. C	29. D	30. A
31. C	32. B	33. C	34. B	35. C	36. B	37. A	38. D	39. C	40. D
41. D	42. D	43. C	44. A	45. A	46. A	47. C	48. D	49. B	50. D
51. D	52. D	53. A	54. B	55. D	56. D	57. C	58. B	59. A	60. B
61. A	62. A	63. A	64. A	65. A	66. A	67. B	68. A	69. C	70. B
71. B	72. D	73. D	74. D	75. A	76. D	77. B	78. D	79. A	80. A
81. B	82. B	83. C	84. B	85. C	86. C	87. B	88. B	89. D	90. D
91. A	92. A	93. A							

Explanatory Answers

1. (A) RBCs are produced in the bone marrow. The process is called erythropoesis.

2. (A) Cells in a single layer is called simple tissue.

3. (C) Ciliated epithelium consists of cells, which lines the Digestive and Reparatory systems.

4. (A) Striated muscle is also called skeletal muscle, voluntary muscle, etc.

5. (B) Non-striated muscle is also called involuntary muscle which is spindle shaped.

10. (A) The cells of adipose tissue are called adipocytes. The cytoplasm of these cells is filled with fat granules.

11. (D) Blood is a fluid connective tissue.

14. (D) Axons of several nerve cells form bundles and are called nerve.

15. (D) Cell wall of collenchyma cells is made up of cellulose & pectin.

19. (D) Trachea also has 'C' shaped cartilagenous rings which prevent the trachea from collapsing.

27. (A) Primary meristem remains meristematic throughout the life of the plants.

28. (C) Meristem that remains embedded within the permanent tissue is intercalary meristem.

30. (A) Parenchyma retains the power of growth and division.

32. (B) Collenchyma, like parenchyma retains the power of cell division.

36. (B) Short sclerenchymatic cells are called sclereids.

37. (A) Succulent stems are present in desert plants and they store water.

42. (D) Xylem tissue is a conductive tissue which transports water from the roots to other parts of the plant.

44. (A) Sieve tubes have sieve plate at its end which have pores to conduct the food material.

54. (B) Xylem is made up of lignin & cellulose which helps to give mechanical support to the plant.

56. (D) In collenchymatous cells the cell wall is made up of cellulose, hemicellulose and pectin, whereas in sclerenchymatous cells, the cell wall is thickened due to lignin deposition.

61. (A) Germinal epithelium is usually present in the gonads.

62. (A) It helps in the diffusion of various substances, as the cells are extremely thin and flattened.

63. (A) It lines the mucous membrane of the respiratory passage and olfactory chambers.

64. (A) Muscle forming cells are called mycoblasts.

65. (A) Adipose tissue is fat storing connective tissue.

69. (C) Cardiac muscles are the muscles that do not get fatigued.

70. (B) The part of myofibril between two adjacent z-lines is known as sacromere.

73. (D) Chondrocytes form chondro-mucoid.

75. (A) About 60-65% of the bone is calcium phosphate.

76. (D) Keratin is scleroprotein (water proof) that forms stratum corneum.

77. (B) Mast cells are modified basophils of blood.

79. (A) Nissle's granules are modified Golgi bodies.

90. (D) Monocytes also differentiate into scavenger cells, which remove the damaged and dead cells to clean the body.

93. (A) Neurons are formed during the embryonic stage. After that, they do not divide and form new cells even if the neurons are damaged.

✦ ✦ ✦

Chapter 3

Diversity in Living Organisms

Synopsis

1. Classification helps us in exploring the diversity of life forms.

2. Aristotle, the Greek thinker, classified animals according to their habitat – land, water or air. The process of classification depends on characteristics. The characteristics in a level is dependent upon those in the previous level.

3. All living things are identified and categorized on the basis of their body design in form and function. The classification of life forms is therefore closely related to their evolution. Charles Darwin first described this in 1859.

4. Robert Whittaker (1959) proposed the '5-kingdom System' based on the cell structure, mode and source of nutrition and body organization.

5. The five kingdoms are Monera, Protista, Fungi, Plantae and Animalia.

6. Scheme of classification is kingdom

   a. Phylum (animals)/division (plants)

      Class

      Order

         Family

            Genus

               Species

7. Woese divided Monera into Archaebacteria and Eubacteria.

8. Monerans do not have a defined nucleus. The mode of nutrition is either autotrophic or heterotrophic. e.g. Cyanobacteria, Mycoplasma, etc.

9. Protista includes unicellular eukaryotic organisms whose mode of nutrition is either autotrophic or heterotrophic. e.g. diatoms, protozoan, etc.

10. Fungi are saprophytic eukaryotic organisms. They have cell walls made up of chitin. e.g. yeast and mushroom.

11. Some fungi lead a symbiotic life with algae. e.g. lichens.

12. The various level of classification of plants depends on well-differentiated components, having special tissues for transport, ability to bear seeds and whether the seeds are enclosed within fruits.

13. Plants that do not have a differentiated plant body belong to Thallophyta. e.g. spirogyra, ulothrix, etc.

14. Plants with a differentiated plant body without a specialized vascular tissue belong to Bryophyta. e.g. moss, marchantia, etc.

15. In Pteridophyta the plant body is differentiated into roots, stem and leaves and has specialized vascular tissue. e.g. fern, marsilea, etc.

16. Thallophytes, bryophytes and pteridophytes are together called Cryptogams.

17. Plants with well-differentiated reproductive tissues that ultimately bear seeds are called Phanerogams (Gymnosperms and Angiosperms).

18. Gymnosperms bear naked seeds and are usually perennial, evergreen and woody. e.g. pine, deodar,etc.

19. Angiosperms bear seeds inside the fruit. Plants with seeds having a single cotyledon are called mono cotyledonous or monocots.

20. Plants having two cotyledons are called dicots. e.g. ipomea.

21. Organisms belonging to Animalia are eukaryotic, multicellular, heterotrophic and mobile. They do not have a cell wall.

22. Porifera includes non-mobile animals having pores and are commonly called sponges.

23. Animals belonging to Coelenterata show body design differentiation and have a cavity in the body. The body is made up of two layers of cells. e.g. hydra, sea anemones, etc.

24. The body of Platyhelminthes is bilaterally symmetrical with no true ceolom. e.g. planarians, liverfluke, etc.

25. The body of Nematodes is triploblastic with pseudo ceolom. e.g. ascaris, wuchereria, etc.

26. Annelids have extensive organ differentiation in a segmented form. e.g. earthworms, leeches, etc.

27. Animals belonging to Arthropoda have open circulatory system and jointed legs. The ceolomic cavity is blood filled. e.g. prawns, spiders, crabs, etc.

28. In Molluscans the ceolomic cavity is reduced. e.g. snails, mussel, etc.

29. Animals of Echinodermata have calcium carbonate in their skeleton and a water-driven tube system. e.g. starfish, sea cucumber, etc.

30. Protochordates do not have a proper notochord at all the stages in their life.

31. Notochord is replaced by vertebral column in adults in Vertebrata. (Pisces, Amphibia, Reptilia, Aves and Mammalia).

32. In Pisces, exoskeleton is made up of scales, endoskeleton of bones and cartilage. They respire by means of gills. e.g. sea horse, anabas, etc.

33. Amphibians have a three chambered heart, mucous glands in the skin and respire with the help of lungs (gills in larval stage).e.g. frogs, salamanders, etc.

34. The animals belonging to Reptilia are cold blooded, have a three-chambered heart (crocodile-being an exception - has four chambers). e.g. snakes, lizards, etc.

35. Aves(birds) are warm-blooded animals and have a four chambered heart. They lay eggs and their two fore limbs are modified for flight.

36. Mammals are warm-blooded animals with a four-chambered heart. They have mammary glands for production

of milk. They are viviparous. e.g. human beings, whales, etc.

37. Duck-billed platypus and Echidna are egg-laying mammals. Kangaroos give birth to poorly developed young ones and nurse them in their pouches.

Multiple Choice Questions

1. Organisms that feed upon decaying matter are called :

   (A) heterotrophs   (B) saprophytes

   (C) myxophytes   (D) autotrophs

2. Psedocoelom is present in :

   (A) Annelida

   (B) Platyhelminthes

   (C) Nematoda

   (D) Protozoa

3. The causative organism of elephantiasis belong to phylum :

   (A) Arthropoda   (B) Protozoa

   (C) Porifera   (D) Nematoda

4. Animals having jointed-legs belong to :

   (A) Arthropoda

   (B) Annelida

   (C) Mollusca

   (D) Porifera

5. Circulatory system in cockroach is :

   (A) open

   (B) closed

   (C) semi-open

   (D) sometimes open & sometimes closed

6. The skeleton of star-fish is made up of :

   (A) calcium phosphate

   (B) calcium carbonate

   (C) potassium carbonate

   (D) potassium chloride

7. The heart of crocodile has _____ chambers.

   (A) 4   (B) 2

   (C) 3   (D) 1

8. Angiosperms are :

   (A) non-flowering plants

   (B) closed seeded plants

   (C) naked seeded plants

   (D) none of the above

9. Which of the following is an egg-laying mammal ?

   (A) Duck-billed platypus

   (B) Kangaroo

   (C) Whale

   (D) Pigeon

10. Cell wall of fungi is made up of :

    (A) suberin

    (B) pectin

    (C) chitin

    (D) cellulose

11. Symbiosis between fungi and algae leads to the formation of :

    (A) algae

    (B) lichens

    (C) fungi

    (D) yeast

12. Locomotive structures found in some protists include :

    (A) muscles

    (B) flagella

    (C) tentacles

    (D) contractile vacuoles

13. Which of the following organs is enclosed in molluscans?

    (A) Heart

    (B) Kidneys

    (C) Gonads

    (D) All of these

14. The chief component of pearls is :

    (A) sodium carbonate

    (B) calcium carbonate

    (C) chitin

    (D) conchiolin

15. The Linnaean system of classification uses _____ as the basis of organism classification.

    (A) leaf anatomy

    (B) flower colour

    (C) sexual organs

    (D) stem and root structure

16. In the Latin name *Salix nigra*, the first name is the _____ and second is the _____.

    (A) genus, species

    (B) family, genus

    (C) common name, scientific name

    (D) species, genus

17. Which of the following is the correct sequence of the taxonomic hierarchy?

    (A) Division, Order, Family, Class

    (B) Division, Class, Order, Family

    (C) Family, Divison, Order, Class

    (D) Class, Order, Family, Divison

18. Which life process is classified as autotrophic in some organisms and heterotrophic in others?

    (A) Hormonal regulation

    (B) Nutrition

    (C) Anaerobic respiration

    (D) Transport

19. What is classification?

    (A) Grouping things together on the basis of the features they have in common

    (B) Grouping things together on the basis of how they respire

    (C) Grouping things together on the basis of how they feed

    (D) Grouping things together on the basis of how they survive.

20. Which is the most commonly used classification scheme?

    (A) Linnaeus five kingdom scheme

    (B) Whittaker five kingdom scheme

    (C) Darwin five kingdom scheme

    (D) Hooke five kingdom scheme

21. Which of these is a kingdom?

    (A) Madelaine   (B) Monera

    (C) Algamus   (D) Litmus

22. The kingdom Protista consists of :

(A) Multicellular organisms whose chromosomes are not enclosed in a nuclear membrane.

(B) Unicellular organisms whose chromosomes are not enclosed in a nuclear membrane.

(C) Unicellular organisms whose chromosomes are enclosed in a nuclear membrane.

(D) Multicellular organisms whose chromosomes are enclosed in a nuclear membrane.

23. What are kingdoms sub-divided into?

(A) Phyla   (B) Genera

(C) Classes   (D) Hominidae

24. Which of these is not included in the kingdom Fungi?

(A) Plants with chloroplasts

(B) Organisms with hyphae

(C) Organisms which grow on tree trunks

(D) Moulds

25. What is a flowering plant , in which the seed is enclosed in a fruit called?

(A) Angiosperms

(B) Gymnosperms

(C) Cryptograms

(D) All of the above

26. Which of the following could be the order of man ?

(A) Mammal   - (B) Chordate

(C) Primate   (D) Homo

27. Which of the following are characteristics of both bacteria and fungi?

(A) Cell wall, unicellular and mitochondria

(B) Cell wall, DNA, and plasma membrane

(C) Plasma membrane, multicellularity, and Golgi apparatus

(D) Nucleus, organelles and unicellularity

28. Which groups of words mean the same thing?

(A) Autotroph and consumer

(B) Autotroph and producer

(C) Heterotroph and producer

(D) Autotroph and carnivore

29. Which of the following is not a kingdom?

(A) Animals

(B) Fungi

(C) Plants

(D) All of the above

30. Which of these terms is used in the classification of species?

(A) Division

(B) Phylum

(C) Class

(D) All of these

31. Locomotion in molluscans is by :

(A) pseudopodia

(B) parapodia

(C) legs

(D) muscular foot

32. The excretory organ in molluscs is the :

(A) malphigian tubule

(B) organ of bojanus

(C) flame cells

(D) nephridium

33. Which of these is a characteristic of a plant?

(A) Photosynthesis

(B) Flowering

(C) Production of seeds

(D) All of these

34. Angiosperms were the first plants to have :

(A) Petals

(B) Seed coats to protect seeds

(C) Fleshy fruit

(D) All of the above

35. Which of the following is not an amphibian?

(A) Lizard   (B) Frog

(C) Salamander   (D) Newt

36. Mammals have :

(A) Hair

(B) Teeth

(C) Mammary glands

(D) All of the above

37. Amphibians usually have _____ legs/feet :

(A) 2   (B) 4

(C) 6   (D) More than 6

38. The flowering plant group, which is the biggest in the plant kingdom is:

(A) Ferns

(B) Angiosperms

(C) Gymnosperms

(D) Moss

39. Algae are similar to plants and were classified together because :

(A) they have true leaves, stems and roots

(B) they make their own food through photosynthesis

(C) they produce seeds

(D) they do not prepare their own food by themselves

40. The study of algae is called :

(A) Psychology   (B) Mycology

(C) Phycology   (D) Microbiology

41. Plants whose seeds have one seed leaf are :

(A) monocots   (B) dicots

(C) ferns   (D) moss

42. Plants whose seeds have more than one seed leaf are :

(A) ferns   (B) dicots

(C) monocots   (D) moss

43. What is a consumer that feeds directly upon a producer called?

(A) Second-order consumer

(B) Third order consumer

(C) First-order consumer

(D) Carnivore

44. What are the consumers that feed on other consumers called?

(A) Herbivores

(B) Carnivores

(C) Abiotic factors

(D) First-order consumers

45. Pseudopodia are the characteristics of which of the following groups of protozoans?

(A) Ciliated   (B) Flagellated

(C) Amoeboid   (D) Sporozoan

46. Algae are included in which of the following kingdoms?

(A) Monera   (B) Animalia

(C) Protistan   (D) Fungi

47. Organisms designated as producers obtain their energy from :

(A) other producers

(B) dead consumers

(C) decomposers

(D) the sun

48. Members of which of the following kingdoms are single cells of considerable internal complexity?

(A) Animalia   (B) Protista

(C) Plantae   (D) Monera

49. Which of the following pairs are most closely related?

(A) Dog & tapeworm

(B) Tapeworm & bacteria

(C) Mushroom & tree

(D) Amoeba & bacteria

50. Organisms in the kingdom Animalia are:

(A) multicellular & heterotrophic

(B) multicellular & autotrophic

(C) unicellular & autotrophic

(D) unicellular & autotrophic

51. A scientific name contains information about its:

(A) family & species

(B) genus & species

(C) phylum & order

(D) class & family

52. Gymnosperms are :

(A) naked seeded plants

(B) open seeded plants

(C) non-flowering plants

(D) none of the above

53. Which of the following is common among plants and animals?

(A) Both are heterotrophic

(B) Both are autotrophic

(C) Both are prokaryotic

(D) Both are eukaryotic

54. The current classification system was devised by :

(A) Aristotle   (B) Plato

(C) Linneaus   (D) Darwin

55. If two organisms are in the same phylum, they must also be in the same :

(A) class   (B) species

(C) family   (D) kingdom

56. Which of the following kingdoms contains 'extremophiles'?

(A) Eubacteria

(B) Archaebacteria

(C) Fungi

(D) Protista

57. Which of the following is not one of the five kingdoms of the Linnaean classification system?

(A) Animalia (B) Monera

(C) Protista (D) Chordata

58. The broadest category of organism in biological taxonomy is :

(A) the phylum

(B) the class

(C) the kingdom

(D) the family

59. Carlous Linnaeus is referred to as :

(A) father of genetics

(B) father of classification

(C) father of biological taxonomy

(D) none of these

60. A collection of population within which interbreeding may occur is called :

(A) genus (B) family

(C) species (D) phylum

61. Father of biology is :

(A) Linnaeus

(B) Aristotle

(C) Von Leeuwenhock

(D) Schleiden

62. Theory of natural selection was proposed by :

(A) William Harvey

(B) Charles Darwin

(C) Robert Hooke

(D) Von Morgan

63. The word species was first proposed by :

(A) Aristotle

(B) Linnaeus

(C) John Ray

(D) Leeuwenhoek

64. 'Systema Naturae, Genera Plantarum', was written by :

(A) Darwin

(B) Linnaeus

(C) Aristotle

(D) John Ray

65. The system of giving two latin names to every organism is called :

(A) dimorphism

(B) binomial nomenclature

(C) trinomial nomenclature

(D) monomial nomenclature

66. The levels in classification are called :

(A) families (B) taxa

(C) orders (D) kingdoms

67. The lowest taxonomic level is :

(A) genera (B) order

(C) species (D) phylum

68. Group of organisms which can interbreed to produce fertile offsprings is called :

(A) genera   (B) family

(C) species   (D) order

69. The sequence of taxa in the animal kingdom is :

(A) kingdom, phylum, class, order, family, species and genus

(B) kingdom, phylum, class, order, family, genus and species

(C) kingdom, phylum, class, family, order, species and genus

(D) phylum, kingdom, class, family, order, genus and species

70. In the binomial system of nomenclature, the first and second names stand for :

(A) genus and family

(B) genus and order

(C) genus and species

(D) species and genus

71. The kingdom intermediate to kingdom Monera and multicellular organisms is :

(A) Fungi   (B) Animalia

(C) Plantae   (D) Protista

72. Five kingdom classification was proposed by :

(A) Hyman

(B) Linnaeus

(C) Whittaker

(D) Aristotle

73. Organisms with a common gene pool are called :

(A) species   (B) genus

(C) order   (D) family

74. A drawback of the 'five kingdom classification', is :

(A) inclusion of unicellular eukaryotes in the kingdom Protista

(B) inclusion of bacteria and cyanobacteria in the kingdom Monera

(C) distinction of the unicellular viruses

(D) inclusion of fungi as the third major evolutionary kingdom

75. Vascular and mechanical tissue is absent in :

(A) Bryophyta   (B) Pteridophyta

(C) Gymnosperms   (D) Angiosperms

76. Cryptogams include :

(A) all flowering plants

(B) all nonflowering plants

(C) all flowering and nonflowering plants

(D) only algae

77. Vascular cryptogams are :

(A) gymnosperms   (B) fungi

(C) bryophytes   (D) pteridophytes

78. Plants producing naked seeds belong to :

(A) angiosperms

(B) cryptogams

(C) gymnosperms

(D) thallophytes

79. Angiosperms differ from gymnosperms :

(A) in the type of secondary growth

(B) in geographical distribution

(C) in the nature and enclosure of ovule

(D) in the dispersal of seeds

80. The most primitive vascular plants are :

(A) cycas   (B) ferns

(C) moss   (D) brown algae

81. Pteridophytes differ from bryophytes in having :

(A) vascular tissues

(B) archegonia

(C) alternation of generations

(D) motile sperms

82. If a seed is defined as an ovule modified as a result of fertilization, one may expect to find seeds in :

(A) gymnosperms only

(B) angiosperms only

(C) all vascular plants

(D) all phanerogams

83. The division of plants into gymnosperms and angiosperms terminates with the suffix 'sperm'. It means that both produce :

(A) motile sperms

(B) nonmotile sperms

(C) ovules and seeds

(D) sporophylls

84. The kingdom with prokaryotic organisms is :

(A) Protista   (B) Monera

(C) Plantae   (D) Fungi

85. A common character shared by pteridophytes and gymnosperms is the presence of :

(A) ovules

(B) vascular tissues

(C) fruits

(D) aplanogametes

86. Pteridophytes differ from thallophytes and bryophytes in having :

(A) highly differentiated plant body

(B) true roots, stem and leaves

(C) well-defined vascular system

(D) all of the above

87. Dominant flora on the present day earth is :

(A) gymnosperms (B) angiosperms

(C) ferns   (D) moss

88. Highly evolved plants in the plant kingdom are :

(A) bryophytes   (B) pteridophytes

(C) angiosperms   (D) gymnosperms

89. Most advanced type of reproduction in plants is :

(A) vegetative   (B) asexual

(C) sexual   (D) budding

90. In angiosperms seeds are :

(A) covered   (B) naked

(C) not formed   (D) none of these

91. The term Thallophyta was coined by :

(A) Engler   (B) Eichler

(C) Endlicher   (D) Linnaeus

92. Motile sperms are absent in :

(A) Rhizopus   (B) Funaria

(C) Ferns   (D) Cycas

93. Fungi differ from algae in being mostly :

(A) heterotrophic   (B) autotrophic

(C) parasitic   (D) epiphytic

94. *Funaria* is a bryophyte because it :

(A) lacks roots

(B) lacks xylem

(C) has dominant sporophyte

(D) has multicelled and jacketed sex organs

95. In which of the following groups would you place a plant which produces spores and embryos but lacks seeds and vascular tissues?

(A) Fungi

(B) Pteridophytes

(C) Bryophytes

(D) Gymnosperms

96. The common character between algae and bryophyta is :

(A) they are autotrophic

(B) vascular tissue is absent

(C) gametophyte is the main plant body

(D) all of the above

97. Double fertilization takes place in :

(A) bryophytes   (B) gymnosperms

(C) angiosperms   (D) pteridophytes

98. The first triploblastic phylum is :

(A) Coelenterata

(B) Platyhelminthes

(C) Nemathelminthes

(D) Both A and B

99. Acoelomate phylum is :

(A) Nemathelminthes

(B) Rotifera

(C) Platyhelminthes

(D) Both A & B

100. All invertebrates are :

(A) acoelomates

(B) coelomates

(C) cold blooded animals

(D) warm blooded animals

101. Nerve cord is in _____ position in invertebrates.

(A) dorsal   (B) lateral

(C) ventral   (D) absent

102. Sponges are lowly organised metazoans because :

(A) number of types of cells are less

(B) absence of nervous system

(C) absence of tissue grade of organisation

(D) all of the above

103. A chamber common to all types of canal systems in sponges is called :

(A) paragastric cavity

(B) radial chamber

(C) excurrent canal

(D) incurrent canal

104. Sponges are not found in :

(A) cold water

(B) sea water

(C) blackish water

(D) sandy shore

105. Cavity present in sponges is called _____

(A) coelenteron

(B) spongocoel (paragastric cavity)

(C) pseudocoelom

(D) schizocoelom

106. The animals which live on the floor of sea are referred to as :

(A) benthic   (B) pelagic

(C) planktonic   (D) terrestrial

107. Water in sponges is expelled through an opening called :

(A) ostium

(B) osculum

(C) excretory pore

(D) mouth

108. Which of the following is a diploblastic animal?

(A) Hydra   (B) Leech

(C) Ascaris   (D) Fasciola

109. Diploblastic, aquatic animals with tissue grade of organization belong to the phylum :

(A) Protozoa

(B) Porifera

(C) Cnidaria

(D) Helminthes

110. In coelenterates, oxygen is carried to tissues by :

(A) blood pigment

(B) plasma

(C) trachea

(D) diffusion

111. This system is absent in aeoelomate and pseudocoelomate animals.

(A) Digestive

(B) Respiratory

(C) Circulatory

(D) Both B and C

112. Majority of flatworms are :

(A) monoecious

(B) bisexual

(C) hermaphrodites

(D) all of these

113. 'Blood fluke' is the common name of :

(A) *Fasciola hepatica*

(B) *Schistosoma haematobium*

(C) *Dugesia*

(D) *T-solium*

114. How does a tapeworm obtain its food?

(A) through blood

(B) through the mouth

(C) through the body wall

(D) alimentary canal

115. Tapeworm has no digestive system because :

(A) it is a parasite

(B) it lives in the intestine

(C) it does not need food

(D) it absorbs its food from general body surface

116. In the phylum Platyhelminthes, the excretory organs are :

(A) nephridia

(B) malpighian tubules

(C) flame cells

(D) green glands

117. Platyhelminthes worms are :

(A) triploblastic, bilaterally symmetrical, pseudocoelomate animals

(B) triploblastic, bilaterally symmetrical, acoelomate animals

(C) triploblastic, bilaterally symmetrical, tricoelomate animals

(D) triploblastic, bilaterally symmetrical, schizocoelomate animals

118. An example of a free-living platyhelminthes with a ciliated body is :

(A) *Fasciola*   (B) *Schistosoma*
(C) *Dugesia*   (D) *Enterobius*

119. Which of the following a is free-living flat worm?

(A) *Planaria*

(B) *Fasciola*

(C) *Taenia*

(D) *Schistosoma*

120. Tube-within-tube plan is shown by :

(A) coelenterates

(B) flatworms

(C) roundworms

(D) sponges

121. The excretory structure in *Planaria* is :

(A) kidney

(B) lungs

(C) gills

(D) flame cell

122. Water vascular system is a distinctive feature of :

(A) Echinodermata

(B) Annelida

(C) Chordata

(D) Mollusca

123. One of the following is a coelenterate :

(A) Sea fan

(B) Sea cucumber

(C) Sea horse

(D) Sea dollar

124. Linear repetition of body parts, called metamerism, is found in :

(A) annelids

(B) molluscs

(C) vertebrates

(D) all of these

125. The only major phylum with pseudo-coelom is :

(A) Platyhelminthes

(B) Nemathelminthes

(C) Annelida

(D) Cnidaria

126. Which of the following is not a typical character of class nematodes?

(A) Syncytial epidermis

(B) Pseudocoel

(C) Nonliving cuticle

(D) Being parasitic only on animals and plants

127. The distinguishing features of a nematode are :

(A) pseudocoelom and flame cells

(B) pseudocoelom and longitudinal muscle in the body wall

(C) flame cells and longitudinal muscle in the body wall

(D) syncytial epidermis and diplo-blastic nature

128. Unique character of Annelida is :

(A) first schizocoelomate major phylum

(B) first to show cephalization and closed circulatory system

(C) first to have brain, nerve ring and ventral nerve cord

(D) all the above

129. The coelom in arthropods is reduced and known as 'haemocoel' because :

(A) coelomic fluid flows in the blood vessel

(B) blood flows in the blood vessels present in the coelom

(C) coelom is filled with haemoglo-bin

(D) blood flows in the coelom

130. Which among the following is true to arthropods?

(A) Unisexual with sexual dimor-phism

(B) Metamorphosis is present

(C) Fertilization is usually internal but in some it may be external

(D) All the above

131. Largest living invertebrate belongs to the phylum :

(A) Arthropoda

(B) Annelida

(C) Mollusca

(D) Echinodermata

132. Second largest phylum in kingdom Animalia is :

(A) Arthropoda

(B) Nematoda

(C) Mollusca

(D) Echinodermata

1. B	2. C	3. D	4. A	5. A	6. B	7. A	8. B	9. A	10. C
11. B	12. B	13. D	14. B	15. C	16. A	17. B	18. B	19. A	20. B
21. B	22. C	23. A	24. A	25. A	26. C	27. B	28. B	29. D	30. D
31. D	32. B	33. D	34. D	35. A	36. D	37. B	38. B	39. B	40. C
41. A	42. B	43. C	44. B	45. C	46. A	47. C	48. D	49. A	50. A
51. B	52. A	53. D	54. C	55. D	56. B	57. B	58. C	59. B	60. C
61. B	62. B	63. C	64. B	65. B	66. B	67. C	68. C	69. B	70. C
71. D	72. C	73. B	74. C	75. A	76. B	77. D	78. C	79. C	80. B
81. A	82. D	83. C	84. B	85. B	86. D	87. B	88. C	89. C	90. A
91. C	92. A	93. A	94. D	95. C	96. D	97. C	98. B	99. C	100. C
101. C	102. D	103. A	104. D	105. B	106. A	107. B	108. A	109. C	110. D
111. A	112. C	113. B	114. D	115. A	116. C	117. B	118. C	119. A	120. C
121. D	122. A	123. B	124. A	125. B	126. C	127. B	128. D	129. D	130. D
131. C	132. C								

Explanatory Answers

1. (B) Saprophytic nutrition is mostly seen in fungi.

3. (D) Two nematode worms *Wuchereria bancrofti* and *Wuchereria malayi* cause elephantiasis (filariasis).

5. (A) Blood flows in open sinuses in cockroach.

7. (A) All reptiles have incompletely divided four chambers except crocodile, which has 4 chambered heart.

8. (B) Angiosperms are flowering plants.

11. (B) Symbiotic association is seen in lichens where algae supplies food to fungi & fungi gives protection to algae.

14. (B) Pearl is produced by pearl oysters which are bivalved molluscs.

16. (A) According to Taxonomy, genus name always should start with a capital letter and species name with a small letter.

18. (B) Autotrophs prepare their own food whereas heterotrophs depend on other organisms.

22. (C) Kingdom Protista is further divided into two Phyla chlorophyta and Protozoa.

24. (A) Fungi are filamentous and donot have chlorophyll.

27. (B) Cell membrane bound organelles are absent in prokaryotes.

34. (D) An organism that feeds directly upon producers is a first-order consumer or a herbivore. A cow that eats grass and a tadpole eating green algae are both first-order consumers.

35. (A) Amphibians can live both in water and on land.

39. (B) Some algae like chlamy-domonas (Green Algae) have chlorophyll and prepare their own food.

43. (C) Herbivores come under 1st order consumers as they feed directly upon autotrophs.

47. (C) Energy for photosynthesis can be derived from sun (photoautotrophs) or from simple inorganic compounds (chaemoautotrophs).

55. (D) Kingdom is further divided into several phyla.

59. (B) Carolous linnaeus introduced binomial nomenclature.

63. (C) Species is the basic unit of classification.

67. (C) Taxonomy is a branch of science which deals with classification of plants and animals.

75. (A) Bryophytes posses only loosely packed parenchymatous cells.

77. (D) Pteridophytes have xylem made of trancheids and phloem made of sieve cells.

78. (C) Gymnosperms have seeds but are not enclosed by fruits.

79. (C) The ovules are orthotropous and naked in gymnosperms.

81. (A) Bryophytes have a central cylinder of parenchyma for conduction.

82. (D) All phanerogams have ovules hence produce seeds.

84. (B) Monera includes bacteria.

89. (C) Fusion of gametes and formation of zygote is the most advanced form of reproduction.

93. (A) Fungi are heterotrophic and algae are autotrophic.

98. (B) Platyhelminthes includes flat worms, which have organ-system organization and are acoelomatic.

99. (C) They have no coelom and the spaces between body organs are filled with a mesodermal connective tissue called parenchyma.

100. (C) Poikilothermic-all invertebrates are cold-blooded animals.

101. (C) Nerve cord is below the digestive system.

103. (A) Paragastric cavity is also called spongocoel.

107. (B) Osculum is an exhalent pore.

108. (A) Hydra has an ectoderm and endoderm with mesoglea in between.

109. (C) Knide in Greek is stinging cells. Cnidaria have cnidoblasts, which inject hypnotoxin into their prey to paralyse it.

112. (C) Both sex organs are present in the same organism-Hermaphorodites.

115. (A) Absence of alimentation is a parasitic adaption.

118. (C) Its body is covered by a ciliated epidermis.

119. (A) Mostly Platyhelminthes organisms are parasites.

120. (C) Round worms (Ascaris) belong to Nematoda.

124. (A) Linear repetition of body parts is because of segmentation.

129. (D) Circulation in arthropods is of open type and the coelom is bathed with blood (haemoglobin is absent in the blood).

❖ ❖ ❖

Chapter 4

Health & Diseases

Synopsis

1. Health is a state of physical, mental and social well-being.

2. Health is influenced by genetic, environmental, social, economical and psychological factors.

3. Personal hygiene includes all the factors, which influence the health and the well being of an individual.

4. Depending upon the duration of diseases they are classified into acute (common cold) or chronic (tuberculosis) diseases.

5. Acute diseases last for a short period of time whereas chronic diseases last longer, sometimes for a lifetime.

6. Diseases may be caused either by infectious or noninfectious agents.

7. Diseases where microbes are the immediate causes are called infectious diseases (common cold) and those, which are mostly internal, are non-infectious diseases (cancers).

8. Infectious diseases include viruses (influenza, AIDS, etc.), some of the bacteria (typhoid, anthrax, etc.), fungi (candidiosis, aspergillosis, etc.), protozoans (malaria, kala-azar, etc.) or some kinds of worms.

9. Diseases, which spread from an affected person to a healthy individual are called communicable diseases. Agents for the spreading of such diseases are usually microbes.

10. Disease causing microbes can spread through air by droplets of saliva (common cold & pneumonia), by water (cholera), by unsafe sexual practices (syphilis & AIDS) or by animals around us (rabies).

11. Animals which act as intermediates for the spread of diseases are called vectors. Mosquitoes are the vectors for the spread of malaria.

12. The signs and symptoms of a disease depend on the tissue or organ, which the microbe targets.

13. Inflammation is the process where an active immune system allots many cells to the effective tissue to kill the disease-causing microbe.

14. The basic principle of prevention of infectious diseases is the availability of proper and sufficient food for every one, public health and hygiene measures that reduce exposure to infectious agents.

15. Human immune system recognizes the infectious microbe and responds to it with greater vigour when an individual is infected for the second time by the same microbe. This formed the basis for development of immunization.

16. An English physician Edward Jenner had introduced the technique of vaccination.

1. What is the cause of infectious diseases?

   (A) Pollutants

   (B) Harmful lifestyle

   (C) Inheritance

   (D) Micro-organisms

2. Which of the following insects carries the virus that causes yellow fever?

   (A) Aedes mosquito

   (B) Culex mosquito

   (C) Similium blackfly

   (D) Putsi fly

3. Which of the following carris the parasite that causes malaria?

   (A) Culex mosquito

   (B) Anopheles mosquito

   (C) Aedes mosquito

   (D) Tse-tse fly

4. What is the name of the parasite that causes malaria?

   (A) Paramoecium

   (B) Plasmodium

   (C) Flavi-virus

   (D) Toxoplasma

5. Which of the following causes amoebic dysentery?

   (A) Entamoeba histolytica

   (B) Giardia lamblia

   (C) Escherichia coli

   (D) Entamoeba coli

6. Which of the following is a cause for elephantiasis?

   (A) Leishmania

   (B) It is genetic in origin

   (C) Mastodonia gigantica

   (D) Wuchereria bancroftii

7. The type of germ that causes ringworm and athlete's foot is :

   (A) protozoa   (B) bacteria

   (C) fungi   (D) algae

8. A condition that interferes with the normal functioning of the body or mind is :

   (A) cancer

   (B) epidemic

   (C) disease

   (D) endemic

9. The disease that is often spread by mosquitoes is called :

   (A) west-nile virus

   (B) tuberculosis

   (C) rabies

   (D) malaria

10. Which of the following diseases does not have a vaccine presently?

    (A) Cold   (B) Flu

    (C) Measles   (D) Mumps

11. Which of the following is a communicable disease :

    (A) Cold

    (B) Flu

    (C) Chicken pox

    (D) All the above

12. A new-born baby can already be suffering from a non-viral disease, which is :

(A) haemophilia   (B) AIDS

(C) polio   (D) measles

13. Dehydration due to diarrhoea can be prevented by taking :

(A) rice

(B) vitamin pills

(C) bread

(D) boiled and filtered water with some salt, sugar and baking soda

14. In acute cases, diarrohea lasts less than two weeks and can be caused by :

(A) infections

(B) food poisoning

(C) medication

(D) all of the above

15. The major cause of diarrohea in children is :

(A) a bacterial infection

(B) a viral infection

(C) antibiotics

(D) food poisoning

16. Which of the following is not a viral infection?

(A) Pertussis

(B) Rabies

(C) Rubella

(D) Chicken pox

17. Rubella is also known as :

(A) Measles

(B) Three day measles

(C) Rubeola

(D) Yellow fever

18. Poliomyelitis virus, which cause infantile paralysis enters the body through :

(A) the skin

(B) the mouth and nose

(C) the ears

(D) the eyes

19. Hepatitis virus is transmitted by :

(A) food and water

(B) intravenous injections

(C) blood transfusion

(D) domestic animals

20. Uncontrolled cell division leads to :

(A) normal growth

(B) cancer

(C) whooping cough

(D) gigantism

21. Which of the following are types of disease-causing agents?

(A) Viruses, bacteria and fungi

(B) Measles, mumps and chicken pox

(C) Cholesterol, saturate fat, and helminthes

(D) All of the above

22. Which of the following body defenses trap, engulf and sweep disease-causing agents towards the body openings?

    (A) Body secretions

    (B) Enzymes and compounds in the blood

    (C) Mucous membranes

    (D) Immune system

23. Which of the following conditions results from having been vaccinated?

    (A) Artificial immunity

    (B) Natural immunity

    (C) Humoral immunity

    (D) Cellular immunity

24. Opportunistic infections that are common among AIDS patients include all of the following except :

    (A) tuberculosis

    (B) toxoplasmosis

    (C) diabetes mellitus

    (D) pneumocystis carinii

25. The common cold is caused by :

    (A) bacterium

    (B) protozoan

    (C) fungus

    (D) virus

26. A person can catch a cold from :

    (A) streaking

    (B) a handshake

    (C) a sudden drop in temperature

    (D) none of these

27. Which of the following may be present in tinned food?

    (A) Staphylococci

    (B) Clostridium

    (C) Salmonella

    (D) None of these

28. Which of these statements listed below is true about a common cold?

    (A) Common cold is not contagious

    (B) The common cold virus does not have its own RNA

    (C) Common cold usually takes two months to clear up

    (D) The common cold virus can leave the body through the mucus of infected people.

29. Jaundice is caused by :

    (A) deficiency of vitamin A

    (B) contaminated water

    (C) bacterial infection

    (D) air pollution

30. Which of the following disease do bacteria cause?

    (A) bacterial   (B) leprosy

    (C) cancer   (D) AIDS

31. Which of the following is an air borne disease?

    (A) Tuberculosis

    (B) Malaria

    (C) Typhoid

    (D) Leprosy

32. Which of the following diseases spreads through infected needles or blood transfusion?

(A) Hepatitis   (B) AIDS

(C) Measles   (D) Polio

33. Vaccination is not available for :

(A) Polio   (B) Common cold

(C) Tetanus   (D) Tuberculosis

34. The disease that can be passed from one person to another is a /an _____ disease.

(A) congenial

(B) non-communicable

(C) inborn

(D) communicable

35. Which of the following is non-infectious disease?

(A) Arthritis

(B) AIDS

(C) Tetanus

(D) Sleeping sickness

36. Vaccination :

(A) develops resistance against the attack of a disease

(B) can control every disease

(C) kills all the disease causing organisms in the area

(D) involves the use of antibodies

37. Infectious diseases spread :

(A) only through mosquitoes

(B) from a healthy person

(C) from a patient to a healthy person

(D) through droplets

38. The bacterium responsible for peptic ulcers is :

(A) Staphylococcus aureus

(B) Streptococcus pneumonia

(C) Helicobacter pylori

(D) Nisseria

39. Acnes is caused by :

(A) bacteria   (B) fungus

(C) protozoa   (D) virus

40. BCG vaccine is for the prevention of :

(A) polio   (B) tuberculosis

(C) tetanus   (D) none of these

41. Which of the following is a communicable disease?

(A) Diabetes

(B) Marasmus

(C) Diphtheria

(D) None of these

42. Dengue is caused by :

(A) fungi   (B) bacteria

(C) virus   (D) protozoa

43. Which of the following is water soluble?

(A) Vitamin A   (B) Vitamin D

(C) Vitamin E   (D) Vitamin C

44. Anthrax is a :

(A) congenital disease

(B) genetic disease

(C) infectious disease

(D) none

45. Rabies is caused by :

   (A) virus   (B) bacteria

   (C) fungi   (D) none

46. Malaria is caused by

   (A) bacteria   (B) protozoa

   (C) fungi   (D) virus

47. Which of the following is a genetic disease?

   (A) Cretinism

   (B) Diabetes

   (C) Haemophilia

   (D) Marasmus

48. Pneumonia is caused by

   (A) fungi

   (B) virus

   (C) bacteria

   (D) none of these

49. The diseases caused by defects that are present right from the birth are known as :

   (A) hereditary diseases

   (B) hormonal diseases

   (C) genetic diseases

   (D) congenital diseases

50. Which of the following is not an infectious disease?

   (A) AIDS

   (B) Lock jaw

   (C) Arthritis

   (D) Sleeping sickness

51. Which of the following is an air borne disease?

   (A) Diphtheria   (B) Pneumonia

   (C) Tuberculosis   (D) All of these

52. Match the following and select the correct answer.

i. Measles	a. protozoa
ii. Cholera	b. virus
iii. Kala azar	c. bacteria

   (A) i - a, ii - c, iii - b

   (B) i - a, ii - b, iii - c

   (C) i - b, ii - a, iii - c

   (D) i - b, ii - c, iii - a

53. Culex mosquito can spread :

   (A) malaria

   (B) filaria

   (C) allergy

   (D) none of these

Answers

1. D	2. A	3. B	4. B	5. A	6. D	7. C	8. C	9. D	10. A
11. D	12. A	13. D	14. D	15. B	16. A	17. B	18. B	19. A	20. B
21. D	22. E	23. A	24. C	25. D	26. B	27. B	28. D	29. B	30. B
31. D	32. B	33. B	34. D	35. A	36. A	37. C	38. C	39. A	40. B
41. C	42. C	43. D	44. C	45. A	46. B	47. C	48. C	49. D	50. C
51. D	52. D	53. B							

2. (A) Mosquitoes act as vector for many diseases.

4. (B) Plasmodium is a protozoan parasite.

5. (A) *Entamoeba histolytica* is also a protozoan parasite in man.

6. (D) Nematode worms are responsible for filariasis.

7. (C) Fungi grows mostly in moist environment.

10. (A) Common cold is caused by a virus.

11. (D) Communicable diseases are those which spread from one individual to the other.

12. (A) Haemophilia is a y-linked genetic disorder.

16. (A) pertussis (Whoophing cough) is a bacterial disease in man.

18. (B) Polio myelitis effects the nervous system.

20. (B) Cancer is formed due to uncontrolled mitotic division.

22. (D) Immune system provides immunity and resistance to defend against various diseases.

23. (A) The immunity that is not acquired by birth is artificial immunity.

24. (C) The AIDS virus attack the human immune system.

27. (B) Clostridium is an anaerobic bacteria which can survive even in vacuum.

35. (A) Arthritis is not caused by an organism.

36. (A) Vaccination is a process in which the person develops antibodies by artificial methods.

39. (A) Acnes is caused by *Acne rulgaris*.

42. (C) Dengue is transmitted by mosquitoes.

45. (A) Rabies (hydrophobia) is caused, by rabies virus.

46. (B) Malaria is caused by the Protozoan plasmodium.

❖ ❖ ❖

Chapter 5

Natural Resources

5

1.   Life on earth depends on resources like soil, water and air.

2.   The outer crust of the earth is called the *lithosphere*.

3.   The air that covers the earth like a blanket is called the *atmosphere*. It prevents the sudden increase in temperature during daytime.

4.   The life supporting zone on earth is known as the *biosphere*. Living things constitute the biotic components of the biosphere.

5.   Uneven heating of air over land and water causes winds.

6.   The atmosphere can be heated from below by the radiation that is reflected back, which on being heated, releases sets of convection currents.

7.   The hot air released from various biological activities consists of water vapour that can expand and cool. This cooling causes it to condense and form rain.

8.   When the temperature of the air is low, precipitation may occur in the form of snow, sleet or hail.

9.   When fossil fuels are burnt they release oxides of nitrogen and sulphur, which dissolve in rain and cause acid rain.

10. Presence of high levels of hydrocarbons forms(unburnt carbon particles) increases the content of harmful substances in air is called air pollution.

11. Water occupies a very large area of the earth surface. All cellular processes take place in water.

12. Water is one of the major resources that determines life on land. The availability of water decides the number of individuals that are able to survive in a particular area.

13. Fertilizers and pesticides, sewage, water released by factories and addition of undesirable substances to water can pollute it.

14. Humus maintains the soil structure.

15. Removal of useful components and addition of harmful compounds, which affect the fertility of the soil, causes soil pollution.

16. Water evaporates and falls on the land as rain and later flows back into the sea via rivers. This is known as *water cycle*.

17. Nitrogen gas makes up 78% of the atmosphere.

18. Carbon is in elemental form in diamonds and graphite. The endoskeletons and exoskeletons of various animals are formed from carbonates.

19. Carbondioxide is kept constant in the atmosphere by the process of photosynthesis.

20. An increase in the percentage of carbondioxide in the atmosphere increases the temperature globally. This is known as *global warming*.

21. Ozone is present in the upper layers of the atmosphere.

22. It prevents harmful radiations from reaching the surface of earth.

23. Chloro fluoro carbons or CFC react with ozone molecules and degrade it causing great harm to people on earth.

Multiple Choice Questions

1. If excessive amounts of hot water are discharged into a lake, the immediate result will most likely be :

    (A) an increase in the sewage content of the lake

    (B) an increase in the amount of dissolved oxygen in the lake

    (C) an increase in the amount of PCB pollution in the lake

    (D) a decrease in the amount of phosphates in the lake

2. All of earth's water, land and atmosphere, within which life exists is known as :

    (A) a population

    (B) a community

    (C) a biome

    (D) the biosphere

3. Which of the following processes provides most of the oxygen found in the earth's atmosphere?

    (A) Photosynthesis

    (B) Aerobic respiration

    (C) Dehydration synthesis

    (D) Fermentation

4. Which of the following pollutants is not present in the vehicular exhaust emissions?

    (A) Lead

    (B) Ammonia

    (C) Carbon monoxide

    (D) Particulate matter

5. Bhopal gas tragedy struck in the year 1984 due to the leakage of :

    (A) methyl-iso-cyanate

    (B) nitrous oxide

    (C) methane

    (D) carbon monoxide

6. Health problems related to air pollution include :

    (A) coughing   (B) asthma

    (C) bronchitis   (D) all of these

7. What is the main source of water pollution in India?

    (A) Municipal sewage

    (B) Bathing

    (C) Industrial discharge

    (D) Both A and C

8. What minerals are found in the runoff from agricultural land and untreated sewage effluents that are responsible for eutrophication of water bodies?

    (A) Phosphorous and carbon

    (B) Nitrogen and phosphorus

    (C) Potassium and arsenic

    (D) Iron and manganese

9. Which of the following indications of the health of a water body is the most widely accepted means of measuring how polluting an effluent is?

(A) COD (chemical oxygen demand)

(B) BOD (biological oxygen demand)

(C) Chloroform content

(D) None of the above

10. Which of the following gases is a CFC that is used in the refrigerators?

(A) Carbon dioxide

(B) Freon

(C) Methane

(D) Ammonia

11. Which sector is the largest emitter of greenhouse gases in India?

(A) Transport

(B) Domestic

(C) Agricultural

(D) Electric power generation

12. Materials of biological origin which are commonly used to maintain and improve soil fertility are :

(A) green manure

(B) biofertilizers

(C) bioinsecticides

(D) Both A and B

13. Which sector is the single-largest consumer of fresh water in India?

(A) Agriculture

(B) Industry

(C) Domestic

(D) Power

14. Water harvesting is :

(A) collection of river water

(B) collection of rainwater in storage tanks or in the soil to recharge ground water

(C) harvesting of water from tube wells

(D) all of the above

15. Which of the following element's oxides contribute to acid rains?

(A) Silicon

(B) Sodium

(C) Oxygen

(D) Carbon

16. pH value of acid rain is :

(A) 11-12

(B) 3-6

(C) 7-8

(D) 10-11

17. Global warming could cause a rise in the sea level because :

(A) oceans expand as they get warmer

(B) glaciers and ice-sheets melt

(C) both of the above

(D) none of these

18. Over the last 100 years global sea level has risen by about :

(A) 20 – 25 cm

(B) 10 – 12.5 cm

(C) 25 – 50 cm

(D) None of the above

19. Climate change may impact :

(A) agriculture natural terrestrial ecosystems and water resources

(B) air quality oceans, and coastal zones

(C) energy and human health

(D) all of the above.

20. What does the term 'NPK' mean ?

(A) Nitrate, Potash & Calcium

(B) Nitrogen, Phosphate & Chromium

(C) Nitrogen, Phosphorus & Potassium

(D) Nitrate, Protein & Vitamins

21. The process of photosynthesis and respiration cause the cycling of _____ through the environment.

(A) carbon

(B) water

(C) nitrogen

(D) hydrogen

22. Phosphates and nitrates entering a lake cause an explosive growth of algae, this is called :

(A) aestivation   (B) mutualism

(C) humus   (D) an algal bloom

23. What is the source of SO_2 emissions?

(A) Agricultural industries

(B) Natural gas processing

(C) Hydro-electric generators

(D) None of the above

24. What is the origin of energy that drives the water cycle?

(A) Trees

(B) Water

(C) Mountains

(D) Sun

25. The process of converting atmospheric nitrogen into nitrates is called :

(A) Nitrogen fixation

(B) Nitrogenation

(C) Nitrification

(D) Denitrification

26. Water is listed as one of the basic :

(A) solid forms of matter

(B) nutrients of cool-aid

(C) needs of animal and plant life

(D) unit of life

27. Which of the following processes is involved in the water cycle?

(A) Evaporation, hibernation and dehydration

(B) Evaporation, condensation, and precipitation

(C) Paddling, swimming and drinking

(D) Bathing, sunning and drinking

28. Acid rain is :

(A) the rain of acids

(B) evaporation of acids from the industries

(C) rain water containing dissolved acids

(D) none of the above

29. What compounds are identified as contributing to acid rain?

(A) Carbon Dioxide

(B) Sulphur oxides

(C) Mercury oxides

(D) Phosphates

30. The largest store of carbon molecules on earth is in :

(A) the atmosphere

(B) fossil fuels

(C) marine sediments

(D) living organisms

31. Some bacteria have the ability to 'fix' nitrogen. This means :

(A) they convert ammonia into nitrites and nitrates

(B) they break down useful nitrogen-rich compounds and release ammonium ions

(C) they convert nitrates into nitrogen gas

(D) they convert atmospheric nitrogen gas into biologically useful forms of nitrogen

32. The conversion of nitrates to nitrogen gas by bacteria is called :

(A) denitrification

(B) nitrification

(C) nitrogen fixation

(D) excretion

33. The conversion of nitrogen gas to nitrates by bacteria is called :

(A) nitrification

(B) nitrogen fixation

(C) denitrification

(D) decay

34. The way in which carbon is used and reused through the ecosystem is called :

(A) energy recycling

(B) the energy pyramid

(C) the biotic/abiotic cycle

(D) the carbon cycle

35. The process in which liquid water changes into gas is called :

(A) precipitation

(B) condensation

(C) evaporation

(D) transpiration

36. The process in which water vapour changes to a liquid is called :

(A) condensation

(B) evaporation

(C) transpiration

(D) precipitation

37. Water that moves over the surface of the ground into lakes and rivers is called :

(A) ground water (B) a water table

(C) run-off   (D) the water cycle

38. The largest reservoir of carbon is the :

(A) soil

(B) atmosphere

(C) ocean

(D) sedimentary rocks

39. What compounds are identified as contributing to acid rain?

(A) Carbon dioxide

(B) Sulfur and nitrogen oxides

(C) Mercury oxides

(D) Phosphates

40. In terms of a food chain or food pyramid, organisms that trap energy, such as plants, are known as :

(A) carnivores

(B) primary consumer

(C) herbivores

(D) primary producers

41. Which of the following lists contain all the ingredients and products of photosynthesis?

(A) Carbon dioxide, water, oxygen and carbohydrate

(B) Phosphorus, nitrogen, water and carbon dioxide and oxygen

(C) Carbohydrates, water, nitrogen, and carbon dioxide

(D) Carbon dioxide, water, ozone, and carbohydrates

42. Why is it difficult to integrate nitrogen gas from the atmosphere into the nitrogen cycle of the biosphere?

(A) Nitrogen is not very abundant in the atmosphere

(B) Few organisms can directly utilize atmospheric nitrogen gas

(C) Oceans quickly absorb nitrogen gas

(D) Living organisms quickly absorb nitrogen gas

43. Which of the human activity has added the most carbon to the atmosphere?

(A) burning fossil fuels

(B) mining fossil fuels

(C) increasing soil erosion

(D) none of these

44. In nutrient cycles, generally, minerals tend to be dispersed through :

(A) plant action

(B) surface and subsurface run-off

(C) evaporation

(D) assimilation

45. Bacterium drives the _____ cycle

(A) carbon   (B) nitrogen

(C) oxygen   (D) energy

46. Oxygen is contributed to the atmosphere by :

(A) green plants

(B) the weathering of rocks

(C) fossil-fuel combustion

(D) all of the above

47. _____ fixes carbon in green plants as simple sugars

(A) Denitrification

(B) Photosynthesis

(C) Carbonation

(D) Bacteria

48. _____ are floating ocean plants of animals?

(A) Plankton (B) Benthes

(C) Terrenus (D) None of these

Answers

1. B	2. D	3. A	4. B	5. A	6. D	7. D	8. B	9. B	10. B
11. D	12. D	13. A	14. B	15. D	16. B	17. C	18. B	19. D	20. C
21. A	22. D	23. B	24. D	25. A	26. C	27. B	28. C	29. B	30. C
31. D	32. A	33. B	34. D	35. C	36. A	37. C	38. C	39. B	40. D
41. A	42. B	43. A	44. B	45. B	46. D	47. B	48. A		

Explanatory Answers

1. (B) The normal flora of the lake is affected due to pollution of the lake by hot water (thermal pollution).

3. (A) Photosynthesis is a biological process which takes up CO_2 and releases O_2.

7. (D) Water is being polluted because of the disposal of sewage, fertilisers, pesticides and industrial waste into water streams.

8. (B) Extensive and uncontrolled growth of diatoms, algae, etc. in water streams is called eutrophication.

9. (B) As eutrophication increases, BOD also increases.

11. (D) CO_2 and CO are green house gases.

16. (B) pH value of acids is always below 7.

17. (C) Due to green house gases, the temperature of the earth increases, which leads to global warming. Due to global warming polar ice caps melt and increase the sea level.

22. (D) Phosphates from detergents and nitrates from fertilizers can enter a lake and cause an algal bloom. This explosive growth of algae provides more food for first order consumers at first, but the algae soon use up available nutrients and die. Their decomposition uses up dissolved oxygen in the water, resulting in stress or even death to other organisms living there.

25. (A) Nitrogen fixation is done by Rhizobium, Azatobacter etc.

31. (D) Nitrogen fixation means conversion of atmospheric nitrogen to salts of nitrogen (nitrates).

45. (B) Bacteria like Rhizobium fixes nitrogen and makes it available to plants.

47. (B) Photosynthesis is a process in which CO_2 is converted to glucose $(C_6H_{12}O_6)$ with the help of H_2O, sunlight and chlorophyll.

✦ ✦ ✦

Chapter 6

Improvement in Food Resources

6

Synopsis

1. Food supplies all the required nutrients for the development, growth and health of the body.

2. Cereals like wheat, provide carbohydrates, pulses (grams) provide proteins and oil seeds provide fats.

3. Hybridization is crossing between genetically dissimilar plants (inter varietal, inter specific or inter generic).

4. Improvement of agriculture is done for higher yield, biotic and abiotic resistance, improved quality grade, adaptability and other factors.

5. Macronutrients are those that are required in large quantities by the body (N, P, K, Ca, Mg, S, etc.).

6. Micronutrients are those that are required in small quantities (Mn, B, Zn, etc.).

7. Manure contains organic matter and supplies nutrients to the soil. It is prepared by the decomposition of animal excreta and plant waste.

8. The process in which waste material is decomposed is known as composting. Composts prepared by using earthworms is called *vermi compost*.

9. Fertilizers are commercially produced and supply nitrogen, phosphorus and potassium.

10. Continuous use of fertilizers in an area can destroy soil fertility and also lead to water pollution.

11. To reduce the harmful effects of fertilizers organic farming (use of biofertilizers & organic manure) should be practiced.

12. Use of wells, canals, river lift systems, tanks, rain water harvesting and watershed management has increased the water availability for agriculture.

13. Mixed cropping is growing two or more crops simultaneously on the same piece of land. For example wheat and mustard are often grown together.

14. Inter cropping is growing of two or more crops in the same field but in a definite pattern. For example maize and soyabean crops are grown alternately.

15. Insects, rodents, fungi, bacteria, etc. cause loss to the stored grains.

16. Animal husbandry is the scientific management of animal livestock.

17. Milk producing animals are called milch animals and those that are used for farm labour are called draught animals.

18. Exotic or foreign breeds have less resistance to diseases when compared to their local counterparts.

19. Poultry is undertaken to increase the production of meat and eggs.

20. Food given to broilers is proteinaceous in nature.

21. Mariculture is done to meet the demands of marine fish.

22. Fish culture is sometimes done in combination with rice crop.

23. Five or six species of fish are raised (grown) in a single pond in order to reduce competition for food. This is called composite fish culture. For example *catlas* (surface feeders), rohas (middle zone) and *mrigals* (bottom feeders) are raised together.

24. Rearing of honeybees is called *beekeeping* or *apiculture*.

25. *Apis cerana indica* (Indian bee), A. dorsata (Rock bee), *Apis florae* (little bee), *Apis mellifera* (Italian bee) are generally used in the commercial production of honey.

26. Italian bees have high honey collection capacity.

Multiple Choice Questions

1. What are the three primary nutrients needed for plant growth?

   (A) Calcium, sulphur and magnesium

   (B) Nitrogen, phosphorus and potassium

   (C) Zinc, boron and copper

   (D) None of these

2. A measure of the acidity or alkalinity of the soil is called?

   (A) Leaching   (B) Soil test

   (C) Soil pH   (D) None of these

3. How many chemical elements are known to be important to plant's growth and survival?

   (A) 16   (B) 13

   (C) 3   (D) 10

4. What is the most popular breed of dairy cattle in North America?

   (A) Jersey

   (B) Holstein

   (C) Ayrshire

   (D) Brown Swiss

5. Where did the Jersey Breed originate?

   (A) The Isle of jersey

   (B) Wales

   (C) England

   (D) France

6. Approximately how old should a cow be when she starts milking?

   (A) 2 years   (B) 1 year

   (C) 6 months   (D) 3 years

7. Manure is a good source of fertilizer but what is the another benefit of manure?

   (A) Water

   (B) Organic matter

   (C) Worms

   (D) Weed seed

8. What would you use to control dicot weeds in a cornfield?

   (A) Cytokinins

   (B) Abscissic acid

   (C) 2, 4, dichloro phenoxy acetic acid

   (D) Gibberellins

9. Which of these crops does not require nitrogen fertilizer?

(A) Corn

(B) Soybeans

(C) Grass hay

(D) Oats

10. What does G.M.O stand for?

(A) Genetically Modified Organism

(B) Growth Maturity Order

(C) Good Maturing Offspring

(D) Gold Medal Order

11. Soil erosion is caused by :

(A) Water

(B) Wind

(C) Poor farming practices

(D) All of these

12. When soil pH is low, which of the following elements can become toxic to plants?

(A) Oxygen

(B) Carbon

(C) Nitrogen

(D) Aluminium

13. Soil includes the decayed remains of organisms known as :

(A) sand (B) humus

(C) compost (D) clay

14. What are the physical aspects of the environment like temperature and wind called?

(A) Biotic factors

(B) Abiotic factors

(C) A community

(D) Niches

15. Crop rotation is an important part of organic farming. Why is mono-cropping problematic?

(A) The crop is vulnerable to organized crop thieves

(B) It encourages the build up of diseases and pests that destroy that particular crop.

(C) If is not economic

(D) None of these

16. Which of the following is not an organic method used to control weeds?

(A) Cover crops

(B) Herbicides

(C) Pre-irrigation

(D) Flame weeding

17. Pests and insects :

(A) eat plants and other crop produce

(B) sting and buzz

(C) eat other insects

(D) destroy bacteria

18. Which of the following factors influences biotic distributions?

(A) Moisture

(B) Wind

(C) Temperature

(D) All of the above

19. The biosphere encompasses the total _____ of living material in a region or the globe.

(A) diversity of species

(B) phyla

(C) animal population

(D) weight

20. Biotic components include :

(A) all plants

(B) all animals

(C) water, air and soil

(D) all the living organisms

21. Which of the following is a natural manure?

(A) Nitrogen cake

(B) Phosphorus manure

(C) Ground water cake

(D) Carbon manure

22. The elements that are taken by the plants from the soil are called :

(A) nutrients

(B) minerals

(C) chlorophyll

(D) pigments

23. Micro-organisms used to increase the growth and yield of crop plants are called :

(A) chemical fertilizers

(B) biofertilizers

(C) organic fertilizers

(D) inorganic fertilizers

24. Which of the following is a fish with fins ?

(A) Oyster

(B) Tuna

(C) Mullets

(D) Bombay duck

25. The fish that feeds on weeds is :

(A) Catla   (B) Rohu

(C) Mrigala   (D) Grass carp

26. "Seed" in fisheries refers to :

(A) fish

(B) eggs of fishes

(C) feeders

(D) none of the above

27. Scientific name of Italian bee is :

(A) Apis indica

(B) Apis dorseta

(C) Apis mellifera

(D) Apis florae

28. Bee-keeping is done for :

(A) honey

(B) wax

(C) both A & B

(D) none of these

29. Which of the following is a disease of poultry ?

(A) Ranikhet

(B) Fowl pox

(C) Fowl cholera

(D) All of the above

30. Milk producing cattle are called :

(A) exotic animals

(B) milch animals

(C) draught animals

(D) buffaloes

31. Jersey cows are preferred to local breeds as they :

(A) have resistance to diseases

(B) need less food

(C) need less maintenance

(D) have long lactation period

32. Compost prepared form earthworms is called :

(A) manure

(B) vermicompost

(C) green manure

(D) fertilizer

33. The crops grown in rainy season are called :

(A) Khariff

(B) Rabi

(C) Crop production

(D) Both A & B

34. Growing two or more crops in the same land is called :

(A) intra cropping

(B) inter cropping

(C) mixed cropping

(D) ultra cropping

35. Which of the following is a weed plant ?

(A) Gokhroo

(B) Parthenium

(C) Cyprinus

(D) All of the above

36. Hybrid is :

(A) homozygous dominant

(B) homozygous recessive

(C) heterozygous

(D) mutant

37. First step to evolve a disease resistant strain is :

(A) hybridization   (B) selection

(C) crossbreeding (D) farming

38. High yielding varieties of crop plants can be obtained through the technique of :

(A) clonal selection

(B) acclimatization

(C) hybridization

(D) pure line selection

39. Undesirable effect of green revolution is :

(A) development of HYV of crops

(B) introduction of agricultural implements

(C) disturbance of food chains

(D) effective control of plant diseases

40. Successive growing of different crops is called :

(A) mixed cropping

(B) crop rotation

(C) intercropping

(D) mixed farming

41. Growing fodder grass with fruit trees is :

(A) mixed cropping

(B) crop rotation

(C) intercropping

(D) mixed farming

42. Disease resistant plants can be obtained through :

(A) mixed farming

(B) hybridization

(C) clonal selection

(D) pure line selection

43. Growing two or more crops in definite row pattern is known as :

(A) intercropping

(B) mixed farming

(C) mixed cropping

(D) crop rotation

44. Crossbreeding between different genera is :

(A) intervarietal

(B) interspecific

(C) intrageneric

(D) intergeneric

45. The crop commonly used for crop rotation is :

(A) legume   (B) cereal

(C) vegetables   (D) all of these

46. Which of the following is true for intercropping?

(A) Seeds of two crops are mixed before sowing

(B) Harvesting and threshing are not possible separately

(C) Pesticides can be easily applied to individual crops

(D) There are no set pattern of rows of crops

47. An exotic breed of cow is :

(A) Jersey   (B) Frieswal

(C) Sahiwal   (D) Gir

48. The major constituent of animal feed apart from water is :

(A) grain mixture (B) minerals

(C) antibiotics   (D) roughage

49. Murrah, Surti and Mehsana are breeds of :

(A) cows   (B) buffaloes

(C) goats   (D) sheep

50. Catla and Rohu are examples of :

(A) marine fish

(B) freshwater fish

(C) brackish water fish

(D) shrimp

51. The process of cross-breeding of two individuals of different varieties is :

(A) artificial insemination

(B) pure line breeding

(C) crossing

(D) hybridization

52. Production of several embryos is possible by the _____ method.

(A) natural breeding

(B) artificial insemination

(C) hybridization

(D) embryo transfer

53. Ranikhet is a disease that effects :

(A) fish

(B) poultry

(C) cattle

(D) sheep

54. The techniques of fish breeding, hatching and growing resulted in _____ revolution.

(A) green   (B) silver

(C) blue   (D) white

55. Bacterial disease of sheep is :

(A) cholera   (B) anthrax

(C) tuberculosis   (D) vibriosis

56. Aseel is a popular breed of :

(A) fowl   (B) cattle

(C) fish   (D) pig

57. Inland fishing refers to :

(A) freshwater fishing

(B) coastal fishing

(C) deep sea fishing

(D) brackish water fishing

58. Which of the following is a micro nutrient?

(A) Potassium   (B) Zinc

(C) Calcium   (D) Magnesium

59. Water is an important source of :

(A) oxygen   (B) nitrogen

(C) hydrogen   (D) copper

60. Which of the following is a synthetic substance?

(A) Farm yard manure

(B) Compost

(C) Vermicompost

(D) Fertilizer

61. The component that causes eutrophication is :

(A) fertilizer

(B) vermicompost

(C) compost

(D) green manure

62. More frequent irrigation is needed by :

(A) clayey soil   (B) alluvial soil

(C) black soil   (D) sandy soil

63. Removal of top soil by wind and water is called :

(A) soil conservation

(B) soil binding

(C) soil erosion

(D) all of the above

64. A legume crop does not require _____ fertilizer.

(A) potassic

(B) phosphatic

(C) nitrogenous

(D) potash

65. Which of the following includes only weeds?

(A) Chenopodium, sunflower and triticale

(B) Amaranthus, chenopodium and convolvulus

(C) Convolvulus, barseem and paddy

(D) Amaranthus, convolvulus and sunflower

66. The herbicide that controls weeds is :

(A) 2, 4 - D

(B) atrazine

(C) isoproturon

(D) all of the above

67. Plants can be made disease resistant by :

(A) breeding

(B) weeding

(C) spraying pesticide

(D) irrigation

68. Living organisms are used in :

(A) vermicompost

(B) inorganic manure

(C) fertilizers

(D) farm yard manure

69. A plant used as rotation crop is :

(A) bengal gram

(B) red gram

(C) groundnut

(D) all of the above

70. The best method to control plant diseases is :

(A) selection of disease resistant varieties

(B) introduction of disease resistant varieties

(C) breeding of permanent resistant varieties

(D) biological control

71. Soil fertility is reduced by :

(A) decaying organic matter

(B) crop rotation

(C) addition of N_2 fixing bacteria

(D) intensive agriculture

72. Humus increases :

(A) water holding capacity

(B) fertility of soil

(C) aeration of soil

(D) all of the above

73. Which of the following is most destructive?

(A) Erosion by water

(B) Wind erosion

(C) Slip erosion

(D) Stream bank erosion

Answers

1. B	2. C	3. A	4. B	5. A	6. A	7. B	8. C	9. B	10. A
11. D	12. D	13. B	14. B	15. B	16. C	17. D	18. D	19. D	20. D
21. C	22. A	23. B	24. C	25. D	26. B	27. C	28. D	29. D	30. D
31. D	32. B	33. A	34. C	35. D	36. C	37. B	38. C	39. C	40. B
41. D	42. B	43. A	44. D	45. A	46. C	47. A	48. D	49. B	50. B
51. D	52. D	53. B	54. C	55. D	56. A	57. A	58. B	59. A	60. D
61. A	62. D	63. C	64. C	65. B	66. D	67. A	68. D	69. C	70. C
71. D	72. D	73. C							

1. (B) Nitrogen, phosphorus and potassium are required for the growth of plants. In their absence plants show stunted growth of shoots, roots, chlorosis, premature withering, etc.

3. (A) Of the sixteen elements required by plants, C, H, O, N, S, P, K, Mg, Ca and Fe are called macronutrients, while B, Mn, Zn, Cu, Mo, Cl are called micronutrients.

7. (B) Manure contains organic matter that forms a part of the humus.

15. (B) All disease causing bacteria, viruses, etc., are very specific to their hosts. They survive in the soil as spores, fragments of hyphae, etc., and cause damage to crops when repeated.

45. (A) Leguminous plants have root nodules that lodge nitrogen fixing bacteria. These plants enrich the nitrogen deficient soil.

61. (A) Fertilizers that reach water sources cause extensive growth of algae. These on decay reduce the oxygen content of the water. This process is called eutrophication.

✦ ✦ ✦

 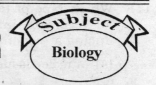

1. Proteins synthesized by the rough ER are :

   (A) exported from the cell

   (B) for internal regulation

   (C) for internal storage

   (D) to digest food in lysosomes

2. Within chloroplasts, light is captured by :

   (A) thylakoids within grana

   (B) grana within cisternae

   (C) cisternae within grana

   (D) grana within thylakoids

3. Ribosomes contain maximum amount of :

   (A) steroids   (B) lipids

   (C) RNA   (D) DNA

4. What is the substance that is used by the cells as an immediate source of energy for them?

   (A) Adenosine triphosphate (ATP)

   (B) Amino acids

   (C) Chlorofluorocarbons

   (D) Phenylalanine

5. Which of the following is absent in erythrocytes?

   (A) Nucleus

   (B) Aerobic respiration

   (C) DNA

   (D) All of the above

6. The plastids which make flowers and fruits conspicuous to animals for pollination and dispersal are :

   (A) chloroplast   (B) chromoplast

   (C) leucoplast   (D) none of these

7. The functional activities of a cell are controlled and directed by the :

   (A) protoplasm   (B) nucleus

   (C) mitochondrion (D) ER

8. If the ribosomes of a cell are destroyed then :

   (A) respiration will not take place

   (B) fats will not be stored

   (C) carbon assimilation will not occur

   (D) proteins will not be formed

9. Which of the following is always non-myelinated?

   (A) axon   (B) dendrite

   (C) both A and B   (D) none of these

10. A tissue is made of :

    (A) cells with similar structures but very different functions

    (B) a diverse group of cells that perform similar functions

    (C) cells with similar structures and functions

    (D) cells with very different structures but the same function

11. Which type of tissue is responsible for receiving, interpreting and producing a response to stimuli?

(A) Muscle tissue

(B) Nervous tissue

(C) Epithelial tissue

(D) Connective tissue

12. Elongation of internodes of the stems of grasses is facilitated by :

(A) apical meristem

(B) lateral meristem

(C) intercalary meristem

(D) secondary meristem

13. The dividing tissue present in between xylem and phloem of the stem in the plants is :

(A) secondary cambium

(B) apical meristem

(C) intercalary meristem

(D) vascular cambium

14. Collenchyma differs from sclerenchyma in :

(A) having suberin cell walls and protoplasm

(B) having lignin cell walls and protoplasm

(C) not having protoplasm and pectin cell walls

(D) having pectin cell walls and protoplasm

15. Which of the following tissues is composed of dead cells?

(A) Xylem   (B) Phloem

(C) Epidermis   (D) Ground tissue

16. Mast cells are found in :

(A) adipose tissue

(B) yellow fibrous tissue

(C) white fibrous tissue

(D) areolar tissue

17. Voraciously phagocytic and actively mobile WBCs are :

(A) neutrophils

(B) basophils

(C) lymphocytes

(D) monocytes

18. The causative organism of elephantiasis belong to phylum :

(A) Arthropoda   (B) Protozoa

(C) Porifera   (D) Nematoda

19. Cell wall of fungi is made up of :

(A) suberin

(B) pectin

(C) chitin

(D) cellulose

20. Which life process is classified as autotrophic in some organisms and heterotrophic in others?

(A) Hormonal regulation

(B) Nutrition

(C) Anaerobic respiration

(D) Transport

21. Locomotion in molluscans is by :

(A) pseudopodia   (B) parapodia

(C) legs   (D) muscular foot

22. Angiosperms were the first plants to have :

(A) Petals

(B) Seed coats to protect seeds

(C) Fleshy fruit

(D) All of the above

23. A scientific name contains information about its:

(A) family & species

(B) genus & species

(C) phylum & order

(D) class & family

24. The broadest category of organism in biological taxonomy is :

(A) the phylum

(B) the class

(C) the kingdom

(D) the family

25. Cryptogams include :

(A) all flowering plants

(B) all nonflowering plants

(C) all flowering and nonflowering plants

(D) only algae

26. Pteridophytes differ from thallophytes and bryophytes in having :

(A) highly differentiated plant body

(B) true roots, stem and leaves

(C) well-defined vascular system

(D) all of the above

27. In which of the following groups would you place a plant which produces spores and embryos but lacks seeds and vascular tissues?

(A) Fungi   (B) Pteridophytes

(C) Bryophytes   (D) Gymnosperms

28. In coelenterates, oxygen is carried to tissues by :

(A) blood pigment   (B) plasma

(C) trachea   (D) diffusion

29. In the phylum Platyhelminthes, the excretory organs are :

(A) nephridia

(B) malpighian tubules

(C) flame cells

(D) green glands

30. Which among the following is true to arthropods?

(A) Unisexual with sexual dimorphism

(B) Metamorphosis is present

(C) Fertilization is usually internal but in some it may be external

(D) All the above

31. A condition that interferes with the normal functioning of the body or mind is :

(A) cancer

(B) epidemic

(C) disease

(D) endemic

32. In acute cases, diarrohea lasts less than two weeks and can be caused by :

   (A) infections (B) food poisoning

   (C) medication (D) all of the above

33. Jaundice is caused by :

   (A) deficiency of vitamin A

   (B) contaminated water

   (C) bacterial infection

   (D) air pollution

34. Infectious diseases spread :

   (A) only through mosquitoes

   (B) from a healthy person

   (C) from a patient to a healthy person

   (D) through droplets

35. Culex mosquito can spread :

   (A) malaria (B) filaria

   (C) allergy (D) none of these

36. All of earth's water, land and atmosphere, within which life exists is known as :

   (A) a population (B) a community

   (C) a biome (D) the biosphere

37. Water harvesting is :

   (A) collection of river water

   (B) collection of rainwater in storage tanks or in the soil to recharge ground water

   (C) harvesting of water from tube wells

   (D) all of the above

38. Materials of biological origin which are commonly used to maintain and improve soil fertility are :

   (A) green manure

   (B) biofertilizers

   (C) bioinsecticides

   (D) Both A and B

39. Phosphates and nitrates entering a lake cause an explosive growth of algae, this is called :

   (A) aestivation (B) mutualism

   (C) humus (D) an algal bloom

40. The largest store of carbon molecules on earth is in :

   (A) the atmosphere

   (B) fossil fuels

   (C) marine sediments

   (D) living organisms

41. The way in which carbon is used and reused through the ecosystem is called :

   (A) energy recycling

   (B) the energy pyramid

   (C) the biotic/abiotic cycle

   (D) the carbon cycle

42. In terms of a food chain or food pyramid, organisms that trap energy, such as plants, are known as :

   (A) carnivores

   (B) primary consumer

   (C) herbivores

   (D) primary producers

43. In nutrient cycles, generally, minerals tend to be dispersed through :

(A) plant action

(B) surface and subsurface run-off

(C) evaporation

(D) assimilation

44. When soil pH is low, which of the following elements can become toxic to plants?

(A) Oxygen

(B) Carbon

(C) Nitrogen

(D) Aluminium

45. Pests and insects :

(A) eat plants and other crop produce

(B) sting and buzz

(C) eat other insects

(D) destroy bacteria

46. Micro-organisms used to increase the growth and yield of crop plants are called :

(A) chemical fertilizers

(B) biofertilizers

(C) organic fertilizers

(D) inorganic fertilizers

47. Scientific name of Italian bee is :

(A) Apis indica

(B) Apis dorseta

(C) Apis mellifera

(D) Apis florae

48. Successive growing of different crops is called :

(A) mixed cropping

(B) crop rotation

(C) intercropping

(D) mixed farming

49. Which of the following is true for intercropping?

(A) Seeds of two crops are mixed before sowing

(B) Harvesting and threshing are not possible separately

(C) Pesticides can be easily applied to individual crops

(D) There are no set pattern of rows of crops

50. Production of several embryos is possible by the _____ method.

(A) natural breeding

(B) artificial insemination

(C) hybridization

(D) embryo transfer

Answers

1. A	2. A	3. C	4. A	5. D	6. B	7. B	8. D	9. D	10. C
11. B	12. C	13. C	14. D	15. A	16. B	17. D	18. D	19. C	20. B
21. D	22. D	23. B	24. C	25. B	26. D	27. C	28. D	29. C	30. D
31. C	32. D	33. B	34. C	35. B	36. D	37. B	38. D	39. D	40. C
41. D	42. D	43. B	44. D	45. D	46. B	47. C	48. B	49. C	50. D

- Enhances the students' reasoning and analysis skills and understanding of subject.
- The exhaustive coverage of mathematics, physics, chemistry and biology give the learners a huge confidence to face the brunt of +1, +2 competition.
- The programme equips the students to post an excellent performance in their regular board exams.
- The extensive assignments pose wide variety of challenges to students in different formats so that they can get accustomed to various competitive examinations.

Assignments

Each lesson in all subjects includes an assignment for the students to answer at home, after studying the lesson carefully. The assignments contain:

> ✔ Multiple choice questions   ✔ Fill in the blanks
>
> ✔ Match the following   ✔ True or false questions
>
> ✔ Reasoning - assertion questions   ✔ Short answer questions
>
> ✔ Numerical problems

The solutions to these assignments are provided at the end of the chapter itself so that the student can check his/her progress.

Test Papers

Each set will have four test papers, one for each subject - mathematics, physics, chemistry and biology. The solutions to the test papers in the first set will be sent along with the second set and the solutions to the test papers in the second set will be sent along with the third set and so on The solutions to the last set's test papers will be despatched as a small booklet.

Application based questions

Questions that require the students to apply information to a situation in order to solve a problem or understand something.

Example :

You are part of your school's science team formed to assess the safety of swimmers diving into the swimming pool. You would like to know how fast a diver hits the water. The swimming coach has a diver perform for the observation. The diver, after jumping from a diving board 3 m above the water, moves through the air with a constant acceleration of 9.8 m/s^2. With the stop watch, you determine that it took 0.78 seconds to enter the water. How fast was the diver going when he hit the water?

Reasoning - Assertion Questions

These questions require the students to understand and analyse the reasons or causes of various phenomena. The student must explain the reasons, identify the evidence or draw conclusions.